LORDS OF THE RIM

Also by Sterling Seagrave

DRAGON LADY
THE MARCOS DYNASTY
THE SOONG DYNASTY
YELLOW RAIN
SOLDIERS OF FORTUNE

LORDS
— OF THE —
RIM

STERLING SEAGRAVE

BANTAM PRESS

LONDON · NEW YORK · TORONTO · SYDNEY · AUCKLAND

TRANSWORLD PUBLISHERS LTD
61–63 Uxbridge Road, London W5 5SA

TRANSWORLD PUBLISHERS (AUSTRALIA) PTY LTD
15–25 Helles Avenue, Moorebank, NSW 2170

TRANSWORLD PUBLISHERS (NZ) LTD
3 William Pickering Drive, Albany, Auckland

Published 1995 by Bantam Press
a division of Transworld Publishers Ltd
Copyright © 1995 Peggy & Sterling Seagrave

Reprinted 1995

The right of Sterling Seagrave to be identified
as the author of this work has been asserted in accordance
with sections 77 and 78 of the Copyright, Designs and
Patents Act 1988.

A catalogue record for this book is available from the British Library

0593 029070

Typeset in 10½/13 Sabon by
Deltatype Ltd, Ellesmere Port, Cheshire
Printed and bound in Great Britain by
Mackays of Chatham PLC, Chatham, Kent

To my sister, Leslie,
who got there long
before the heavens fell.

ACKNOWLEDGEMENTS

This book was written with a lot of help from Peggy Seagrave. Much of the research and collection of materials was done by Elizabeth Murray in London and Edward Leslie in the United States. Scores of others in Asia provided material and insights, particularly in Thailand and Indonesia, but sensibly prefer to go unnamed.

I owe a debt of gratitude to the faculties of SOAS, the School of Oriental and African Studies in London, the University of Hong Kong, the University of Singapore, and Cornell University, who have done so much in recent decades to expand our knowledge of the Overseas Chinese.

At the School of Oriental and African Studies, I would particularly like to thank Dr Hugh D. R. Baker, head of the Department of East Asia; Dr R. G. Tiedermann, Lecturer in the History of the Far East; and Charles d'Orban, former librarian of the Chinese Section, now at Cornell's Watson Library.

At the University of Hong Kong, Vice Chancellor Wang Gongwu has produced invaluable books on the sociology of the Overseas Chinese and the merchant culture of China, and has encouraged the work of others. Thanks also to Professor S. G. Redding for his help and encouragement.

At Cornell, John Badgley was a great help on many occasions.

At the British Library Oriental Collection and India Office, thanks to Hamish Todd; Dr Frances Wood, Head of the Chinese Section; Dr Henry Ginsburg; and Mrs Beth McKillop.

Thanks as well to the library at SOAS; London University Library, Senate House; British Library, Bloomsbury, British Library Oriental Collections and India Office Library; British Library Newspaper Library, Colindale; Westminster Central Reference Library, The London Library at St James's; and the British Association of Chinese Studies.

Many individuals provided valuable material, including John and Dorothy Sawyer, Barbara and Laura Saurborn, Carline and Robert Lewis, Helene and Pierre Solane, Leah and Jerry Garchik, Eric Seagrave, Paul Manson, Anthony Grey, Julian Holstein, Dimon Liu, and Colonel Denny Lane.

'*Nowhere in the world are there to be found people richer than the Chinese.*'

— Ibn Batuta (fourteenth century)

'*I know not whether most to admire the Chinese for their many virtues or to despise them for their glaring defects . . . their industry exceeds that of any other people on the face of the earth, they are laborious, patient and cheerful; but on the other hand they are corrupt, supple and exacting, yielding to their superiors and tyrannical to those who fall into their power.*'

— Sir James Brooke, Raja of Sarawak (nineteenth century)

TABLE OF CONTENTS

PROLOGUE

INVISIBLE CHINA

Be so subtle that you are invisible.
Be so mysterious that you are intangible.
Then you will control your rivals' fate.
— Sun Tzu, *The Art of War*

WHEN THE 1990S BEGAN, THE WEST WAS SO SPELLBOUND BY THE economic threat of Japan that it took a while to realize there were more important things happening next door in China. What was stirring in China was potentially the greatest consumer boom in history. Editors of *The Economist* deemed it 'the most significant development since the industrial revolution', and the best economic news since the nineteenth century, in a world that desperately needed just such a boost. While we were looking the other way, China had already become the third largest economy in the world, after the United States and Japan. By 2010, the World Bank predicts that China will be number one (if Japan has its way, the United States will be number three). By 1994, China's growth rate reached 19 per cent, three years running. Astonishingly, the South China coastal provinces of Kwangtung and

Fukien, where most of the world's Overseas Chinese originated, were growing nearly twice as fast. While the West crawled through interminable depression, dramatic developments all over Asia made it clear that global changes were occurring in the balance of wealth and power. The force behind most of these changes, in China and around the Pacific Rim, was and is the enormous vitality and wealth of the Overseas Chinese, a people of whom we know surprisingly little. In fact, the Overseas Chinese are a separate world force, Offshore China, if you will. This book is an effort to fill that void.

Offshore China is an empire of fifty-five million people, intricately interlaced by systems of guilds, benevolent societies, tongs, triads, *kongsi* and name-and-place associations, which, individually and together, supply the personal connections and financial linkages that make the Overseas Chinese such a potent force. It is an empire without borders, national government or flag. It is deliberately opaque – an invisible empire of conglomerates. In recent decades, more than a hundred large corporate conglomerates have emerged in South East Asia (not counting Hong Kong and Taiwan), nearly all owned or controlled by ethnic Chinese, a number of them US-dollar billionaires. They live and work in Indonesia, Malaysia, Thailand, but all have their roots in South China. In keeping with tradition, these billion-dollar corporations are passed down from father to son like neighbourhood stores. They are run by the super-rich heads of secretive Chinese commercial syndicates, some of which (like the Hokkien and Teochiu) have been in existence for more than a thousand years. These are the Lords of the Rim.

Chinese have been much more successful outside China than inside. The mandarin bureaucracy of imperial China and the cadre bureaucracy of the communists suffocated economic activity. You had to leave China to make it big. The fifty-five million Overseas Chinese represent only 4 per cent of the population of China. How can fifty-five million expatriates drive the modernization of an impoverished continental giant with a population of 1.2 billion? The answer is that they command resources far beyond their numbers. The GNP of the Overseas Chinese who live in Asia is $450 billion, a quarter bigger than China's. They dominate the economies of every country on the Asian side of the Rim, with the exception of Japan and the Koreas. Their combined leverage far exceeds that of Japan's corporate shoguns. Per capita, Taiwan alone has bigger hard currency reserves than Japan. Bank deposits in Taiwan exceed $330 billion, and Taiwan is only a small corner of Offshore China.

The Overseas Chinese have one of the world's deepest wells of liquid capital. A Singapore banker estimates they control liquid assets of as much as $2 trillion, not including securities – assets that are salted all over the world, out of reach of any predatory regime. Japan, with about twice as many people, had only $3 trillion in assets in 1990. While the Japanese economic miracle was achieved under tight government control, the Overseas Chinese did it furtively, as immigrants or sojourners in hostile foreign lands.

The Overseas Chinese are a prosperous multinational middle class with a small superclass on top. Those who have made it very big are different from Western billionaires; true, they have business acumen and organizational ability, but they also have a knack for finessing political patronage and monopoly concessions from difficult governments. As events have shown, success in Asia is all but impossible without a special skill for bribery and patronage. It is a fact of life.

The South Seas (Nanyang) were colonized by the Overseas Chinese starting more than two thousand years ago. Today, no economy in the region can function without Chinese involvement; in most cases a government would cease ticking if the Chinese kicked out the life-support plug. There is no place were the Chinese are not to be found; they are the fuel that drives new turbines and old jungle jitneys.

These expatriate wizards did not create the boom in South East Asia or in Mainland China, but they were uniquely placed to take advantage. It was the pace of change that surprised everyone. Crucial was the Western pullout at the end of the colonial era, and the convulsive changes in ownership during and after the Second World War when old money fell into new hands – usually Overseas Chinese hands. The war shook loose great sums of white and black money not in circulation previously. Property was orphaned. Flight capital from Maoist China looked for new homes, and nervous Overseas Chinese assets sought better hiding-places. So much money was in flux that unusual opportunities arose. The Overseas Chinese were there to grab them.

Then Western and Japanese investors alike discovered that they needed Overseas Chinese to gain access to South East Asian markets. In country after country, the doorkeepers were Chinese, and nothing could be done without their intervention, at a price. At the very moment that Asia began to emerge as the world's most dynamic market, the revolution in information technology brought high-speed finance. Crucial changes came from falling regulatory barriers, tumbling telecommunications and transport costs, and freer domestic and international capital markets. Boundaries between national financial markets dissolved. As the barriers came down, Overseas Chinese financial syndicates, with ancient networks already in place, were the first to turn the Rim into a borderless economy.

The boom in Mainland China is a desperate attempt by the communist regime to cling to power by opening the moongate to capitalism. A special invitation was issued to Overseas Chinese money and management savvy. It was not lost on Beijing that South China was the ancestral home of a fabulously rich offshore people. Venture capital, factories, expert managers and trade poured into the People's Republic from expatriate Chinese investors in Hong Kong, Taiwan, Singapore, Indonesia, Malaysia, Thailand, the United States, Canada and Europe.

Offshore China is not rich merely because it is clever and industrious beyond belief. Its power is not based only on a rare ability to save and invest. It rests also on unusual ethnic solidarity, underground networks, political pragmatism, exceptional information, and the capacity to adapt quickly – faster, even, than the Japanese.

The work ethic of the Overseas Chinese rests on two principles: the obsessive pursuit of individual wealth is respectable because it benefits your family and your community; and it is honourable to protect personal wealth from confiscation by moving it offshore. Today it is estimated that 60 per cent of the world's money is in hiding offshore. A lot of it is Overseas Chinese money.

Financially and organizationally, the Overseas Chinese dominate the entire Pacific Rim, the world's biggest market and cheap labour pool. They are the biggest investing group on the Mainland and, if China holds together, their influence and leverage will be immeasurably enhanced. The longer term outlook is that the Overseas Chinese

will greatly increase their commercial lead over the rest of the world –
and if the West does not prepare for that possibility, it is in for a major
shock.

Rather than rest on their laurels, the Overseas Chinese have been
invigorated by the challenge of the opening of China. Although
China's government has been feuding with its businessmen for
thousands of years, methods developed by the Overseas Chinese for
doing business with hostile foreign regimes in adopted countries work
remarkably well in dealing with Beijing. The central government of
China has a long and dark history of extreme tyranny. It was this
tyranny that created the Overseas Chinese in the first place.

Just how did the Overseas Chinese come to exist and to grow so
powerful? That is what this book is about. *Lords of the Rim* is part
economic analysis, part Pacific Rim history, part chronicle of flamboyant characters and the fortunes they won, lost and won again.
Spanning thousands of years, it encompasses stories of murder and
betrayal, bravery and corruption, of triads, syndicates, kingmakers,
merchants, emperors, generals, spies and pirates.

Part One, 'Roots', sweeps from the eleventh century BC to the
seventeenth century, exploring the extraordinary course by which the
empire came to be. Part Two, 'Empire', travels along the Pacific Rim
itself, from Thailand, Indonesia and Malaysia, to Singapore, Hong
Kong and Taiwan and, via the United States and Canada, back to
Mainland China itself, to trace this new world where men of wealth
and power only become wealthier and more powerful. This is both
history and cautionary tale – for the strategies which have proven so
successful for so long for the Chinese are just as effective today.

To begin at the beginning, however, we must go back to the Duke of
Chou, who first started the feud between government and merchants,
and thereby set off a movement south . . .

PART ONE
ROOTS

CHAPTER 1

THICK FACE, BLACK HEART

IN ONE OF THE MOST FAMOUS SCENES FROM CHINESE LITERATURE, the crafty Ts'ao Ts'ao is besieging a town when his supply officer points out that they are running short of food, and asks what to do. Ts'ao Ts'ao orders him to give the troops short rations. 'They won't like that,' the supply officer says. 'I'll take care of it,' Ts'ao Ts'ao assures him. When the soldiers did complain, Ts'ao Ts'ao called in his supply officer. 'I want to borrow something of yours to quiet the men. Your head. I hope you won't mind. I've made provisions for your family.' Executioners dragged the startled officer outside and decapitated him. His head was impaled on a pole and displayed to all the troops with a sign: 'Supply Officer Wang Hou – punished for stealing from the granary and giving the troops short rations.'

Such treachery was the rule rather than the exception in China, at least in the view of its victims, particularly the merchants, shopkeepers, bankers and entrepreneurs. Their hard-earned wealth and stocks of valuable commodities made them the targets of unscrupulous government ministers, bureaucrats and thieving generals. China's rulers had nothing but contempt for people involved in business. They were to be used and discarded, like Ts'ao Ts'ao's supply officer. Merchants were often rounded up and expelled from North China to settle 'barbarian' lands of Yueh, south of the Yangtze. It was an easy way to cancel whatever debts the rulers and their mandarins had accumulated, and to explain away whatever mistakes they had made in handling the economy. In this way, it was tyranny that caused thriving colonies of merchants to occupy secluded enclaves along the South China coast, where they began venturing overseas, and building the maritime trade networks that evolved into today's great Overseas Chinese offshore powerbase.

The whole story of the Overseas Chinese thus begins with this ancient feud between money and power, and with victimization by regimes that claimed celestial virtue to hide cosmic corruption.

It was not always that way. Once upon a time, there was a golden age when China's rulers were sages, and all was in peace. Or so we are told. Only when this tranquil paradise fell apart did a double standard come into place, with virtue cloaking treachery. But many things in China are not what they seem. It helps to have a quick look at the good old days, to see if they were really that good, and what price was paid for such perfection.

Ancient China is often portrayed as a land of forests and marshes filled with brigands, warlords and magicians. Actually, the north never had many trees, because forests could not develop on its rich loess soil. Big marshes existed only near the coast, around the delta of the Yellow River. There were only a few forests in the north-west, on mountain ranges that made the regions of Shansi and Shensi into natural fortresses. The original home of the people we call the Han Chinese was here on a plateau of loess along the oxbows of the Yellow River. Loess was a fine powder blown down from the steppes by the wind over the ages. Erosion carved it into deep canyons, pocked with caves where humans had sheltered since the last ice age. According to tradition, civilization began here when Yu the Great, founder of the Hsia Dynasty, invented agriculture, irrigation and writing. The golden age of the Three Dynasties (Hsia, Shang and Chou) seemed to be only myth until the 1930s, when oracle bones, tortoiseshell and inscribed bronze ceremonial vessels were unearthed that proved the existence of Shang (1523–1028 BC) and Chou. The chief Shang deity, Ti, represents the neolithic individual who first discovered how to domesticate red millet, which made settled civilization possible along the riverbanks. Ti (god) became synonymous with T'ien (heaven), which was occupied by the glorious ancestors of the élite who ruled these ancient fortified villages as vassals of the Shang kings.

For five centuries, the Shang kings controlled a large area in northern China, appointing relatives to administer clusters of villages that were beyond their immediate control. These relatives owed their loyalty to the king, but each enjoyed sovereignty over his own domain. They protected the farmers, who provided the food upon which everyone depended. As most people were fully occupied just getting enough to eat, and surpluses were regarded as royal treasures, agriculture was the centre of all life and ritual. Precious surplus grain was stored in the fort, to be doled out during winter or hard times, and careful records were kept to ensure that nobody cheated or stole to enrich himself at the expense of the community. Members of the nobility were among the few who could read and write, which is why it is usually said that in ancient China scholars ruled farmers. It is closer to the truth to say that they were warriors who had been taught to read and write by a few scholars among them. When these nobles went to war they did so in chariots, riding across the bare loess soil armed with bows and arrows and accompanied by groups of peasant footsoldiers bearing pikes. During royal hunts, the footsoldiers were taught to obey signals on drums, gongs and whistles.

Unfortunately, by the eleventh century BC, the Shang kings had gone soft and developed bad habits, including heavy drinking and orgies. This offended the leaders of the warlike Chou people, prudish teetotallers who lived along Shang's western desert frontier. One day they stormed into Shang and took over, in order to set things straight. Eventually, the Chou conquered Shang's vassal states and neighbouring tribes, an area larger than France, Belgium and the Netherlands combined. Their control extended south to the Yangtze River basin. Like the Shang Dynasty before them, they kept a royal domain around their capital at Sian, and divided the rest of North China into states and fiefdoms ruled by relatives or obedient vassals. Although Shang had been a loose confederation of states, Chou was a rigidly centralized regime.

Each vassal gave his own ministers an estate, and each minister in turn gave his officials and military commanders their own manors, where they could collect tribute from subordinates on down the line to the peasants tilling the soil. Tribute was paid by the peasants in the form of homespun cloth and bushels of grain. After taking a certain percentage, the rest of the cloth and grain was passed up the line to the next superior, ultimately reaching the king's own warehouses. Surplus commodities were for the king to redistribute as he saw fit, during times of scarcity, hardship or famine. Chou officials kept a scrupulous tally of bushels, so anything missing could be reported immediately to the king's ministers.

Few dared to steal, because the kings and dukes of Chou were quick to punish, and their punishments were extreme. They gave the death penalty for practically everything, including throwing a drinking party. Alcohol was allowed only in sacrificial ceremonies. 'If it is reported that a group is drinking together,' the king said, '. . . seize them all and send them to [the capital] and I will kill them.' China sobered up fast and went on the wagon for two hundred years. The Chou kings cleared up any confusion about what was right and what was wrong by killing everyone who offended them in any way. 'Small faults should be punished severely,' they said, 'then, if small faults are inhibited, great crimes will not appear.' It did not take long for the message to sink in. 'All those who are insubordinate . . . particularly administrators and minor officials . . . when they deviate and introduce innovations . . . quickly put them to death.' Sons who did not show proper respect, fathers who ignored family responsibilities, all faced execution along with robbers and traitors. Lesser punishments included branding the face and cutting off the nose, feet or genitals. Women were not spared, especially 'a woman with a long tongue'.

The rule of thumb in Chou was overkill. Use a grindstone to crack an egg. When simple laws were vigorously applied, 'people will completely abandon their errors . . . and become tranquil and orderly.' It worked. After several decades of terrible killing, everyone got the message and 'a great peace' settled over China. The golden age had returned.

Not everybody was happy living under such a humourless regime. Uncounted refugees fled into Manchuria and Korea, and from there small numbers crossed the strait to Japan. Others fled north into the steppes or west into the deserts, where they were taken in by the nomads, and south across the Yangtze into the warm moist lands of hill-tribes and coastal folk who were of a gentler Tai/Shan stock. So the exodus began.

Fear was the key. Absolute certainty was the method. After the deaths of the first two Chou kings – King Wu and King Wen – one of the most admired men in Chinese history, the Duke of Chou, took over. When his opponents rose in rebellion, the Duke and his armies flattened them, and completely obliterated fifty rebel states. Their surviving families were moved to a new city where they could be watched closely. The Duke of Chou did not take chances. He, too, believed in overkill. He is considered a sage not because of his methods but because of his results.

One result was that the Chou Dynasty reigned for a thousand years, until 256 BC, longer than any Egyptian or European dynasty. Many elements of the Chou system of government persisted in China for the next two thousand years.

This suggests that the Chou got it right. Confucius and others regarded the first Chou rulers as masters of discipline and common sense, and tried to follow their example. When Confucius was appointed chief justice and prime minister of one of the feudal states, his first act was to execute somebody, which focused everyone's attention very quickly.

After witnessing the extreme punishment meted out by the Chou rulers, everyone in ancient China – farmers, artisans, merchants, soldiers and nobles alike – fell into the habit of making excessive public demonstrations of courtesy and obedience. Absolute submission was practised by all citizens. The idea was to be highly visible when you were submissive, and absolutely invisible at all other times. This is sometimes called 'keeping a thick face'. The further you were down the pecking order, the more you grovelled. The king grovelled only before his ancestors. Scholars expressed their submission in clever ways, sprinkling their conversation with quotes from previous rulers, sages or celebrated ancestors, like church deacons spouting biblical fragments. Social behaviour became extremely stylized. Epigrams were everything. The outward expression of submission was a game – a game of survival – that became China's national pastime. It remains so to this day.

Chou was able to control such a large area because of its family network. Everyone related to the ruling family, or bound to it by marriage, formed a web of power that extended down through all the smaller states. Government was a closely held family corporation. Security was in the hands of the king's own brothers. Only the Chou clan (and a few descendants of the earlier Shang rulers), were considered proper Chinese. All others were serfs, farm animals.

Because family ties were so important, they were traced back to distant ancestors, to establish seniority over other families. Kings were unique because their ancestors were past kings, now demigods in heaven. The strong early Chou kings accepted this, and got on with the job. Weak kings, who came along later, were forever propitiating the spirits, burning joss, and became so preoccupied that they left earthly matters to their ministers. Oracle bones were used to communicate with the dead, to ask advice by divination. Specially chosen bones were engraved with a simple question and burned; the yes or no answer was determined by observing the direction of tiny grooves produced by the fire. Some bones had better yes or no properties than others, so they were used more than once. In this way professional diviners were able to rig the outcome, to encourage or discourage particular royal decisions.

Lesser nobles believed that they, too, were endowed by their ancestors with supernatural charisma. To reinforce this message, some of them invented ancestors going back thousands of years to the millet god, Ti. One family cleverly changed its name to T'ien, meaning heavenly. What their ancestors thought of that is not recorded on any of the oracle bones found so far.

When it is said that the Chou Dynasty reigned for a thousand years, it is literally true, but after only four of those ten centuries the tight grip of the Chou kings went limp. From then on they were only figureheads, who depended on their sacred position to command respect. For a few centuries, nobody dared insult them in the face. China's golden age was degenerating into foppery, fuzzy-mindedness and intrigue. Tyranny was being overwhelmed by corruption. This did not mean an end to tyranny. It only meant that tyranny was applied for increasingly corrupt reasons. China's golden age was effectively over (if, in fact, it had ever existed), but nobody yet realized it, because one of the most corrupt elements was false virtue.

Just how silly things had become is illustrated by a famous incident that took place as two rival armies were preparing to do battle by a river. On one side, the current Duke of Chou (a pale shadow of his great forerunner) rode up in his heavily ornamented chariot and saw that the enemy was busy fording the river. 'My lord,' said one of the duke's officers, 'we should strike now while the enemy is defenceless. We can achieve a mighty victory.'

'That's outrageous,' snorted the duke. 'The rules of chivalry clearly state that we must give our adversary a proper chance to prepare his force, before we engage.' When the enemy completed the river crossing and regrouped to attack on the field of battle, the chivalrous Duke of Chou and his army were completely annihilated.

If the original Chou rulers really had been able to influence matters from heaven, doubtless they would have put many of these descendants to death immediately. As it was, left to their own devices, their descendants did themselves in. After the eighth century BC, China's golden age turned to lead. 'All-Under-Heaven was in chaos.'

The bare historical details are well known: attacks by nomads caused the frightened Chou kings to move to a more secure capital at Loyang, where it became clear to everyone that they were powerless. Their greedier vassals began to covet wealth and power for themselves. In the Spring & Autumn period that followed (722–481 BC), chivalry and virtue were replaced by wickedness and conspiracy. Officials and lesser aristocrats dropped all pretence of virtue and jockeyed ruthlessly for territory and leverage.

Virtue was kicked off like tight ballet shoes. Corruption, bribery and conspiracy were rampant. From the throne down, everyone avoided problems by giving lavish gifts as bribes. Once bribery began you could never stop it, for 'the one who rewards becomes tired, but the receiver is never satisfied.' Bribery became institutionalized in China. To guarantee their survival, rich men sometimes even showered money on the poor, which shows how desperate things had become.

It was a time of social and economic cannibalism. No man was safe from his relatives. For most of China's aristocracy, there was only downward mobility. Rulers ate their own young, or were devoured by them. When the blood-letting was done they had wiped each other out in an orgy of class suicide. Like gorged leeches, a few powerful clans remained in seven big states and several minor principalities. They hired the best generals and strategists they could find, and prepared their armies for a great showdown – a bloody period known as the Warring States.

During Warring States, ruling groups typically consisted of a despotic local king or duke and his chancellor, plus a grand secretary who handled daily administration. Next came a high priest for religious ritual, a general (Tiger Retainer) and a supervisor of dogs. The main requirement for all these jobs was cunning. Only a pretence of morality was maintained for the sake of etiquette. Behind each thick face beat a black heart. With so much at stake, the slightest miscalculation could lead to disaster. In such violent times, it was observed, only two things really counted: war and food. War was constant, so the clever manipulation of spies, diplomats and armies was entrusted to strategists and professional spymasters. As rival states became ever more ruthless, the black arts were highly prized. Government worked by intrigue, bribe, fraud and deceit. Chariots were useless at a time of backstabbing. When treachery failed, overwhelming violence was carried out by armies of up to half a million soldiers, newly armed with crossbows. While these numbers are impressive, however, they are misleading. What good were so many soldiers when the generals were easily bought and sold, and changed sides instantly?

One historic consequence of this power struggle was that ambitious nobles hired talented commoners for the first time to administer their territories. This created a new class of scholar-bureaucrats called *shih*. Originally, scholars served only as priests or tutors; they were experts on morals, omens, sacrifices, and etiquette, much like the legal profession today. Some *shih* were the lesser sons of minor nobles, but the great majority were smart commoners recruited for their skills and energy. During the turmoil of Spring & Autumn and Warring States, they became the administrative élite of China. They were the only ones who knew how to get things done. Kings and dukes had power and glory, but *shih* had talent and brains. Gradually, many ancient domains came to be run by such talented men of obscure origin. To call them civil servants is misleading because they were neither servants nor civil. They are still running China today, as cadres and bureaucrats. They can be very dangerous enemies.

In ancient China, such ambitious and often unscrupulous men wandered from state to state looking for official posts as advisers or strategists. Many were professional talkers who fascinated rulers with their conspiracies. When their schemes worked, they found employment. When they failed, they were pickled, boiled or minced. Rewards were so great that such risks were worthwhile. In China of the Warring States, there was no patriotism, no virtue, no chivalry, and only fleeting loyalty. Such men served two or three rival masters at once, and vanished by night. It was difficult to distinguish between scoundrels and bureaucrats. They looked and acted the same, had the same manners, and were equally arrogant, grovelling, cruel, and obsequious, in turns. Often these bureaucrats rebelled against their masters and simply took over. Some ended up running Chinese states the size of France, commanding huge armies in bloody infantry warfare.

Also among the educated commoners were many talented entrepreneurs and businessmen, who siphoned off commodities from government warehouses; their illicit profits made them wealthy and powerful men, able to steer political events behind the scenes. They invested secretly in merchant ventures, paying for a ship, a barge, a caravan or a pack train. In this way they became brokers of luxuries imported from distant places, including gems and pearls, carved ivory decorative objects, hardwoods, aromatics and aphrodisiacs. Sometimes these men were employed as powerful bureaucrats or magistrates. They had much in common with professional merchants, but they operated under cover of official roles and guises. As such, they often made use of their government positions to interfere with rival entrepreneurs, and to prey upon merchants in general.

Burdened with such bloody-minded rulers and scheming bureaucrats, it is no wonder that the people of China mourned the passing of the golden age. Under the original Chou kings, your head might be in constant peril but your purse stayed in its place. Nobody toyed with your family, people paid their bills or else, and bribes or kickbacks were unheard of. There was a nostalgia for serious authoritarian rule –

old-fashioned tyranny – as opposed to the more recent variety of hopelessly corrupt tyranny.

In the old days, while the government was harshly repressive and intolerant, merchants had had no choice but to be relatively straight-forward, and to live on very small margins. All that had since changed. Rulers and bureaucrats had become so venal that they resented ordinary merchants as unfair competition. Perhaps this was inevitable. Merchants craved wealth in order to gain power, while officials craved power in order to gain wealth. Of the two, officials had the advantage because they made the laws and controlled the police and the army. It became official doctrine in China that merchants and shopkeepers were only to be despised, squeezed and preyed upon. So it is hardly surprising that, in self-defence, China's merchant class came to regard all politics as money-politics. They fought back by becoming equally venal. Corruption was not a disease that merchants were in danger of catching, for it was the liquid in their gene pool. Everyone was contaminated already at birth. Merchants who, for their own reasons, personally remained virtuous, still had to make provision for the greed of all around them. When they talked about the golden age being over, they were not mourning its passing but acknowledging a fact of life, which justified all manner of mischief.

The government struck back harshly. Those who paid bribes (and those who balked at paying bribes) were rounded up and expelled to the barbarian lands of the south, with all their relatives. A different kind of China would be born below the Yangtze, in a place called Yueh. And from there, these clever exiles would venture abroad, to become the Overseas Chinese.

On our way south to Yueh with them, it helps to stop here and there, to pick up a few stragglers, to listen to their bizarre tales, and to receive some advice from fugitive *shih* strategists.

CHAPTER 2

A STEW OF HOUNDS

WU TZU-HSU WAS A MAGNIFICENT SURVIVOR. BUT IN THE END HE could not save himself from being stuffed into a leather body-bag. He also introduced the world to Sun Tzu, the legendary strategist who became a role model for every ambitious Overseas Chinese. Both men lived during the turbulent years of Spring & Autumn, when great amounts of manpower and resources were expended in struggles between China's feudal kingdoms. Early on, when his father and brother were beheaded by the king of Chu, young Wu Tzu-hsu fled from state to state, pursued by his father's killers, at times having to beg for food. In 519 BC he reached the state of Wu, which straddled the lower Yangtze. Its capital, Wu Hsieh (Suchow), was a centre of silkworm cultivation; clustered around a sugarloaf hill where a pagoda-shaped palace overlooked rivers, ponds and wooded lakes in all directions, it was a rich and beautiful kingdom. The sibilant Wu dialect spoken today in the Shanghai region gets its name from this ancient state.

When he arrived in the kingdom, Wu Tzu-hsu went directly to the king and begged him to finance a punitive campaign against Chu, to avenge the murders of his father and brother. The king refused, but his half-brother, Prince Kuang, offered the fugitive a post as his personal advisor. The prince needed a special kind of advice because he was plotting to murder his brother and seize the throne for himself. After giving the plot some thought, Wu Tzu-hsu recommended preparing a dish fit for a king, in this case a fresh-caught bream poached in white wine, ginger and lemon grass, and stuffed with a dagger, which would make a deep impression on the royal stomach. It took five years to prepare the banquet properly and to find the right psychopath to serve the dish. Well ahead of time, to avoid being identified with the conspiracy, Wu Tzu-hsu resigned his post to take up farming. In 514 BC, the king was dethroned by the stuffed bream, and after a lavish funeral Prince Kuang crowned himself King Ho-lu. His ambition realized, he recalled Wu Tzu-hsu from his farm and named him prime minister. It was a successful partnership, because King Ho-lu was a dynamic and intelligent man who appreciated shrewd advice and acted upon it forcefully. One of Wu Tzu-hsu's first proposals was that the king read a new treatise on warfare and espionage written expressly for him by the man we know as Sun Tzu.

One reason we know so little about Sun Tzu is that the Chinese often change their names. They do this for many reasons, among them the desire to enhance their public image and self-esteem, while shielding themselves from bad luck. Sun Tzu's family is said to have once ruled as dukes of Ch'en. After a palace *coup*, a young son of Duke Ch'en fled for his life, along with other members of his clan. When they reached the coastal kingdom of Ch'i, on the Shantung peninsula, they thought it would be prudent to change their name. However, wanting everyone to know their aristocratic origins, they took the name of T'ien (heaven), which is pronounced like Ch'en but written differently. The family became very prominent. One branch eventually seized power and ruled Ch'i for many years. Over five generations, the branch we are following became military commanders. Around 547 BC, General T'ien Shu made himself famous in Ch'i by successfully invading the small neighbouring kingdom of Lu, birthplace of Confucius. He was rewarded with the bestowal of the new surname Sun and was given the revenues of the city of Tung-an as his fiefdom.

In short, General T'ien Shu became Sun Shu, Lord of Tung-an, and settled down in the palace to raise a family. Around 535 BC, a son was born called Sun Ch'ang-ch'ing. He would later became famous as Sun Tzu, Master Sun.

Their good fortune did not last long because the ruler of Ch'i was fickle. After only a few years as Lord of Tung-an, General Sun had to flee for his life, escaping with his family by wagon southward to the kingdom of Wu near the mouth of the Yangtze. Crossing the great river, they took up residence on a small country estate about ten *li* (about three and a half miles) west of the capital. The general's son grew up there in black-soiled farmland, among waterways crowded with ducks and geese. He was expected to follow in his father's military footsteps, and was carefully tutored in statecraft, military tactics, strategy, conspiracy and the running of spies. As he mastered these concepts, his journal grew into a treatise called *Ping Fa* or *The Art of War*, which contained the distilled wisdom of centuries of warfare and intrigue, as passed down to him by his father.

He wrote these precepts in the traditional form of epigrams, using a squirrel-hair brush and ink on thin strips of bamboo, the characters running from top to bottom. The strips were then bound together with silk cord to make a book, a secret manual of tradecraft for use during his studies and later in his professional career.

By the fifth century BC, armies in the rival Chinese states had grown in size to several hundred thousand men, including porters and carters. They went on distant campaigns lasting weeks or months. Such campaigns had to be planned intelligently. War had become so complex that success could only be achieved with a coherent strategy, including espionage, intelligence, subversion, operations, logistics and administrative procedures down to the last mule. Sun Tzu was the first to bring together the accumulated wisdom of centuries of warfare and intrigue, interpret it in surprisingly humane terms, and produce such a coherent theory.

As exiles tend to cluster in tiny circles, soon after Wu Tzu-hsu arrived in the kingdom and became prime minister, he made the acquaintance of young Sun and his father. Sun the younger was hoping to find a post in which he could begin a military career. He showed *The Art of War* to Wu Tzu-hsu in the year 512 BC. The prime minister recommended it to King Ho-lu. The king was impressed and summoned Sun to a royal audience.

'I have read your treatise,' said the king. 'Will you give me a demonstration of the proper training of troops?'

'Yes,' replied Sun.

'Will women suffice?'

'As you wish.'

The king sent 180 palace ladies to the courtyard, where Sun divided them into two companies. He appointed the king's two favourite concubines as officers. While the king watched from a high terrace, each of the women was given a halberd and shown how to hold it.

Sun then asked, 'Do you know your front from your back, and your left hand from your right?'

The women replied yes.

'When I order the drums to sound the advance, move forward. At the order, "left", turn toward your left hand, at "right" turn toward your right hand, and when I say "retreat", turn back.'

The women agreed.

Having made the rules perfectly clear, Sun called for the palace executioner and had him stand by with his sword. He then repeated his instructions several more times, explaining them patiently each time. Then he ordered the drummer to sound the order 'Face right'. The women burst out laughing.

Sun said, 'If rules are not understood and orders are not clear, the commander is to blame.' Twice more he repeated his instructions, then gave the order for a left turn. Once more the women giggled.

Sun said, 'When orders are clear but are not carried out, the officers are to blame.' He instructed the executioner to behead both company commanders.

The king was stunned to see his two beautiful favourites forced to kneel before the executioner, and quickly sent an aide to Sun with a message: 'I already know you are a brilliant general, but without these two concubines my food will lose all its flavour. Please spare them.'

Sun sent back the message, 'I have been appointed commander, and a general in the field is not bound by orders from his sovereign.' He had the young women beheaded, and chose the next two concubines as company officers. This time, when he gave marching orders, the women quickly turned left or right, advanced or retreated without uttering a sound, and knelt or stood as they were told.

When he was satisfied, Sun sent a message to the king, saying, 'The troops are ready for inspection. You can now expect them to go through fire or water.'

'You may go back to your quarters and rest,' replied the king. 'I have no desire to inspect them.'

Sun said, 'The king is only interested in theory, not in the real thing.'

Thoroughly convinced of Sun's seriousness and skill, King Ho-lu appointed him chief strategist and commander-in-chief of Wu's armies.

Until recently, this famous anecdote, recounted by historian Ssu-ma Ch'ien in the first century BC, was all we knew about Sun Tzu, apart from surviving fragments of his treatise. It was not at all certain whether these thirteen brief chapters were authentic, who the author really was, or exactly when he lived. Nobody was really sure whether someone called Sun Tzu had ever existed. Chinese historical documents, including the writing of Ssu-ma Ch'ien, were anecdotal and imprecise. In the 1950s, a Chinese historian suggested that the real author of *The Art of War* was Sun Pin, a strategist who lived about a century later; as an act of filial piety, or as a bit of deception to throw off his own enemies he might have attributed the treatise to one of his ancestors. In the absence of anything more concrete, scholars favoured this Sun Pin explanation, and the identities of Sun Tzu and Sun Pin became mingled.

Then, Chinese archaeologists who opened a two-thousand-year-old tomb in Shantung discovered a magnificent hoard of ancient military texts, including missing pieces of Sun Tzu's *The Art of War*, and a completely different treatise by Sun Pin. These discoveries prove that Sun Tzu and Sun Pin were real characters and that each wrote an *Art of War*. We can also be more confident in deducing certain biographical details about Sun Tzu.

After being made chief strategist and commander-in-chief by King Ho-lu, Sun worked closely with prime minister Wu Tzu-hsu and another member of the king's cabinet named Po Pi, a tricky fellow whose father had also been murdered by the king of Chu. We know only the bare outlines of their military campaigns. To avoid the destruction caused by full-scale war, Sun Tzu set up a network of spies and informers, and sent secret agents of various types into enemy states around Wu. When there was no alternative to combat, he mounted a successful attack on Chu, took one of its districts, and captured two renegade nobles who had become a great nuisance. Delighted with these triumphs, King Ho-lu was all for pressing on. But Sun Tzu told him, 'Our men are tired. The time is not right. Let us wait.'

The following year, 510 BC, Sun and the army of Wu again invaded Chu, this time seizing two districts. The next year they struck in another direction, attacking and defeating the southern state of Yueh.

A year later, a Chu army commanded by Lord Nang struck back, but was completely routed by Wu defenders led personally by Sun's colleague, prime minister Wu Tzu-hsu. This string of victories enhanced King Ho-lu's reputation as a great leader and a man of action, and distressed his neighbours. Enjoying the celebrity, King Ho-lu waited anxiously to teach the king of Chu a final lesson. When three years had passed, he reminded Sun Tzu: 'Before, you told me the time was not ripe to attack the Chu capital. What about now?'

'Their commander, Lord Nang, is a greedy man,' Sun replied, 'and both the kingdoms of Tang and Tsai bear him a grudge. If you want to attack in strength, first win over these other kingdoms.' This strategy, called Fire-in-the-Lake, gets its name from trigrams in the Book of Changes; it mingles opposites such as fire and water, making friends while attacking enemies. King Ho-lu took this advice and authorized Sun Tzu to make a secret alliance with the rulers of Tang and Tsai.

Then, just as the main forces of Wu were preparing to cross the river and invade Chu, King Ho-lu's rash and aggressive younger brother, acting on his own, led a flanking army of 5000 men into Chu and defeated an insignificant enemy force. This spoiled the element of surprise, so Sun Tzu's main army had to fight five tough battles before reaching the enemy capital. By the time they entered the city, the Chu king had escaped. They pursued him as far as the kingdom of Sui, where Sun Tzu sent in some poisonous propaganda: 'The runaway king of Chu exterminated all the descendants of the Chou Dynasty in his realm.' This was a terrible accusation. The Chou kings had fallen on hard times and were now little more than religious figures, guardians of ancient traditions, regarded as a moral force. To persecute them or their relatives was unthinkable.

The people of Sui were suitably shocked, and discussed whether to put the fugitive Chu king to death or turn him over to his pursuers. But after consulting an oracle they changed their minds and refused to surrender him.

Meanwhile, in the fallen capital of Chu, Sun's colleague Wu Tzu-hsu was grimly avenging his murdered father and brother. Unable to lay hands on the fugitive king, he exhumed the body of the king's predecessor – the ruler who had put his father and brother to death – and gave the corpse three hundred lashes, defiling the body. No doubt this was immensely gratifying, but it went against all propriety and could dangerously provoke the spirit world.

As word spread of this dark deed, the duke of the rival state of Chin declared angrily, 'Although the king of Chu was in the wrong, the actions of this minister are unacceptable, so we must go to Chu's defence.' The duke sent 500 chariots and infantry to aid Chu, and after six months of bitter fighting, they defeated the Wu army and its commander-in-chief, Sun Tzu.

King Ho-lu lingered too long in the conquered capital, enjoying the spoils of victory. During his absence, his impetuous younger brother took the opportunity to seize the throne of Wu, intending to declare himself king. King Ho-lu had to withdraw his occupying forces from Chu to put his own house in order. The prince fled into exile.

All this quarrelling further whetted the appetites of Wu's enemies. While everyone was distracted, the fugitive king of Chu recovered his throne as if he had never been away. Two years later, Sun Tzu devised a new strategy and Wu Tzu-hsu launched a fresh invasion that put the king of Chu to flight again. Historian Ssu-ma Ch'ien sums up: 'Thanks to the stratagems of Sun Tzu and Wu Tzu-hsu, the state of Wu defeated powerful Chu in the west, awed Ch'i and Chin in the north.' But the fighting was not finished.

At a time when all kings were dangerously unpredictable, the kings of Yueh were considered especially so. Their kingdom was in 'barbarian' country below the mouth of the Yangtze that today includes Chekiang, Fukien and Kwangtung provinces. For generations they had worn outrageous tattoos, cut their hair unfashionably short, and preferred to live rough 'in brambles and weeds', earning a reputation as wild men. The royal succession of King Kou-chien provided a chance to catch Yueh off-guard. Sun Tzu was instructed to plan the campaign. Inflated by recent victories, King Ho-lu unwisely insisted on leading the invasion personally. As Sun Tzu observed, 'the men of Wu and Yueh hate one another,' which made the outcome unpredictable.

The chief strategist of Yueh, the wily Fan Li, was Sun Tzu's most capable adversary. True to form he contrived a devilish twist. He scoured Yueh's dungeons for condemned men and offered them a deal in return for richly rewarding their families. As the convicts were doomed to be put to death anyway, they readily agreed. When the Wu army was poised to strike, the convicts all marched out in front of them and – with a great shout – cut off each other's heads. So dumbfounded were the Wu officers and men that Fan Li was able to launch a surprise attack on their flank and defeat them. During the confusion a poisoned arrow struck King Ho-lu in the hand, making him mortally ill. As he lay dying, he asked his son Fu-ch'ai, 'Will you forget who killed your father?'

'I will never forget,' the young prince swore.

That night Fu-ch'ai became king of Wu. He offered his father's prime minister, Wu Tzu-hsu, half his kingdom as a reward for supporting his right to inherit the crown. Wu Tzu-hsu thanked him, but graciously refused to accept. Offended, the singleminded young king became suspicious and chose the greedy and ambitious Po Pi as his prime minister instead.

After gaining this surprise victory over Wu, Fan Li warned the king of Yueh not to provoke further trouble. 'Weapons are unlucky, war is evil, and this feud with Wu is a minor matter. If you pursue an evil goal with unlucky means, risking your life for something minor, you insult Heaven and risk defeat.' The brash young king ignored him, began another campaign, and was defeated.

'I should have followed your advice,' he told Fan Li.

The strategist replied: 'One who overcomes vanity earns Heaven's help, one who turns disaster into victory earns men's help, and one who lives modestly earns the earth's help. Be humble, send Wu rich gifts, and if all else fails offer yourself as a hostage.'

Wagonloads of tribute from Yueh soon arrived in Wu, and particularly valuable gifts were secretly sent to Prime Minister Po Pi, who was dazzled. He decided to urge peace. Wu Tzu-hsu warned, 'The king of Yueh is just trying to buy time,' he said. 'If you do not destroy him now, you will regret it.'

Instead, King Fu-ch'ai took Po Pi's advice and chose peace. Five years passed, and the king of Wu began to feel cocky. He foolishly decided to atttack the state of Ch'i. Wu Tzu-hsu warned that behind his submissive mask the king of Yueh was secretly preparing to pounce. 'He eats only one dish at each meal. He shows exaggerated concern for his subjects. Odd behaviour like this means he is preparing his people for something. He is a cancer in our stomachs, a menace to us as long as he lives. Ch'i is only a disease of the skin. It is wrong to attack Ch'i before we destroy Yueh.'

When the king ignored his advice, Wu Tzu-hsu tried again. 'An unruly and insolent people should be wiped out, leaving no seeds in the soil. This is how the Shang Dynasty succeeded. I beg you to deal first with Yueh.'

Annoyed by this continual contrary advice and interference, King Fu-ch'ai sent Wu Tzu-hsu away from court on a trivial mission. While he was absent, Prime Minister Po Pi slandered him, saying that Wu Tzu-hsu was 'hot-tempered, stubborn and suspicious' and might start a rebellion. Indeed, spies reported that Wu Tzu-hsu had sent his son to live with friends in an enemy state, a potentially ominous move. That was enough for King Fu-ch'ai, who took off his sword and sent it to Wu Tzu-hsu with the command: 'Kill yourself with this.'

Seeing calamity ahead for the kingdom of Wu, and having no alternative according to the etiquette of the day, Wu Tzu-hsu committed suicide. Before doing so, he asked that a sapling be planted on his grave. When it had grown, it was to be made into a post and placed atop the city wall, with his skull mounted on the top so that he could witness the destruction of Wu by Yueh. Infuriated by this parting insult, King Fu-ch'ai had the dead man's corpse sewn up in a leather bag and thrown into the river, whereupon the spirit of Wu Tzu-hsu avenged him by raising mighty waves that caused many deaths.

Observing all this from neighbouring Yueh, chief strategist Fan Li advised his king to wait three more years to further allay suspicion. Exactly three years later, when the king of Wu was away from his capital, Yueh launched a surprise attack, defeated the Wu army and killed the crown prince. Nine years later, Yueh's armies struck again and completely overwhelmed the kingdom of Wu, absorbing it into Yueh and putting King Fu-ch'ai to death.

The feud between Wu and Yueh had lasted for thirty-seven years. Sun Tzu's opponent Fan Li, who ultimately succeeded in destroying Wu, was one of the few men involved in this long conflict to survive and prosper. Fan Li understood the perversity of human nature, so he realized that being a great hero was extremely dangerous. He turned down all rewards and honours and, when nobody was looking, slipped away secretly. In a letter explaining his decision to a friend, he said: 'When all the birds are killed the good bow is put away. When the cunning hares are dead, the hounds are made into stew. The king of Yueh with his long neck and predatory mouth is a good companion in time of trouble, but not in time of peace. You, too, had better leave.'

Gathering his jewels and other treasures, he set out in a flat-bottomed boat with his sons and a few followers, crossed rivers and lakes to the north, and never returned to Yueh. When he reached the state of Ch'i in Shantung, he changed his name to Master Wineskin, meaning he was infinitely adaptable. As a farmer on the coast, he worked hard with his sons, amassing property and gold. The people of Ch'i, impressed by his intelligence, wanted to appoint him prime minister. Fan Li rebuffed them, saying, 'No good ever came from nobility and fame.' He handed all his money to friends and neighbours and once again slipped away quietly with a few favourite jewels, resettling in Tao, a big city where a man could remain invisible, while getting rich. This time he called himself Lord Chu, bought and sold commodities, raised cattle, and made huge profits, until again he was rich and famous. Now too old for people to envy, he died peacefully. Today his stylized image hangs in Chinese stores all over the world, whose owners hope to match his adaptability and financial success, if not his invisibility.

What became of Sun Tzu we can only guess. He ceases to be mentioned in Ssù-ma Ch'ien's anecdotal histories. When King Fu-ch'ai succeeded to the throne and demanded Wu Tzu-hsu's suicide, Sun Tzu may have thought it prudent to take early retirement. It seems likely that he withdrew to his family's country place west of the capital, to devote the rest of his life to writing and refining the eighty-two chapters of his treatise. Like his rival Fan Li, Sun was always secretive and mysterious. A philosophy of invisibility runs through his *Art of War*. Being conspicuous makes you vulnerable. If you are invisible, your power is increased tenfold.

Certainly, he was exasperated by the vanity of his monarch. In his text, Sun repeatedly criticizes rulers and generals who drag out military campaigns in hope of eventual success – as the war between the kingdoms of Wu and Yueh was endlessly prolonged. 'Hostilities may exist for years while one strives for a single day of victory . . . Such a general is no commander of men, no help to his sovereign, no master of victory.' Implicitly, he is also saying that such a monarch is a burden to his people. In one of the chapters recently discovered in Shantung, titled 'Questions of King Wu,' the king asks Sun Tzu which one of the feuding ducal clans was going to inherit the kingdom of Chin. The analysis that follows reveals Sun's fundamental humanism. One group taxed unfairly, was disproportionately rich, and kept too large an army. 'Being too rich and their armies too large, the rulers too proud and their officials too extravagant, they expect to be victorious in every war – and therefore they will be the first to perish.' One by one he discounts the others, for the same reasons: too rich, too proud, too extravagant. Finally he comes to the Chao clan, who rule fairly and levy no taxes. 'Being modest, keeping few soldiers, living frugally, and ruling wisely over bountiful people – they . . . will survive victorious.'

Sun Tzu is remembered not for military victories, which were hampered by a small-minded, egocentric monarch, but for his genius in emphasizing the importance of mischief, cleverness and common sense in human conflict – as opposed to brute force. Not just in war but in diplomacy, commerce and all other endeavours. Foreknowledge, deception and other elements of the black arts must come into play to achieve success with minimum damage and hardship. Only when cleverness fails should violence be used, and then with maximum surprise, maximum ingenuity, and maximum force, to achieve a quick and overwhelming victory. No halfway measures are acceptable.

After many centuries of inspiring kingmakers, generals and spies, Sun's message was lost on the nineteenth century's Clausewitz, Moltke, and the iron generals of Total War, who were too fascinated by industrial technology, military hardware, logistics, and sheer destructive power. Nevertheless, much of what Clausewitz admired about Napoleon's use of paramilitary units, surprise and evasion, probably came from the Corsican's early reading of the first Western translation of Sun Tzu, by J.J.M. Amiot, a French Jesuit scholar in China, which was in circulation in Paris when Napoleon was a young officer.

This preference for cleverness over brute force has earned Sun Tzu a prominent place ever since on the bookshelves of diplomats, generals and corporate planners. Filled with terse and provocative aphorisms, *The Art of War* is as closely studied by Asian investors and businessmen today as it was earlier by Mao Tse-tung, Ho Chi-minh and Vo Nguyen Giap. The Japanese say, 'Politics is business, business is war.' If the marketplace is a battleground, requiring strategy and tactics, Sun Tzu wrote the bible:

Bait them with the prospect of gain, bewilder and mystify them.
Use anger to disrupt them, humility to make them arrogant.
Tire them by running away, cause them to quarrel among themselves.
Attack them when they do not expect it, when they are least prepared.
Be so subtle that you are invisible.
Be so mysterious that you are intangible.
Then you will control your rivals' fate.

We can easily see how a grasp of Sun Tzu helps Asian politicians and CEOs confuse and manipulate their Western counterparts in the international marketplace.

Use espionage and mystification in every enterprise.
All life is based on deception.

When all the human instruments of spying, deception and mystification are in place and functioning smoothly, he said, this is the Celestial Web.

Sun Tzu's treatise remains inaccessible to many Western readers because of its identification with warfare and its aura of Oriental mysticism. That is easily fixed by eliminating the military jargon that has been used in the classic translations, most of them done by military men. Plain English works wonders. Even after reading *The Art of War*, many military thinkers failed to grasp that to Sun Tzu war was failure. *Winning* was all important, but the *art* of war was to win without battle. Sun Tzu never talked about 'fair rules' or a 'level playing field.'

> Everyone says victory in battle is good, but it is not.
> A general who wins every battle is not really skilful.
> To make your enemy helpless without battles is the secret.
> It is better to preserve a nation intact than to destroy it.
> To overcome rivals without fighting is the summit of skill.

If battle could not be avoided, then every deceit and ploy should be used to mislead, anger and confuse the enemy, before dropping the very heavens on him. There was a time for overwhelming force. All other possibilities must first be exhausted, including turning and running.

Among Sun's most diligent practitioners today are the Japanese. They had been avid pupils of Sun down the ages, until the nineteenth century, when they became fascinated by the industrial revolution, and the Prussian military model of Total War. In 1945, they abandoned Clausewitz and Moltke at Hiroshima and rediscovered Sun Tzu. With Sun's guidance, they re-established Japan's Greater East-Asia Co-Prosperity Sphere without firing a shot.

No group has been more effective in applying Sun Tzu's ideas to daily life, to commercial strategy and business operations, and to survival itself, than the Overseas Chinese, who have always found themselves mangled between the gears of East and West. To him they owe much of their success in coming out of the mangle controlling the gears and owning much of the machinery. These were lessons that the Overseas Chinese had to learn the hard way. After repeatedly being persecuted in their adopted countries, they became particularly expert at invisibility. While the Duke of Chou is their sworn enemy, Sun Tzu and Fan Li are their natural allies.

In recent years there has been an explosion of interest in Sun Tzu in Asia and the West. Hundreds of articles and many new editions have appeared in China, Japan and Taiwan. In Beijing, conventions are held and seminars given on the study of Sun Tzu. In the West, five new English-language versions of *The Art of War* have been published, along with a flurry of books applying Sun Tzu's precepts to business activities. It is part of the wave of excitement about new Asian markets, where Westerners must grapple with the challenge of 'unfair' Oriental competition, and learn to recognize and deal with Asian methods and mystification. Sun Tzu is the best place to start. He has done much to make invisibility and mystification part of Asian culture, a barrier that the West senses but finds difficult to penetrate. The art of the chameleon.

To the sage himself, one ancient Chinese source adds a final epitaph: 'Outside the Wu Gate of Wu Hsieh [Suchow], at a distance of ten *li*, there was a large tomb which is that of Sun Tzu.' Nobody has found it.

CHAPTER 3

SWEET REVENGE, EATEN COLD

HE WAS BORN IN INTERESTING TIMES, WHEN CAPTAINS AND soldiers were smeared on the leaves and grass. Quick and clever, Sun Pin might have been a successful magician or Taoist shaman, but his ancestor was Sun Tzu, which gave him a very high opinion of himself and provoked dangerous envy. His birthplace was a country manor on the Shantung peninsula, in the state of Ch'i, one of several kingdoms still contending for power in the final stages of Warring States, just before all of China was swallowed up by the state of Chin.

Ch'i was famous for its sorcerers and magicians, many of whom lived along the coast or on the magic mountain, Mount T'ien, whose summit was close to heaven. The capital, Lin-tzu, was a city of 70,000 households, or roughly 350,000 individuals, which, even allowing for boasting, was pretty crowded. In its streets they said the crowds were so thick on a hot day that 'when they shake the sweat off, rain falls'.

Sun Pin lost his parents at an early age and was raised by an uncle who was an official in the state bureaucracy. After they took the wrong side in a power struggle, the family fled into exile and Sun Pin became separated. Eventually, the boy found refuge in a secluded hermitage

called Ghost Valley, where he was taken as a pupil by the famous
Taoist hermit known as the Master of Ghost Valley. In those days,
rustic martial arts academies were all over the place. The best path for
upward mobility was a career winning battles for greedy but incompetent kings. Even Confucius was expected to give advice on military
strategy, and was no laggard when it came to conspiracy. When Sun
Pin was a boy, the role model was Wu Ch'i, a ruthless soldier-
statesman whose enemies surprised him at a funeral and perforated
him with arrows. Sun Pin was planning a similar career with a better
ending. He had a natural advantage, for any king or general would be
honoured to have Sun Tzu's direct descendant as his protégé.

Ghost Valley was a fine beginning. Among the other students was
P'ang Chuan, who became commander-in-chief of the king of Wei.

Disciples were pitted against each other in solving Taoist riddles, in
wargames, or in hand-to-hand combat. Sun Pin and his fellow student
P'ang Chuan became arch-rivals. The dashing Sun Pin was supremely
confident, and usually victorious. This had a demoralizing effect on
P'ang Chuan, who became sullen, and finally resigned from the
academy to return to his native state, Wei. There he joined the army,
proved himself in battle, and was promoted to general.

Sun Pin continued his training at Ghost Valley, where over the years
visitors came away with stories of his cleverness, originality and
prowess. The king of Wei heard these reports, and after learning that
they had been classmates, asked General P'ang Chuan to invite Sun Pin
to court, where he might give them advice on strategy. P'ang Chuan
was furious and tried to dissuade the king, pointing out that Sun Pin
was a native of Ch'i, their enemy, so his advice would be suspect. But
the king insisted and a royal invitation was despatched.

When Sun Pin arrived at Ta Liang, the capital, the king was
immediately impressed by his wit and bold ideas. They discussed Wei's
overall military strategy, and Sun offered clever suggestions. The king
was so pleased that he wanted to make Sun a staff officer, but P'ang
Chuan – jealous of the attention – persuaded the king to settle instead
for the title 'guest officer'. A welcoming banquet was thrown for Sun,
and he joined the king's inner circle.

In time this news reached Sun's relatives in Ch'i. They sent a
messenger to Wei to invite him home for a reunion. Sun was delighted.

It had been years since they had been separated. But it would have been graceless to ask for leave so soon after accepting the king's appointment. He wrote a reply promising to visit at the first opportunity, and sent a messenger off with the letter and a generous gift of money. As this was a family affair, he did not report it to the king.

P'ang Chuan had been eating bitterness. Here came this vainglorious puppy, the swaggering hero from Ghost Valley, performing conjuror's tricks to steal the teeth from his mouth and break his rice bowl. Already Sun had taken P'ang Chuan's place as the king's favourite. Something would have to be done to put the puppy in his place. The solution presented itself when one of P'ang Chuan's spies ambushed Sun's messenger and brought back his letter promising to visit Ch'i soon.

P'ang Chuan showed the letter to King Wei, pointing out that only an ingrate and scoundrel would plot to leave immediately after being taken into the king's deepest confidence – unless, of course, he was a secret agent planning to reveal Wei's military secrets to the enemy commanders of Ch'i.

The king was reluctant to judge his new adviser too hastily, for the letter might be counterfeit. Surely Sun Pin was not really thinking of leaving so soon. P'ang Chuan hurried to Sun's chambers and warmly encouraged him to visit his family, promising that King Wei would be very sympathetic. Encouraged, Sun went directly to the king and requested leave. Instead of kindness, the king flew into a rage. He ordered Sun taken to the dungeon and prepared for execution. P'ang Chuan suggested a lingering punishment instead. The king left matters in his hands.

In the dungeon, P'ang Chuan took charge. On his orders, the jailers strapped Sun down on a stone bench and tattooed his face with two ideographs on each cheek, the four together reading: *ssu-t'ung wai-kuo* or 'Treacherous Collusion with Foreign Kingdom'. Having this tattooed across his cheeks would make it impossible for Sun ever to show his face in polite society, or to obtain a job of trust from any royal court.

Taking up a butcher knife, the jailers then sliced the tendons below each kneecap, crippling him for life. He would be able to move around only by dragging his legs. Mutilation was routine punishment for criminals in ancient China. Cutting off the left foot at the ankle was one of several kinds of amputation. Iron was expensive, only then coming into use in weapons and farm implements, so leg-irons were a luxury. It was simpler to hobble a man by cutting off a foot. This limited movement, but still allowed a man to be worked to death in construction gangs building roads or walls of packed dirt.

When he recounted the story of Sun Pin, historian Ssu-ma Ch'ien expressed dismay that such a brilliant strategist would allow himself to be tricked in this manner, but the young man had not yet learned the importance of invisibility. When men were competing for posts throughout the Warring States, it was sometimes necessary to be conspicuous.

Now his only hope lay in deception. As one Chinese account goes, while Sun lay in the dungeon recovering from his mutilation, he rubbed slime in his hair and smeared his face with blood and mucus. He screamed, wept, laughed hysterically and jerked in convulsions until P'ang Chuan decided to put his insanity to the test. Delicious food was brought, but Sun knocked the dish away and ate his own faeces. This repelled even P'ang Chuan, who ordered the crazed prisoner kept out of sight from then on. P'ang Chuan soon lost interest. As months passed, guards paid less attention when the madman dragged himself around. He was even permitted to drag himself into the sunshine.

Nearly a year after his mutilation, Sun overheard that an emissary from Ch'i was paying an official visit. Although he did not realize it, his rescuers were on their way. The visit of Ambassador Ch'un Yu-k'un was cover for a cloak-and-dagger operation by secret agents in his entourage. Word of what had befallen him had reached Sun's family in Ch'i, and they had reported this to a powerful relative, Prince T'ien Ch'i, who discussed it with their king. The king of Ch'i was incensed. Calling in his ministers, they devised a plan. A look-alike was found and a cash settlement was arranged whereby the double agreed to take Sun's place.

When the diplomatic mission reached Wei, Ambassador Ch'un kept the court banqueting all night while his agents substituted the look-alike and spirited Sun Pin to safety. Disguising him as a pregnant woman, they sped across the border in a covered chariot.

When they arrived in Ch'i, he was taken to his cousins, who nursed him back to health. His face was permanently marked by the tattoos, and his legs were all but useless. He could never again move without crutches and braces. With bitter humour, he re-christened himself Sun Pin – Sun the Kneecapped, Sun the Legless, Sun the Cripple. When he was introduced to the commander-in-chief of the army, Prince T'ien Ch'i, who had contrived his rescue, the prince took an immediate liking to Sun, and the two were said to have spent three days and nights drinking and talking. The prince insisted that Sun remain permanently as a guest in his palace, where there were servants to look after his needs, and numerous concubines. It was the beginning of a lifelong friendship.

Prince T'ien often gambled with other nobles on chariot races in which they pitted their own teams of horses, but he usually lost. Watching the races, Sun Pin observed that the teams, which were ranked as first, second and third string, did not differ greatly from one stable to another. Mediocre in one was the same as mediocre in another. After that, it was simple arithmetic. He told Prince T'ien Ch'i, 'If you bet heavily on the next race, I will show you how to win.'

Sun then told him, 'Match your weakest team against his first, your best against his second, and your second best against his weakest.' The prince readily agreed and wagered with his king on the best two out of three, as Sun had instructed. The prince lost the first, but he won the next two, bringing him a thousand pieces of gold. Immensely pleased, he introduced his protégé to the king, who was fascinated to hear a first-hand account of Sun's physical ordeal. After discussing espionage and warfare with him, the king made Sun a staff officer on the spot.

Sun's life now entered a productive new phase. His early years had been spent in the reckless pursuit of glory, for which he had paid a terrible price. He would spend the rest of his days in solitude, becoming his ancestor's most ardent pupil.

Several years later, in 353 BC, the kingdom of Wei – where Sun Pin had been crippled – attacked an outlying district of the state of Chao, with General P'ang Chuan leading the attack. The government of Chao appealed to its ally, Ch'i, for help. The king of Ch'i called in Sun Pin and asked him to take charge and hurry to Chao's defence. Sun thanked him for the honour, but explained, 'It would not be appropriate; a cripple cannot lead an army, and I have been marked for life as a convict.' Instead he offered to serve as strategist and chief-of-staff under Prince T'ien Ch'i.

To keep off his legs, Sun set out for the front in a specially built wagon. The prince wanted to strike directly at the enemy force, now deep in Chao territory. Sun advised against a headlong attack. 'To unravel tangled yarn, one does not grasp the entire skein. To ward off a tidal wave, one does not stand in its path. Strike at an undefended place. Then, when the antagonists grow tired, you will control the outcome.' The prince was puzzled, so Sun explained: 'At this time Wei and Chao are busy fighting each other. Wei's special forces and shock troops are all in the field, leaving their capital city guarded only by the old and the weak. Why not march quickly toward the capital, and take control of the main roads and lines of communication? Everyone will think we plan to attack their capital while it is undefended. To save it the Wei army must disengage from Chao and hurry home. We will be waiting in ambush for them. In one stroke we can relieve Chao and hit Wei when they are weary and frantic.'

The prince followed Sun's advice. P'ang Chuan and his army were forced to break off their invasion of Chao and hurry home, blundering into Sun Pin's well-prepared ambush. They were badly beaten. P'ang Chuan barely escaped with his life.

Sun Pin had dealt a humiliating blow to his mortal enemy. His strategy became famous in Chinese military annals, where it is called 'Besiege Wei to Rescue Chao' (the tidy epigram, *wei-Wei chiu-Chao*'). Let the enemy strike the first blow, allow it to go by unobstructed, avoid the predictable response and instead hit his weakest point at a time of your own choosing. Alternatively, hit 'that which he values most' – strike his homebase or kidnap his favourite concubine. In 1938, Mao Tse-tung used Sun Pin's tactic against Japanese troops attacking a communist base: '. . . leave some of our forces in the base area to keep the enemy busy while our main force attacks the Japanese base; this will oblige him to withdraw, employing the tactic *wei-Wei chiu-Chao*.'

During the next thirteen years, Chinese sources mention Sun Pin and Prince T'ien Ch'i taking part in a number of campaigns, but details are missing until the great battle of Maling in 341 BC, when Wei attacked the kingdom of Han. General P'ang Chuan was again in command of Wei forces, accompanied by Crown Prince Shen. Han urgently appealed to Ch'i for aid. Prince T'ien Ch'i suggested using the same strategy that had worked before, attacking the undefended capital of Wei to force General P'ang Chuan to break off his siege and hurry home. Sun Pin listened to the discussion silently, smiling to himself. The king asked him to explain his amusement.

'Why hurry?' asked Sun. 'The siege has just begun, so Han is not yet weary. If we take the pressure off Han too quickly, they might send their armies against us.' Sun Pin was well acquainted with treachery.

'However, let us promise to help Han, so that they will take heart and defend themselves with a will,' Sun said. 'When both Wei and Han are tired, we can still intervene.'

This agreed, they took their time making preparations. Ever more anxious appeals came from Han. When Sun Pin's spies brought evidence that both combatants were growing weary, Prince T'ien Ch'i set out with Sun Pin at the head of an army of a hundred thousand men, including chariots, cavalry and ten thousand crossbowmen. As before, they marched toward the capital of Wei. News of their approach caused panic, and the king sent an anxious message to General P'ang Chuan ordering him to interrupt the siege of Han and hurry back with his army.

P'ang Chuan was furious. 'That puppy Sun Pin is trying the same trick again. The king gives me no alternative, but I will be watching closely as we return. This time there will be no ambush.'

When Sun Pin's spies reported P'ang Chuan's anger, he chuckled. 'We will use his rage against him.'

'How can we bait the trap this time?' asked Prince T'ien Ch'i.

'Everyone thinks we are cowards because we avoid fighting whenever possible. This is only wisdom, but they mistake it for cowardice. So we will use our enemy's folly to trick him, by making him believe that our men are all deserting.' He surveyed the landscape. 'We are deep in enemy territory. Let's have our secret agents spread news that we are thinking of turning back because of heavy desertions.'

That night, Sun Pin gave orders for each man in the army to make a separate cooking fire, lighting up the sky and leaving a hundred thousand small burnt patches. The second night, deeper in enemy territory, he ordered only fifty thousand cooking fires. The third night thirty thousand.

At a reckless pace, P'ang Chuan and his army were catching up, but with growing fatigue. Each day, as his vanguard came upon another Ch'i bivouac site, they reported many fewer cooking fires. Mass desertions were evidently cutting Sun Pin's huge force down to a small, ragtag remnant. P'ang Chuan always considered the Ch'i people cringing curs, so he was pleased with himself. 'As soon as they heard I was coming, most of their officers and soldiers fled!'

Wei's Crown Prince Shen, still wet behind the ears, tried to warn him: 'But the men of Ch'i are notoriously deceitful, and that cunning Sun Pin is commanding the army. We should be careful.'

'This time I will get even,' P'ang Chuan replied. He hastily departed with only lightly armed troops on a forced march.

By then Sun Pin had found a suitable spot near Maling. It was a gentle valley between two hills, with a single trail down the middle, and numerous knolls, grave mounds, dykes and other obstacles on either side that would conceal his archers. At the far end of the valley was an ancient tree with a broad trunk. Sun ordered his men to cut saplings and build a barrier across the trail beyond the tree. Then he hid five thousand crossbowmen on either side of the trail for several hundred yards leading up to the tree. The remainder of his infantry and cavalry took cover in woods at the opposite end of the valley; they would allow P'ang Chuan's army to enter, then close the trap.

When everyone was hidden, Sun Pin had the bark peeled off the trunk of the great tree, and in charcoal wrote the big ideographs: P'ANG CHUAN DIES HERE. His crossbowmen were ordered to fire when a torch was lit beneath the tree. Sun Pin then retired to wait for his enemy.

As expected, P'ang Chuan's force reached the valley at Maling that evening. When alerted to the barricade ahead, he took it as a laughable attempt by the fleeing Ch'i army to block pursuit. As he approached, he saw something daubed on the tree's bare trunk. Curiosity got the better of caution. Lighting a torch, he read his own epitaph – just as ten thousand crossbowmen discharged their bolts. The Wei vanguard sprouted quills like porcupines. Dozens of bolts pierced P'ang Chuan, turning him into a human pincushion. Far to the rear, the Ch'i infantry and cavalry fell upon his men. P'ang Chuan's last words are said to have been: 'That puppy! I've made his reputation.'

Taking full advantage of the victory, Sun Pin and Prince T'ien Ch'i destroyed the Wei army and captured Crown Prince Shen, sending him back to Ch'i, where he was executed.

Fame being fleet of foot and only loyalty faster, the Battle of Maling was hardly over when the two heroes found themselves feared and their achievements despised. Success is a dangerous thing in China, perhaps everywhere. Fan Li could have warned them about what happens when hounds are no longer needed to hunt hares.

On their way home, Sun Pin warned Prince T'ien that he might have to stage a pre-emptive *coup*. Spies told them that during their absence, rivals at court had persuaded the king of Ch'i that the two heroes were now too dangerous to be trusted. When your rivals claim that you are plotting to seize power, Sun said, one of your few options is to do exactly that. The king ordered the city gates closed to block their return and refused them entry to the capital.

Because of Prince T'ien's failure to take the initiative, it was by then too late for a *coup*. The two men withdrew to a distant garrison to consider the future. Eventually, Prince T'ien accepted an invitation to go into exile in the state of Chu to the south. The prince became the lord of Kiangnan, on the south lip of the Yangtze, with crippled Sun Pin as his silent partner.

There in the garden each morning as he grew old, doubtless chuckling to himself, Sun Pin brushed eighty-six chapters of ideographs down hundreds of bamboo slips, to leave behind a small reminder of his passing. For more than two thousand years they were lost, and Sun Pin became the god of invisibility. But recently in Shantung, when his complete treatise was found along with fragments of Sun Tzu's *The Art of War*, Sun the Kneecapped literally came back from the grave.

CHAPTER 4

ELIXIR OF YOUTH

WHEN HE GREW BORED BROKERING PEARLS AND JADE BACK IN THE third century BC, Lu Pu-wei – East Asia's first big capitalist magnate – decided to take over the most powerful state in China using only his wits and the perfume of money. By extraordinary guile and the application of Sun Tzu rules, he made himself the real power behind the throne. For over two thousand years (until the 1930s) he was the only tycoon to serve as China's prime minister. To top that, it is generally accepted that Lu secretly fathered China's First Emperor. This may reflect badly upon the emperor, but it has given Chinese businessmen something to gloat about.

Orthodox Confucians see Lu as one of the greatest villains in their history. Merchants regard his bastard son, the First Emperor, as their nemesis, because he expelled many thousands of merchant families from North China. This began the mass migration southward into Yueh that ultimately produced the Overseas Chinese. Perhaps it was a blessing in disguise.

Merchant Lu started life as an importer. In ancient times, just like today, wealthy Chinese craved luxuries from distant places, foreign goods brought to China by caravan, pack mule and ship from the South Seas and beyond: precious stones, ivory, camphor wood, exotic furs, aphrodisiacs. How far back this trade first began is anyone's guess, but the cowrie shells used as currency during the Shang Dynasty before 1500 BC could only have come from the Indian Ocean. We know that North China traders imported goods from Eurasia, Indochina and India during the Chou Dynasty. International trade boomed during Spring & Autumn when ships from Yueh below the mouth of the Yangtze carried Chinese goods to South East Asia and brought back local products and articles purchased from Arab, Phoenician and Indian traders. However, for a very long time knowledge of the outside world remained the trade secret of maritime traders, overland merchants and brokers such as Lu, who bought cheap and sold dear.

The idea for his hostile corporate takeover of Chin first occurred to Merchant Lu in 267 BC, while he was throwing a party at a mansion in the city of Hantan in the state of Chao. Among his guests was the teenage son of a lesser concubine of the crown prince of Chin. The boy, who was not very bright, had been sent to Chao to fulfill one of those non-aggression pacts of the day, in which royal families despatched relatives to be the hostages of their enemies. Lu recognized immediately that this boy was a rare commodity. After befriending the lad, and winning him over completely with a stunning gift of five hundred gold coins, Lu made a discreet trip to Chin. There, by the donation of a small fortune in pearls and gemstones, he persuaded the childless wife of the crown prince to adopt the concubine's son, thus legitimizing him as a potential heir to the throne. Then Lu gave the crown prince himself a huge sum in gold to designate this boy as his royal heir. The crown prince also agreed to make Merchant Lu the boy's official tutor, which gave Lu the run of the palace, where he could easily double or triple his fortune in no time by insider trading. As conspiracies go this might sound complicated, but no more so than building a house of cards. Lu had a knack for such things.

To put it in business terms, Lu was investing heavily in Chin state futures. This shows amazing foresight on his part, because Chin had a powerful army and would soon overcome all its Warring States rivals to create the first Chinese empire, and Lu was to play a biological role in this historic event. The reigning king of Chin was very old. It was only a matter of time before the crown prince would inherit the throne, and Lu's speculative investment in the boy would then pay off.

Meanwhile, Lu had a beautiful young concubine, Lady Hsia, who was in perpetual heat. He was the only one who knew that she had just become pregnant. The moment the teenage prince saw her, he fell in love with Lady Hsia and begged Lu to let him marry her. Lu was fond of the girl himself, but his devious mind came to his rescue and he granted the boy's wish. Their wedding took place immediately and a few months later, in 259 BC, the bride gave birth to a son. Her dimwitted husband accepted the child as his own and called him Prince Cheng.

When the elderly king of Chin expired eight years later, the crown prince mounted the throne, but conveniently died of an upset stomach within the year. As arranged, he was succeeded by Lu's youthful protégé. Within three years this luckless fellow died too, and was succeeded by little Prince Cheng – the secret child of Merchant Lu.

While the boy grew up, Lu served for ten years as his regent and as prime minister of Chin. Already a very rich man, he took the title of marquis and assigned himself ten thousand slaves.

He also set about fixing the image of Chin state. Because of its location on the north-western frontier, where nomadic tribes posed a constant danger, Chin had become the most powerful kingdom in China militarily, but its people were considered vulgar and uncouth. To improve this image, Lu invited three thousand scholars, artists, philosophers, poets, orators and celebrities from other states to come and live in the Chin capital at his expense. While he fed and entertained them, he asked them to compile their most brilliant ideas in an encyclopaedia, which became China's first integrated full-length book, the *Spring and Autumn Annals of Master Lu*. Lu was so proud of it that he offered a thousand gold pieces to anyone who could think of something brilliant to add. Nobody took up his offer.

While this makes Lu seem a bit frivolous, his shrewd administration as prime minister and regent brought Chin much closer to the moment when it would overrun the last of its neighbours and unite China under a central regime. Lu's story is all the more extraordinary because he was a crude, uneducated, self-made man. Most commoners who attained high position had outstanding educations. Lu's case is also exceptional because the state of Chin was the stronghold of the Legalists, who regarded all commercial people as parasites. Mandarins condemned Lu for starting out in life as a crass merchant, but others pointed out that many bureaucrats were not as competent as merchants. A jealous noble was told point blank: 'You cannot win a contest of power with Lu, so you curse him as someone lacking propriety.'

His bastard son mounted the throne of Chin as a teenager in 246 BC. Lu became worried that the young man might discover that his prime minister was still having an occasional romp with the royal mother, Lady Hsia. A way had to be found to make the perpetually amorous queenmother self-destruct. After searching far and wide, Lu hired a young man that the great historian Ssu-ma Ch'ien describes as having an enormous penis. To get the attention of the queenmother, Lu commanded the young stud to walk naked around the palace garden with a wagon wheel mounted on his permanent erection (even great historians are given to occasional exaggeration). Excited palace ladies spread the news like windblown sand.

When the queenmother showed immediate interest, Lu gave the man to her as a love slave. He recommended shaving the paramour's head and plucking his eyebrows, to make him look like a palace eunuch. Wickedly, Lu then let the young ruler know that his mother was keeping a false eunuch, and that the lovers were plotting against him. The stud and all his relatives were arrested and executed, and Lady Hsia was sent to live out her days locked up in a remote palace. Lu himself also came under suspicion. When the monarch turned twenty-one and began to take power into his own hands, he fired Lu as regent, degraded him to commoner, and banished him to distant Szechuan in disgrace. On his way there, fearing he would be assassinated, Lu swallowed poison. After his death, extreme vigilance was exercised to keep businessmen from ever again gaining control of the government.

In 221 BC, sixteen years after the suicide of Merchant Lu, having conquered all rival states, the ruler of Chin declared himself China's First Emperor (Shih-huang-ti). Brief though it was, his reign changed China dramatically. When he unified the country all the old feudal barriers collapsed and social mobility became easier. The north-west and west were incorporated, and China expanded militarily north-east to Korea and south all the way to Vietnam.

Apart from its military tradition, Chin was a well-run state, with a legal system of terrible effectiveness. While other states had been weakened by intrigue, the entire population of Chin was divided into groups of five or ten families, in which all members were responsible for the wrongdoing of any individual. Punishment was severe. Aside from beheading, those guilty of treason were boiled alive, cut in two at the waist, or torn apart by chariots. A death sentence could be commuted if you submitted to castration. As scholars have pointed out, in nineteenth-century England you got the death penalty for stealing five shillings' worth of shop goods. The difference in Chin was that laws applied to rich and poor alike. Although the rich evaded punishment in the usual manner, the idea itself was highly original.

Many of the actions of the First Emperor were inspired by his brilliant and tyrannical prime minister, Li Ssu. For one, he persuaded the First Emperor to end the feudal system, which had been a major source of corruption. All the former state rulers and their noble dependents, some 120,000 families in all, were pensioned off and moved to palaces built for them in the capital, where they were kept under strict surveillance. The empire was partitioned into thirty-six commanderies ruled by a triumvirate of a civil governor, a military commander and an imperial inspector. Each commandery was divided into counties run by magistrates. These posts were salaried rather than hereditary. In this way, the entire empire could be ruled from the centre, where the emperor had a monopoly on punishment and patronage.

Ending the feudal aristocracy provoked a famous confrontation. At a banquet in 213 BC, scholars wished the First Emperor 'long life', but one crusty Confucian warned that the new empire would not last long if the emperor failed to restore the hereditary privileges of the noble families. This annoyed Prime Minister Li Ssu. He cursed scholars for 'studying the past to criticize the present', confusing and agitating ordinary people, and endangering the empire. To eliminate such provocation, Li Ssu went on, all books should be burned, except those in the imperial library. Anyone who failed to turn over all his books and records within thirty days should be arrested, tattooed across the face as a criminal, and put into forced labour. Then anybody who read books without authorization should be beheaded along with all his relatives. The emperor agreed, and to emphasize his decision, he took off the offending scholar's hat and urinated in it.

This was not the only time in Chinese history when books were banned, burned or rewritten, and scholars put to death. Many emperors saw to it that records were rewritten to conform to their views. Books themselves were not what Li Ssu objected to, but their use by scholars to criticize and subvert the regime. This incident fixed for all time the First Emperor's image as a tyrant.

Despite this nasty reputation, he accomplished much, building great roads, walls, palaces and irrigation projects, some continuing in service to this day. Highways stretched 6,800 kilometres, nearly double the road system of the Roman Empire. Chin's victory brought in vast treasures and made possible the use of prisoners as slave labour on a mammoth scale. Military campaigns and great building projects were carried out simultaneously. General Meng T'ien, the most famous of Chin's commanders, built the Great Wall and a three-lane north–south highway to Inner Mongolia, in places 24 metres wide. Some shorter sections of the Great Wall had been built in earlier times, but Meng T'ien built new walls to join them all together. When finished, the Great Wall stretched 2,600 miles from the desert west of Sian across the mountains to Liaotung near Korea. 700,000 men were put to work building and furnishing the First Emperor's tomb, which included a magnificently crafted terracotta army.

The First Emperor also conquered the feisty independent kingdom of Yueh, along the coast of the Yangtze River, which had been Sun Tzu's chief adversary. While everyone else was busy building the Great Wall, digging canals, cutting roads, spying on enemies and firing the terracotta army, the emperor was colonizing Yueh and the rest of South China with tens of thousands of criminals, riff-raff, merchants and shopkeepers, who were forcibly expelled from the north with their entire families. The idea was to clean out all commercial people from North China and ship them south to repopulate Yueh with ethnic Chinese. There, among the hills and wetlands of modern Chekiang, and in the pocket valleys of coastal Fukien and Kwangtung, environmental conditions were suitable for traditional North China agriculture. Few merchant families escaped the First Emperor's dragnet: lowly stallkeepers, prosperous middlemen, rich entrepreneurs, everybody was loaded onto carts and sent away south, giving the coastal bulge of South China the characteristic commercial personality it has today. This would become the great seedbed of the Overseas Chinese.

Merchants were targeted because of the longstanding official prejudice against commerce in any form. North China had always been an agricultural civilization run by a fastidious feudal bureaucracy. Orthodox Confucians assigned merchants to the bottom of the social heap, lower than peasant farmers, lower than artisans, lower even than soldiers, down on a level with criminals. Merchants were dangerous because they were greedy, ruthless, unpredictable, and predatory, and lived by different rules. National prosperity was based on agriculture, not commerce, and there was something unfilial, venal and dangerous about the way many merchants made their living. The bottom line was that farmers and artisans were producers, while merchants produced nothing and made their living by profiteering at the expense of others. While not all merchants or shopkeepers were predatory, many were prepared to withhold grain in the face of famine to drive prices up.

One imperial minister complained that peasants were always being squeezed between the avarice of the government and the avarice of merchants: 'Sometimes taxes are collected unexpectedly; if the orders are issued in the morning, farmers must be prepared to pay by evening. To meet this deadline they have to sell their possessions at half price, while those who have no possessions to sell have to borrow money at two hundred per cent interest. To pay back the loan eventually they must sell their fields and dwellings, sometimes even their children or grandchildren. The big merchants deal in superficial luxuries and lead an easy life in the cities. Taking advantage of the urgent demands of the government, they sell commodities at double the normal price . . . Without experiencing the farmers' sufferings, they make vast gains. Taking advantage of their riches, they associate with kings and marquises. Their power is greater than that of government officials, and they try to outdo each other in spending their profits. They wander idly around, roaming as far as a thousand *li* . . . They ride in fancy carriages, wear shoes of silk, and trail white silk garments. It is no wonder that merchants take over farms, while farmers become vagrants drifting from place to place.'

Then, as today, merchants were always seeking to subvert officials; and many bureaucrats were only too willing to be tempted. Even the highest mandarins were prepared to make exceptions for very rich merchants, providing they played by certain rules and were painstakingly discreet in their loans, bribes, kickbacks, gifts and other inducements. In the end, those with money and those with power were mutually dependent. The all-too-human craving for luxuries created a dangerous addiction. Better to blame merchants for profiting from bad habits, than to blame mandarins for allowing the addiction to develop in the first place. Expelling all merchants to the south also cancelled many unpaid debts.

Most dangerous politically were the venture capitalists, educated officeholders or members of the nobility with a knack for secret investing and commodity trading, hidden behind layers of intermediaries. Shadowy investors and commodity brokers like Merchant Lu had been able to buy serious political power.

To keep merchants from gaining influence through bribery, political appointments or social status, strict controls were applied to all visible sources of income. New laws were drafted that put this prejudice into action. Official antagonism towards merchants and entrepreneurs hardened into formal government doctrine during the Han Dynasty, and has been a cornerstone of every subsequent central regime in China. Merchants as a whole were ostracized from North China politics for the next two thousand years, until Deng declared that 'to get rich is glorious'. This only forced businessmen to be more devious, keeping multiple ledgers. Thicker face, blacker heart. They were especially hated because they were chameleons: hard to detect, mobile, resilient and in a pinch able to grow a new tail.

The First Emperor's loathing for merchants was strikingly inconsistent on one point. He was a sucker for any promoter of everlasting life. He made frequent trips to Shantung and other parts of the empire where there were sacred mountains, seeking the elixir of immortality. As he travelled around his realm, the emperor became fascinated by the rugged beauty of the Shantung coast, and the sea beyond. He sent thirty thousand families to colonize a stretch of that coastline.

Shantung was famous for its magicians and sages. They spoke of potent plants from islands in the ocean, possessing narcotic properties that might contribute to longevity or immortality. The First Emperor expressed regret that he could not go to sea himself in search of such ingredients. One magician, Hsu Fu, asked for permission to set out, 'after due purification', to find three mountainous islands inhabited by the immortals, who might be willing to part with some elixir. The emperor agreed to underwrite the expedition at huge cost, and Hsu Fu embarked with a fleet of oceangoing sailing rafts and three thousand carefully chosen young men and comely girls as colonists. They took along 'large quantities of seeds, and of the five grains, and artisans of every sort,' and never returned. Some think they settled in Taiwan, Guam, Japan – or even North America.

The First Emperor probably concluded from this costly experience, that there were strong similarities between magicians and merchants, but he never stopped searching for the elixir. During a visit to Shantung in the summer of 210 BC, the First Emperor fell ill and died. By the time the funeral cortège travelled hundreds of miles inland to his magnificent tomb, the body was decomposing. To protect the emperor's sacred image, the smell was hidden by rotting fish, carried in other vehicles in the procession. They might have saved themselves the trouble, for in North China noses have never really been sensitive to the stink of corruption.

No sooner was the First Emperor dead than an evil court eunuch persuaded the elderly Prime Minister Li Ssu to join in a plot to place Prince Hu-hai, a younger son, on the throne instead of the eldest son. Li Ssu discovered he had been tricked when he was arrested and given the five punishments: in front of a mob in the public market his face was tattooed, his nose cut off, his feet cut off, his genitals cut off, then his torso sliced in half at the waist.

The folly did not stop there. When the easily manipulated Second Emperor had been in power for only three years, his chief eunuch presented a deer to the assembled court and called it a horse, a gag in which all the courtiers joined. This trick and several others convinced the Second Emperor that he was hallucinating, so he abdicated. The chief eunuch, who had 'the head of a man but the voice of a beast', then provoked a fake uprising, which panicked the bewildered Second Emperor into committing suicide. The eunuch replaced him with a royal nephew. After gaining the throne, this Third Emperor feigned illness and, when the evil chief eunuch came to visit him, stabbed him to death. But only forty-six days after the Third Emperor gained the throne, his government was toppled by a rebel army made up of convicts, slaves, ruined farmers and other desperate victims of the regime.

The Chin Empire, which had forever changed the face of China and given it a name, had lasted only fifteen years. In the end, the only ones who really benefited from its tyranny were the thousands of merchant families the First Emperor had expelled to the south, for it was there that the elixir of youth had been all along.

CHAPTER 5

THE MAN WHO DISCOVERED EUROPE

THE GREAT WALL AND OTHER MONUMENTAL WORKS OF THE FIRST Emperor were the product of vast numbers of enslaved artisans, dispossessed farmers, bankrupt merchants, prisoners from fallen kingdoms, ex-soldiers of shattered armies, bureaucrats in disfavour, and common desperadoes – all eating bitterness while they toiled. So it is hardly surprising that from their midst came those who rose up and overthrew the First Emperor's bungling descendants. A convict started the revolt with members of his chain gang. Liu Pang, a dirt farmer in charge of a slave labour unit on the imperial tomb, led a ragged army in the first big peasant rebellion of Chinese history. What Liu Pang lacked as a military man he had in boundless quantities as a politician. 'While you generals know how to command soldiers,' he said, 'I know how to command generals.' In 202 BC, after disposing of his rivals, Liu Pang mounted the throne as the first ruler of the Han Dynasty, and the first peasant emperor of China. He promptly reintroduced the feudal system, and put members of his family in charge of China's riches and strategic resources. In return, he expected them to defend the throne. To make sure nobody challenged his right to rule, he trumped up treason charges against his ablest commanders and had them executed. Other officers fled into exile.

After seven years of absolute power, Liu Pang died. When his heir died young, the boy was followed by Liu Pang's widow, Empress Lu, one of only three women to reign alone in China's long history. During the next four centuries, eleven male heirs of the Liu family succeeded to the throne. Several tried to be models of the Confucian ideal of service to the people. Ordinary life got much better. Granaries and treasury overflowed. Two emperors, Wen-ti and Wu-ti, were men of exceptional energy and military skill. Wu-ti aggressively pursued a policy of expansion, so by the first century BC the Han Dynasty ruled an area larger than the Roman Empire.

'When Han arose, all within the seas became one; customs bridges were opened . . . Rich traders and great merchants drifted about over the empire. There was no article . . . which was not circulated, and what one desired one could obtain.'

This was the first time China looked outward. As the Han domain spread far and wide, ambitious young men began careers as explorers. One who ventured bravely across the steppes of Central Asia in 139 BC – fourteen centuries before Marco Polo and sixteen centuries before Columbus – 'discovered' Europe, the Mediterranean, and the Atlantic Ocean. Thanks to Chang Chien's reconnaissance, nomad raids diminished and the first garrisoned Silk Roads were established between China and the West. Another trade route through Burma to Siam and India (long used secretly by Chinese merchants) was officially identified. And the sea route from South China across the Indian Ocean to Arabia and Africa was found to be seeded already with small Overseas Chinese merchant colonies more than two thousand years ago.

Before Chang Chien's secret mission, the Chinese government knew and cared little about what lay beyond its borders. The treeless steppes spread like a broad superhighway from Mongolia to Bulgaria, the killing field of wild nomad cavalries. As far back as 3000 BC, merchants in Mesopotamia, Persia and India started long-distance caravan trade with each other around the Asian mountain ranges. Raiding these caravans and isolated trading posts provided an easy source of food and luxuries to the nomads. Over the ages they struck in wave after wave, from the Cimmerians and Scythians to the Huns and Mongols. They swarmed out of nowhere, massacred villages on the edges of the steppes, then vanished.

On China's borders, the most aggressive of these nomads were the Hsiung-nu, who ruled the wastes from the Pamirs to Siberia. They led as many as three hundred thousand horsemen at a time in homicidal raids on border cities, killing for fun. The Chinese were unable to wage long punitive campaigns deep into the deserts or steppes because hundreds of wagon teams were needed to carry provisions for as little as three months. When they withdrew, the nomads simply resumed their guerrilla raids. In the Han Dynasty a new alliance of Hsiung-nu tribes brought a fresh wave of fear to outlying districts. At first the Han emperors chose the soft weapon, by sending frightened princesses to the nomad Son-of-Heaven, or Shan-yu, but efforts to buy a lasting peace failed because centuries of conflict had made a tradition of treachery.

Prospects improved when Emperor Wu-ti learned of a split in nomad ranks. A prisoner reported that the Hsiung-nu had murdered the ruler of the tribe called the Yueh-chih, and disgraced his spirit by using his skull as a drinking cup. The Yueh-chih, who had then fled westward across the desert with a burning grudge, might now be willing to ally with China against the Hsiung-nu.

The emperor decided to send a secret agent to sound them out. Among the officers who applied for the job was Chang Chien. A tough and intelligent soldier, he was a perfect scout because his good nature assured him of a warm welcome wherever he went. He was given the official role of ambassador and set out with a retinue of a hundred, guided by a Hsiung-nu prisoner named Kan-fu, an expert archer who knew secret sources of water in the desert.

Personally, Chang Chien was motivated by curiosity as much as by ambition. At a time when expanding the empire was a fashionable idea, a poor but talented man could make his fortune while satisfying his own craving for adventure.

Few Chinese had ever gone by choice into the steppes, or across the trackless wastes of the Takla Makan and Gobi deserts. During times of chaos and insurrection, educated Chinese mandarins or generals sometimes defected to the nomads or to the southern barbarians.

Mountain passes in the north, west and south were convenient doorways to safety. 'North we can flee to the Hsiung-nu,' it was said, 'and south to the Yueh.' They took a bit of Chinese culture with them into places where nomads drank fermented mare's milk and never bathed or washed their hands. Happily, what many of them found on arrival was not as barbaric as they expected. The cultured tutor of a Han princess given in marriage to a Hsiung-nu chief praised the nomads for their ancient customs and exceptional loyalty. Much that seemed elegant about Chinese society, he said, was mere infatuation with luxuries, disguising men and women who murdered their own flesh and blood, and sometimes ate their livers.

'Just because the Chinese wear hats,' he said, 'what does that make them?'

Chinese traders knew the way into these remote and dangerous areas. Bolder merchants could make big profits from border trade, and get around Han laws that prohibited the sale to nomads of precious iron, crossbows, and other weapons. There was a thriving black market along the frontiers. So many people were involved that in a single year Emperor Wu-ti had five hundred traders beheaded for dealing in contraband.

Chang Chien's party travelled west for many days, crossing deserts and mountain ranges until, deep in nomad territory, they were ambushed and taken before the maximum leader, the Shan-yu. He thought their whole mission was ridiculous: 'Do you suppose that if I tried to send an embassy to the kingdom of Yueh, that the Han would let my men pass through China?'

He put Chang Chien under house arrest for the next ten years, looked after by the faithful servant Kan-fu. To help pass the time, Chang Chien was given a beautiful nomad wife, who bore him a strapping son. Eventually, the warriors stopped guarding him closely, and Chang Chien fled with his wife and son and servant to continue his sacred mission to the west.

Riding as fast as they could to Ferghana, in what is now Tadzhikistan and Uzbekistan, they were made welcome by its king, who provided them with guides and interpreters for the next leg of their journey. Eventually, Chang Chien caught up with the displaced Yueh-chih people, the original goal of his secret mission. He found

them totally changed. In the intervening years, they had captured the
rich region of Bactria south of the Oxus River and made themselves its
new rulers, living a sensual and indulgent life at the expense of its
people. The last thing they wanted was to forfeit this pleasant existence
to resume their old blood feud with the Hsiung-nu. As to avenging their
dead king whose skull had been used as a drinking cup – his son was no
longer interested.

Bactria, which sprawled from the Caspian Sea down past the Hindu
Kush to the frontier of India, had just been abandoned by the Greeks as
the last vestiges of Alexander the Great's empire collapsed. There were
still many Hellenes in Bactria, so at this moment ancient China was
brushing its fingertips against those of ancient Greece. Chang Chien
learned things no Chinese officer before him had ever known. After a
year in Bactria gathering exotic intelligence, he resigned himself to the
failure of his original mission and began the long trek back to China,
hoping that the things he had heard about the West would keep his
head on his shoulders. He took a route from Afghanistan through the
Hindu Kush, along the northern slope of the Himalayas to eastern
Tibet. He planned to give the Hsiung-nu a wide berth and re-enter
China from Tibet, through the territory of the less dangerous Chiang
barbarians. But as he and his tiny party were crossing the high desert
above the great salt marsh called Lop Nor, a lunar landscape well
known in those days only to small herds of wild Tibetan ass, he was
ambushed once more by the wily Hsiung-nu and detained for another
year.

The leathery old Shan-yu who had been his host during his previous
captivity chose that awkward moment to die. A rival chief attacked
and set himself up as the new ruler of the nomad federation. In the
midst of this turmoil, Chang Chien once again fled into the night with
his family and his trusty servant.

Reaching the imperial court after an arduous mission lasting thirteen
years in all, Chang Chien regaled Emperor Wu-ti for days and nights
with his reports of places far and strange. Instead of losing his head, he
was rewarded with the post of palace counsellor. Kan-fu, the former
slave, was given the title 'Lord Who Carries Out His Missions'.

Chang Chien told the emperor about the nomads, the great Takla
Makan desert, and the isolated mountain valley of Ferghana where

people raised 'horses so magnificent that they sweat blood'. After Ferghana, he reported, all the rivers flowed west into the Caspian and Aral seas, where there were many potential allies against the Hsiung-nu. He talked at length about the Wu-sun nomads, who could muster thirty thousand mounted archers. They were led by Kun-mo, a legendary warrior who, as a child, had been left in the desert to die but was saved by vultures that fed him meat, and wolves that suckled him. Beyond were other nomads, with ninety thousand mounted bowmen, and around the Aral Sea were the Yen-tsai with one hundred thousand archers. Together they could form an army nearly a quarter of a million strong.

The emperor listened spellbound to Chang Chien's accounts of Bactria, and a kingdom to the south-west called Persia, whose people lived in walled cities and kept records by writing horizontally on strips of leather. Among the Persians were merchants from Mesopotamia, and from a great western sea, the Mediterranean. Beyond, in a region that was very hot and damp, were giant birds that laid eggs as big as cooking pots. Still farther, beyond the Mediterranean, were other countries and a great ocean.

'In my travels, I saw bamboo canes and cloth from our regions of Chiung and Shu [Szechuan],' Chang Chien told the emperor. 'When I asked how they obtained such articles they told me "Our merchants go and buy them in the markets of India." ' India, he had learned, was a hot, wet kingdom on a great river south-east of Persia, whose people rode war elephants into battle. 'Now if the Indians obtain trade goods from south-western China, they cannot be far. Instead of trying to reach India by crossing the deserts or the mountains to the west, a more direct route would be south by way of Shu.'

Chinese merchants, he had learned, regularly crossed through mountain passes into Burma to obtain jade, rubies and sapphires, although they kept their sources secret. Lu Pu-wei, the merchant who had fathered the First Emperor, had made much of his initial fortune by brokering jade and rubies from these places.

Because many of the people Chang Chien had encountered in the west were militarily strong but lived in poverty, he proposed offering them treasures from China in return for an alliance. The prospect of becoming rich, he reasoned, would persuade them to attack the

Hsiung-nu. China would become secure, and her frontiers and trading networks could be extended far to the west. The fame and prestige of the Han Dynasty would be spread all over the world.

In recognition of his many discoveries, Chang Chien was given the title Marquis Po-wang ('Broad Vision'). He took part in various military campaigns against the Hsiung-nu, but misfortune struck when he arrived late at a rendezvous, and found that his general's army had been wiped out. Disgraced and sentenced to die, Chang Chien was allowed to live only on the condition that he pay a stiff fine and give up his noble title.

A chance to redeem himself came when Emperor Wu-ti asked him to set out once again far to the west to secure the alliance he had proposed with the Wu-sun nomads in Turkestan. He was to offer their leader, Kun-mo, rich gifts and bribes to attack the Hsiung-nu from the rear. A treaty between China and the Wu-sun would intimidate everyone, the emperor said, and they would all grovel at China's feet and send tribute.

This time Chang Chien went well prepared, with three hundred soldiers, six hundred horses, tens of thousands of cattle and sheep, and wagonloads of gold and silk as gifts. When the caravan reached Turkestan, Kun-mo was thunderstruck by the sight of these riches but refused to consider an alliance. Chang Chien stopped his men from unloading: 'The Son of Heaven sent me with these gifts, and if you do not prostrate yourself immediately to receive them, I will take them all back!' This was too much for the ragged nomad chief, who threw himself down and offered to sign anything. Before he could change his mind, Chang Chien returned to China with the treaty and was rewarded with the title Grand Messenger. He died peacefully a year or so afterward, happy and revered, one of the world's great early explorers.

Thanks to his pioneering travels, sweetened with the bribes only an emperor could dispense, emissaries arrived in China from India and Persia. For the first time, China established diplomatic and trade relations with nations on the Caspian, the Black Sea, the Mediterranean, and the Indian Ocean, countries that a few years earlier only her much-despised merchants had known existed.

Han's new nomad allies, attacking from the west, helped defeat the

Hsiung-nu. Emperor Wu-ti personally led a victory parade to celebrate the triumph.

Eager to acquire Ferghana horses for his own stables, Wu-ti found the breeders reluctant to share their treasured steeds, so in 104 BC he despatched a large Chinese military force beyond the Pamirs, where they had little difficulty persuading Ferghana's rulers to change their minds.

Once China's desert frontier was secure, four international trade routes came into regular use – two Silk Roads, north and south of the Takla Makan desert, a Jade Road through Burma to India and Siam, and a sea route across the Indian Ocean. Merchants from Roman Europe could venture safely along caravan routes guarded by Han army outposts, stopping in oases where they mingled with Chinese traders. Bolts of shimmering silk became the luxury item most sought after by Roman women.

But the achievements of the Han Dynasty came at a very high price. Although Wu-ti was praised as a man who 'loved greatness and enjoyed military deeds', his military campaigns drained the treasury, dragooned thousands of farmers into the army, emptied the granaries, made taxes unbearable, and ended one of China's longest periods of wealth and stability.

After turning briefly outward, China turned inward again; men with broad vision and grand schemes were replaced by narrow men intent upon discipline. Centuries would pass before China's rulers would once more look abroad.

CHAPTER 6

CHILDREN OF YUEH

CHINA'S SPLIT PERSONALITY — ONE MOMENT INWARD-LOOKING
and tyrannical, the next outward-looking and gregarious — derives
from the opposite natures of its north and south. The central
government has mostly been located in the north or has been
dominated by northerners. The south was long considered just
barbarian wilderness, full of wild animals and uncultured people. The
word for barbarian was *yueh*, and everything south of the Yangtze was
lumped together under the name Yueh. In Sun Tzu's day, it had been
the independent kingdom of Yueh, but after its conquest by the First
Emperor, Yueh became a dumping ground for undesirables. When
emperors expelled criminals and merchants from the north by the tens
of thousands, they were sent to Yueh the way doomed Russians were
sent to Siberia, or British convicts to Australia. The lowlands they
entered were inhabited by a different people, tribes of Tai Shan stock,
with hill-tribes such as the Meo and Yeo at higher altitudes. We know
little about them. They were displaced from the good agricultural land
by the aggressive incoming Chinese, who built a different sort of life for
themselves in the south. Far from the scrutiny of the central regime,

opportunities for profit were unlimited. Men were free to carry on all kinds of forbidden commercial activities. This tide of outcasts, hustlers and survivors blended with Yueh's original population to become the patchwork of dialect groups that we see in South China and the Overseas Chinese today. It is a hybrid culture with an 'offshore' mentality based on smuggling. More than 90 per cent of all Overseas Chinese today come from the coastal provinces of Chekiang, Fukien and Kwangtung – what was once ancient Yueh. They are the children of Yueh, very different from today's narrow and suspicious northerners; southerners are chronically wary and resentful of Beijing, and vice versa. As they put it, the north craves power to get wealth, the south craves wealth to get power.

Two thousand years ago, historian Ssu-ma Ch'ien said the north was 'small, crowded, and often suffered from flood and drought.' The people were 'frugal, cautious and afraid of trouble.' They 'accumulate wealth by spending little on their food and clothing.' By contrast, southerners were 'indolent and easy-going.' Everything was in abundance. 'For food they had rice, for soup they had fish . . . Fruits and shellfish were so plentiful there was no need to buy them . . . there were no hardships from failure of crops.' Southerners did not save, so while they did not suffer from cold and hunger, neither were there any great families 'worth a thousand catties of gold'. That would change.

As ever stricter controls were applied to commerce by North China regimes, initiative was smothered. This prevented China from experiencing anything like a Renaissance until the last decades of the twentieth century. The current boom in Mainland China is being inspired, financed and managed by the Overseas Chinese. They are the engine behind the boom, and if China blows apart it will be somewhat their doing. All of China's new Special Economic Zones are located in South China for good reason – to capitalize on the craving of the Overseas Chinese to return to their roots, and to put their wealth into their ancestral villages. In a deeply satisfying way, China is being lifted into the present and nudged into the future by the children of Yueh, the descendants of people condemned and expelled from the north many centuries ago.

In Sun Tzu's day the people of Yueh had a reputation for being rude, rough, tricky, and excellent seafarers. Yueh had been vaguely known to North China as far back as the Shang Dynasty, when the north imported exotic southern products such as rhino horn, elephant ivory, kingfisher feathers, tortoise shells, jade and pearls. The earliest inhabitants in the Canton area were the Pai, a tribe of Tai Shan people. Around 1100 BC, they built a walled town on the site of Canton, which eventually became the capital of South Yueh, with Foochow serving as the capital of North Yueh. Along the heavily indented coast between the two were many good harbours, each with its settlement. It was in Yueh's harbours that sea trade first developed in East Asia. Seafarers from Yueh traded with outposts of the Chou Dynasty along the lower Yangtze. Strong Yangtze River sailing rafts and fishing boats ventured onto the ocean as cargo vessels and coastal warships. A large fleet of ocean-sailing rafts was built by the king of Yueh in 472 BC, towards the end of Sun Tzu's lifetime, and some might have crossed the Pacific to North America on the strong, favourable currents flowing in that direction. We know that ships from Yueh sailed to Korea, Japan and Siberia, and south to Java and Sumatra. Some spent years trading in the Indian Ocean.

The ancient Taoist recluse Hsu Wu-kuei once exclaimed: 'Have you not heard of the wanderers of Yueh? When they sail several days away from their country, they feel lucky to encounter any old friend. When they have been absent weeks or months, they are surprised to meet anyone they have ever seen before. By the time they have been away for a whole year they have gone so far they are astonished to see anyone who even looks Chinese. The longer they are gone, and the farther they go, the more homesick they become.'

Had Yueh remained an independent state, it could have been one of the world's great maritime cultures, like that of the Phoenicians. Because they were involved in foreign trade rather than domestic buying and selling, the people of Yueh were different. They had to deal over long distances with unpredictable dangers, so they became more adventurous than their landlocked North China relatives. They are still among the planet's leading shipowners and seafarers today.

Yueh bloodied many noses during Warring States. Inevitably, a day would come when the north would punish and overwhelm the barbarian upstart. In 219 BC, the First Emperor sent Chin armies into Yueh with five hundred thousand men, accompanied by war junks topheavy with marines. Yueh became un unwilling slave of the Chinese Empire. When Chin collapsed, Yueh resumed its independence, but a century later in 112 BC, Emperor Han Wu-ti sent another navy and two thousand men. This completed the subjugation of Yueh, although underground resistance continued for a long time. The most warlike tribes from the Fukien coast were forcibly transported to the bleak interior of north-western China, where they were never heard from again. Over the next three centuries, Yueh, like the American West, was completely overwhelmed by settlers. As the Chinese took over the best land, the original inhabitants of Yueh were assimilated or moved south-west into the highlands. Once the lowlands became saturated with Chinese, the Tai continued on a slow migration west to Yunnan and south into Burma, Laos and Siam.

When the Chinese controlled everything as far south as Hainan Island, they ceased to regard the area as barbarian. The label 'Yueh' continued to be used only for people farther south in the Red River basin, who resisted all Chinese attempts at permanent conquest. The word Yueh evolved into Viet, so it is still in use today, but for a different group of people. The genes of the original inhabitants of Yueh live on in the mingled blood of South China and the Overseas Chinese. The distinctive dialects of South China today – Hokkien, Hokchiu, Teochiu, and so forth – are a blend of the native tongues of Yueh with those of the immigrants from North China.

South China remained rustic because nobody in North China was interested in financing improvements. The south was a fruit to be squeezed and eaten. Of its cities Canton was the biggest, with Amoy, Hangchow and Foochow catching up slowly. Because it was in their blood, as banished merchants or shopkeepers, most people in the south became involved in trade. When farmers prospered they entered the rice trade; when artisans retired they opened shops. Rivers and harbours became packed with boatpeople and seafaring traders, pirates and smugglers. Everyone wanted to be left alone to get on with making a living. Wealthy families in the cities secretly financed the business activities of maritime traders who were linked to them by blood, marriage, clan, name-association, secret society, or native place. They invested in ships, crews, cargoes and operating capital. Huge profits were made, but they kept their involvement with merchants a secret. The secrecy and furtiveness that surrounds all Overseas Chinese business activities today has a very ancient history.

South China became independent again when the last emperors of the Han Dynasty lost their grip, and the empire broke up into the Three Kingdoms. The final collapse of Han in AD 220 was followed by four centuries of genocide. North China was levelled by nomads who galloped around killing for fun, gouging out eyes and cutting off tongues.

The rich fled first. They had the money to go in style. Whole villages and entire clans moved out, taking all their servants and neighbours, and their private armies. Millions of refugees crossed the Yangtze to safety in the south in one of history's biggest stampedes. The arrival of these rich and manipulative refugees changed the south. They easily took over many of the best jobs as office-holders and government advisers. They brought with them the worst elements of Confucian social hierarchy. Exaggerated personal loyalty was part of it.

Since the Stone Age in China, the family had been the bedrock, the basic corporate unit. Hierarchy was not invented by Confucius, just glorified by him. Ancient China's rank-conscious society sustained itself according to a rigid pecking order. Beginning at the bottom, each community was subservient to a family patriarch, a village patriarch, and a provincial patriarch culminating in the emperor. Originally, a poor man with talent could rise high in government, but the Han Dynasty dragged on so long that the system calcified into a cold-hearted hereditary bureaucracy. Families of officials had such a grip on power that they were able to remain in position even as dynasties rose and fell. These great northern families kept hoards of gold bars and owned vast expanses of real estate, worked by serfs. From time to time, they cannibalized each other. With the destruction of the north by nomads, the tradition of family loyalty died out in North China, but was transplanted to the south by the rich refugees. They used ritual loyalty to maintain control like the Sicilian or Corsican Mafia. For the first time in South China, which had been so freewheeling, power and wealth became identified with family and connections. To enhance their prestige, these incoming northern families lied about their genealogy and built ancestral halls adorned with portraits of phony ancestors.

What was done by the rich was imitated by the poor, so family arrogance, in the guise of virtue, became universal in South China. What in the north ultimately had been loyalty to the emperor, in the south became loyalty to local godfathers. Outwardly, everyone at least acted loyal and submissive.

Once they were firmly established in South China, the northern families set about taking over the livelihoods of all the weaker people around them. This was not easy because there were many commercial warlords already in place. Powerful families, clans and mafias became involved in flat-out, predatory commerce, not just rural horsetrading. They told each other, 'Commerce is war!'. This made them more aggressive, more imaginative, more greedy, and led them to invest big sums in expanding their market share. Never was there enough market share, enough financial security for the family or clan, so among these northern interlopers, greed remained forever unsatisfied. They kept at it until they self-destructed. Fierce loyalty was not just family glue but also commercial glue, binding together ruthless clans of moneylenders, banking clans, smuggling clans, rice brokers, silk merchants, gold traders, and clans dealing in merchant shipping and foreign trade. Whole communities of human beings were attached to each other by the code of loyalty and the tyranny of trust. No matter where you travelled, no matter how far, no matter how many years passed, you belonged to a secret organization. What started as loyalty ended as dried blood.

The most successful families recognized a dangerous contradiction in money-making. The moment wealth was achieved and acknow-ledged, energy faded and failure began. They called it the Three-Generation Curse: one generation sacrificed everything to get rich, the second lost momentum, the third blew it. So no matter how much money these families had, they practised extreme frugality. 'They never look down, but they pick up; They never look up, but they take down.' They allowed themselves no leisure. Children were told of a dying man unable to speak. He kept raising two fingers. Then his family noticed there were two wicks in the oil lamp. When was one pinched out, he died smiling.

Confucianism sanctified and reinforced this discipline and hier-archy, so that profits were not taken out of the hands of elders and squandered by young fools. The Western idea of deficit spending is regarded by Chinese with astonishment and horror, as a form of self-swindle. It should only be done with other people's money.

One way to dodge the Three-Generation Curse was never to admit that an objective was achieved, to train each new generation as if prosperity was forever somewhere down the road. Wealth was kept hidden, rich men dressed in threadbare gowns, everyone worked in shabby storefronts, feigning poverty. This contributed to the widespread impression that merchants were too uncouth to bathe.

Merchants had to be unusually tenacious and calculating because they operated under very difficult conditions. Risk-taking was condemned by Confucians, but as born gamblers, Chinese believed that fortune only rewards those who dare. They made every effort to be calculating, hence their endless fascination with Sun Tzu's *The Art of War*. They adopted the God of War, Kwan Ti, as the God of Wealth. They taught themselves to stay invisible. Only those who remained invisible could expect to hold on to their wealth in the face of continual extortion by imperial eunuchs and bureaucrats.

Among poor Chinese in the south, the family also came first, but for other reasons. It was the only reliable economic unit. All family income went into a common treasury that was administered by the current patriarch. Each member received an allowance for expenses. If the family prospered, all benefited; if fortunes declined, all suffered. So for humble poor as well as predatory rich, the family was a closely held corporation with a reinvestment incentive, like a rolling tontine. Unlike a Western tontine, where benefits go to an ever-diminishing number of participants as they die off, the Chinese tontine requires continual reinvestment that is passed from generation to generation. Secondary benefits expand outward in concentric circles from family to clan, from native village to native district, and so on. Like a circus net, this web of responsibility was always there. When famine struck, rich peasants in a village were obliged to help the poor. When a village became exhausted, its survivors moved to other villages, which were morally bound to help them, according to the invisible filaments of family, clan and district, that connected them in a magic circle.

When this magic circle expanded to include a number of enterprises beyond the family, clan or village association, the bigger organization was called a *kongsi*, a form of corporation. *Kongsi* were created to exploit industrial and commercial operations that might include mines, factories, plantations, or merchant fleets. They were organized along the lines of miniature republics to help all members survive and prosper. Members shared in gains and losses, as if the *kongsi* were a family. To protect its financial interests, each *kongsi* had a private army. Some *kongsi* armies had as many as six to ten thousand paramilitaries. *Kongsi* doubled as labour unions and employment agencies. Chinese who went overseas without their families regarded their *kongsi* as a substitute for the family. Their only protection against persecution was the *kongsi* defence force.

Between the end of the Han Dynasty and the beginning of Tang, while North China suffered, South China enjoyed unparalleled prosperity. Foreign products, fashions and customs experienced great popularity in China. Canton exported porcelains and silk to the Mideast and East Africa, and imported frankincense from Arabia and Somalia. As more southern families became involved in financing trade, new ports in Chekiang, Fukien and Kwangtung prospered.

Everyone remained intensely wary of government intervention. The only communities to escape continual bureaucratic interference were those tucked away in remote coastal enclaves, where they could smuggle in foreign luxuries or deal in the black market, without tax or supervision. These havens of free enterprise, the secluded harbours of ancient Yueh, are still the homebase of the Overseas Chinese.

Corruption spread to all levels of southern bureaucracy. The craving for prosperity was contagious. Government officials and gentry, forbidden to be involved in commerce, invested secretly. When they retired, even high mandarins went into business.

Clandestine maritime trade depended on official collusion. Cargo manifests were forged, and import and export duties were 'adjusted' accordingly. All this was done by customs officials in return for a percentage of the merchant's profits. Many officials received regular protection money. When the government occasionally cracked down, heavy taxes and penalties forced merchants underground. Officials inflated bribes to match the risk.

Nobody was safe from extortion of some form. It was the easiest way to earn a living. Mandarins concentrated their extortion on the very rich, but everyone, rich or poor, tried to obscure how he made extra income. Bureaucrats had little time to carry out their proper duties, because they were involved in a perpetual act of levitation, hiding secret deals. Scratch the surface of any of them, and beneath was the ruthless appetite that propels hungry men out of oblivion.

'Senior interpreters working for government officials recruit crews and go to sea,' a chronicle said, 'to trade for brilliant pearls, glass, strange gems and other exotic products, exchanging for them gold and silks. When they arrive, officials of those countries provide them with food and handmaidens. They may sail part of the way home on merchant ships belonging to foreign barbarians but these barbarians sometimes rob or kill people to get more profit. Travellers may also encounter storms and drown. Even if nothing dangerous occurs, they may be away for several years. As for the great pearls they acquire, these can measure as much as two inches in circumference.'

After China was reunified by the Tang Dynasty, all eyes became fixed on the splendid northern court, but the most important commercial centres remained on the south coast: Yangchow, Chuan-chou, Chiao-chou (Teochiu), and Canton. Foreign merchants came to them in ever-increasing numbers. Canton became home to a large community of Arab and Hindu traders; by 880 there were one hundred and twenty thousand Muslims, Jews and Persians living there, with thousands of other merchants from Indonesia, Ceylon and India. Every major port had foreign quarters with their own rulers, bazaars, and temples.

Under Tang, Buddhism was all the rage. The earliest Buddhist arrivals were Indian merchants, who brought along their own monks. Buddhist pilgrims from India followed, buying passage on Chinese trading vessels. The craze reached a peak when Tang emperors competed with merchants to build the most lavish pagodas. The construction of so many created a frenzied market for imports of incense, ivory, statues, gems and religious paraphernalia.

The Tang court's taste for the exotic made it impossible to pretend that trade did not exist. The money being squandered by the Tang emperors and their entourage caused a boom in trade across the Indian Ocean and Eurasia. In the imperial love-nest at Chang-an in the north-west, concubine Yang Kuei-fei had lichees brought to her daily by pony express all the way from Canton, a distance of 1500 miles. This self-indulgence allowed power to fall into the hands of the imperial eunuchs, who ran the imperial household. Eunuchs murdered two emperors and installed puppets. Rebellions broke out. As the empire again fell apart, local warlords collected taxes and started their own kingdoms. The province of Fukien on the coast, once the heart of northern Yueh, briefly became independent.

This chaos ended in 960, when a scholar-general named Chao K'uang-yin conquered most of the warlords and founded the Sung Dynasty, which lasted nearly two hundred years. Militarily, Sung was one of the weakest regimes in Chinese history. They bought off the nomads by paying annual protection money, including two hundred thousand bolts of silk. A southerner complained: 'Our enemies become richer and more aggressive. The more they get, the more contemptuous they become . . . Though we work hard all year round, we never have a full stomach.'

Sung solved its problems by throwing money at them. Intelligentsia were subsidized. Bureaucrats received food and wine allowances. Yet Sung was the first Chinese government to accept openly the importance of commerce to the success of the nation. Sung government ministers openly invested. In AD 987, the Sung court itself sent four fleets to the South Seas to buy drugs, ivory, rhino horn, pearls and other luxuries, bypassing the middlemen.

These and other efforts to make the central government self-sustaining were part of radical reforms introduced by a remarkable southern prime minister, Wang An-shih. For the first time, the state engaged in trade, buying and selling commodities at the cheapest prices in the most convenient market, making a profit in the process. This temporarily ended the provincial tribute system, by which the central government had previously acquired what it needed. To encourage private business, the government actually gave loans to small urban and regional traders through state-owned pawnshops. Wang also introduced government loans to poor farmers, as well as price-stabilization, land reclamation and a professional army. He proposed a land survey to make property taxes more equitable. These unprecedented reforms angered big land owners and syndicates of private pawnbrokers. When a new emperor came to the throne in 1086, Wang's enemies ganged up and his reforms were ended.

Once Wang was out of the way, a very modern notion caught on: the

only way to become wealthy was to spend. The Sung Dynasty quickly
went bankrupt, and in 1127, nomads galloped in to pick over the
remains, captured the Sung emperor and took him hostage to
Manchuria. One of his brothers, Kao Tsung, rallied grassroots support
and set himself up in South China as Southern Sung (1127–1276). He
was a clever man, choosing able ministers and manipulating opponents
with flattery. He also chose Hangchow as his capital; located in the
prosperous Yangtze delta, it was protected by broad bays and
waterways that stymied nomad cavalry. This was the only time a
Chinese imperial capital had been near the sea, smack in the brainpan
of Ancient Yueh, and it had a dramatic effect. Attention focused on
maritime and foreign trade rather than North China's traditional
preoccupation with agriculture and defensive fortifications. In a very
real sense, Yueh had never died, just gone underground. With Southern
Sung, Yueh sprang back to life.

Hangchow, an old Yueh port and the southern terminus of the
Grand Canal, was richly endowed. It had 'vegetables from the east,
water from the west, wood from the south, and rice from the north.'
Most foreign trade poured through the nearby Fukien port of Chuan-
chou, just to the south, enriching the treasury of Southern Sung
through customs duties. The welfare policy of the Southern Sung
government made this one of the most humane periods in China's
history. The population ate better than ever before, thanks to a new
variety of rice imported from Cambodia, which made possible two and
even three annual crops. Sung shipbuilders, carrying on a direct
tradition from Ancient Yueh, were the most inventive and successful
the world had ever seen. Enormous ships were built, propelled at sea by
huge lug sails and on the waterways by manpowered paddle wheels.
Many had five decks, rising 100 feet above the waves. Their crews were
usually members of the same extended family, who were born, lived
and died abroad. They had their own shipboard vegetable gardens,
musicians, actors and harems. A writer in 1178 said, 'The ships which
sail the southern sea are like houses. When their sails are spread they
are like great clouds in the sky. A single ship carries several hundred
men, and has in the stores a year's supply of grain. Pigs are bred and
wine fermented on board.'

The Southern Sung navy controlled the high seas, guarding sea lanes to Japan, Korea and the South Seas. At major trading centres all over South East Asia and the Indian Ocean, where in the past there had been only small groups of Chinese merchants mixed in with the Arabs, Persians and Indians, large colonies of Overseas Chinese now bloomed. They came from Fukien, Kwangtung, Chekiang, and ports along the lower Yangtze. They spoke languages that were incomprehensible to the people of North China. The children of Yueh had been liberated by Southern Sung, and could now come and go as they pleased.

Inside South China itself, the population swelled, market towns became boisterous cities with a million inhabitants. An urban middle class took shape in a noisy ghetto hodgepodge of wealthy merchant families, prosperous shopkeepers, and successful vendors. Sung China was at bottom a culture of wholesalers, shippers, warehouse owners, brokers, travelling salesmen, seafarers, smugglers, gangsters, shopkeepers and peddlers. Unlike North China, wealth and self-indulgence were not limited to the ruling dynasty, its nobility and its mandarins. In South China, anybody who had energy, connections, brains and cunning, could make it. Luxuries were necessities. Wealth alone became a legitimate measure of a man's worth, providing he then put moneymaking behind him, bought a fine estate, and set himself up as fake Confucian gentry. For added insurance, merchant families educated hand-picked family members to reach literati status, so they could get government jobs and shield the family's questionable enterprises. If nobody knew you paid for your title, you could have all the titles you wanted. For the first time in China, the celebration of wealth was a national obsession. Eight hundred years ago, in twelfth-century China, to get rich was glorious.

Why not? Southern Sung emperor Kao Tsung said, 'The profits from maritime commerce are very great. If properly managed they can amount to millions . . . Is this not better than taxing the people?'

Seafarers and merchants had been spreading this philosophy around the Pacific Rim for more than a thousand years. But the argument of the First Sung Emperor gave legitimacy to the South China Ethic. Emphasis on the good life left a lasting impression on the coastal populations. Later, when they had to flee overseas, they took the ethic with them.

Regrettably, the good times did not last. When in the thirteenth century the Mongol cavalries exploded out of nowhere and swept across Asia, cutting down everyone before them, they were bogged down by South China's marshes, paddy fields, waterways and forests. By then the south was so densely populated that murder became time-consuming. Citizens of Southern Sung rallied and put up armed resistance. It took the Mongols more than a generation to subdue the south.

When the end came, with the fall of the capital at Hangchow in 1279, it was due to the treachery of an Arab merchant named Abu Shou-keng. His family had been trading in Canton for generations. A Chinese who visited their mansion in the twelfth century wrote that they 'lived a life of luxury far exceeding the level permitted under the law. However, since the local government was interested in encouraging more traders to come and since the family involved was not Chinese, it did not wish to concern itself with the violation.'

Abu was the government official in charge of merchant shipping at Chuan-chou, China's largest port, and the boss of the big Muslim community there. Thanks to the wealth and power his family had accumulated, he was able to use treachery to gain control of the major trading syndicates operating between Chuan-chou and South East Asia. For thirty years, he controlled hundreds of merchant ships and fleets of giant war junks. When the Mongols were finally poised to overrun the coast and to sack the cities of Southern Sung, Abu concluded that 'war is bad for business' and made them a deal. In return for surrendering his ships and submitting to the khans as a fellow Tartar, he was made an admiral of the Mongol navy, and given the job of destroying the remaining Sung fleets. In the process, he was allowed to keep the property of his rivals.

Thanks to Abu's treachery, in the final battle off Canton in 1279, the Mongol armada captured eight hundred Sung warships. The becalmed flagship of the nine-year-old Sung emperor was too sluggish to escape in the fog with the rest of the imperial squadron. The boy and all his ministers and their families threw themselves into the sea and drowned.

The Mongol conquest reintegrated north and south, and Mongol garrisons were based in all Chinese communities. Tyranny returned with a vengeance. Whole cities were slaughtered in reprisal for staging uprisings against the Mongol occupation.

Unlike the Confucians, however, the Mongols were not opposed to private enterprise. When they encouraged maritime trade, the economy of the south slowly revived. Private shipowners, who otherwise would have engaged in smuggling and piracy, were given concessions by the Mongols to transport grain by sea to the north, and fortunes were made. A courier system was introduced, with two hundred thousand horses, which helped more distant regions to revive. The Grand Canal was repaired and improved. However, the Mongols were whimsical and inconsistent. When they followed the Sung practice of issuing paper money, they flooded China with the notes, devalued the currency, then refused to exchange worn-out notes for new. Merchants first prospered, then suffered great losses. In anger they began to finance determined rebellions. The Mongol warriors were growing soft from the good life in the south. Living in peace, they fell into bad habits. The fruit they had eaten was overripe. In 1368, the last of the khans withdrew to the desolate steppes.

Southern Sung had survived in peace and prosperity for a hundred and fifty years before being swept away by the Mongols. That it lasted so long is astonishing. It was anti-military, when China was constantly threatened by nomad invasion. It was extravagant and humane and fun-loving, when all around were predatory. Following the Mongol victory, the former Southern Sung capital of Hangchow was visited by Marco Polo. He saw the extravagance still clearly visible. 'The inhabitants take such delight in ornaments, paintings and elaborations that the amount spent on them is something staggering. The natives of [Hangchow] are men of peace, through being so cosseted and pampered by their [emperors] who were of the same temper. They have no skill in handling arms and do not keep any in their houses. There is prevalent among them a dislike and distaste for strife or any sort of disagreement. They pursue their trades and handicrafts with great diligence and honesty. They love one another so devotedly that a whole district might seem, from the friendly and neighbourly spirit that rules among men and women, to be a single household. They are no less kind to foreigners who come to their city for trade.' He was awed by the 'marvellous great shipping' in South China's ports. On the Yangtze 'more dear things, and of great value, go and come by this river, than go by all the rivers of the Christians together, nor by all their seas.' In its lower reaches alone, he estimated there were fifteen thousand ships, not counting rafts.

Of Southern Sung as a whole, Marco Polo prophetically remarked, 'I give my word that the men of [Southern Sung], if they were a war-like nation, would conquer all the rest of the world. But they are not war-like. I can assure you rather that they are capable merchants and skilled practitioners of every craft.' As a tool of conquest, the children of Yueh simply preferred economic tactics to military strategies. According to the South China Ethic, business is war.

CHAPTER 7

SANBAO THE SAILOR

OF ALL THE CHILDREN OF YUEH, ONE OF THE MOST EXTRAORDINARY, and one of the most influential in opening up the doors of the world to the Chinese, was the man known as Ma Sanbao.

To start with, this Ming Dynasty admiral was over eight feet tall, and said to be five feet around the middle. His spectacular naval expeditions from China to East Africa and Arabia in the first decades of the fifteenth century, at the head of the biggest armadas the world had ever seen, assure him a brief mention in most encyclopaedias. Most likely, he is also the real source of the legend of Sindbad the Sailor.

The children of Yueh had just been through convulsions. The 'most savage and pitiless race known to history' – the Mongols of Genghis Khan – had swept across China, murdering millions and incorporating prosperous Southern Sung into an empire stretching from Korea to the Danube. After all this genocide the Mongols' Yuan Dynasty lasted little more than a century. By 1348, the Chinese were in open revolt. A rough peasant named Chu Yuan-chang led a ragtag army to seize the old southern capital of Nanking on the Yangtze; thirteen years later, he took Peking, proclaiming himself the first Ming emperor, under the name Hung Wu.

The founder of the Ming Dynasty was one of the ugliest men who ever lived. Like the peasant founder of the Han Dynasty, he had great magnetism, luck and timing, distrusted intellectuals, and was mercilessly cruel, even to his closest supporters. Since the Duke of Chou, Chinese governments had not become gentler. Anything short of despotism was seen as an invitation to chaos. The first Ming emperor's biggest innovation was to flog his own ministers to death. In the past, gentlemen were ordered to commit suicide, not humiliated in public. Emperor Hung Wu made public spankings routine. Mandarins accused of errors were tied down on their stomachs, their robes hoisted to expose their buttocks, and a whip laid on. Few survived. Ming court officials faced each day with dread. But bribery and corruption stopped. Because of perpetual fear, the outward manifestation of poverty became ingrained more deeply than ever in Chinese life; today many first-generation Hong Kong millionaires still slouch around their mansions and high-rise offices in soup-stained singlets and Uncle Ho thongs, keeping up the pretence of poverty in front of nobody.

For a while under Southern Sung, the people of South China had enjoyed unprecedented freedom to get rich and openly squander their wealth on luxuries. But under the brutal early Ming emperors, China's ruthless ancient feud between businessmen and bureaucrats resumed. It was a coldblooded cycle. First, merchants were used to help consolidate the wealth of the state. Then they were denounced as scoundrels and thrown into dungeons, where they were tortured into revealing the hiding-places of their treasure. After a suitable delay for everyone to forget, surviving merchants were 'rehabilitated' so that the state could again benefit from their wealth and energy – only to be jailed and tortured once more as the cycle was repeated. In modern times this has also happened repeatedly to Overseas Chinese communities in Indonesia, Malaysia, Thailand and the Philippines. On the communist Mainland, the get-rich policies of Deng represent a vast rehabilitation, after the great purge of capitalists under Mao.

In the early years of the Ming Dynasty, the new regime needed the help of merchants to restore prosperity and to refill the empty treasury. This was repulsive to Emperor Hung Wu. A northerner who had grown up in poverty, he was a deeply suspicious man who despised merchants and the way they manipulated their wealth. When he seized power, South China was plagued by pirates, and Vietnam remained stubbornly independent. The emperor blamed coastal businessmen for provoking much of this unrest. In his view, they were no better than pirates; in fact, many engaged in piracy whenever they thought they could get away with it. True to form for the children of Yueh, the coastal population as a whole remained estranged from the central regime. As an old Chinese folk song expressed it, 'Powerful as the emperors are, what has that power to do with me?'

After securing his throne, Hung Wu spent the rest of his reign ruthlessly squeezing wealthy families, particularly native banking chains and rich South China merchants who had enjoyed centuries of unrestricted trade under Southern Sung and the Mongols. Many wealthy people who lived on or near the coast – and who had formed the economic backbone of Southern Sung – had no alternative but to flee offshore, taking their treasure with them, along with their relatives and followers. They joined the small colonies of Chinese expatriates in southern Japan, Taiwan, the Philippines, Indochina, Siam and the Malay archipelago. Others were betrayed by competitors before they could escape.

During Southern Sung, the Overseas Chinese had taken shape as a significant community of expatriates. They were no longer isolated communities of merchants linked together by maritime trade networks. Under Southern Sung, they gained the freedom to move back and forth to South China, and no longer felt the need to be clandestine. Commerce became open. But the greed and extortion of the Ming Dynasty sent a wave of panic down the coast, provoking what can only be described as a mass migration offshore. Scores of wealthy families fled with hundreds of ships and thousands of followers. Their arrival in the balmy harbours of the South Seas disrupted existing arrangements between Chinese merchant chiefs and local Malay, Arab, Hindu or Buddhist rulers. In some cases, the newcomers seized power and set themselves up as warlords, displacing rivals and establishing piratical control. Only in Japan were they kept in check by the samurai of powerful local clans. The lasting effect of this flight offshore during Ming was once more to give the Overseas Chinese an air of habitual clandestineness. As if, given the choice, they would rather smuggle than trade openly, rather deal in black money than white: a people perpetually on guard against treachery. It is an image they have kept to this day. And it is not paranoia.

The mass exodus of so much treasure offshore aroused imperial rage. The Ming court made it a crime for Chinese to travel abroad, so those who were already overseas were afraid to return home. This turned a large number of temporary Chinese sojourners into permanent expatriates.

While he professed to have no interest in foreign conquest, the emperor and his sons were determined to recover the capital that had fled offshore. Orthodox Confucian mandarins at court proposed eliminating the problem once and for all by putting all foreign import-export trade back as a strictly controlled government monopoly, known as the 'tribute system'.

Hung Wu gave his toughest sons military command of frontier regions in North China to defend against the Mongols, and expected them to come to the rescue of Nanking if help was ever needed. When his chosen heir died young, Hung Wu picked a grandson to replace him and tried to protect the boy by having all possible rivals murdered. When the crown prince ascended the throne at age sixteen, one of his uncles, Duke Yan, rebelled and marched on Nanking at the head of his northern army. After three years of fighting, Nanking fell in 1402, and the young emperor vanished when the palace burned down. Regicide was shameful, as was usurpation, so it was put about that the boy was hiding among the Chinese communities overseas. His uncle, the usurper, proclaimed himself the new emperor under the name Yung Lo, and made a great show of searching for his missing nephew. Yung Lo assembled a spectacular fleet of junks and sent them on seven great voyages as far as Africa. They carried gifts to foreign rulers, obliging them in return to send envoys to China bearing tribute and confirming Yung Lo's heavenly mandate.

Command of the fleet was given to one of Yung Lo's favourites, the giant Muslim eunuch Ma Sanbao – Ma of the 'Three Jewels'. The title was a wordgame of the sort Chinese love. In polite society, it referred to the *trir-atna* of Buddhism: the Gautama, the doctrine and the believers. In vulgar circles, it referred to Ma's being a superb warrior despite having no testicles and penis ('Three Jewels' or 'Thrice Precious'). By giving him this title, the emperor figuratively made him whole again.

Ma Ho, as he was orginally called, was born in 1371 to a poor ethnic Hui family in Yunnan, a high plateau with rolling green hills and terraced rice paddies sprinkled with mauve and white opium poppies. The Hui were Chinese Muslims of Mongol-Turkic mix. During previous centuries, the Islamic faith had swept across Eurasia. There were many Turkic Muslims in the Mongol cavalries, because the khans regarded all people of the steppes as Tartars, as opposed to alien Chinese. When the Mongol horde overran Yunnan, Ma's great-grandfather was posted with a Mongol garrison at Kunyang on Lake Tien Chih. The boy's grandfather and father had since made a pilgrimage overland to Mecca. Their travels aroused curiosity in the village and contributed much to young Ma's education. He grew up speaking Arabic and Chinese, learning much about the world to the west and its geography and customs.

Chinese soldiers were sent to expel the Mongols from the south-west. On rampages through towns and villages across the countryside, they caught every male adult and child and cut their sexual organs off, to terrorize the population into submission. Among the Chinese forces were officers charged with recruiting promising eunuchs as servants for the court. In 1381, when Yunnan was pacified by an army under General Fu Yu-te, ten-year-old Ma was one of the boys mutilated. When he did not bleed to death or die from infection, and proved to be of exceptional intelligence, he was chosen to be trained for the imperial household. Two years later, he was assigned to the retinue of then-Duke Yan, who would later usurp the throne as the emperor Yung Lo.

By his early twenties, Ma was already over seven feet tall, his gigantism caused by a deficiency of male hormones after emasculation. An unusually clever army officer, he studied Sun Tzu and Sun Pin. In addition to his great height, he featured a high, broad forehead, small nose and glaring eyes. He looked like the very personification of Kwan Ti, the God of War (by no small coincidence also the God of Wealth). His family records say, 'He had a voice as loud as a huge bell. He knew a great deal about warfare and was accustomed to battle.'

An impressive figure in every way, Ma accompanied the duke on a series of military campaigns, and his crafty handling of strategy against the Mongols outside the Great Wall from 1393 to 1397 made him a hero. When the duke usurped the throne, Ma played a crucial role in the southern expedition leading to the capture of Nanking. After the duke proclaimed himself Emperor Yung Lo, he gave Ma supreme command of the thousands of eunuchs in the Imperial Household Agency, who served the throne as a secret service. This was a position of enormous leverage, not unlike a pope appointing a new Vatican chief of Opus Dei. Eunuchs had been a chronic problem in China. As the imperial quartermasters, they sought control of patronage and tributary trade, relying on their own intelligence service to pursue a wide range of clandestine sources of revenue in China's provinces and overseas.

Along with the new post, Ma was given the grand surname Cheng, officially becoming Cheng Ho, and soon afterward he was chosen to head the biggest naval expedition in history up to that time. Over the next twenty-eight years (1405–33), Cheng Ho commanded huge fleets that visited thirty-seven countries, from Champa to India, and along the Persian Gulf and the Red Sea to the coast of Kenya.

The word junk, which comes from the Malay work *djong*, meaning any large vessel, usually conjures up an image of a creaking, high-pooped scow with tattered sails. This was far from the case in Cheng Ho's day. Although Chinese shipwrights were mostly illiterate, they invented watertight compartments, the lee board, the centreboard, the balanced and slotted rudder, the windlass, and many other major innovations. Until the modern period, China had more vessels afloat than all the rest of the world, and by far the biggest ships of the time. In 1420, the Ming navy dwarfed the combined navies of Europe.

By July 1405, a great fleet was ready. Most were armed merchantmen dragooned into service by imperial command. The smallest were one-masted ships around 56 feet long that served as water taxis (of Columbus' three ships, two were less than 50 feet long). War junks, which had to be fast and manoeuvrable, were of middle size, at 180 feet overall by 68 feet in beam. The largest in Cheng Ho's armada were great treasure ships over 300 feet long and 150 feet in beam, the biggest being 440 feet long and 186 feet across. Most of the treasure ships were built expressly for these voyages at the Dragon Bay shipyard near Nanking, the remains of which can still be seen today. Chronicles of the Ming Dynasty described sixty-two of these great ships in all, each with nine masts and crewed by five hundred men.

All classic Chinese junks were bright white, each hull coated with lime mixed with poisonous oil from the seed of *sryandra cordifolia* to protect the wood from worms. Friar Odoric of Pordenone marvelled, 'all the vessels are as white as snow . . .' To find their way, they all had eyes painted on the bows; to frighten enemies, the war junks were decorated with tiger heads, while their marines wore tiger masks complete with whiskers. Some ships had stables for cavalry, while others were tankers that topped up with fresh water from streams near anchorages. By tradition, a little mud from wells at home was tossed into the water tanks to keep the germs and bugs familiar.

When it was fully assembled, Cheng Ho's first fleet included 27,870 men on 317 ships. Sailing together, they covered the sea from horizon to horizon. This mission was under the control of the imperial corps of eunuchs, so among the officers aboard were seven grand eunuchs, ten ranking eunuchs, and fifty-three ordinary eunuchs. There were two brigadiers, ninety-three captains, one hundred and four lieutenants, one senior secretary of the Board of Revenue, two protocol officers, five astrologers and one hundred and eighty doctors. Experienced Chinese merchant skippers steered by secret navigational manuals called rutters and charts drawn on silk with rectangular grids, at a time when Europeans were still arguing over biblical geography. Courses were set with a magnetized needle floating on water in a circular box. Speed was calculated by throwing an object over the bow and walking with it to the stern while reciting a formula. The ships had names such as *Pure Harmony*, *Kind Repose*, *Lasting Tranquillity*, *Peaceful Crossing* and *Pure Durability*. Cheng Ho's flagship was called the *Star Raft*.

Each voyage began in autumn from the shipyard at Dragon Bay. They sailed down the Yangtze to near what is now Shanghai, where sacrifices were made to the goddess of sailors. From there, it took eight weeks to reach Taiping anchorage, near Amoy in Fukien, one of China's great merchant shipping harbours. There they waited for the north-east monsoon to arrive in December. When the monsoon began, Cheng Ho's fleet sailed south to Qui Nhon in Champa – bypassing hostile Vietnam – then to Java, where they remained four months waiting for easterly winds.

Several who took part in Cheng Ho's voyages kept notes. One found the islands of Indonesia like 'floating green shells'. Java, he said, was a particularly violent place, where all males wore knives and used them at the least provocation, and public executions were frequent.

The South Seas might be a mystery to the emperor and his court, who were inlanders, but they were no great mystery to Cheng Ho and the commanders of his armada. By then, coastal Chinese had been trading privately with South East Asia and the Indian Ocean for over a thousand years, since Ancient Yueh. Chinese junks commonly visited Vietnam, Cambodia, the Philippines, Siam, Java, Sumatra, and had ventured beyond to Ceylon, India, Persia, Arabia, even reaching Africa. A voyage from India to Africa and back was not as intimidating as it might seem, thanks to the regular cycle of monsoons, which had been understood and used for roundtrips by the Phoenicians. Although Chinese dynasties rarely showed any interest in foreign geography or foreign affairs, and private trade was usually illegal, it had been underway routinely for centuries. The Overseas Chinese are not a modern phenomenon.

In the 1320s, when Wang Taiyuan travelled from Taiwan and the Philippines around South East Asia to India, he observed that it was as simple as travelling 'between east and west prefectures'. Harbours along the way were crowded with merchants from India and the Middle East, while Overseas Chinese communities were still relatively small. Detailed records of their colonies were not available for good reason. Since foreign travel usually was illegal, Overseas Chinese kept their movements secret to avoid official retribution. Ming hostility to private commerce caused a sharp drop in the flow of all kinds of luxury imports to which wealthy Chinese had grown accustomed. One of the biggest markets for imported luxuries, ironically, was the emperor's own family and its dependent nobility. Only the wealthy could pay for them.

When he usurped the throne, Emperor Yung Lo tried to boost his damaged prestige by a display of China's might, and by bringing foreign ambassadors to his court. While Chinese were not allowed to go to foreign countries to engage in trade, foreigners could come to China. Foreign trade was allowed as long as it was disguised as tribute. Local officials were given the authority to decide whether prospective traders were 'legitimate' or 'troublemakers', and this left a lot of room for manoeuvring by 'vested interests' and bribery. Foreign merchants who posed as official envoys were allowed to give 'gifts' to the emperor and his family in return for the right to engage in trade discreetly while travelling around China as sightseers. The flow of foreign luxury goods was to be controlled as a state monopoly by the emperor's eunuchs. Critics of the emperor could have access to these luxuries only if they first submitted to him. This gave Yung Lo a powerful weapon of patronage.

To get physical control over foreign trade, Admiral Cheng Ho had to remove a powerful Chinese trade syndicate boss who had taken control of one end of the Strait of Malacca, through which most merchant shipping passed.

Historically, control of the Strait was contested by the rulers of Java, Sumatra and the Malay Peninsula. Java was divided into two different kingdoms, one Hindu, the other Muslim. Hindu Majapahit controlled eastern Java, Madura and Bali, plus part of the Malay Peninsula and Borneo. The west end of Java was ruled by Islamic Surabaya. A lot of Muslim merchants lived there. Some had spent years in China, then moved to Java as intermediaries between Chinese trade syndicates and Arab or Persian merchant syndicates in the Middle East. Mingled with them in Surabaya were prosperous Chinese traders from Kwangtung, Fukien and Chekiang, some of whom had become Muslims, the better to fit in to their adopted communities.

On the neighbouring island of Sumatra, the west end was controlled by Muslims, while the east end was largely Buddhist under the influence of Siam. At Palembang were thousands of Chinese in the biggest Overseas Chinese settlement of its day. Some were descendants of traders who had been coming there for centuries. Most did not intend to stay, but were trapped by the new Ming regulations forbidding foreign trade and travel, and were afraid to go home. Here also was a large floating population of armed Chinese freebooters who engaged in both trade and piracy. Such people could be found all around the South Seas, and up the China coast as far as Kyushu in Japan. They belonged to different syndicates, depending upon their clan loyalties and their mutually incomprehensible languages. Those from Chekiang and Fukien provinces had godfathers based in Amoy or Chuan-chou or Ningpo, and other harbours along the rugged coast.

Those from Kwangtung also spoke different dialects, depending on whether they came from the Pearl River in the west or the Han River in the east. Isolated by geography and by language, each dialect group had its own commercial network of financiers, merchants, shipowners, crews, middlemen, accountants, warehousemen, shopkeepers, stevedores and coolies. These South China networks stretched from Japan to the South Seas. Nobody outside the dialect group could join – a characteristic that still strongly marks the Overseas Chinese business community today.

The most powerful man in Palembang was Chen Tsu-i, a Cantonese-speaking merchant prince from the Pearl River delta, who had fled China with his family in the early 1370s to escape being arrested and fleeced by the first Ming emperor. He had brought his hoard of treasure with him. Thousands of followers came after him in their big armed junks and smaller smuggling vessels. Reaching the Malacca Strait, which was ideal for ambushing passing ships, Chen Tsu-i seized Palembang and made it his new base.

Many of the Overseas Chinese in Palembang were very rich, and had fled there with their whole households to escape Ming tyranny. Whenever a ship belonging to strangers passed by, Chen immediately offered them a deal, or robbed them of their valuables. His pocket navy was big enough to overwhelm armed traders sailing in convoy. He had seventeen large war junks, each with hundreds of men aboard. Other traders and their families lived on smaller ships, or in houses on stilts by the water's edge.

The cost of outfitting Cheng Ho's voyage had been underwritten by one of Chen's old business rivals, Hsia Yuan-chi, a rich mandarin who sought to ingratiate himself with Emperor Yung Lo by helping to pay for the naval assault on Palembang. If all went well, Hsia stood to profit greatly from his increased influence at court.

Cheng Ho avoided a confrontation on the outward voyage, but left secret agents to infiltrate Chen's base. There was also the spectacle of the great white fleet passing by, filling the entrance to the Strait. So in July 1406, Cheng Ho caught the easterlies and sailed past Palembang to Lambri and Semudera, then into the Indian Ocean. After stopping briefly in Ceylon, they went on to Calicut on the south-west coast of India, the domain of the 'Sea King', Malayalam. From December to

March, they remained at Calicut, giving local dignitaries presents of gold-embroidered silks, and trading Chinese goods for those of the Western world. So many Chinese articles were for sale that it took three months just to unload and put prices on them.

The Chinese found Calicut amusing: the king was Buddhist and a vegetarian, while most of the rich were Muslims and did not eat pork. Otherwise, it was a Hindu country where the ox was sacred, and a whitewash made with ox-dung was smeared on all the temple walls and as a cosmetic over the skin of the Sea King and his chiefs. Many residents were wealthy because foreign ships brought goods there from all over the world, which the government taxed. In a curious form of justice, the rich owned coconut plantations, while poor criminals were boiled in coconut oil: it was a place of extremes. The Sea King himself was delighted to become an ally of China, and prepared a golden girdle set with precious gems as his tribute to Emperor Yung Lo.

In March, envoys from Calicut, Semudera, Quilon, Malacca and several countries in the Middle East boarded the treasure ships to return with Cheng Ho to China. *En route* there was unfinished business.

In Palembang, Cheng Ho's lead squadron of war junks met head-on with the fleet of Chen Tsu-i. Cheng Ho demanded his surrender. Chen pretended to comply, while preparing a counter-attack, but Cheng Ho's spies had subverted another rich Chinese trader, Shih Chin-ching, who knew Chen's strategy and betrayed him. A sharp battle followed. Chen's ships had thousands of armed men aboard, ready to fight, but Cheng Ho's war junks were armoured with sheet iron, and carried giant crossbows, trebuchets and guns, flaming arrows, rockets, flame-throwers and bombs. His commanders avoided close combat, using giant claws to hold the enemy ships away while setting them afire by means of flaming bolts from crossbows. Five thousand 'pirates' in all were slain, ten of Chen's big war junks were burned, and seven others badly damaged. Chen and his two chief lieutenants were captured alive, but little of his treasure was recovered. Either there had been ample time to disperse it throughout his clan and syndicate, or he had never kept it in one place.

Cheng Ho's fleet caught the south-west monsoon around Singapore island and arrived back in the Yangtze in July. Chen was taken to

Nanking, where the emperor had him executed in October 1407. Trader Shih, who had betrayed Chen by warning Cheng Ho in time, was appointed 'official pacification commissioner' of Palembang, meaning he was put in charge of humbling its Chinese community and assuring its future loyalty to the Ming throne, rather than to Siam. The victory did much to enhance Ming prestige, but more had to be done before control of the Strait could be guaranteed.

Cheng Ho's second voyage began immediately, with 248 ships sailing to Calicut to deliver gifts and greetings at the coronation of a new Sea King. On the way home, the fleet stopped in Java, where Cheng Ho dethroned the king of Muslim Surabaya, and replaced him with a relative of the king of Majapahit. Despite Ming insistence that China was not interested in foreign conquest, this at least qualified as intervention.

Cheng Ho's third voyage left Nanking in September 1409, with only forty-eight ships but thirty thousand men, bound for the Strait of Malacca to put in place the final element of Ming southern strategy.

Malacca was a drowsy port on the west coast of the Malay peninsula across from Palembang in Sumatra. For centuries it had been under the domination of Siam, which controlled the peninsula as far as Singapore. China had been warring with Siam and the Tai kingdoms for many years and now sought to outflank them in the south. This had been engineered during Cheng Ho's first two voyages, by planting agents along the coast who arranged for the Siamese vassal at Malacca to be murdered. His throne was taken over by a Chinese-backed usurper. With Palembang in Ming hands on one side of the Strait, a Chinese puppet in control at Surabaya and another installed at Malacca, eastern and western approaches to the Strait were secure. The emperor ordered Cheng Ho to bestow upon Malacca's new king two silver seals, a mandarin's hat, a girdle of office, and an embroidered silk robe. The admiral was to declare the town a city-state under Ming protection, after which Siam would not dare to attack.

The new ruler of Malacca forced all passing ships to enter his harbour and pay taxes on all trade goods, exactly what had been done by Chen, the late Chinese warlord at Palembang. The difference was that Malacca's ruler paid homage to the Ming throne.

Malacca was a convenient place for the Chinese to set up a regional warehouse of trade goods, to be distributed to nearby countries by Cheng Ho's smaller squadrons. 'By the king's residence there is a large river with a wooden bridge,' a Chinese visitor wrote, 'on which are more than twenty pavilions, trading every kind of article . . . Whenever the treasure ships of the Middle Kingdom arrived there, they at once erected a line of stockading like a city-wall, and set up towers with watch-drums at the four gates; at night police patrolled with bells; inside was a second stockade containing warehouses and granaries; all the fleet's money and provisions were stored in them. The ships which sailed to various countries returned to this place and loaded goods, waiting till the wind was favourable.'

The admiral's next stop was Ceylon. Near the Buddhist centre at Galle, he staged a great exhibition of Chinese products, including textiles, silk embroidery, gold and silver candlesticks, incense burners and other ceremonial articles. Hearing of so many luxuries, the king of Ceylon began to scheme about the goods remaining in the holds of the Ming ships. When the Chinese came back on their return voyage and Cheng Ho let his men go ashore, they came under attack by an army of fifty thousand men. A series of battles followed, climaxing in a midnight showdown. The king was captured and taken to China, with his family and ministers, arriving in Nanking in July 1411. After they were presented to the emperor, Yung Lo set them free and had them escorted home.

Now that the Ming navy was fully in control of the Strait of Malacca, Emperor Yung Lo ordered the arrest of Hsia Yuan-chi, the rich mandarin who had underwritten part of the cost of the first voyage. He had promised more than he could deliver.

Two years later, in the autumn of 1413, Cheng Ho set out with sixty-three ships and nearly thirty thousand men on his fourth and most ambitious voyage so far, sailing all the way to Arabia. Reaching the Persian Gulf, they put into the island of Hormuz, a major centre for sea-trade. From Hormuz they coasted around the Arabian boot to Aden at the mouth of the Red Sea. This excellent harbour was crowded with Arab *dhows* and gorged to overflowing with products from Europe, the Middle East and Africa, including caged wild animals of every description.

While Chinese and their junks were not new to the Red Sea, the sight of sixty-three big white-hulled ships decorated with wild eyes, red sails and silk pennants at each mast, and thousands of marines wearing tiger masks and bamboo armour, sent a frisson up the coast. During subsequent months, nineteen countries sent ambassadors to board Cheng Ho's ships with tribute for Emperor Yung Lo, topped by a giraffe presented by the king of Bengal. Yung Lo was astonished by the giraffe. One of his mandarins had the wit to observe that it resembled a mythical *chi-lin*, which appears only to rulers of perfect virtue. It was for having such presence of mind and silvery tongues that emperors surrounded themselves with mandarins.

In 1417, after two years in Nanking and then touring other cities along the Yangtze, the foreign envoys assembled and were escorted home by Cheng Ho with another great white fleet. On this trip, the admiral sailed down the east coast of Africa, stopping at Arab trading ports in Mogadishu, La'sa, Malindi and Mombassa, causing wild hysteria. They sailed on to Zanzibar and the Mafias, and may have reached Mozambique before turning home.

When a sixth voyage left Nanking in 1421, Cheng Ho did not join them until later. The emperor's health was failing, there were problems with the Mongols, and the emperor had decided to move the capital back north to Peking.

On this voyage, squadrons again visited the African coast. But after only ten months away, Cheng Ho returned to China early and was appointed military commander of the Nanking district, making him watchdog over the former southern capital, to guard the emperor's back. Emperor Yung Lo died on 12 August 1424. His policy of backing these great sea expeditions immediately came under attack. There was intense hostility to Cheng Ho, in part because his court eunuchs had a monopoly on all tribute, foreign trade, and imperial patronage. Nevertheless, in 1430 Cheng Ho was commissioned to undertake a final voyage. Now sixty years old and feeling the enormous burden of his weight, Cheng Ho revisited the Persian Gulf, the Red Sea and Africa, filling his holds with giraffes, elephants, and some of the products of the Renaissance in Europe.

What happened to him after this seventh voyage is not known. Jealous mandarins opposed to the court eunuchs destroyed most records and tried to shatter the stelae commemorating his voyages.

Luckily, they missed several, and there is much to remember him for. He sailed the longest distance of anyone in the world until then. He created a set of twenty-four surprisingly accurate navigation maps. He brought back to China many prosaic but important discoveries, such as eyeglasses. Although his voyages were intended to restrict trade to official patronage channels, they actually had the result of making many more Chinese familiar with the possibilties of travel and trade, so that after his death there was a dramatic increase in the number going abroad to become part of permanent Overseas Chinese communities.

With the death of Emperor Yung Lo, Ming vitality ended. After twenty years of fighting with Vietnam, China was defeated and the Ming navy lost three hundred junks. Failures piled up. Weak emperors were preoccupied with domestic intrigue. It became a capital offence to build a sea-going junk with more than two masts. Whoever went to sea in such ships, for whatever reason, was considered a pirate. Within a few decades, the Chinese forgot more about shipbuilding than the West had yet learned. A golden age of seafaring ended.

Today, Cheng Ho is virtually unknown in the West. In Asia he lives on, celebrated by the Overseas Chinese. Six images of the admiral are preserved in temples in the region. There is a Sanbao Harbor, a Sanbao Pagoda, a Sanbao Town. In Indonesia, Chinese go every year to Tajue Temple to pay homage on the anniversary of Cheng Ho's first visit. In Malacca the oldest well is called Sam Bao Kung. In Thailand incense is burned for him at San Pao Temple.

At the opposite end of the Indian Ocean, Arab and Persian storytellers tell of the fantastic seven voyages of a Muslim sailor of Eurasian blood named Sindbad – or was it Sanbao?

CHAPTER 8

CHAIRMAN OF THE HIGH SEAS

DURING THE NIGHT OF 29 APRIL 1661, A THICK FOG CREPT OVER the two Dutch forts in Taiwan. 'As soon as the fog lifted,' recalled a German mercenary, 'we perceived such a fleet of Chinese junks that we could not even estimate their numbers, much less count them . . . No-one knew whether they had come as friend or enemy.' Inside Fort Zeelandia were eleven hundred armed Europeans. Previous encounters had led the Dutch to believe that Chinese made poor soldiers. So they were completely unprepared for the disciplined marines of a half-Japanese, half-Chinese merchant pirate named Coxinga. The smaller of the two forts was quickly captured. Fort Zeelandia itself, on an island guarding the harbour, was more secure. Coxinga sent Governor Coyest a polite ultimatum: the Europeans could sail off unharmed with all their goods, or be destroyed; all he wanted was the fortress.

Misjudging his adversary, Coyest chose to fight. Coxinga urged him to reconsider: 'I realize that since the Dutch have come here from so great a distance to carry on trade, it is their duty and obligation to do whatever they can to preserve their fortress. This devotion pleases me, and I see no guilt or misdeed in it; I hope that you will not be afraid . . .

When I say something the whole world has confidence in me, and knows that I shall keep my word. I am inclined neither to lie nor to deceive. You people must understand my intentions.' The Dutch fought stubbornly for months till a European deserter showed the Chinese how to get in the back way. Good to his word, Coxinga still let the Dutch go with all their men, but kept half a million guilders worth of goods as punishment for their folly.

Men whose word could be trusted were as rare as ever, nowhere more so than in Peking, where glorious treachery in the two hundred years since the death of Emperor Yung Lo was the long shadow cast by cosmic virtue. The last Ming emperors were flaccid incompetents. Government was run by masters of deceit like Wei Chung-hsien, the most notorious Grand Eunuch in Chinese history, who had had himself emasculated to avoid a gambling debt. Such men were the archvillains in South China's struggle to free itself from the tyranny of the throne. Coxinga became the first great hero to emerge from the Overseas Chinese syndicates when he turned Taiwan into an independent offshore nation.

For centuries, the Ming Dynasty had tyrannized the coast. Trading syndicates fought back with pocket navies and insurgent armies of ten thousand men or more, even threatening Nanking. The Ming labelled them pirates. But in China you have to be careful who you call a pirate.

The Ming had outlawed private foreign trade in order to secure a lucrative monopoly for the throne. Privately owned merchant ships were prohibited from sailing to foreign lands. Anyone caught offshore was a criminal. Tribute missions could only enter legally at Canton, where they came under close bureaucratic scrutiny. Their cargoes and envoys were then escorted overland to the imperial capital. Many harbours were garrisoned and all illegal private shipping approaching them was seized. These measures drove sea traders to greater feats of resourcefulness, creating a lively black market from Japan to Java.

Whenever officials looked the other way, smuggling resumed. Ming was attempting to suppress a merchant culture that was much bigger and more enterprising than it realized. Chinese trade syndicates covered all of East Asia, with resident agents in Japan, South East Asia and the Indian Ocean. Large Overseas Chinese communities thrived in

Kyushu and the Ryukyus, in Luzon, Borneo, Sulu, Siam, Sumatra and Java.

In Siam, the royal court was authorized to send only one tribute fleet to China every three years, but the king actually provided documentation for two or three fleets each year, composed of Chinese junks with Chinese crews, and financed by Chinese merchants living in Siam. Most got through to discreet harbours where magistrates were paid off. As these fleets yielded profits of 300 per cent, the forfeiture of a few old junks from time to time made little difference.

By 1500, European traders were becoming active in the China Seas, and dealing directly with Chinese and Japanese syndicates. European demand for Chinese products spurred black-market activity. Overseas Chinese at Patani in Malaya arranged the speedy entry of Dutch cargoes to Fukien by greasing the eunuch in charge of maritime customs. When the governor of Fukien tried to stop them, merchants and gentry protested to the court, the governor was arrested, and he then committed suicide in prison.

China's central government was ill-equipped to deal with the challenge. Peking was landlocked physically and mentally. For it the sea posed problems, not opportunities. When Ming finally relaxed its ban, it went about liberalization in a niggardly way that caused an explosive increase in corruption. Chinese were licensed to trade privately overseas, but only under strict controls in designated ports. Success became a matter of licensing, bribes and kickbacks. The murderous rivalry over kickbacks between palace eunuchs and grand mandarins continued. Court officials were at the top of a pyramid of profiteering. They opposed complete regularization of trade because it would have made kickbacks unnecessary.

The exuberance of the coastal trade and the extreme avarice of Peking made this arrangement highly unstable. By interfering continually in routine procedures, Chinese bureaucrats created an imperial protection racket. A Dutch trader complained that officials in Peking were 'more like merchants than like princes'. When traders balked at being squeezed, reprisals followed. Leaders of long-established trading syndicates were suddenly branded pirates, and armies were sent to destroy them. They fought back, and for more than a hundred years a state of wild rebellion prevailed along the coast below the mouth of the Yangtze.

The leading players on the 'pirate' side were the people of Fukien, particularly those from Amoy, who had the most successful trading syndicates in East Asia. Their godfathers were as much at home in Sumatra, Luzon or Kyushu as they were in Amoy. Each syndicate was set up as a *kongsi* with its own army and navy. Each had treasuries of gold bars from which they bribed imperial officials. Other treasuries were kept overseas so that betrayals had limited effect. This remains standard procedure among Overseas Chinese today.

Their natural allies were the Japanese. The China trade was a major source of wealth for Japanese *daimyos* and samurai adventurers in Kyushu, nearest to China. During the Tang Dynasty, trade between China and Japan had boomed. When Ming tried to confine foreign trade to tribute missions, Japan responded aggressively with pirate raids, in league with Chinese syndicates headquartered on islands near Nagasaki. Japanese marauders joined Chinese in pillaging the wealthy south bank of the Yangtze from strongholds on islands off Chekiang that were beyond the reach of all but the most determined imperial forces.

The south bank of the Yangtze, called Kiangnan, was densely populated, inhabited by rich and cultured families. In the 1500s, the nearby port of Ningpo became a hotbed of smuggling. Chusan Island off Ningpo and the adjacent harbour of Chapu were pirate strongholds. In spring and autumn, prevailing winds made it easy to sail here from Japan. The surrounding tidewater country was criss-crossed with waterways, providing easy access to sampans, barges and shallow draft junks.

Chusan Island was headquarters for one of China's most successful maritime traders, Hsu Tung. As a young man from a village in Anhwei, he was jailed for smuggling and became friends with his cellmate, a trader from Amoy. Following their escape, Hsu Tung joined his cellmate's Amoy syndicate and climbed to the top of its maritime empire. One of his fellow villagers, Wang Chih, who represented the syndicate in Malacca, arranged one of the first Portuguese voyages to Japan. The next year he brought Japanese traders directly to Chusan Island. Promoted to Hsu Tung's right-hand man, Wang Chih took over handling all financial matters, and served as chief strategist in negotiations with Peking.

In return for full legalization of trade, the two men offered agents of Grand Secretary Yen Sung a major share of their profits. Yen Sung was a man of insatiable greed, whose assurances of good faith could result in an individual being tortured to death with all his children and grandchildren. Corruption started at the very top, with Grand Secretary Yen Sung and his son, and continued downward into every province. Regional bureaucrats had to maintain a constant flow of expensive gifts to the grand secretary or risk losing their heads. Hsu Tung was unable to meet the grand secretary's price. When their negotiations broke down, the scene was set for a bloody showdown. The grand secretary sent a military force to destroy the smuggling base, and Hsu Tung was trapped and murdered. Wang Chih fled to Japan, and became the new overlord of the maritime empire; indeed, he may have planned it that way. He was not a saint – he routinely betrayed rivals to the Ming government, while keeping their ships and trade goods – but thanks to a pact with Japan's Lord Matsuura, Wang Chih had a secure base in the Goto Islands off Nagasaki. While others did the fighting and looting, he stayed secure in Japan, blandly petitioning the Ming government for permission to trade legally.

Grand Secretary Yen Sung turned Wang Chih's fate over to an unusual bounty hunter. Hu Tseng-hsien was one of many investigators for the Censorate, the internal security watchdog responsible for policing the Ming bureaucracy, but he was from the same village in Anhwei where Wang Chih had been born. By accident of birth, he was plugged directly into the pirate network. Hu was quickly promoted to general in charge of all Chekiang province.

Extermination of the pirates had been tried repeatedly without success. In *The Art of War*, Sun Tzu prescribed two choices: the direct, which usually took the form of military liquidation campaigns, ending in failure, and the devious, which was preferred. Everyone in China sought to avoid confrontation, preferring to compromise until some opportunity arose to outwit an opponent. Deceit was the answer. So, as his weapons General Hu chose insincerity, poisoned wine, and treachery. Even pirates can be startled by the depths of a man's dishonesty.

His first step was to send agents to negotiate personally with Wang Chih in Japan. Because they were from the same village, Wang Chih was willing to listen. That was his first big mistake.

As an opening gambit, several of General Hu's secret agents stayed in Japan as hostages for the duration of their talks, in exchange for Wang Chih's godson, Wang Ao. General Hu entertained the young man and quickly plumbed his weak character. He told the godson that he had to demonstrate his sincerity to Peking by betraying a few comrades. Foolishly, Wang Ao blurted out that one of his godfather's biggest rivals, pirate leader Hsu Hai, was preparing to pillage the coast.

Hsu Hai was a former Buddhist monk whose fellow pirates thought he could see the future by divination. His force landed at Chapu harbour and set out to loot the Kiangnan countryside. In their path General Hu placed a boatload of poisoned wine. A few pirates partied, but the rest moved on. After months of looting and kidnapping, they had amassed so much booty that a thousand sampans trailed behind them through the waterways. When Hsu Hai and another leader quarrelled and went off in different directions, General Hu seized the moment to send in agents to make a deal. They began by revealing that Wang Chih's godson had betrayed all of them, as part of a secret Ming deal with their godfather in Japan. Since Hsu Hai and Wang Chih were 'as close as teeth and lips', this news came as a bit of a shock. General Hu's agents recommended plea-bargaining. They hinted that Hsu Hai's other rivals were also making deals to save their own skins. This so enraged Hsu Hai that he agreed to make a deal himself if General Hu could provide him with adequate financial guarantees. Gold and silks would have to be delivered to his Japanese samurai comrades, so they could go home in style. General Hu immediately informed the rival pirates that Ming government agents were seen carrying gold and silks into Hsu Hai's camp.

The general then stunned them all with an offer of absolute amnesty for everyone who agreed to lay down arms, followed by individual commissions as officers in the Ming army. Anybody who preferred to leave China would be given boats to carry their loot back to Japan. As intended, this invitation totally confused the pirates – a fine example of Sun Tzu mystification. Some were eager to accept amnesty, while others were frantic to go.

General Hu's agents hinted to Hsu Hai that there was no reason why he should let all the pirates leave when he could take their loot for his own use. Hsu Hai jumped at the chance and ambushed his rivals.

During the confusion, General Hu destroyed all of Hsu Hai's riverboats. This rattled the pirate leader, who withdrew to consider his predicament.

General Hu pressed him now, promising to memorialize the throne personally, and to ask the emperor to grant him a full pardon if Hsu Hai lured all his rivals into a government trap.

Completely bewildered, Hsu Hai agreed, and the rival pirate gangs were lured into Chapu harbour and slaughtered. When Hsu Hai then demanded that General Hu confirm his amnesty and keep all his other promises, he found that he was completely circled by government troops. Moments later, they attacked. Hsu Hai was pursued to a stream where he drowned himself, with some help. His head was removed for display in Peking.

As a climax, General Hu then persuaded the throne to offer a special amnesty to the merchant warlord in Japan, Wang Chih, if he returned to China and turned himself in. Wang Chih regretted the decision, for the emperor changed his mind and had him beheaded. For all his cleverness, General Hu was relieved of command, tried on charges of corruption and abuse of authority, and beaten to death in prison. This was the way of Ming. And Han. And Chin. And Chou.

Now one would think that with this kind of background, nobody in his right mind would ever again trust China's central government. Alas, folly never ceases, for now a great hero was about to come onstage, and a new Ming emperor brought a new supporting cast of villains.

Heirs to the Chinese throne were suckled until puberty. A palace eunuch named Wei Chung-hsien attached himself to the wet nurse of the heir apparent, because she had status as a secondary mother. The adolescent heir was led astray by Eunuch Wei, who served as the boy's pimp and procurer. The boy became so preoccupied with self-gratification that when he ascended the throne as Emperor Hsi-tsung (1621–1627), he left all administrative details to his Grand Eunuch. Wei followed in the footsteps of Grand Secretary Yen Sung by taking control of every kind of corruption in Peking. A group of scholar-officials tried to stop him, but were outwitted at every turn. Soon the Ming Dynasty was near bankruptcy. Bandit gangs in the north-west, and Manchu and Mongol armies in the north and north-east, made it clear that Ming's days were numbered.

Profiteers scrambled to take advantage of the growing incompetence of Peking. Along the coast, aggressive Western merchants pressed for advantages. The Dutch East India Company attacked Macao, and occupied the Pescadores Islands in the Taiwan Strait. The Ming court wanted the Dutch to leave, but the Dutch would only negotiate through Li Tan, the Overseas Chinese merchant warlord who had succeeded the late Wang Chih.

Li Tan had been the head of the great Amoy maritime trade network for thirty years. Among Western ship captains he was called Captain Andrea Ditties, because anywhere you went from Surabaya to Nagasaki, if you wanted to buy needles and thread or other little necessities of life, you could find those ditties in one of the general stores run by Li Tan's syndicate. Before 1600, Li Tan had been 'Captain China' of the twenty-six-thousand-strong Overseas Chinese community in Manila, mostly Hokkien from Amoy. The Spanish in the Philippines resented his wealth, his immense property holdings, and the fact that many of them owed him serious money. As a form of debt-rescheduling, they provoked a quarrel that led to Li Tan's arrest and sentencing to the galleys. The Spaniards seized all his property in the islands, including more than forty thousand gold bars rumoured to be only a small part of a huge mountain of gold and silver ingots he had hidden. The arrest of Li Tan and the seizure of his properties outraged the Hokkien community in Manila. Li Tan was the head of their *kongsi* – a *kongsi* that had been in existence for more than a thousand years. The gold mountain belonged to all of them. In Peking, Ming eunuchs stayed well informed about this dispute. In 1603, a group of imperial household eunuchs went to Manila to search for the rest of Li Tan's 'gold mountain'. The arrival of these exotic creatures, dressed like dancing lampshades, alarmed the rustic Spaniards. They panicked and massacred twenty-four thousand of the twenty-six thousand Chinese in Manila.

Li Tan had other gold mountains stashed in Amoy and Japan, so after his escape from the Spanish galleys in 1607, he moved his headquarters to Hirado and Nagasaki, where he resumed his role as chairman of the China Seas.

As the Portuguese took over Japan-China trade, Li Tan formed an alliance with them, and he was also careful to cultivate good business relations with the Dutch and British. When the Dutch asked him to negotiate with the Ming court over their occupation of the Pescadores, Li Tan sailed down from Hirado with a small fleet of his own war junks.

Age was catching up with him, so he brought along his chosen successor. Cheng Chilong was a cunning young man from Amoy. He was impossibly sly, a born deal-maker who could not help playing all sides against the middle. As a youth he had been sent to Macao to work for his uncle. There, his charm and quick-thinking made a big impression on the Portuguese, who baptized him Nicholas Gaspard. Cheng also worked for the Spaniards in Manila and the Dutch in Taiwan. By the age of nineteen, he knew his way around the China Seas and was ready to shake silver apples from the moon. One day, he arrived in Hirado as *comprador* of a Portuguese fleet. Li Tan already had a son of his own, but he recognized in Cheng the cunning, audacity and negotiating skill that had served him well in his own career. He took Cheng on as a protégé, and brought him to the Pescadores. It was young Cheng who worked out an agreement between Ming officials and the Dutch, which involved the transfer of a very large sum of gold into the coffers of Grand Eunuch Wei.

When Li Tan died of old age in August 1625, Cheng had gone to Japan in advance so that he could grab the leadership and cut out Li Tan's son. As word spread that he was the new overlord, the Ming court sent an agent to persuade him to switch sides, betray all his associates, and become a flunky of Grand Eunuch Wei. It was a replay of General Hu. Doubtless, Cheng was tempted, but after a heated family argument, he and his family decided that the Ming throne was not worth saving. They decided to stick together, to expand their grip on the offshore trade network, and to challenge the Ming fleet patrolling the Fukien coast.

In December 1627, a squadron of war junks commanded by the Chengs routed the Ming fleet and successfully occupied Amoy. As soon as he was ashore, Cheng was informed that leaders of other Hokkien syndicates were not willing to accept his domination. Tough as they all were, they were unprepared for the depth of Cheng's treachery. What better rebuttal than to strike an immediate bargain with the Ming? In return for being allowed to keep control of the Amoy maritime trading network, Cheng doublecrossed all his Hokkien friends and exposed them to Ming persecution. As a bonus, he was permitted to take over not only Amoy but the adjacent coastal valleys that were the ancestral homeland of all Hokkien dialect speakers. This brought the whole Hokkien trading system into Cheng's hands, along with all the estates, mansions, properties and other holdings amassed by powerful families over previous centuries, including a castle built out over the sea at An-p'ing-chen, which he made his personal headquarters. Cheng was given Ming military rank, free government provisions, cargo and war junks, and the free use of the imperial militia. As a lifelong pirate, his ultimate Ming accolade was to be named 'Admiral in Charge of Pirate Suppression'.

Cheng now had a near monopoly of Chinese trade with Japan, Taiwan and South East Asia as far as India. He had leverage with the Portuguese in Macao and Nagasaki, with the Dutch in Taiwan, and the Spanish in Luzon.

A major drought that year, 1628, caused many North Chinese to join bandit forces in the north-west, or to flee south to join Cheng's private army in Fukien. By the 1640s, the Ming were pleading with Cheng to send his personal army and that of his brother to fight the invading Manchu. They did so, but without conviction, for Cheng was already marinating a new deal with the enemy.

When the alien Manchu gained control of Peking in 1644, remnants of the Ming court fled south to seek refuge with Cheng in his coastal redoubt. A new Ming capital was established at Nanking, and in return for defending the city, Cheng was made an earl. His brothers, to no-one's surprise, were in command of defences on the south bank of the Yangtze, where the Manchu somehow managed to get their first foothold. After the fall of Nanking, the Cheng brothers escaped easily by ship, taking another Ming pretender, Prince Tang, to Foochow, where they had control. The prince found himself an uneasy guest.

With all North China in Manchu hands, the South China coast became the heart of Ming resistance. The Manchu could easily have been stopped by naval forces at the Yangtze, for they had little competence on the water, and South China could again have become a separate empire. But in less than five years, resistance shrank to a fingernail paring of coast and offshore islands. Warlord Cheng, far from putting up a spirited defence, was preparing to switch his allegiance to the Manchu in return for holding on to his commercial and military independence.

He ran into an unexpected problem – his son.

Coxinga was by all accounts an unusual character from birth; many thought he was supernatural. It was said that strange lights glowed in the sky when he was born on 28 August 1624, at the Overseas Chinese stronghold in Hirado. His Japanese mother was a member of the Tagawa clan, so to this day Coxinga is as much a legend in Japan as in China. His birth is commemorated by a stone marker on the beach at Hirado, and he is a major figure in Japanese literature. His mother named him Fukumatsu, but among the Chinese boatpeople in Hirado harbour he was always Cheng Sen, an ideograph with three trees meaning luxuriant foliage. At six, he was taken away from his mother to his father's new base in China. There he lived the life of a young prince in the stolen castle over the sea. Boats tied up in its inner courtyard. His father had a bodyguard of Portuguese-speaking Africans who charged into battle shouting 'Santiago'.

The boy showed great aptitude for classical learning. At the age of twenty-two, a handsome, charismatic young man, bursting with force and patriotism, he was presented by his father to the current Ming pretender, Prince Tang. The prince was so taken that he immediately bestowed on him the family name of the Ming dynasty – Chu – by way of informal adoption. Because nobody could actually speak the sacred name, the young man was called 'Lord of the Imperial Surname' or *Kuo-hsing-yeh*, which Westerners spelled Coxinga.

In theory, the pretender and his court were safe in Foochow, for to reach it Manchu armies would have to cross a range of mountains or sail down the coast. Unlike his father, who was a born turncoat, Coxinga regarded himself as a champion of China, fighting alien invaders. He urged Prince Tang to rush a large military force to block a mountain pass that was the only overland route into the coastal sanctuary. The grateful prince made Coxinga an earl and a field marshal, and sent him personally with an army to guard the pass.

This made things awkward for Coxinga's father, who had planned to invite the Manchu through that pass when the time was ripe.

In the summer of 1646, Ming hopes dimmed when Manchu armies

achieved sweeping victories in nearby Chekiang and Kiangsi. As Cheng Senior was not willing to lead military campaigns inland, the pretender set out himself at the head of an expeditionary force. The moment he was gone, Cheng sold out. He withheld supplies and food from his son's army at the mountain pass, so they were obliged to return to Foochow. A Manchu army quickly marched through the unguarded pass and captured the pretender, and by prior arrangement Cheng surrendered Foochow to them.

The Manchu had made Cheng Senior lavish promises. They had agreed not to interfere with his coastal domain, but they insisted on his accompanying them to the northern capital. To his surprise, when they reached Peking they gave him only the minor title of viscount-third-class, and confined him to a mouldering villa under close guard. Prospects were not good.

Coxinga felt betrayed. He saw himself as China's saviour. Hurriedly raising an army of his family's followers, he took control of a number of cities along the coast. His mother, who had come over from Japan the previous year, was in Amoy when Coxinga's father allowed the Manchu troops to take control of the island stronghold. Most of the defenders fled, but Coxinga's mother was captured and gang-raped. She then committed suicide, plunging a samurai short-sword into her stomach and leaping from the city wall.

All over China, generals with thousands of troops were switching to the Manchu without a fight. When he learned of his mother's death, Coxinga went to a Confucian temple, burned his scholar's robes, denounced his father's betrayal, and declared war on the Manchu. Coxinga's resistance became the only coherent, sustained effort to reverse the Manchu victory. He had his own agenda. Ming pretenders were not a part of it. When another pretender was enthroned in Kwangtung in 1648, Coxinga merely sent congratulations (and in return was named a duke).

Coxinga attracted universal support, but his talents were political and organizational, not military. He had charisma, family name and connections, and he projected a powerful aura that drew experienced men to him. He was a severe but impartial disciplinarian, executing even close relatives for dereliction of duty. With strict training and organization, Coxinga's army and navy became unusually effective.

Initially, his campaign against the Manchu was so successful that enemy troops in one besieged city were reduced to cannibalism.

They did everything they could to buy him off. His father, still under glorified house arrest in Peking, wrote letter after letter urging his son to submit, warning him between the lines. Coxinga ignored the letters and devoted his attention to the civil and military reorganization of his coastal stronghold, which was to be the heart of a new independent South China – this time with strong maritime trade and political connections to Japan, the Philippines and South East Asia.

In 1658, Coxinga was ready to attack. He set out at the head of an army, a hundred thousand strong, and a navy of a thousand ships, heading up the Yangtze to lay siege to Nanking. Many government garrisons along the way joined him. Nothing stood in his way.

The prospect of Coxinga capturing Nanking greatly alarmed the Manchu. Reinforcements were rushed south.

Coxinga was a talented naval commander, able to wield combined naval and marine forces intuitively, with great success. But in siege conditions inland, he was out of his element. He could easily have stormed the reduced garrison at Nanking, giving himself a great symbolic victory, but, unwisely, he rejected the advice of his chief of staff, and decided to starve the garrison out.

A Belgian priest in Nanking described how, 'When the city had been besieged only twenty days . . . a large number of inhabitants died of hunger every day, and many, despairing, hanged themselves . . . there were only five hundred real [Manchu] troops in the garrison . . . other members of the garrison were Chinese.'

Meanwhile, by forced march, Manchu reinforcements arrived, including large numbers of Mongol cavalry. They spied on Coxinga's forces, saw them to be offguard – soldiers were gathering firewood, trenches were deserted, troops were amusing themselves. Knowing the Chinese well, the Manchu attacked immediately and took the front encampment. Other Manchu poured from the city to do battle. Coxinga's men were caught completely by surprise and suffered a great defeat.

Stopped on the verge of triumph, Coxinga withdrew his huge fleet downriver, and the Manchu hurriedly assembled eight hundred vessels to follow, which was their own mistake. At sea off Chekiang, Coxinga utterly destroyed them, taking four thousand Manchu prisoners. He sent them back to Peking, after ordering their ears and noses cut off.

Determined now to set up a secure permanent base, Coxinga gathered his followers in a fleet of nine hundred ships and twenty-five thousand marines, and crossed the strait to Taiwan. He had detailed intelligence on the island from a Chinese interpreter who had worked for the Dutch. A large fleet from Batavia had just departed. Early in the morning of 30 April 1661, Coxinga's invasion force ghosted through the fog to anchor off Fort Zeelandia. The Dutch held out for nine months.

Victory on Taiwan was sweet and sour. In Peking, the vengeful Manchu chained his father around the neck and ankles and put him in a dungeon to receive the 'death of a thousand cuts'. It was commuted to beheading, but he was first given the pleasure of watching two of his infant children beaten to death against a wall.

Coxinga began colonizing the independent kingdom of Taiwan as the heart of a new offshore empire that would soon include the Philippines. He had kicked out the Dutch. Next, in reprisal for the 1603 massacre of Manila, he would boot out the Spaniards. In warning he sent a Dominican priest to Manila to demand that the Spanish submit to his rule. Their response was to expel all Chinese – more than thirty thousand people – from the islands. Fearing murder, many fled into the jungles. Those caught outside Manila's Chinese ghetto (the Parian) were immediately beheaded. All remaining Chinese were put aboard ships and forced out to sea on punishment of death.

Then fate intervened. Coxinga's headquarters at Fort Zeelandia, near present-day Tainan, was a mosquito-infested malarial swamp, attractive at first to Dutch lowlanders but a bad choice for a new capital. On 23 June 1662, at the age of thirty-eight, Coxinga – the first great hero of the Overseas Chinese – came down with the most dreaded form of cerebral malaria. After weeks of agony, interspersed with the outbursts of raving typical of the disease, he suddenly died. Contemporary Manchu and European sources piously attributed his death to insanity, brought about by heavenly punishment for a demon from hell.

Deflated by the loss of their great hero, some of his officers gave up the struggle and surrendered to the Manchu.

That same year, just before Coxinga's death, a general who had defected to the Manchu, made one of history's most senseless proposals. In order to cripple rebel support, he suggested that the Manchu oblige all inhabitants of the China coast, including the provinces of Shantung, Kiangsu, Chekiang, Fukien and Kwangtung, to move inland a distance of ten to fifteen miles. This had a negligible effect on the rebels militarily or commercially, but it brought disaster to millions of ordinary Chinese, uprooting farm families from fertile river valleys along the coast and forcing them onto barren hillsides inland, depriving artisans and shop-keepers of their places of livelihood, and condemning hundreds of thousands of women and children to become homeless refugees. This policy remained in effect for nineteen years, from 1662 to 1681. Normal life on the coast took centuries to recover. Even the rural people of coastal China became permanently estranged from Peking. They still are today.

Coxinga's gallant but hopeless rebellion spawned many anti-Manchu secret societies that are celebrated to this day in books and movies. His death on Taiwan, and the Manchu displacement of millions inland, was followed by a great exodus of boatpeople and refugees to all sanctuaries offshore. As they fled they took their secret alliances, signals, tattoos and codes of conduct with them, into Overseas Chinese communities around the world. As an independent state, Coxinga's offshore empire did not die. It just became invisible.

PART TWO
EMPIRE

CHAPTER 9

PORTS UNKNOWN

————————————

IT IS TIME TO EXAMINE THESE OVERSEAS CHINESE COMMUNITIES more closely, to explore how they worked and what made them so strong, so tightly knit, and so invisible. The answers are the same as they were four hundred years ago, so rather than track events in a strictly chronological manner from 1500 to 1900, we will approach the questions topically, as in a Chinese banquet, figuring out what is in each platter as it comes to the table.

When Europeans first arrived in Asian waters, they were intent on conquest and armed trade, and failed to see that they were blundering into a great cobweb of Chinese commercial networks. What they found – or thought they found – were small Hindu, Buddhist and Muslim kingdoms, which they were able to conquer and colonize, then defend against rival European merchant navies. In most ports there were ghettos of Chinese traders, but no hint that they were outposts of powerful syndicates based far away in the harbours of South China. Much of what went on in South East Asia was kept out of sight, as rainforest creepers spread their threads through the mulch to feed on the roots of other plants. Unknown to the colonials, these syndicates had long ago divided South East Asia into commercial territories and were engaged in a perpetual, often vicious, struggle to wrest control from one another. The punitive voyages of Cheng Ho, and the brief prominence of Coxinga, were rare public glimpses of this furtive struggle. Just as their ancestors had been expelled from North China, most of these Overseas Chinese traders were refugees.

Refugees had been leaving South China for the Indies in small waves since Yueh was overrun by Chin armies at the end of Warring States. More fled when Chin collapsed and Han armies reconquered the south. In the ninth century, following the collapse of the Tang Dynasty, the massacres of the Huang Chao uprising caused thousands more to emigrate. There was a haemorrhage of refugees when the Mongols overwhelmed Sung and turned much of China into a wasteland. The characteristic disobedience of the south coast repeatedly made it a target of repression during the Ming Dynasty. And after the Manchu ordered all coast-dwellers to move inland, the end of Coxinga's rebellion provoked a mass exodus.

Given their attachment to their ancestral villages, many of the refugees eventually went home. They saw themselves not as permanent emigrants, but as temporary sojourners.

Natural calamities caused others to leave. When people in North China fled south to escape flood, drought or famine, many of those already in the south were pushed out. South China had its own droughts or floods every few years. More than twenty-three million died on the coast in the famines of 1846, 1849 and 1877.

Finally, there were the commercial refugees. To keep from being fleeced by their own government, the most dynamic entrepreneurs in the south often fled offshore, at least temporarily. When nearby islands proved insecure, they shifted their treasure and their bases overseas to Japan, Indochina and the Malay archipelago.

Mixed in with the refugees were boatpeople who migrated season-ally, like great flocks of birds, up and down the coast from Hangchow to Sumatra. Few records exist of these comings and goings because, from the viewpoint of China's imperial bureaucracy, emigrants and boatpeople did not exist. They were nonpersons.

The exit points for most of these refugees were secluded harbours between Hong Kong and Shanghai, where it was always possible to find passage on a family-owned junk, loosely belonging to one of the *kongsi* confederations of local traders. The southern coast is a series of blue-on-blue capes cut off from the rest of China by rugged mountains through which there are few passes. Here, rivers flow south-east to the sea, cutting deep valleys. Their deltas form natural harbours that are difficult to reach overland. This is one of the most beautiful regions in China. Since ancient times, because of their isolation, these river valleys and the headlands, islands and bays between them have been sanctuaries for renegades, pirates and smugglers. Each river valley developed its own culture, and its own loyalties. Great legends were born when Coxinga gave them common cause against the Manchu. Folklore made Amoy and Swatow the mother lode of all Overseas Chinese triads. Even gangsters in Canton and Shanghai, who speak entirely different dialects, trace their mythic and spiritual origins to this incubator. To understand the social and business networks of Overseas Chinese as far away as the Belleville ghetto in Paris, you have to trace the root systems back here.

Most Overseas Chinese say they come from Fukien, Kwangtung and Chekiang provinces, along this coast. But to say that someone comes from Fukien is like saying he comes from Europe. What really matters is your ancestral village. Anyone else is a foreigner.

Surprisingly, their ancestral villages cluster in only a few districts around four river deltas. Three of these are in Fukien province: the Min River flows into the sea at Foochow; the Chiu-lung empties near Amoy; the Han River begins in Fukien, then crosses the border into Kwangtung before reaching the sea near Swatow. So while the city of Swatow is in Kwangtung province, the Han River links it to Fukien. The fourth delta is the mouth of the Pearl River below Canton.

The people living in these four river deltas each speak a different dialect, as unlike one another as German, French and English. People from Foochow speak the Hokchiu dialect. Those from Amoy speak Hokkien. Between Foochow and Amoy, they speak Henghua. The people of the Pearl River delta and Canton are often lumped together as Cantonese, although they speak a number of dialects of which urban Cantonese (Yueh) is just the major one. Most of the early Chinese immigrants to North America came not from Canton itself but from a group of ancestral villages south-west of the city, where they spoke a different dialect called Taishan.

Along the Han River at Swatow in eastern Kwangtung province, 170 miles north-east of Canton, they speak Hoklo but call themselves Teochiu, from the name of a riverside town that used to be the major port in that area, a thousand years ago. It has since been superseded by Swatow. The Teochiu people are culturally unique. They operate what many consider to be the richest, most powerful underworld network on earth, one of the world's first multinational corporations. Tightly organized and intensely loyal, all the Teochiu in the world today are linked by common dialect and common origin to seven village districts around Swatow. This is one of the great spawning grounds of what officials regarded as piracy, smuggling and black marketeering.

All these tribal groups have written Chinese script in common, but their local dialects are mutually unintelligible. Many also speak Mandarin, the dialect of the national capital and imperial bureaucracy, because fluency in Mandarin was necessary to qualify for civil service exams and government jobs. Their coastal dialects intensify the clannishness of each group, creating an exclusive membership that is exported to Bangkok, Singapore, Toronto, Seattle, Amsterdam, and elsewhere in the world. These dialects evolved from a blend of the ancient tongues of Yueh with the dialects of various Chinese expelled from the north. Each mix developed in the isolation of a separate valley girded by mountains, where the local aberrations were preserved like jars of pickled vegetables.

The central government, always suspicious of the unruly coastal provinces, deliberately neglected them. Happy to be left alone, the inhabitants of the coast became completely self-sufficient, relying on their local ties of family, clan, county and dialect. When they left China to live or work in foreign cultures, these loyalties went with them and became more pronounced. All who left the Middle Kingdom without permission were considered traitors, so China's rulers never concerned themselves with the welfare of citizens living abroad. To look out for themselves, Overseas Chinese formed their own organizations: native place associations; surname groups; dialect groups; business guilds; athletic clubs; religious groups; benevolent societies, tongs and triads. To outsiders, the proliferation of so many public and secret Chinese organizations results in a confusing welter of names and identities. But that is the whole idea. Traditionally these organizations have been obsessed with secrecy and mystification in order to protect themselves and their members from persecution by the central government, by regional warlords, or by rival groups. In the West, triads and tongs easily became confused with guilds and *kongsi*. So some simplification is called for. The key is that, beyond the magic circle of the family/clan, the most powerful group is the native place association. All the other organizations, such as triads, are merely spin-offs or overlays.

The Teochiu dialect group, for example, has seven native place associations, one for each of the seven *hsiens*, or village districts, in the Swatow region. The most powerful are Mei Hsien, Chin Hai, Yao Ping and Chao Yang. As more successful members move up the hierarchy of each *hsien* association, they become senior officers controlling or influencing the affairs of all their members. At the top in each country is an overall Teochiu Association, a council of leaders from each *hsien* association. These are paternalistic civic associations that look after the business affairs, financial needs and social welfare of their many members, but each Teochiu *hsien* association has its own enforcers, paramilitaries who make up a secret private army numbering in the thousands. Because these associations exist in countries all over Asia and the West, and their private armies have been involved historically in a broad range of clandestine activities, the worldwide total of Teochiu paramilitaries may be several hundred thousand.

In English, these secret armies are commonly known as syndicates because each handles the covert business operations of a separate *hsien* association. Collectively, the seven Teochiu syndicates have become known popularly as the Chiu-Chao Brotherhood, or simply Chiu-Chao, the Cantonese pronunciation of Teochiu, which is used by the Hong Kong police in their criminal records and by Hong Kong newspapers. Elsewhere in the world they are most often called Teochiu, and have a somewhat better image. For simplicity's sake, this book will refer to the dialect group as the Teochiu, and to their secret commercial armies as the Teochiu syndicates.

The Teochiu themselves number many millions, but the exact total outside China can only be estimated roughly, because of the lack of precise census data in many places. While they are the richest of the Overseas Chinese and are the majority Chinese population in Thailand, they are only the second largest in Hong Kong, Vietnam,

Singapore, Malaysia, Canada and the United States. In the course of
their day-to-day activities in South East Asia and elsewhere around the
Pacific Rim, Teochiu syndicates have been massively involved in rice
smuggling, drugs, and all other conceivable rackets. Many of these
activities have been going on for centuries and are not in any way
unusual for the region. Nor are they necessarily seen by Asians as being
criminal. A sense of scale can be drawn from the international heroin
trade out of the Golden Triangle, dominated by four or five of the seven
Teochiu syndicates, which in the 1990s is thought to be worth
something on the order of $200 billion a year in black money. Not all
Asian heroin is smuggled or brokered by the Teochiu – Hokkien and
other syndicates move large quantities of Golden Triangle drugs
through Taiwan, for instance – but Teochiu have the lion's share.
People who are not sympathetic to its activities consider the Teochiu
Brotherhood to be the biggest criminal organization in the world.
Those who do benefit from it see the matter differently.

Every dialect group contains any number of big and small triads,
some tracing their roots to Coxinga, who was a Hokkien. Because of
their shared interest in fighting the alien Manchu, many dialect groups
on the coast were temporarily allied with the Hokkien in backing
Coxinga. Together they called their anti-Manchu organization the
Hung-Men (Hung League) after the first Ming emperor, whose reign
title was Hung Wu. Hung also means red, which Chinese regard as the
colour of hope, so the Hung League is often referred to in Western
sources as the Red Gang. While this sounds colourful and gangsterish,
it is neither helpful nor entirely accurate.

After the death of Coxinga, five militant monks associated with the
Hung League inspired fresh outbreaks of anti-Manchu conspiracy.
They became heroes to generations of Chinese, and their adventures
have been dramatized by puppet shows at village fairs, travelling acting
troupes, movies and television, and inspired (if that's the word) the
long-running American TV series, *Kung Fu*. Members of the Hung
League spread down the coast and set up branch organizations
throughout Asia and the Pacific, using the ancient symbolism of the
triad, an equilateral triangle with sides representing Man, Heaven and
Earth. Its three parent organizations were the Heaven and Earth
Society (T'ien-ti Hui), the Three Dots Society (San-tien Hui) and the

Three Harmonies Society (San-ho Hui). Native populations and Western colonials were often terrified of the triads, attributing to them all manner of sinister murders, extortion, kidnapping, gold hoarding, drug smuggling, protection rackets, counterfeiting, and abduction of village girls for brothels. On the positive side, they provided expatriate members with the social services usually denied them because they were Chinese. The Teochiu triads (distinct from other Teochiu organizations) are considered by the Hong Kong police to be the most secretive, exclusive and dangerous. On the other hand, Teochiu civic associations are among the most public-spirited social organizations in Thailand. They lend their members seed money to start businesses, help to arrange marriages and funerals, set up schools so that Chinese children receive education along traditional lines, build hospitals, and back charities.

Confucian hierarchy is tight. Each Chinese family and clan had its elders, each guild its chief, each triad its boss, while umbrella organizations in each country, such as the dialect group associations – Hokkien, Teochiu, Hakka – were overseen by a grand patriarch. He was usually the richest tycoon in that country, and was subservient to an international godfather, who might be based in the ancestral village, or (since the communist takeover) in Taipei, Hong Kong, Bangkok or Singapore. For example, most Chinese in Paris today come from a small town in Chekiang province, and settled in the Belleville ghetto after the French Jews who lived there were deported and killed during the Nazi occupation. Other French were not eager to move into the Jewish ghetto while the Nazi curse was still upon it, but the Chinese had no such qualms. Many years later, when their feuds in Paris upset the French government in 1993, their godfather was imported from Chekiang to resolve the disputes and to calm his flock. It worked like magic. Tradition, combined with economics, gives the international godfather profound leverage. When the head of a dialect group dies or retires, his designated successor becomes the overlord of subsidiary groups all over the world.

Loyalty and discipline within a dialect group are maintained by *shinyung*, or trust, the superglue used to guarantee repayment of unsecured, informal loans, and to guarantee silence and invisibility. This form of trust is an absolute, and today is in increasingly short supply in the West, where nuclear families routinely disintegrate. To survive and prosper under tyrannical dynasties, or in permanent exile, Chinese family and clan elders had to apply very strict rules of trust. Just because you spoke Teochiu or Hokchiu did not automatically make you a member of the in-group, or a fully-fledged member of the family enterprise, or entitle you to the real or implicit benefits of the tontine.

To begin with, you had to be from the same native place – the same county if not the same village, and either the inner or outer circles of the same clan. Next you had to demonstrate your trustworthiness, your *shinyung*. Nobody was born with it. Not even family members had it automatically. Boys or young men who wished to go into the family business had to serve a long apprenticeship, during which their abilities and their trustworthiness were closely observed. Only those who repeatedly demonstrated absolute *shinyung* were then permitted to join the business, or to become part of a network.

Later, after the Pacific War, as tradition began to unravel around the Rim, and a new generation of Overseas Chinese challenged the behaviour of their elders during the occupation, *shinyung* loosened up somewhat. In business it continues to be vital, but collateral – especially offshore collateral – has begun to take its place to guarantee loans. Traditionalists feel that things have changed too much; too much interest in passing fashion, and sophistication, distract new generations from their deeper commitments. But compared to Westerners in general, and to Americans in particular, even the most urbane and progressive Overseas Chinese is a long way from abandoning his patrimony.

Confucians speak loftily about *shinyung*, but feuding between the paramilitary syndicates of dialect groups has always been fierce, provoking clan wars that could be murderous and end in open combat. This ruthless and bloody rivalry divided East and South East Asia into Chinese commercial territories many centuries before Westerners arrived. The port of Chuan-chou was China's busiest port for generations, during which the Henghua dialect group was riding high. This was the group eventually taken over by the Muslim trader Abu, who betrayed Southern Sung to the Mongol invaders. After Mongol rule collapsed and Chuan-chou silted up, the port of Amoy became favoured by the Ming Admiral Cheng Ho, and the Hokkien dialect group of Amoy (and Coxinga) gained the upper hand till the twentieth century. Since the Second World War the Teochiu have taken the lead from their main bases in Swatow, Hong Kong and Bangkok.

Although they are no longer the richest, Hokkien continue to be the most numerous and widespread of all Overseas Chinese, and are in the majority in Taiwan, the Philippines, Indonesia, Singapore and Malaysia. Amoy, their homebase in Fukien province opposite Taiwan, is a superb harbour on the south-west coast of an island called Mansion Gate (Hsiamen or Xiamen), literally guarding the approaches to the 'mansion' of the Hokkien in the Chiu-lung River valley. Since the 1300s, the Hokkien had become the most powerful Overseas Chinese dialect group, but during the Second World War they were singled out for victimization by the Japanese, particularly in Singapore and on the Malay Peninsula, where they were slaughtered. Because Thailand sided with Japan, its Teochiu population came out of the war virtually unscathed, and at least in part because of the growth of the Golden Triangle drug trade, vastly richer.

The majority of Chinese in Indochina are Cantonese speakers from the Pearl River delta, but since the Vietnam War they have been persecuted, expelled and reduced in numbers. The remainder of the Overseas Chinese, scattered all over the world, are Hakka, Hokchiu, Henghua, and Hainanese, plus a large number of Wu speakers from Chekiang province and urban Shanghai.

The Hakka people are distinctive because they are latecomers from far inland. According to tradition, they originated to the north in arid Shansi Province, but to escape the Mongol invasion they fled south to the mountains of Kiangsi. The Han River begins near the border of Kiangsi, so it was natural for the Hakka to haul their mountain rice downriver to sell to the Teochiu, who marketed it by boat along the coast. Gradually, Hakka formed a subordinate relationship with the Teochiu and accompanied them to Hong Kong and Hainan Island. When the Teochiu became the principal rice marketers in Vietnam, Thailand and Malaya, many Hakka went with them, becoming the fourth largest Overseas Chinese group, after the Hokkien, Teochiu and Cantonese. The Hakka have enjoyed a disproportionate amount of influence because they have produced many gifted and aggressive leaders, including the republican revolutionary Dr Sun Yat-sen, and Singapore statesman Lee Kuan Yew.

On the bottom rung, the Hainanese are actually a mixture of dialect group refugees who fled over the centuries to Hainan Island, the smuggling centre on the edge of South China that thrived on illicit trade from the South Seas. There they resumed life-as-usual, joining various syndicates in voyages of piracy and trade during each monsoon season. Typically, their junks carried cargoes of silk and porcelain south to exchange for food, medicinals and aphrodisiacs. Between ports, the junks stopped to barter with coastal villages, anchoring close to shore while the crew beat gongs to alert merchants and housewives. Along the Borneo coast, Chinese who settled among the Dayaks collected swallow nests from giant caves, to supply the Mainland market in bird's nest soup. Many gathered plants, bark, reptiles and mammal parts thought to have properties as sexual stimulants or prolongers. For many isolated South Seas islanders, the Chinese arrived like cosmic aliens, their first contact with the outside world.

Goods the Chinese purchased in the islands came from the trading monopolies of petty rulers. Each *tuan*, *dato* or *raja* had men collect and stockpile goods they knew the Chinese wanted. Often there were local Chinese residents who made a living as the intermediaries for this trade. In bigger ports, Muslims and Indians controlled retail, so Chinese concentrated on wholesale. Although there might be fewer Chinese than Muslims in the harbours of Java and Sumatra, their syndicates had thousands of junks plying the seas between Ceylon and the Yangtze. Teochiu smuggling junks were in continual motion around the islands like mosquitoes over a stagnant pond. It served their commercial interests to remain clandestine, and to do things at night, not only because they were outlaws in the eyes of imperial China, but because they were in continual warfare with their own Overseas Chinese rivals.

This is why their networks were like a giant gossamer spider's web when the first European armed traders arrived on the scene, and why centuries were to pass before Westerners recognized that some local Chinese shopkeepers were actually representatives of great multi-national trading houses, as powerful in their way as their own East India companies, and far older.

While many of their commercial operations were carried out in a clandestine fashion, they were only 'smugglers' or 'pirates' in the view of central regimes or colonial governments that were unable to tax and regulate them. Only renegades indulged in outright piracy. Most Chinese saw themselves simply as free agents engaged in inter-island or coastal trade, doing what they could to avoid customs duties, kickbacks or squeeze. In Asia, free trade is taken to mean exactly that. So smuggling was an honourable pursuit in the face of predatory rulers. In this book the term 'smuggling' is used in that sense.

Against this background, the arrival of Europeans was a mixed blessing. On the one hand, they introduced positive Western attitudes towards commerce, and provided stable colonial regimes where trade could go on in broad daylight. Excited by the opportunities, many Chinese left Kwangtung and Fukien to join their relatives in the new colonial settlements. On the other hand, racism and commercial envy provoked a great deal of friction, and bloodshed.

Sir James Brooke, the White Raja of Sarawak, spoke for many when he said: 'I know not whether most to admire the Chinese for their many virtues or to despise them for their glaring defects . . . their industry exceeds that of any other people on the face of the earth, they are laborious, patient and cheerful; but on the other hand they are corrupt, supple and exacting, yielding to their superiors and tyrannical to those who fall into their power.'

Though the Overseas Chinese provided wholesale access to a wide range of Chinese products including tea, silk, dyes, ink and paper, their syndicates also competed with Westerners in buying up South East Asian commodities such as spices, sugar, tobacco, tin, rubber and forest products. Colonial authorities tried to restrict them to trading in Chinese products, and to confine them in their ghettoes. These ghettoes of ten thousand people or more were completely self-governing under the leading merchant, whom the Westerners commonly called 'Captain China'.

Native élites, afraid that they would lose their own patrimony, blocked Overseas Chinese from buying land. The constant danger of persecution persuaded the Chinese to keep their wealth in gold, gems and hard currency, rolling it over by short-term investment, moneylending and, later, modern banking. Much of their lending went to spendthrift locals, who used the money to buy property, then forfeited the land to the Chinese when they were unable to repay. Thus, by roundabout means, Chinese prohibited from directly buying land ended up acquiring great estates. In this way, Fukienese immigrants in the Philippines became the biggest landowners after the Catholic Church.

The vitality Raja Brooke spoke of was not easy to repress; their dexterity in moneylending gave the Chinese abnormal influence and led to reprisals and massacres. A few years later, after a Hakka gold-mining *kongsi* tried to murder him, Brooke himself led a pogrom that killed two thousand of the five thousand Chinese in Sarawak.

Officers of the Dutch East India Company tried to suppress Chinese competition by labelling them 'smugglers' and obliging them to pay extortionate fines. In 1740, the Dutch decided that any Chinese in the islands who could not prove he was making an honest living would be sent to Sri Lanka as a slave. When the Chinese objected and rose in rebellion, the Dutch became enraged and slaughtered thousands in a dark episode known as the Batavian Fury. Javanese enthusiastically joined in the massacre. More than ten thousand Chinese were murdered. The sugar industry, dependent upon the old Chinese infrastructure, collapsed. To restock the islands with labourers, the Dutch governor-general of the Indies sent ships to make slave-raids on the coast of Fukien and Kwangtung provinces. The Spanish in the Philippines also kidnapped thousands of Chinese to work as slaves on the estates of the Catholic Church. By the nineteenth century, millions of Chinese were being imported to all the colonies to work as coolies in mines and plantations. Native populations of South East Asia were unwilling to work for wages away from their home villages. Westerners themselves were reluctant to put their hands to physical labour. Chinese filled the gap, while carefully demonstrating humility.

Everywhere, colonial administrators also found that they needed the Chinese as middlemen, or *compradors*. So long as they remained submissive and inconspicuous, there was no serious trouble. But racial hatreds lay just beneath the surface.

In Borneo, Chinese working in various mining *kongsi* became one-third of the population. Some of their leaders grew so rich that they

rivalled the sultans who had sold them their mining concessions. In
1823, when the sultans 'resold' these concessions to the Dutch, the
Chinese *kongsi* resisted, only to be massacred. By 1880, their numbers in
Borneo had dropped by one hundred thousand. Many Chinese industries
in South East Asia were taken over by Western colonials in this way.

All this acrimonious history was what made Singapore such a
refreshing exception. Singapore had been founded by Stamford
Raffles, an unlikely player. The son of a sea captain, he'd grown up in
poverty and quit school at fourteen to support his mother and four
sisters by working as a clerk for the British East India Company. In his
spare time, he studied natural history and languages, and by twenty-
three was assistant secretary with the colonial government of Penang
Island at the north end of the Strait of Malacca. Raffles learned Malay,
and in 1811, sailed with the viceroy of India, Lord Minto, on a raid
against Dutch–French forces in Java. Receiving much of the credit for
Britain's success in taking Java, at age thirty Raffles was appointed its
lieutenant-governor. A fair-minded man, he immediately introduced
reforms to improve conditions for the Javanese. However, the East
India Company had no interest in oppressed natives, and Raffles was
recalled to London. There, he surprised critics by becoming a social
lion and gaining a knighthood. Hastily posted back to obscurity in
Asia, he found himself downgraded to overseer of a pepper port in a
Sumatra backwater, where he watched the Dutch regain possession of
the archipelago. Raffles pleaded for action, and was given command of
a squadron which he sailed to the old port of Tumasik, on a low-lying
island at the south end of the Strait. There, on 29 January 1819, he
established a garrison he called Singapore.
    Singapore is usually thought to have been nothing but a mangrove
swamp before Raffles picked it up for a song. A thousand years before
Raffles, and many centuries before Admiral Cheng Ho dropped his
hook off Malacca up the coast, however, the island was already a
thriving entrepôt. Tumasik (Sea Town) was an important Malay-
Chinese-Arab trading port as far back as the Roman Empire.
According to a visitor in 1349, Malays there lived 'mixed up with the
Chinese'. In the late fourteenth century, the town was destroyed by
raiders from Java. After that, Tumasik survived only as a sleepy fishing

village, while its Arab and Chinese traders moved to Malacca, to trade under the protection of Cheng Ho's war junks.

When Raffles founded Singapore, only one hundred and twenty Malays and thirty Chinese were living there. The rest had left for Malacca five hundred years earlier. By 1823 Singapore had ten thousand inhabitants, one-third of them Chinese, mostly Hokkien and Teochiu. Six years later, the Dutch conceded all claims to Tumasik, and the sultan of Johore gave the island to Britain.

Singapore drew Chinese from all over the South Seas. Unlike the hostility of Manila and Batavia, Singapore's experience was of unique co-operation. The colonial administration was relatively benign. And when Chinese community leaders decided that Britain's commercial and legal systems were definitely superior, the Overseas Chinese became the world's most enthusiastic practitioners of capitalism. They had been looking for just such a haven. Singapore succeeded as few places ever have.

Most of those who came to Singapore were peasants, shopkeepers and urban workers. Everyone's goal was to make a fortune, send remittances home, burn joss to the spirits, and plan a spectacular funeral. Nobody was there for fun, but you could eat magnificently in Singapore, and gamble. Inevitably, the rival dialect groups feuded, so the Hokkien were forcibly separated from the Teochiu and the Hakka.

The opening of the Suez Canal in 1869 and the advent of steamships greatly increased Singapore's importance. Industrial demand for tin and rubber brought a boom. Cheap labour was urgently needed, so European managers imported millions of coolies. Even Chinese scholars were kidnapped. Fortunes were made buying and selling coolies. The coolies themselves had to pay back their travel, board and lodging, with 10 per cent interest. At their destinations they were sold again. Their first year's wages had to go to the shipping agents. The trade slowed only when there was a resurgence of Yellow Peril panic, leading to new immigration restrictions in the United States, Canada and Australia.

During the same period, three million other Chinese who were not coolies embarked for ports unknown when the Manchu regime ended imperial prohibitions on foreign travel. For the first time Chinese women were able to join their husbands, so future generations of Overseas Chinese would be born abroad.

As South East Asia became swept up in the industrial revolution, a money economy grew. Growing middle-class prosperity in Europe and America increased demand for sugar, tea, coffee and spices. Anxious not to compete with home industries, colonial governments concentrated on raw materials and did not encourage manufacturing. Singapore and the Malay States depended heavily on exports of rubber, transplanted from Brazil. To supply the growing demand, more Chinese arrived. Between 1920 and 1930, another two million Chinese left the Mainland for the Malay Peninsula alone.

Britain's policy of unrestricted immigration also brought thousands of Tamils from South India and Sri Lanka, so that by 1921 Chinese and Indians together outnumbered the Malays. Only Malays were eligible for the Civil Service, and only Malays could buy agricultural property, but they felt overwhelmed on their own turf. The British kept the races separate, but it was a delicate balancing act.

In all of South East Asia, the Overseas Chinese population as a whole topped four and a half million by the 1930s. Britain then introduced strict quotas in Malaya, not provoked by racial sensibilities but by the Great Depression and the collapse of the rubber trade. This placated the Malays somewhat, but they saw that they were being excluded from the new prosperity.

Some newly rich Chinese liked to flash their money around, rubbing noses in it. Penang and Singapore already had a few Chinese millionaires. They built mansions, bought hand-built limousines, and imported French cognac by the crate. Tan Kim Seng, Tan Tock Seng and Whampoa were all nineteenth-century tycoons. Fluent in English, they cultivated connections with Western merchants and British officials. While they were the most conspicuous successes, hundreds of other Chinese were moving discreetly into the millionaire bracket. Just how many was astonishing.

Malaya's first internationally famous Chinese tycoon was rubber baron Tan Kah Kee. As a young man in the 1890s, he left Amoy for Singapore to work with his father in the rice trade. When his father went bust, Tan Kah Kee borrowed money from his Hokkien clansmen to start a pineapple plantation and cannery. Planting rubber trees between his rows of pineapples, he became a very rich man. Soon after, as one of the wealthiest and most powerful Hokkien, a kingpin of the

Amoy syndicates, Tan returned to China to build a primary school that grew into Amoy University.

When the Western market for pineapple collapsed with the First World War, Tan adroitly moved into the shipping business. He leased ships to the French government to move supplies in the Mediterranean, and when the vessels were sunk by German torpedoes, he collected much more than they had cost. By war's end, he owned three mansions and a Daimler limousine.

The postwar rubber boom greatly enlarged Tan's personal wealth and his business holdings. In a burst of enthusiasm, he borrowed lavishly. By 1925 his interest payments were so great he was borrowing just to pay them. In the Crash of 1929, his empire collapsed. Or so it seemed.

Tan was said to have 'lost his fortune', but nothing of the sort happened. He always kept his personal assets separate from business liabilities, so he remained a rich man. All he lost were heavily mortgaged factories and commercial properties that he had bled dry. His timing was brilliant, for all his bad paper was lost in the blizzard of the Depression. Tan 'retired' from industry, but he continued to be the energetic patriarch of the Hokkien community. He also became a role model, and 'creative bankruptcy' became a standard procedure for many Chinese on the way up.

Today, Western intellectuals and economists like to attribute such success to the virtues of Confucianism. On its own, Confucianism never generated aggressive economics, just the opposite. Its chief benefit to the Overseas Chinese in Singapore and elsewhere was that it reinforced family and community discipline and hierarchy, so the strict protection of family assets made further capitalization possible.

The extraordinary success of Overseas Chinese in modern times has occurred in countries where authoritarian Western governments kept order and encouraged commerce. Chinese gravitated to places like Singapore because there the public acknowledgement of greed was part of the West's work ethic. Western colonials were every bit as determined as the Chinese to make it big quick, and go home. But their family and communal ties gave the Overseas Chinese many advantages over individualistic Westerners, whose family bonds were breaking down as the twentieth century progressed.

The clincher came when the West's colonial outposts in South East Asia suddenly, unexpectedly, lost everything. The lightning Japanese conquest in the Second World War, as everyone knows, caught colonial governments unprepared, poorly armed, half asleep, facing the wrong way. In a matter of weeks, the wealth of centuries of Western colonial development was up for grabs. Estates, homes, industries, banks, plantations, overflowing warehouses and all manner of personal resources – everything was presumed lost to the Japanese. Yet when the Pacific War was over and the Japanese had gone home, a very large part of the lost Western colonial wealth remained in Overseas Chinese hands, not Japanese. Some of the biggest fortunes among today's Overseas Chinese tycoons began in this dark manner, and the story remains little known and less understood. The proper person to tell it is Tsuji Masanobu, who played a key role.

CHAPTER 10

THE CANNIBAL

IN A NATION WHERE RULERS AND ENTREPRENEURS ARE TRADITION-ally at odds, such as China, greed is the opposite of virtue. In a nation where rulers and entrepreneurs collaborate, such as Japan, greed is easily confused with patriotism. Add an overdose of military ambition and the effect is intoxicating. Tsuji Masanobu blended these elements with Messianic energy and visionary genius. For a while, he was one of the most dangerous men on the planet. He was involved in some of the Second World War's boldest exploits, including the escape of General Honda Masaki from Allied encirclement in Burma; he was personally responsible for the grisly purges of civilians in Malaya and Singapore during the war; and it was he who contrived the nightmare bloodbath of Overseas Chinese known as *Sook Ching*. When he was not busy watching his men murder Chinese, Tsuji was cutting deals with Chinese gangsters and entrepreneurs. Thanks to such deals, many Overseas Chinese collaborators emerged from the war rich men, future leaders of the Pacific Rim. Tsuji, not incidentally, was a cannibal; in Burma he hosted a dinner party where the main course was the liver of a captured American pilot.

By the 1920s, Japan was ready for Tsuji. All people are vulnerable to what Carl Jung called 'psychic epidemics'. Nobody upsets the Japanese more than they upset themselves. When they are calm, they are among the world's most rational people, but they are completely irrational about vengeance. They feel like perpetual victims, intimidated by the group, policed by samurai, ruled by tyrants who hide behind silk screens. In the nineteenth century, when Commodore Perry's gunboats forced it to open up after centuries of deliberate isolation, Japan for the first time felt abused by Westerners, and although they suffered much less at Western hands than the Chinese did, they could not endure humiliation with the same fortitude. Tsuji, the superpatriot, made it his mission to exact revenge.

Yamagata Aritomo and other far-sighted Japanese military leaders saw to it that they paid particular attention to Western arms and methods, and closely studied the German army model. While rational Japanese were fascinated by their great experiment with industrialization and demo-cratization, Tsuji and others used modernization as a cover to build a separate military power base for conquest on the Asian mainland.

As the twentieth century dawned, Japan emulated the West by becoming an aggressive imperialist power. In 1895, she took Taiwan from China. As spoils of war in 1905, she got from Russia the lower half of Siberia's Sakhalin peninsula, the lease of Manchuria's Liaotung peninsula, and most of Russia's Manchurian investments. In 1910, she annexed Korea. German holdings in the Pacific and in Shantung were seized during the First World War, along with the big German naval base at Tsingtao. By 1920, Japan was a major imperialist power in North Asia.

Further conquest of the mainland appealed to Japanese gangsters, militarists and patriots alike. For Tokyo's growing economic needs, conquest was imperative. As her industry grew, Japan's need for raw materials became urgent. Her population outgrew domestic agricul-ture. Need for food imports became pressing. In the minds of some Japanese, these needs became mixed with the craving for conquest, domination and revenge.

While Siberia was seen by some as the logical target, China was given the highest priority: most of Japan's foreign investments were concen-trated there. In 1901, the Foreign Ministry offered to train, protect and subsidize any Japanese prepared to do business in China or Korea.

The War Ministry persuaded members of the *zaibatsu* merchant dynasties (including Mitsui, Mitsubishi and Okura) to set up a company called Heavenly Peace to promote arms sales to Chinese warlords and revolutionaries. After the Manchu downfall in 1911, Tokyo undermined each new strongman, to keep China from being reunited. Japanese agents of the paramilitary sects Black Ocean or Black Dragon backed rival warlords and provoked demonstrations.

Japanese were encouraged to emigrate to Manchuria, to run confiscated farms and commercial properties. Seeding Manchuria quietly enlarged Japan's presence on the Asian mainland. Not counting soldiers, a million Japanese moved to North Asia to make their fortunes, eight hundred thousand to Manchuria alone. There, in an area the size of New England, much of it covered with red sorghum, life was good, thanks to strict secret police control and terrorist suppression of the Manchu population. Colonists lived better than Japanese at home.

An unexpected boost to Tokyo's ambitions came when the First World War distracted Europe, leaving the China trade to America and Japan. The United States was Japan's best export customer, and American trade with Japan was considerably larger than its trade with China. This could have become the constructive partnership of the Pacific Rim – but Washington and Tokyo were more interested in competing over China. Like jealous young suitors in a brothel, both America and Japan were convinced that they had a 'special relationship' with China. For centuries, Japan had been China's frequent partner, but no matter how often they co-operated, China could never agree about who was to be on top. Before the 1890s, China had always had a superior attitude, and Japan became resentful of every imagined slight. Co-operation is not a concept that comes easily to countries spellbound by absolutism.

After the First World War, when Europe returned to Asia's markets, Japan saw it as unfair competition. She could no longer survive without China's raw materials. If the West regained dominance, Japan would be elbowed aside. If Tokyo grabbed complete control, her trade and industry would be secure. The Chinese would not play along. With the end of dynastic rule and the beginning of republican government, nationalism flooded down the Yangtze. There were boycotts of foreign goods, and protests against foreign meddling. Tokyo could not decide whether to allow her position in China to deteriorate, or to force China into a submissive role, as she had Manchuria and Korea. In Tokyo boardrooms, there was a lot of frustration, followed by agreement. Immediate action would be taken by all the conglomerates. In this hypnotic Japanese manner, military, corporate, government and underworld appetites converged.

Unlike Japan's military, which was fascinated by the destructive power of the industrial age, the *zaibatsu* were avid practitioners of Sun Tzu, content to influence events obliquely. Civilian governments consistently favoured big business over the military. Defence budgets were cut, the size of the army reduced, naval construction slowed. This had a predictable effect.

Rightists were alarmed. Society was becoming too bourgeois, merchants too powerful, youth too vulgar. The feudal system, with its paternalism toward peasants, had been replaced by an industrial culture that trapped labourers in conditions of slavery. In these grim conditions, socialism and communism were taking hold. Growing food riots and strikes convinced patriots that the only solution was 'the blood of purification' – a return to ancient values and authoritarian rule. Since 1900, secret organizations of superpatriots had multiplied, dedicated to domestic terrorism and foreign conquest. Business and political leaders were assassinated in spectacular ways, attracting attention to the political views of the killers. Japanese politicians were depicted as slaves of greedy businessmen. Curiously, the huge fortunes of Japanese army generals, and their methods of acquisition, never became a major political issue.

The sumo match between overlarge army and overweight business came to a thudding climax with the Great Depression. Massive unemployment in Japan was followed by famine. Villages starved, workers were on breadlines. Rightwing Japanese portrayed the Depression as a plot by Western racists. Militarists decided to seize what they needed or wanted in North Asia. Caution ceased to be their main concern.

Japan's obsession with North Asia was out of control. Only this would satisfy military needs, business needs, social needs, and appease the craving for revenge that energized the nobility, the *zaibatsu*, the military, the secret societies and the underworld. They were convinced that the West had deliberately blocked their search for raw materials and marketplaces, for racial reasons. The ultra-right had long planned for this moment. To them, coexistence was irrelevant. Government leaders who disagreed would be assassinated.

The stronghold of this extreme thinking was not Japan, but Manchuria. Japan's Kwantung army, which occupied southern Manchuria, was allowed such an independent position after 1919 that it became a rival power base to Tokyo, a separate command, not subject to scrutiny by civilian politicians and Tokyo government officials. This put Kwantung officers in a position to traffic in heroin and to extort money, goods, land and favours from the Manchurian population, without supervision.

The decision to make the Kwantung army independent turned out to be an act of suicidal folly. With uncontrolled power and unprecedented access to wealth, its officer corps became insatiable, recklessly plotting conquest on the mainland. It was unnecessary to refer their plans to Tokyo. They conspired with generals at home to trigger martial law and eventually to bring about the installation in Tokyo of a military dictatorship. They were able to carry out terrorist acts inside Japan through cells of military fanatics who craved a return to purified authoritarian rule.

One of the Kwantung army's first major conspiracies was the killing in 1928 of the Manchurian warlord, Marshal Chang Tso-lin. Then, in 1931, the Kwantung army staged the phony Manchurian Incident, declaring that Chinese soldiers had dynamited the south Manchurian Railway and attacked Japanese guards. The army said it had no choice but to occupy Mukden. Actually, the bomb plot had been the work of young officers in Tsuji's group, including his *alter ego*, Ishiwara Kanji. A brilliant graduate of staff college, Ishiwara had spent three years studying in Germany, where – like so many Japanese officers – he had become infatuated with the concept of Total War expounded by Clausewitz and refined by Moltke. On his return to Japan, Ishiwara became a flamboyant instructor at staff college. To young Japanese officers, it was intoxicating to think in terms of total destruction, purification by fire, complete annihilation of the enemy, and mass suicide for mythic ends. These apocalyptic visions stirred the primal juices of supermen.

Central to Ishiwara's vision, and to that of Tsuji and other hotbloods, was that Japan must save the world from misguided ideologies, including parliamentary democracy. Their mission involved Total Wars against Russia, Britain and America. Entire societies would be incinerated. Like the metal of meteorites folded into katana swords, the people of the world would be melted and reforged under Japan's hammer. The Kwantung army would lead the way. A first step was for China to welcome Japanese domination in Manchuria.

The West did nothing. When the seizure of Manchuria was not repudiated, militarists concluded they could contrive further 'incidents' and take Chinese territory at whim.

Following its annexation, Manchuria became the main supplier of heroin down the China coast, displacing the Shanghai-based Green Gang. The gang's Ku brothers, one of whom ran the Shanghai waterfront while the other served on Generalissimo Chiang's general staff, negotiated an accommodation with the Japanese army that persisted until 1945, covering drug distribution and the swap of American Lend-Lease materials. In the 1930s, Japan earned over three hundred million dollars a year from distribution and sale of Manchurian opium and heroin. To this point, the role of South East Asia was only as a market for Japanese products and a secondary source of raw materials. Investment south of the Yangtze was haphazard.

A sudden thrust south from Manchuria by the Kwantung army in 1933 gave Japan control of the frontier province of Jehol, just north of Peking. This led to a humiliating 'truce', in which China agreed to a demilitarized zone covering the few miles between Peking and the Great Wall.

Poised for further action on the outskirts of Peking, the Kwantung army prepared for a decisive blow. In July 1937, Japanese troops opened fire on Chinese units near the Marco Polo Bridge outside Peking, putting the blame on the Chinese. In 'reprisal', Japanese armies quickly overran Peking, Nanking, Shanghai, Hankow and Canton, gaining control of most of the China Coast. Inner Mongolia and the north-western provinces of Shansi and Shensi were also invaded. When the Nationalist government fled inland to Chungking, and Generalissimo Chiang refused to accept Tokyo's terms, Japan installed a puppet regime at Nanking under Wang Ching-wei. Kodama Yoshio, the Black Dragon leader, was assigned as Wang's 'special bodyguard'.

Despite stunning military victories, success eluded Japan. The drive in China bogged down. Japanese contempt for Chinese soldiers blinded them to the real dangers, which had nothing to do with soldiers. Years earlier, Foreign Minister Shigeru had opposed military intervention in China: 'Almost all other countries, like human beings, have only one heart, but China has any number. Where there is only one heart, one has but to crush it in order to throw the whole country into a state of paralysis . . . China, having many hearts, would still maintain a "pulse" . . . it would be impossible to put all of [her hearts] out of action with a single blow.'

Financing such an open-ended war was an unbearable burden that the militarists had not foreseen. By the end of 1937, over seven hundred thousand Japanese troops were stuck in China, at a cost of five million dollars a day, and mounting. By 1938, rationing and other emergency measures had to be introduced to put Japan on a war footing. National debt skyrocketed. After 1938, Japanese forces in China had to forage for what they needed to survive. Tokyo was heading for disaster, and the Pacific War was still three years away.

As the stalemate dragged on, reserves of foreign currency and raw materials evaporated. Tokyo was dangerously dependent on imports from Western-controlled markets, including oil supplies from the Dutch East Indies. A strike south would enable Japan to guarantee supplies of oil, rubber, tin, bauxite and other strategic materials and foodstuffs from the islands and mainland of South East Asia. The Japanese navy had always favoured a strike south. Now the army agreed it was the only way to rescue Japan's economy.

The strike south was not the result of decades of careful planning. It was ingenious and stunning, but hastily contrived. The master plan, in which Tsuji was prominently involved, called for a surprise blow followed by a quick negotiated settlement, which would guarantee Japan raw materials she needed from that area. It was a disastrous miscalculation, inadequately prepared. Comparatively few Japanese had gone to the South Seas since the Meiji Restoration had freed them to travel abroad. Mitsui and Mitsubishi had set up plantations. During the rubber boom, a few Japanese had gone to Malaya, followed by Japanese *zaibatsu* and banks, which gave loans to their own nationals. By the late 1930s, there were forty thousand Japanese scattered across six countries from Burma to the Philippines, mostly small traders. They ran specialty shops, dental or medical clinics, and lived apart, making no effort to assimilate. Thousands of Japanese women also worked in brothels all over Asia, run by Muraoka Iheiji, a member of Black Dragon, who used them to bring pressure and gather intelligence. He gained the co-operation of clients by generous distribution of Spanish fly.

The main obstacle encountered by Japanese business across the region was the Overseas Chinese. Most retail and wholesale trade, and natural resources, were in Chinese hands. Japanese wholesalers had no choice but to use Chinese distributors. In an effort to gain their co-operation, the Japanese offered them special discounts and rebates. Business friendships developed. But Japan's brutality in China soured relations with Overseas Chinese everywhere around the Pacific Rim. To win them over, Tokyo distributed masses of propaganda. When that failed, secret agents began collecting information about relatives of Overseas Chinese trapped inside Occupied China, preparing for reprisals and extortion.

One of the leaders of the anti-Japanese fund-raising campaigns in South East Asia was the retired rubber baron Tan Kah Kee. Tan was chairman of a Singapore-based federation of Chinese relief organizations raising money to help war refugees back home. Big population centres around Foochow, Amoy and Swatow – home to most Overseas Chinese – had been badly damaged by bombers before they were overrun by Japanese troops. Tan's group had branches all over the archipelago. Never before had all the Overseas Chinese communities around the Pacific Rim united in a single organization with a single purpose. They were anxious to direct aid to their own native districts, but much of their financial help went to China as a whole, in a rare display of national identity. The Nationalist government of the Kuomintang was a major beneficiary, and in return the KMT had endorsed Tan's chairmanship. By 1941, Tan's organization had given the KMT more than seven million dollars, including one night's takings from thirty-eight Singapore brothels. The British allowed Tan to continue fund-raising, on the condition that no money went to military purposes, and neither anti-Japanese speeches nor boycotts of Japanese goods would be encouraged.

With KMT approval, in 1940 Tan organized a tour of unoccupied China for Overseas Chinese. Arriving in Chungking, he was completely disenchanted by Nationalist officials including Generalissimo Chiang Kai-shek. When Tan told the generalissimo that he intended to visit Mao's headquarters at Yenan, Chiang became enraged, shrieking in a falsetto about the communists' treachery and lack of patriotism. Continuing to Yenan nevertheless, Tan was impressed by the integrity and efficiency of Mao and his civil and military leaders, compared to the KMT. When he returned to Chungking, he told a large audience about Mao and the Red Army energetically resisting the Japanese, and denounced the KMT's distortion and manipulation of events in China. At a private audience, Tan told the generalissimo that the KMT needed to reform itself. He carefully avoided denouncing the corruption of Chiang's own inner circle. Again the generalissimo flew into a screaming rage.

The moment Tan left Chungking, he was denounced by the KMT in the international press as 'a running dog of the communists'. (Meanwhile, to be sure, the KMT had its own secret deals with the Japanese, but – as Chiang Kai-shek liked to put it – the Japanese were only a disease of the skin, while the communists were a disease of the heart.)

Tsuji's strategic planning focused on Tan's area – the triangle from Singapore to Rangoon to Manila. Relations with Washington were deteriorating, but President Roosevelt's actions were limited by the passing of tighter neutrality laws by Congress. Britain's appeasement of Hitler at Munich led Tokyo to believe that she, too, could achieve her goals without Western military intervention. That October, Japan seized the city of Canton and isolated British Hong Kong from the Mainland. Early in 1939, Hainan Island and the Spratleys were taken, putting Japanese forces only 700 miles from Singapore.

Thanks to intense lobbying in Washington by Madame Chiang Kai-shek and her brother, China's Foreign Minister T.V. Soong, and with help behind the scenes from well-connected Americans, President Roosevelt found ways to get around Congress and actively to aid Chungking. The Burma Road permitted the overland transport of American Lend-Lease supplies, for which no payment was seriously expected. Roosevelt secretly enabled active-duty US army and navy pilots to serve as mercenaries in China. Crated aeroplanes previously sold to Britain were rerouted to Burma to be assembled for the Flying Tigers. Roosevelt's unusual moves were to some extent the result of Chinese coercion, to which he was sensitive because of his family's early involvement in the China trade. The Soongs were seeking any way possible to get the US locked into conflict with Japan.

Actually, US trade with Nationalist China was minimal, while US trade with Japan was increasing steadily. Despite intense efforts by the China Lobby to arouse opinion in favour of Chungking, most Americans remained isolationist even after the war began in Europe. In 1939, however, the Soongs and the China Lobby persuaded Roosevelt to have Secretary of State Cordell Hull denounce the 1911 commercial treaty with Japan. This he could do without congressional approval. US embargoes of Japanese goods went into effect. These embargoes created a dilemma. The stalemate in China put Japan in a position where she had to either abandon the China campaign at great loss of face or go on to seize all South East Asia, to obtain its oil and raw materials. The US embargoes forced her to make the only decision possible.

As Professor Ienaga Saburo affirmed in 1992, 'There was no reason why Japan had to fight a war against America. It was not inevitable . . . At the time the United States and Japan began negotiations to resolve their [trade] conflict, America accepted Chinese requests and demanded that Japan withdraw its forces from the whole of China. The army could never accept this, not after the enormous sacrifices they had made and the gains so bloodily won.' So when Roosevelt gave in to the Soongs and to the China Lobby, war with Japan became unavoidable.

Although failure in China had been predicted all along, the Japanese army could not accept or admit failure – first, because it was Japanese and, second, because it was an army. An army that had grown lush and self-indulgent with its own Manchurian domain. The Kwantung army's sole reason for existence was as an occupation force. To feed the beast, the war had to be continually expanded. The army boasted that they could still negotiate their way out of a confrontation with the West, once they were firmly in control of South East Asia. Having assassinated their most outspoken critics and terrorized others into silence, the militarists got their way.

Timing was crucial. In April 1940, Hitler's blitzkrieg began and France and Holland fell. That June, Tokyo signed a treaty of friendship with Bangkok. At the same time, the Japanese army occupied the northern part of French Indochina to block Chinese supplies by way of the Kunming-Hanoi railway line. Under pressure from Berlin, Vichy

France agreed to Japanese control of the entire colony. In return, Japan allied itself with the Axis bloc.

Roosevelt reacted by freezing Japanese assets in America and declaring an embargo on all oil shipments to Japan. This committed the High Command to the strike south. Not to challenge the United States now meant bowing to economic extortion, which Toyko could do to others but not permit others to do in return. Diplomatic negotiations with Washington continued, but Prime Minister Konoe was forced to resign in October 1941 to make way for his war minister, General Tojo Hideki.

Attitudes in Tokyo and Washington were now irreconcilable. Months before Pearl Harbor, the arrow had already left the bow.

Both countries had delusions about China. Roosevelt's infatuation was never rational. Some of his closest advisers were receiving discreet favours from the Soongs; others, like General Claire Chennault, were directly on Soong payrolls. Those working for Chennault, such as journalist Joseph Alsop, were locked into the Soong food chain. American passions were being inflamed by a multi-million-dollar propaganda campaign financed by US aid funds doubled back by the Soongs. The magazines and newspapers of China-born Henry Luce and other publishers hugely exaggerated the significance of the China market and ridiculed the fighting abilities of the Japanese. In response to this relentless orchestration, Americans voted Madame Chiang the woman they most admired. She embodied the 'special relationship' Americans were assured that they had with China.

Japan's delusions were of a different kind. Part of her difficulty in China was that no consistent military strategy was followed except the crudest form of Total War bombardment, destruction and seizure. Because great military ambitions are accompanied by great egos, there was no agreement on how to proceed. Having forsaken cleverness, industrial-strength onslaught was used. In a chronic state of military excitement, everything was justified including acts of utter barbarity. The effect of such extraordinary barbarity was to make cruelty routine. It is not that Tsuji and his fellow officers were irrational, or in any way abnormal; but what was normal had changed.

Strangely, it was still intended to be a quick, limited war, because with Japan already facing economic collapse, it lacked the resources to fight a long war against America. Here was irrationality. The United States had nearly twice the population, seventeen times the national income, and seven times the industrial potential. After ten years of economic crisis and crippling war costs, Tokyo did not even have the resources for a short war against America. Rather than admit failure, it would gamble on the strike south rescuing Japan. There was always a possibility that lethargy, equivocation and self-interest would keep America from becoming more directly involved.

They might have succeeded had they avoided Pearl Harbor. That gave Roosevelt a device to unite public opinion behind a declaration of war. Army strategists also failed to anticipate the great problems they would have commandeering South East Asia's resources once they were there. In short, they utterly failed to factor in the Overseas Chinese.

The strike south went ahead with stunning speed. The day after Pearl Harbor, Japanese troops landed in Thailand, the Thai government surrendered and declared war on the Allies. Two days later, sailing from Singapore to block a Japanese landing on the Malay Peninsula, Britain's *Prince of Wales* and *Repulse* were sunk by planes based in Indochina. Japanese troops moved swiftly down the peninsula, many of them on bicycles, as other forces invaded Burma and Sumatra. By the end of December 1941, Hong Kong, Guam and Wake had fallen, and the Japanese were invading the Philippines. On 9 March 1942, resistance collapsed in Java, Bataan surrendered on 9 April, Corregidor on 6 May. Five months after Pearl Harbor, Japan controlled most of East Asia.

The conquest succeeded quickly because of the suddenness and ferocity of the attacks, backed by superiority in numbers, élite troops, and air and naval strength, against puny colonial forces that in many cases had nodded off. The colonial governments were preoccupied with the war in Europe.

Only in early 1941 was a Japanese intelligence officer actually sent to tour the Malay Peninsula. In October 1941, a Japanese consulate was opened in Chiengmai and a rush of tourists arrived to spread through Siam and Burma. The Japanese army Special Service Agency, which handled espionage, exploited underworld connections. Black Dragon Kodama had his own network in South East Asia, and assisted agents from Section Eight of the General Staff. He personally financed the

Shanghai office of Kempeitai counter-intelligence. The chief steward of
the British Officers' club in Singapore was a Japanese colonel. Other
agents running hotels in the East Indies offered special rates to Dutch
soldiers. A former Kempeitai officer explained after the war that, 'Spies
were generally gangsters. Bright gangsters. Paper money had no value
for them. They wanted opium.'

By this point, Colonel Tsuji was a godhead. Exceptionally intelligent, cunning, ambitious and ruthless, he saw himself as a military
genius and hero, like the legendary samurai Musashi. As the 'god of
operations,' Tsuji headed the team that planned the Malayan
campaign, and as director of military operations for General
Yamashita's 25th Army, he personally saw his plans carried out.
Always flamboyant, he liked to disguise himself or his troops,
sometimes having them wear Siamese army uniforms. He had many
enemies among his own peers and was transferred frequently. Later, he
was blamed by many Japanese for some of the war's miscalculations
and worst excesses. A close associate of Kodama and other underworld
leaders, he was involved from the beginning in the looting of South
East Asian businesses, banks, Buddhist temples and wealthy individuals.

To motivate his men for the Malayan campaign, Tsuji wrote an
inflammatory pamphlet and had forty thousand copies circulated. It
contained guidance on everything from constipation to emperor
worship. A lot of it made sense. Or seemed to. He informed his readers
that the countries of South East Asia had been seized by a 'handful of
white men', and their millions of inhabitants had been exploited for
centuries. These native people anxiously awaited Japanese help to
achieve 'national independence and happiness.

'. . . like a man strangling his victim with a soft cord of silken floss,
America has been prohibiting the export to Japan of oil and steel . . .
More than a hundred thousand of your comrades have perished on the
mainland; the greater part of the armaments with which Chiang Kai-
shek killed those men was sold to him by England and America.
England and America . . . dread the thought of any solidarity between
Asian peoples, and . . . all their policies have been directed towards the
instigation of war between Japan and China.

'. . . When you encounter the enemy after landing, regard yourself as an avenger come at last face to face with his father's murderer . . . If you fail to destroy him utterly you can never rest in peace.'

Tsuji reminded his men of the great sacrifice of the Forty-seven Ronin in avenging the death of their master in the eighteenth century, and left them to ponder a few lines of verse:

> Corpses drifting swollen in the sea-depths,
> Corpses rotting in the mountain-grass—
> We shall die, by the side of our lord we shall die
> We shall not look back.

Tsuji intended to let the Overseas Chinese know that their masters had arrived. Since the 1890s, the Japanese had tried to persuade all Chinese to get behind Japan's leadership in the struggle with the West. Few Chinese, at home or abroad, trusted Tokyo. After centuries of coping with their own bureaucratic treachery, the Chinese had few illusions about Japanese leadership. Educated Chinese knew that the Japanese viewed them as hopelessly, biologically corrupt. Perhaps, but they were far from stupid. They saw through Japanese propaganda about Asian harmony, and understood long before the West did that militarists working with gangsters had used the Kwantung army to seize power in Tokyo. Thus, in their eyes, the Japanese army had become a gangster-terrorist army, no better than the KMT – but much more ruthlessly efficient.

Failing to persuade Overseas Chinese not to participate in boycotts of Japanese goods, and not to remit money to the nationalist or communist leadership in China, Japan resorted to bribery, intimidation, extortion and secret deals with Overseas Chinese businessmen. Once in control of cities in Fukien and Kwangtung provinces, the Japanese were able to threaten reprisals on families in the ancestral villages.

Japanese agents infiltrated Overseas Chinese secret societies and triads. They started duplicate societies with the same names and hand-signs. The strike south was followed by gruesome mass killings of Chinese who had taken part in anti-Japanese boycotts. Tsuji's technique was terror, mass rapes of the wives and daughters of middle-class Chinese and Westerners, mass beheadings, and vivisection on fully conscious Chinese prisoners. To make certain that new

Japanese officers did not hesitate to carry out atrocities, they were obliged to undergo brutal exercises to dehumanize all contact with Chinese. Japanese seldom misbehave individually, they tend to do it collectively. The training worked so well that, as one Kempeitai officer boasted: 'If more than two weeks went by without my taking a head, I didn't feel fit. Physically, I needed to be refreshed.'

In Singapore, on 17 December 1941, the governor asked Tan Kah Kee to provide a Chinese labour force to dig trenches for air-raid shelters and to mobilize the Chinese population. Worried about Japanese reprisals, Tan at first refused, but a thousand young Chinese began training. The British – never certain they could trust the Chinese – did not give them weapons until two weeks before the island fell. Tan believed that the British were forcing the Chinese to commit suicide by giving the Japanese an excuse to punish the whole Overseas Chinese population. Seriously frightened, Tan left secretly for Sumatra on 12 February 1942, without even saying goodbye to his family. Six days later, General Yamashita's army swarmed over the island. Tan spent the war in Java under a pseudonym, protected by wealthy Hokkien confederates. While he was away, as he had predicted, the worst happened.

After the British surrendered, the Japanese began summary executions. Anyone who did not grovel, and many who did, were shot or beheaded on the spot, their heads displayed on pikes in Singapore's markets. In a city as gentle and civilized as Singapore, the sight of decapitated heads completely unnerved the population. Kempeitai agents conducted house-to-house searches. Anyone found hoarding was shot. The first targets were British who had eluded capture, Chinese who had taken part in the defence, civil servants and others who had worked for the British, members of the KMT, their rivals in the Malayan Communist Party, and members of Chinese secret societies identified by their tattoos. This was not enough for Tsuji. The 25th Army intended to move on to Sumatra immediately, but he insisted that they should first carry out an additional campaign of retribution. The army had come directly from China, where its men had encountered great hostility in the countryside.

Tsuji's purge was to be called Operation Sook Ching (purification or ethnic cleansing). Its primary targes were the Overseas Chinese.

'Who are the "Overseas Chinese"?' Tsuji asked rhetorically. 'From [the time of Kublai Khan's invasion of China] the Chinese began to emigrate in large numbers to South Asia, and gradually, rising from humble positions as clerks, errand-boys or coolies, they became men of wealth, and by deceiving the naturally lazy natives and colluding with the British, Americans, French and Dutch, they increased their economic power, and today there are in this whole area some five million Chinese colonists. They contribute military funds to Chungking, but most of them are either led astray by Chungking propaganda or are forced by [secret societies], whether they wish it or not, to make those contributions. We must offer to these people the opportunity for self-examination and guide them over to our own side. Two points, however, should be noted: first, that these people, by a variety of clever schemes, concerted with the European administrators, are steadily extorting money from the native population, and that the greater part of the natives' resentment is directed against them rather than against the Europeans; and secondly, that for the most part they have no racial or national consciousness, and no enthusiasms outside the making of money. Consequently, you must realize in advance that it will be difficult, by merely urging them to an intellectual awareness of themselves as members of an Asian brotherhood, to enlist their co-operation in any scheme which does not promise personal profit.'

All male Chinese on the island aged between eighteen and fifty were ordered to assemble in five locations by noon 21 February, with severe punishment for anyone who disobeyed. Each Chinese walked past a row of hooded informers, mostly Japanese agents, but including captured Chinese defenders or triad members who gave information to save their lives. Some were women or children avenging themselves for earlier mistreatment, or trying to gain merit with the conquerors. When a hood nodded, a man was dragged away.

The condemned were stamped on their skin with a triangular ink chop. Others were stamped with squares and released. They took pains not to wash the patch for months till the mark became invisible. For six days, those waiting had no food, water or toilets. A total of 70,699 Singapore Chinese were taken off for torture or killing. When they began, the mass executions lasted many days, sometimes with Tsuji watching closely. Those who were not shot, bayoneted or beheaded were roped together and taken out to sea on barges off Blakang Mati, Changi or Siglap. At

Changi, where the water is shallow for hundreds of metres out, and fishermen's cane weirs extend here and there in random patterns, the barges had to go very far out to find deep water. More than twenty thousand Chinese were roped together in this way and towed out into the sea lanes off Singapore, where they were forced overboard. Those who did not drown immediately were machine-gunned.

At Tsuji's urging, Sook Ching was extended then to the Malay Peninsula. In Malay towns and villages, it began the same way, with hooded informers and lists. Then the Kempeitai lost patience and began indiscriminately killing all Chinese they could find in the quiet kampongs, rubber plantations and tin mines. At a typical village, thirty soldiers rounded up several hundred Chinese and Malays, and marched them to a paddy field, where they were forced to kneel. Each soldier stepped forward in turn to behead a victim with a sword or stab him with a bayonet. Corpses were thrown into village wells to contaminate the water supply. Babies were flung into the air and stabbed as they fell. Groups of Chinese schoolchildren screamed for mercy as they were hacked to pieces. The bloodbath continued through March with estimates of forty thousand slain. General Manaki, who was present, insisted later that Sook Ching was the worst Japanese excess during the Malay campaign. But all South East Asia has grim memories of the Japanese conquest. Those Overseas Chinese who survived were completely alienated. Hundreds of men and boys fled into the jungle to join the communist-led resistance movement. After Sook Ching ended, severe repression continued, but without Tsuji's grisly signature.

Among the prominent Singapore Chinese arrested were bankers, tycoons, journalists and educators. Threatened with death, and in some cases tortured, they were forced to organize a pro-Japanese Overseas Chinese Association to raise fifty million Straits dollars as a 'gift' to Emperor Hirohito, to compensate for their earlier anti-Japanese activities. The campaign fell short by twenty-two million Straits dollars, but a compromise was worked out. The Chinese tycoons would be allowed to borrow the balance from the Yokohama Specie Bank, to be paid in twelve months with a very modest 6 per cent interest.

Although Sook Ching ended, the horrors were not over. Hundreds of thousands from all ethnic groups were dragooned into slave labour battalions and forced to work under killing conditions on the Burma-Thailand 'death railway' and other projects. Tattooed Japanese *yakuza* served as recruitment officers. A quarter of a million Indonesians, and similar numbers from Korea and every other conquered country served as forced labour all over Asia, the men as coolies, the women in brothels. Tens of thousands were whipped to death as they toiled. Others died of disease, hunger or exhaustion.

Despite the immediate military success of the strike south, the Japanese occupation of South East Asia was a disaster. The main purpose had been to rescue Japan from economic collapse by seizing control of South East Asia's oil and other raw materials. This was a complete failure. First, the Japanese discovered that the region's resources were controlled by the Overseas Chinese, or could only be obtained with their co-operation. Most Overseas Chinese had been alienated by Tsuji's Sook Ching and similar terror campaigns in Mainland China or in other conquered countries. To rectify the situation, cleverness was needed, not terror. Japan's best brains, technicians and financial managers were busy in North Asia and the Home Islands. Little talent could be spared for South East Asia.

With centuries of experience in undermining and corrupting bureaucrats and conquerors, the Overseas Chinese helped make South East Asia and the China coast a terrible drain on the Japanese war machine, weakening Tokyo as the Allied counter-attack gathered momentum.

No development capital could be provided by Tokyo. It had to be raised in South East Asia from loot, extortion or the hijacked bank deposits of local populations. The occupied countries also were to be self-sufficient in consumer goods. Accordingly, the *zaibatsu* – Mitsui, Mitsubishi, Sumitomo, Nomura and Hitachi – took over Chinese, Dutch, British and American firms, tried to exploit strategic resources, and set up monopolies in commodities. Mitsui's monopoly of salt and sugar, and Mitsubishi's monopoly of rice, drove long-established Chinese merchants out of business. Prices shot up. Japanese sale of operating licences to Chinese and native entrepreneurs led to universal corruption. Malayan tin production nearly collapsed. Indonesian tea cultivation fell by half. The result was unemployment, inflation, hunger and hoarding. Japanese banks moved in to rescue (or exploit) the situation. Lotteries and gambling farms were started in an effort to lure black money out of Overseas Chinese hiding-places.

Japanese officials became involved with local underworld figures and war profiteers. A former Kempeitai agent explained after the war that, 'In big cities or large villages, there were always pariahs. We'd find them and train them, threaten them, cajole them. We'd tell them, "If you take the wrong course, we'll kill you, but if you do what you're told, you'll have to build warehouses to hold your fortune." We'd bring out the opium. "I'll do it!" they'd say in a minute. Every day we received large amounts of the drug . . . The opium came down from staff level at division headquarters. The better we did, the more opium came.'

New guild associations set up by the Japanese to co-ordinate the supply of strategic materials, created a booming black market, manipulated behind the scenes by Chinese racketeers. Taking advantage of the desperation of the Japanese, Chinese opportunists secretly provided them with huge supplies of hoarded food or strategic materials. Although the Chinese and native élites continued to live well, famine spread throughout South East Asia, and rice became as valuable as gold. The conquerors then found themselves in the awkward position of having to ask Chinese rice smugglers for help. Teochiu traders had always controlled the rice market in Thailand and Vietnam, and a large part of the rice trade in Malaya and the Dutch East Indies. During the war, Teochiu bosses in Penang and Singapore handled the southern end of a coastal junk traffic that brought in over 3,000 tons of black-market rice from Thailand each month. These junks left the west coast of Thailand and sailed the opium route down the Malay Peninsula into the Strait of Malacca, bribing Japanese officers in Penang and other ports to look the other way. When the Japanese came to them for help, the Teochiu were 'officially' mobilized – that is, they went into business with the Japanese. Thanks to this rice partnership with the enemy, the Teochiu gained a commanding position over rival Hokkien rice traders in Malaya and Indonesia after the war.

As Chinese collaborators began to solve Japan's supply problems, the Japanese encountered the second great obstacle of their southern misadventure: getting the strategic materials home. At first, American submarines were unable to stop Japanese ships because of defective torpedoes. By mid-1943, the technical problem was solved and the submarine blockade became complete. Japanese shipping was unable to go north of the Philippines, and their occupation of South East Asia went completely sour. Warehouses now crammed with strategic materials collected dust. The Japanese army was unable to secure an overland route through South China until Operation Ichigo in 1944, when it was already too late.

Corruption was in full flower. A Japanese naval officer confirmed that right-wing Japanese financial groups and the military were in league in the Indies. When the army built a road to an airfield, Japanese construction firms owned by underworld figures charged their own government astronomical sums, which were appropriated by the military and vanished. Such budget items were 'special military expenditures'.

After fifteen years of conquest on the Asian mainland tied to 'rescuing the Japanese economy', most proceeds were sidetracked by military officers, gangsters, and corrupt *zaibatsu* executives whose connections went all the way into the imperial household. It is a wonder the war did not collapse earlier. Japan's overextended armies were experiencing their first outright defeats at Imphal, Kohima and Myitkyina. Concentrating on blocking MacArthur instead of Nimitz, the Japanese navy experienced catastrophic losses. The submarine blockade caused economic defeat long before the first atom bomb was dropped.

The Pacific War left twenty million dead in Asia, more than half of them Chinese, plus three million dead Japanese. A few Overseas Chinese amassed fortunes in looted gold. Other tycoons trace their fortunes to working as trading agents for the Japanese. Depending on who you were, it was the worst of times or the best of times.

For Colonel Tsuji, it was both — but his story is not over yet.

CHAPTER 11

THE DURIAN TREE

THE FRUIT CALLED THE DURIAN IS AN ACQUIRED TASTE. IT IS HUGE, the size of a football, with green crocodile skin. Even before it is opened, the fruit gives forth a rich, pungent smell, like overripe limburger cheese, and for a few weeks each year, neighbourhoods stink until boys have stripped the fruit from the durian trees' limbs. If you like the smell, you love the taste. Many Thais are connoisseurs. Westerners hold their noses and make rude remarks. If you eat durian, the smell comes out your pores for days, and is difficult to explain. It is illegal to take them aboard a plane.

Intertwined with many durian trees are strangler fig vines, slowly making their way up the trunks like pythons, their coils eventually almost enclosing the host tree. At some point over the years, the fig actually becomes stronger than the durian. It is no longer possible for one to survive without the other.

That is the situation now between the people of Thailand and the Teochiu. Although most Overseas Chinese around the Pacific Rim are Hokkien, in Thailand the majority are Teochiu. There are more Teochiu in Bangkok than any other city on earth including Hong Kong and Swatow, where they all came from. They exploit and depend upon the Thai economy and own its biggest banks and enterprises, as the fig exploits and depends on the durian. Over hundreds of years, the Thai government, the aristocracy, and the armed forces have depended upon Teochiu patronage, as the durian depends upon the fig. Teochiu secret armies control most of the international heroin trade flowing out of the Golden Triangle. This probably makes the Teochiu the world's richest tribe, in terms of black money. They have been in business a lot longer than the Columbian cocaine cartel and they have been rolling over vast sums since the boys in Medellin and Cali were going to mass on their mothers' hips. Nobody knows how much the Teochiu have salted away in offshore accounts the world over: they have their own banks, which rank among the world's most prosperous. Hong Kong police files describe the brotherhood as the most clannish, secretive and powerful of all Chinese secret societies. It is the ultimate Chinese tontine.

The Teochiu saga reveals much about the dark side of the Overseas Chinese syndicates. It is both illustrative and cautionary to observe how they gained oblique but profound control of Thailand, sustained that control over centuries, and in recent decades have found new ways to maintain their grip. From their primary bases in Thailand and Hong Kong, the Teochiu ran a truly vast international smuggling network in the old days, dealing chiefly in rice and drugs, but today also dealing in a broad range of commodities, electronics and weapons – helped by the fact that Teochiu are the second largest Chinese group in Vietnam, Malaysia and Indonesia. They are not the only smugglers, to be sure. What is true of the Teochiu and their methods is also true in varying degrees of the Hokkien, Hakka and other Overseas Chinese, wherever they operate as traditional syndicates – which is just about everywhere, including New York City, Los Angeles, Sydney and Vancouver. The fact that there are thousands of innocent Teochiu all over the world who do not participate in these tribal operations does nothing to diminish the manipulative role of the mainstream.

They owe their rise in Siam to a half-Chinese general named Taksin, who reunited Siam after Burmese invaders sacked the capital in 1767. Taksin had become a general the easy way. His father was a Teochiu businessman who grew rich because he outbid Chinese rivals to get a royal tax farming monopoly, which licensed him to collect taxes for the king (the successful bidder agrees in advance to pay the king a certain amount for the year; whatever more he can squeeze out of the population, he gets to keep). Thanks to his father's connections, young Taksin rose rapidly to the top. Making himself king, Taksin surrounded himself with Teochiu advisers who received noble titles. They in turn saw to it that their Teochiu cronies were given royal monopolies over trade and rackets. In this manner, the Teochiu long ago gained high positions in Siam's aristocracy, government, commerce and industry. In the twentieth century, the Teochiu stayed in control, despite the arrival of large numbers of Chinese migrants speaking other dialects.

While Thailand prides itself on never having been under the direct rule of a European colonial power, its people have lived under indirect rule by Overseas Chinese for centuries, however well disguised. Compared to the rest of South East Asia, the Thais have coexisted with the Overseas Chinese in remarkable harmony. However, it has only been possible with a lot of money changing hands under the table. Crucial to this arrangement is the fact that the Chinese in Thailand are different psychologically from those who run Mainland China itself. As coastal hybrids, the Teochiu, outcasts in their own homeland, never wanted direct rule in their adopted home. They were content to control the economy.

Like the Teochiu, the Tai people of Siam could trace their roots back to ancient Yueh. The Tai were originally various tribes of subsistence farmers in river valleys south of the Yangtze, who were pushed into the highlands of southern and south-western China by migrants from North China. Many Tai went farther to Burma, Laos and Annam. In this region of mist-shrouded karst formations with small river valleys, or *mongs*, the Tai grew rice. The hills above them were sprinkled with the villages of slash-and-burn hill-tribes who grew small amounts of opium poppies for their own amusement. Each *mong* was a mini-principality of farmers and artisans, ruled by a leading family, and protected by a clan of hereditary warriors. The kingdom of Nanchao, which flourished from the eighth to the thirteenth centuries around Lake Tali in Yunnan, included many of these Tai principalities. The Tai themselves showed little interest in dominating their non-Tai neighbours, preoccupied as they were with feuds among their own ruling princes. In the thirteenth century, they established a small kingdom at Chiengmai, and another farther south at Sukhothai, called the kingdom of T'ien (heaven), which is also rendered Hsien, Shan, or Siam – hence the original name of the nation. Sukhothai was a crossroads for Chinese caravans travelling south to trade each year.

Hundreds of Chinese traders were in business in Sukhothai before Cheng Ho's voyages in the fifteenth century. When the capital was moved south to Ayutthaya, the role of special counsellor to the king was usually given to the shrewdest and most powerful Chinese merchant. Siamese kings were energetic entrepreneurs in their own right; they had the good business sense to tap into the Overseas Chinese commercial networks. In return for helping the king enlarge his personal wealth and that of his relatives, the Chinese adviser to the throne got special concessions that he could keep or distribute as patronage to his own followers. Siamese armies (much more vigorous in those days under Chinese commanders) conquered most of Laos above the Mekong, most of the Malay Peninsula down to Singapore, the Mon territory on the Bay of Bengal, and humbled the once-great Khmer civilization to vassal status.

Ayutthaya was in the rice-rich basin of the Chao Phraya River. A Dutchman who visited in 1633 said the capital was on 'a little round island, encompassed with a thick stone wall, about six English miles round, the Suburbs are on the other side of the river, closely builded, and full of Temples and Cloisters lying in a flat and fruitful country.' The king himself engaged in trade, 'which brings him in incredible profit.'

Most Siamese kings gladly accepted vassal status toward China, which enabled them to send tribute missions to the king of heaven that were tax-free trade in disguise. Although only one tribute mission was authorized every three years, the Thai king sold scores of licences, and left it up to Chinese syndicates to smuggle the goods into China or swallow the losses. In addition to real and phony tribute missions, the king had shares in four hundred large junks plying the waters to Swatow and everywhere in between. These junks were operated by Chinese, crewed by Chinese, and had Chinese accountants aboard. Really successful Chinese brokers were ennobled, which made them members of the aristocracy, and bound them to the king like Siamese twins joined at the purse. Ruler and merchant together became so rich that this arrangement lasted for six hundred years.

In the old days with so much fertile, well-irrigated farmland available, most Siamese peasants were satisfied to spend their lives at home, with their families beside their spirit houses, growing rice and catching fish in a low-tension culture. The only way to get anything done was to let the Chinese do it, so by the late 1600s, Chinese were serving as chief justices, governors and customs officials. The Chinese population grew to ten thousand, with three thousand concentrated in the capital.

The wealth of Siam attracted unwelcome attention, however. In the late sixteenth century, Burmese armies on elephantback overran Ayutthaya. The Siamese rallied and forced them to withdraw, but when the Burmese came back in the eighteenth century, the Siamese were busy quarrelling among themselves. Thanks to treachery, the invaders sacked Ayutthaya, and destroyed the archives. The Siamese army under General Taksin withdrew to lick its wounds; the defeat by the Burmese sobered him up, and a few months later Taksin counter-attacked and forced them to go home.

When Taksin had made himself king and installed all his Teochiu cronies as nobles and advisers, he moved the capital downriver to Thonburi, closer to the sea. All three thousand Chinese merchants from Ayutthaya hurried after him and settled on the opposite bank of the Chao Phraya River in a snake-infested swamp called Sam Peng (Three Banks) – meaning an oxbow in the river. Malays, Japanese, Portuguese and Dutch built their own ghettoes near by.

Following a series of battles with regional warlords, Taksin united Siam, and after reigning for fifteen years he turned command over to two ambitious Chakkri brothers. The reason for the change? Taksin wanted to concentrate on his recent discovery that he was a saint, a *bodhisattva*. It was like announcing that he could fly by waving his arms. It is a common affliction in South East Asia. His own ministers had the demented Taksin taken into protective custody, and one of the Chakkri brothers, part Chinese with a Chinese father-in-law, agreed to become the new king, Rama I. He helped ex-king Taksin pass quickly into nirvana by having him beaten to death with a fragrant sandalwood club. For good measure, Rama I purged all the habitual conspirators surrounding the throne. When the killing was done, he moved the capital across the river to Sam Peng and made the Chinese shift outside the south-west gate of his new palace. This placed his citadel safely inside the oxbow – its exposed side facing mudflats filled with vipers. The Chakkri Dynasty still reigns today, though just barely.

The new capital was called Krung Thep, City of Angels. Westerners use the name Bangkok, for the wild plums that grew there. Its Chinatown is still called Sam Peng, a crowded ghetto cut here and there by oozing sewage canals lined with neon brothels, gambling joints and gold shops, the backstreets full of barefoot children. At night it is still worth your life to pick your way through the maze. Despite inflation, you can still have someone murdered in Bangkok for two dollars.

After King Taksin pointed the way, there was a flood of Teochiu migrants. Rama I imported thousands of coolies to dig canals that served as highways around the capital. By 1821, the Chinese population was nearly half a million, mostly Teochiu in Bangkok. Most Hokkien immigrants headed for southern Siam, where they engaged in tin mining with their relatives in the Malay States.

The Teochiu concentrated around Bangkok because the economic favours of the royal court brought huge profits. Thanks to their aristocratic connections, the Teochiu were able to 'outbid' rival Chinese in auctions for Royal monopolies of gambling, opium, liquor, tax farms and other concessions. A northern provincial governor once explained the bidding process in simple terms. A powerful Teochiu merchant with good connections made gifts to bureaucrats, nobility and army officers, assuring him of favourable consideration when the bids came in. Nobody sought to make top bids. Instead, the Teochiu guaranteed that over the contract period certain people in the hierarchy would receive more services from them than they could from rivals. Franchisers did not pay the throne a percentage, just an agreed annual amount plus bribes. The higher the bribes (in services and money), the lower the actual bid. Typically, nobles wanted a new mansion, free play at a gambling club, and an endless supply of little boys or girls. Once the franchise was granted, more kickbacks were paid. If everyone was satisfied, the monopoly was renewable for another period. Having sold their influence, government officials vigorously backed the Chinese syndicates in whatever way they wished to abuse their monopolies. As time passed, the variety of concessions increased, until all manner of products, exports and services were franchised. The court tossed franchises on the water like breadcrumbs, and the Chinese gulped at them like hungry carp. There were a lot of carp in Bangkok. In the mornings and evenings they came by the thousands to the murky surface of the *klongs* to gasp for air, mouths working like a choir singing a Teochiu oratorio.

As the number of Chinese in Bangkok grew, so did their feverish commercial activity, until they directly or indirectly controlled all of the country's trade from top to bottom.

They ran the monopolies and controlled the rackets. Once a fortune was made, profits were invested in rice milling, shipping, construction or other legitimate businesses. Families who made it this way often adopted Siamese names. (Chinese who took such names had to pick them off an official list. Even if the name sounded Tai, everyone who counted knew who was Chinese.) They owned vast tracks of paddy, but did not farm themselves. In the early nineteenth century, the chief export was sugar, introduced from Kwangtung. Other Chinese owned tobacco and cotton plantations. They did all the chicken and pig breeding and slaughter. Piglets and chicks were sold to Siamese farmers, who fed them till they were ready to butcher, then – because they were Buddhists – sold them back to Chinese to do the killing.

In the south, Hokkien triad leader Khaw Soo Cheang married a rich Siamese woman and went into business hauling produce by junk from Penang to sell at mining ports. In twenty years, he became so rich that he bid for the tin monopoly. He was also granted sole right to farm taxes in Ranong, a smuggling town on the Burma-Siam border. Khaw was so ruthlessly effective that the throne rewarded him with a noble title and made him governor of the region. He married his children to nobility and to rich Chinese traders in Siam and Malaya, their children became genteel – and in this way, a dangerous Chinese was assimilated into Siamese society. There was always room for Chinese to make their fortune. But they had to play by certain rules to help the Siamese maintain the pretence that they were still in charge.

With its economy, throne and nobility largely in Chinese hands, Siam effectively became (after Coxinga's Taiwan) the world's second

Overseas Chinese state – if a strangler fig can be considered a proper tree. Then Westerners interfered.

Rama IV and his son fended the West off with concessions of trade and territory. Parts of the Malay Peninsula and the Shan States were relinquished to Britain, and the French were given Laos and Cambodia. In 1896, the French and British generously agreed to keep the remainder of Siam as a buffer between them.

Western treaties were imposed that pre-empted many Chinese enterprises. Chinese were left with only the domestic rice monopoly, opium and the rackets. To compensate for their losses, the throne enlarged the racket franchises, for gambling, brothels and alcohol. The Chinese best equipped to get these were underworld syndicates.

The Coolie Boom in the last decades of the nineteenth century altered the delicate balance and made the Siamese nervous. For the first time, large numbers of women arrived, so fewer Chinese would be assimilated by intermarriage. A Chinese national identity began to emerge with the construction of the first community-wide organization, Tien-hua Hospital, followed by a Chinese Chamber of Commerce, guilds, newspapers and schools where children were removed from Siamese culture and taught a Chinese curriculum in dialects.

The government felt threatened. Traditionally, Overseas Chinese were outlaws, unrecognized by any Chinese imperial government, and without any sense of themselves as nationals. But now they were being hustled by republican fund-raisers to see themselves as Chinese rather than as Teochiu or Hokkien. In 1909, the Manchu government declared that all persons born of Chinese fathers were Chinese nationals, no matter where they had been born or lived. After six hundred years of cohabitation, the Overseas Chinese in Siam were becoming subversive.

In 1910, when Rama VI ascended the throne at the age of twenty-nine, the ancient collusion broke down. An Anglophile educated at Cambridge and trained by the British army, he was estranged from the traditional system. When he commanded courtiers with Chinese blood to move to one side of the throne room, 90 per cent of the courtiers did. It was obvious that the Chinese did not only control the economy, but the inner circles of the royal court. The young king could either get into bed with the Chinese, as had his royal ancestors, or he could break with tradition and see where that got him. To attack such a fixed arrangement was very brave, very foolish – or both. The king made no effort to disguise his antagonism. He was going to level the playing field. But this was not a playing field.

It was a particular sore point that the Chinese had always paid a lower head-tax than the poorest Siamese. When Rama VI decreed that henceforth all residents would pay the same tax, triads rioted in the streets, the bloody violence convincing the king that the Chinese were a malevolent force.

After brooding on the matter, the king published in the Siamese press a bitter indictment titled *Jews of the East*. The greatest similarity between Chinese and Jews, he said, was their racism. No matter where they lived, Chinese remained loyal only to their own kind, and only so long as it suited their selfish interests, driven by greed. Their sole purpose was to amass as much money as possible and then leave. They felt no obligation. They expected every privilege and evaded every responsibility. To them all non-Chinese were barbarians to be robbed, cheated and exploited. He mentioned the bogus insurance companies run by Chinese, and the creative bankruptcies they engineered to fob off debts while protecting their personal wealth. He said they sucked money out of Siam and other Asian countries and remitted it to their families in China, not out of charity but to salt it away. One day, he concluded, there would be a reaction against them everywhere.

As a reminder that he was not lacking in power himself, the king presented the most powerful Chinese families in his realm with a sword, 'as a token of my presence.' He ended the practice of ennobling Chinese. He also tried to build a new power base of his own by strengthening the army and navy. This opened a Pandora's box, creating a third force with an agenda of its own, underwritten by Teochiu powerbrokers. For poor but ambitious Siamese, the reborn armed forces became the only path to status. In 1912, the king provoked jealousy by creating his own personal paramilitary force, the Wild Tiger Corps, and a disgruntled group of regular army and navy officers tried to assassinate him. Its failure made the plot seem insignificant, but its true significance was that it had discreet Chinese backing. If their grip on Siam was going to be challenged, they were going to fight back, using the king's own weapons.

In 1925, the crisis deepened when Rama VI died and was succeeded by a much weaker man who tried to reverse his predecessor's policies and return affairs of state to his corrupt royal clique. This endangered the ambitions of a new hard core of army officers who made common cause with members of the Teochiu underworld. In June 1932, army tanks rumbled into *coup* position, government leaders were seized, and an ultimatum delivered to the king, denouncing corruption in the 'royal clique'. The *coup* leaders wished the king to remain as a constitutional monarch. Rama VII accepted and no blood was shed.

Once power was in its hands, the junta fragmented into quarrelling conservative, radical and military factions. Noisiest were the radical intellectuals, led by a young French-educated lawyer named Pridi, who hoped to introduce Utopian social changes that would benefit ethnic Siamese at the expense of the Chinese. A faction of conservative monarchists had been included to lend the junta an air of legitimacy, but they were allies of the Chinese financiers. Muscle was provided by the Tank Corps, led by colonels called the Four Tigers. They had only contempt for Pridi's radicals, but not one colonel yet felt strong enough to take power alone. As their figurehead, they chose Field Marshal Phibun, a vain, high-strung man with lush features and what an astrologer called 'a rare ability to see wrong as right'.

During a monsoon, it has been observed, 'If a tiger, a cobra and a missionary find themselves under the same umbrella, the missionary is usually the first to leave.' Pridi was no exception. He was no match for tigers or cobras. Chinese-backed conservatives (the cobras) portrayed him as a Marxist lunatic, and Pridi was forced into exile. The army did not like Marxists, but within its ranks were a great many poor nationalists who saw merit in Pridi's efforts to benefit Siamese peasants. They took their revenge by booting out the conservative royalists.

The tiger now had the umbrella to itself, and invited the missionary back. Pridi returned from exile and rejoined the government. But he would remain a perpetual victim.

In March 1935, the throne was further weakened when Rama VII, never happy in the job, abdicated in favour of his ten-year-old nephew, Prince Ananda, educated in Massachusetts and Switzerland. One week before the young king arrived for his first visit, the army staged another *coup* to block an alleged Chinese plot. The timing gave the impression that the king endorsed the takeover, when in fact he was a hostage of circumstance. The purpose of the latest *coup* was to tighten the grip of pro-Japanese military officers on the eve of the Second World War.

Preparing for its conquest of South East Asia, Tokyo held out the prospect that Bangkok could regain control of the entire Tai linguistic area, including Laos, parts of southern China, and the Shan States of British Burma. In expectation of that great day, and to emphasize its traditional claim, the country's name was changed to Thailand.

Fear of Japan caused many Overseas Chinese to seek Thai citizenship, but they found themselves blocked by new requirements of military or government service, and fluency in colloquial Siamese. Chinese schools and newspapers were closed. Police raided triad headquarters and private homes. Community leaders were jailed, deported or assassinated, and just before Pearl Harbor, three defiant Teochiu leaders were arrested. When the Japanese army arrived, prominent Chinese fled upcountry, many of them joining the underground Free Thai movement started by Pridi, who was working with Allied intelligence. Others collaborated with the Japanese.

The outcome of Thailand's ongoing power struggle with the Chinese begun in 1910 by Rama VI, ultimately depended on who won the war, but the actual victor was completely unexpected. As the Japanese army stormed from Thailand into Burma, its commanders invited their Thai counterparts to occupy the Shan States. The Shan city of Kengtung became headquarters for the Thai Northern Army of General Phin Choonhavan, military governor of what was to be called the United Thai State. For him it was the chance of a lifetime. Phin was one of the army junta that had seized power in Bangkok in 1932 and installed Marshal Phibun. His Chinese connections were so good, and he was so deft at manipulating people, that by the time the Japanese arrived in 1941, he was commander of the Northern Army, whose zone of responsibility included Chiengmai and the Thai sector of the Golden Triangle. Chiengmai is Thailand's G-spot, the centre of all gratification in guns, drugs, girls, teak, gems and jade. Whoever controls Chiengmai as governor or as chief of the Northern Command, controls the cookie jar. Opium proceeds provided General Phin with limitless resources that were not subject to government oversight. Thanks to his excellent high-level connections in Thailand's Teochiu syndicates, the general was able to build a power base fuelled by drugs and rackets that after the war ushered him and his subordinate officers into absolute power in Thailand at the head of military dictatorships for most of the next half century. As we will see, Phin's romance with the Teochiu mafia made a love baby of the drug trade, and led to its explosive growth to what is now over 2,600 tons of opium per year, which generate billions of dollars in black money worldwide.

It was no coincidence that Thailand's army occupied the Shan States and gained access to the finest opium-growing area in the world. Colonel Tsuji and other planners of the strike south were intimately linked to the Japanese and Chinese underworlds. They had long been involved in marketing Manchurian opium throughout East Asia, and both the Japanese army and the Nationalist Chinese government actively engaged in opium and heroin traffic during the war. The KMT sold crudely processed brown heroin directly to the Japanese army of occupation.

For his part, General Phin contacted the Nationalist Chinese in Yunnan in April 1944, and arranged to meet General Lu Wi-eng, commander of the KMT 93rd Division. In secret talks between the KMT and the Japanese, in which General Phin and Colonel Tsuji participated, it was arranged for the KMT to smuggle American Lend-Lease supplies to the Japanese. Five years later, when Mao was victorious in China's civil war, remnants of this same 93rd Division, escaped into Burma's Shan States. There they seized control of the best opium-growing areas in the Golden Triangle, and resumed a lasting military and commercial alliance with General Phin in Thailand – all made possible by Japan's wartime intercession.

But before looking at the consequences and leaving Colonel Tsuji behind, we must allow him his last flourish. By then, Tsuji had shifted his attention to Burma. In 1944, he visited General Phin in Kengtung, then helped General Honda Masaki escape encirclement by Allied forces. To celebrate this and other feats of daring, Tsuji invited fellow Japanese officers to a banquet at which the main course was the liver of a captured American pilot. In the summer of 1945, he was arrested by the victorious Allies and charged with cannibalism, but he escaped, and hid for months in Thailand posing as a Buddhist monk, protected by General Phin Choonhavan. Since the 1920s, Tsuji had been intimately acquainted with the KMT secret police boss, Tai Li, and making contact with KMT intelligence officers in Bangkok early in 1946, Tsuji arranged to be smuggled to Chungking. There, he personally gave Generalissimo Chiang the idea of using defeated Japanese soldiers against Mao's communists, to save China from being overrun by the Reds. The generalissimo was greatly excited by the possibility of saving himself and his regime in this way, with Japanese military help. Working through Tai Li and the American naval intelligence officer in Chungking, Milton 'Mary' Miles, Chiang Kaishek secretly contacted General Charles Willoughby, MacArthur's G-2 in Tokyo. Both MacArthur and Willoughby were lifelong ultra-conservatives with a visceral loathing for Marxism and a deep-seated fear of the consequences of a communist victory on the Mainland. As part of the deal, Generalissimo Chiang persuaded General MacArthur to release a group of senior Japanese war criminals – all friends of Tsuji – who had been imprisoned by the Americans in Sugamo Prison. When these men were freed, they paid the KMT government a huge undisclosed sum from looted war booty, which was tantamount to Hermann Goering paying David Ben Gurion to get him off the hook at Nuremberg. These men then became leaders of postwar Japan and founders of the ruling Liberal Democratic Party.

During his stay in Chungking, Colonel Tsuji was not punished by the generalissimo for Sook Ching or for any other atrocity, but spent his time translating a book about Mao's stronghold in China's north-west frontier, in preparation for the arrival of his promised Japanese war veterans. The mercenary deal ultimately fell through, but Tsuji was given first-class passage home to Tokyo, where he was greeted with enthusiasm by his liberated comrades, and joined them as a celebrity member of parliament. General MacArthur and the occupation government did not prosecute him for eating the American pilot's liver. On a visit to Hanoi a few years later, Tsuji vanished. Evidently, one of his Overseas Chinese victims had at last got his revenge.

But there was more to be heard yet from Tsuji's friend in Thailand . . .

CHAPTER 12

SILK BOOTS

ON THE EVE OF BUDDHA'S BIRTHDAY EACH YEAR, MONS ALL OVER
Thailand and southern Burma purchase caged birds from pet shops in
public markets, and the next morning set them loose all at once. A
handsome, big-boned, gentle people who were living there long before
the Tai and Burmans came down from the north, the Mons still occupy
much of the area between Bangkok and the Bay of Bengal. When the
birds are given their freedom, the air is filled with the whoop of wings
as they go off in all directions.

When the Pacific War came to an end, many Americans were in
favour of liberating all of Asia, the way Mons and other Buddhists
liberate birds. It was a golden opportunity to free a large part of the
human race from European imperialism, and to bestow the blessings of
democracy. In that immediate postwar atmosphere, Bangkok took
pains to look democratic, liberal and anti-fascist. Pridi, the Free Thai
hero, briefly became the head of a popular government. But as the Cold
War took over, America switched signals. All the birds were put back
into their cages. The Thai army returned to dictatorial power in 1947
after an absence of only two years, and resumed its takeover of

Overseas Chinese assets, using clever and unscrupulous Chinese to undermine their own people.

The historic significance of this event is that the same scenario was to be repeated with variations in country after country around the Rim, as classic Asian authoritarian rule returned dressed in the costume of Western-style democracy. In South Korea, Taiwan, Indonesia, South Vietnam, Burma, the Philippines and Thailand, military regimes ruled more or less openly, while in Japan the ruling LDP was founded and run by the Class-A war criminals released from Sugamo Prison. Not wanting to acknowledge the true nature of these regimes, the West – America in particular – welcomed them as anti-communist bulwarks, and declared that there was no basic contradiction between authoritarian rule and democracy, for one would lead inexorably to the other as living standards improved. Make the regimes rich, and it followed that prosperity would trickle down to all, as surely as day follows night.

Not so easily fooled, the Overseas Chinese took a different approach, which grew out of many centuries of sour experience with despotism. As the Chinese knew, military regimes were expert at breaking kneecaps, and nailing victims to tree-trunks, not at keeping multiple ledgers. Bearing baskets of fruit, great sums of black money and access to offshore accounts, the Chinese made themselves indispensable to the new regimes, showed them how to fleece their citizens, how to usurp and manage former colonial assets, how to lure foreign investment, how to play lucrative games with gold trading and foreign exchange scams, and how to salt the looted proceeds abroad. In Indonesia, the process happened quite differently than in Thailand, so the two countries provide startling insight into the true workings of Asian economics, the real role of Overseas Chinese syndicates, and the financial politics of the Pacific Rim.

Once more the frontman in Thailand was to be the wartime collaborator Marshal Phibun, who gained American support by sending a token force of Thai troops to Korea. Behind him, as before, was a junta of army officers – but this time there was no question as to which group was in control. They were General Phin Choonhavan's clique, veterans of the Japanese-backed takeover of the opium-rich Shan States.

Gathered around General Phin were ambitious and aggressive officers drawn from his wartime Northern Command. For the next fifty years, they took turns running Thailand – among them General Phao (1947–1957), Field Marshal Sarit (1957–1963), General Krit (1964–1976) and General Kriangsak (1976–1980). Some were Phin's subordinates; others (like Phao) were married to Phin's daughters. After a brief respite for parliamentary democracy in the early 1980s, they recaptured power through their army protégés. Phin's son, General Chatichai Choonhavan, inherited the powerbase, became prime minister himself, and during the 1990s remained a leading right-wing powerbroker in Thai politics.

Switching allegiance from Tokyo to Washington, Phin's men turned Thailand into America's closest ally in South East Asia, while they enriched themselves beyond belief supplying the global heroin trade, in collaboration with Overseas Chinese syndicates.

In the process, General Phin and his circle successfully completed the leverage takeover of most Chinese assets in Thailand: not by seizure of ownership, which would have been counterproductive, but by interposing themselves in the ancient system of kickbacks. Phin and his men quietly assumed the role of *uparat* – the supremely lucrative position of intermediary between the throne and the Chinese community, a role passed down for centuries. While the king was kept in position largely for symbolic purposes and to deflect attention, the Chinese were squeezed by Phin's clique as they had never been squeezed before. Much of this was accomplished by his Thai–Burmese son-in-law, Phao, using terror, torture, extortion and murder. While he was upcountry during the war, Phin had arranged for Phao to act as aide in Bangkok to Marshal Phibun. Phao saw to it that his father-in-law's wishes were conveyed to the marshal and that the general was kept intimately informed of developments in the capital.

During their occupation of the Shan States, Phin and his troops had taken part in a number of atrocities. The civilian Pridi government, which took over so briefly at the end of the war, charged them all with war crimes: Marshal Phibun was charged, his aide, Phao, was fired. General Phin was recalled and fired, and the Shan States were given back to Burma. Phin's Northern Army was demobilized in the field, without even transportation back to Thailand, and so, stranded, they turned to banditry, stripping Shan villages and heading home with a vengeance. The officers felt cheated, careers in jeopardy. When they reached Bangkok, they gathered around General Phin and plotted revenge.

Some of Phin's followers still commanded troops in and around Bangkok. 'I discovered that almost all of them wanted to see this [civilian] government overthrown,' Phin explained later. His first move was to persuade the Thai judiciary to drop all war crimes charges against them. A few weeks later, in 1946, the judges declared it was 'unconstitutional' to try Phibun and his aides for war crimes, and they considered themselves exonerated. In army ranks, this made General Phin more popular than ever.

Next, he called a secret meeting of all top army commanders in the capital region and outlined his plan to seize power. All but two agreed to take part. Those two were warned to be silent, Phin said, 'otherwise they would be killed.'

Son-in-law Phao was all in favour of a *coup*, because it would put the Chinese business community at their mercy.

Even the levelheaded Colonel Sarit was afraid that his career was doomed if Pridi's civilian leadership continued. Since the first military *coup* in 1932, the army had gained tremendous economic influence. Chinese entrepreneurs no longer found it adequate to cultivate only the aristocracy; now they had to have army officers on the payroll as well. There was intense rivalry among Chinese to win the favours of the most talented or upwardly mobile officers. Sarit, born in the dry, impoverished north-east, had showed so much promise as a youth that he had been taken up by the Teochiu businessmen who ran the North-east Rice-Millers Association. They'd underwritten his military schooling and his early years as a cadet, spread grease so that he rose quickly, and saw to it that he could afford his own large following. A popular Thai saying goes, 'It is a happy man who can put gold Rolexes on all the hands in his pocket.'

The opportunity to get rid of Prime Minister Pridi came when young King Ananda (Rama VIII) died from the accidental discharge of a revolver in his bedroom. Rumours were deliberately spread that Pridi had been involved in a conspiracy to murder the young king. Most army men shared the opinion that Pridi was a dangerous leftist, so they were easily convinced that he was somehow connected to the king's death (Pridi's only military support was in the relatively small Thai navy).

In November 1947, General Phin's forces occupied radio stations, the central telephone exchange, and the Ministry of Defence. Prime Minister Pridi fled for his life, and Marshal Phibun was again set up as a window-dressing dictator. Behind the scenes, Phin's group staged a series of mini-*coups* and assassinations to get rid of rivals in the military and police establishments. Phin then 'accepted' the post of army commander-in-chief, and his follower, Sarit, became the general commanding the Bangkok area, including the First Infantry Regiment, the main *coup* force controlling the capital. Phin's son-in-law, Phao, became deputy director of the national police. Other key military and intelligence posts were also filled by Phin's men.

Only two years earlier facing trial for war crimes, Phin was now an anti-communist hero to the dominant new group at the American embassy. His position secure, he turned his attention to subverting every Chinese enterprise he could get his hands on.

There had been many fruitless attempts in the past to wrest the rackets and monopolies out of Chinese hands. Thailand produces some of the world's finest rice, called jasmine or perfumed rice because of its fragrance, and the rice monopoly alone was worth many millions of dollars each year. Teochiu families were endlessly scheming to take over each other's mills, rice barge fleets, and offshore junk squadrons. In the Bangkok area alone, there were eighty rice mills to fight over. Thanks to the wartime deal the Teochiu cut with the Japanese military occupation in Indonesia, Singapore and Malaya, the rice merchants of Thailand had a tight grip on the entire South East Asian rice trade at the war's end. Rice was urgently needed all over Asia, and only Burma and Thailand had a surplus. Their peace treaty with Britain obliged Bangkok to export a certain quantity of rice free to Malaya and to other countries. Teochiu brokers evaded this by drastically reducing their declared stocks and turning the rest over to affliliated Teochiu smugglers to be sold at hugely inflated prices on the black markets in those same hungry countries. Officially, this left Thailand with barely enough rice for her own needs. The charade was so obvious that it provoked bitter resentment against the Chinese, and plans had been

made under Pridi to nationalize the rice industry. A few days later, the
chairman of the government committee involved received a fuseless
bomb in the mail, with a note warning that a fused device would be sent
if the nationalization plan went through. The Ministry of Commerce
hastily announced that rice was 'now flowing smoothly once more', so
there was no need to make drastic changes.

Phin and his son-in-law Phao approached the Overseas Chinese
problem in a highly original way. Using extortion and murder, Phin
seized control of one of Thailand's five most powerful Teochiu
underworld syndicates, while son-in-law Phao took over another.
These five syndicates, which make up the core of the Teochiu
Brotherhood, control the drug trade from North Thailand down to
warehouses in Bangkok, then by ocean-going junk or steamer down
the west coast to Penang and Singapore, or from the east coast to Hong
Kong and Taiwan. Although there are many free agents in Thailand
running minor quantities of heroin to Hong Kong and other points by
plane, the majority is shipped by the Teochiu. Geographically, control
of drugs inside Thailand is vested in regional kingpins whose Teochiu
families have fought it out with rivals to gain control of a district. In
their area, they ruled both drugs and rackets. Beyond their immediate
territory, they negotiated with the parent Teochiu organizations that
link Thailand to Hong Kong. Phao and Phin gained control of two of
the five large syndicates in Thailand by displacing the old leaders with
new bosses who were willing to take a back seat in return for military
and police protection.

With the help of other turncoats, Phin and Phao forced out existing
franchise holders in all the rackets. Phin used the War Veterans
Association, which he controlled, to extort soft-drink franchises for his
army followers, and in return for getting General Sarit the national
lottery monopoly (a ready-made vehicle for patronage), Phin formed
an alliance with Sarit's sponsors, the North-east Rice-Millers Association, to squeeze out their rivals. This proved such a success that a
similar deal was made with the Chinese North-east Sawmillers
Association. Both deals bound Sarit tightly to Phin. The following
year, Phin's War Veterans Association took over control of Thailand's
pig-butchering monopoly, but allowed the Chinese to continue
running it. Ultimately, this led to a takeover of the entire pork trade, a

wholly Chinese enterprise. While each business continued to be operated by Chinese, Phin's men gained positions in top management.

Phin had picked Phao to marry one of his daughters because, even as a young man, Phao was extraordinarily cunning. He matured into an abnormal predator. Phao made use of his post as deputy director of national police to arrest and murder rivals and political opponents, including four former cabinet ministers and the chief of detectives. Parliament tried to block his blatant drug trafficking by giving the job of intercepting smugglers to the navy, a stronghold of educated anti-Phin, anti-Phao elements, and in 1951, forces led by the navy attempted to destroy Phin and his clique by staging a *coup* of their own. Failing to kidnap Phin and Phao beforehand – a fatal mistake – the navy arrested Marshal Phibun during a shipboard ceremony and held him hostage aboard the battleship *Ayutthaya*.

Showing his contempt for the navy and for Marshal Phibun, Phin had his air force sink the battleship, leaving it up to the ageing figurehead to swim to shore. Fighting raged through Bangkok, but General Phin was victorious. In the aftermath, the navy was reduced to little more than a coastguard, on strict orders not to interfere with the diesel-powered junks hauling heroin to Hong Kong and Taiwan.

The navy's failed *coup* cleared the way for Phin to come completely out of the closet. He named himself Vice Premier, an entirely fitting title, and in another appropriate move had himself appointed the head of the Economic Coordination Council. He also promoted himself to Field Marshal, and gave his four sons-in-law cabinet rank as deputy ministers for Agriculture, Communications, Commerce and Interior. General Sarit took Phin's place as army commander-in-chief. General Phao became director-general of police, and immediately enlarged the police force to gain a tighter control of the drug trade. Sarit and Phao had roughly equal commands, with forty-five thousand soldiers and forty thousand police. But while Sarit was content with the bloated salary and benefits he received as head of the national lottery, Phao became insatiable.

Some of Phin's financial success has been credited to his 'adopted son', Udane Techapaibul, a handsome, urbane Teochiu businessman who is said to have engineered many of these boardroom takeovers of Chinese businesses. As a young man, Udane had been informally adopted by General Phin because of his uncanny grasp of the secret inner-workings of Chinese community networks. Udane was the son of a pawnbroker who owned an opium den and shares in manufacturing rice whisky. With Phin's backing, Udane started his own liquor business and was phenomenally successful in cornering a large part of the market. He then went into lumber, importing, banking and insurance, with similar success. After the war, when Phin came to power, Udane became managing director of the organization that oversaw the sending of remittances to China, head of the government sugar corporation, and the government rice consortium, and an officer of the Teochiu Association and particularly of the Chao-yang Hsien Association – one of the most powerful Teochiu native place tontines. This had the salubrious result that Phin's 'adopted son' headed the government rice consortium, while a son-in-law controlled all rice smuggling.

On the surface it was one big, successful family. However, a bitter struggle was developing between Phao and Sarit over the drug trade. It was largely a difference in style. Phao was surpremely vulgar. Sarit was a self-made patrician. They kept separate camps. Phao was based at Field Marshal Phin's mansion on Soi Rachakrul, while Sarit maintained his following at a villa on Soi Si Sao Theves.

The 'Rachakrul Ratpack', as it was discreetly known among the embassies, included Field Marshal Phin and his family and followers, many of them Chinese. The Si Sao Theves Group ('Seesaw Thieves' in the embassies) had Sarit as leader, backed by a circle of formidable senior officers.

Between them, these two groups now had control of the world's wealthiest Overseas Chinese community, not to mention navies, tourism, temples, brothels, palaces (and one of the world's great cuisines). But they chose to quarrel over drugs.

The Golden Triangle was about to become the world's largest source of heroin. The big change began in 1949, when the civil war in China ended with Generalissimo Chiang fleeing to Taiwan. KMT army remnants bottled up by communist forces in Yunnan escaped into Burma, where they seized control of the best high-altitude poppy-growing areas in the Shan States. This was the same KMT 93rd Division that had sold American Lend-Lease supplies to the Japanese.

It was now under the command of General Li Mi. Since Generalissimo Chiang laboured under the delusion that he could recover the Mainland, General Li Mi was ordered to stay in the Shan States, and to sustain his army by taking over all opium tar marketing, and to escort each year's bounty to Thailand, where it could be processed into morphine base or various grades of heroin and brokered by the KMT to Teochiu syndicates for export.

Senior members of General Li Mi's staff have each said on separate occasions that Li Mi received this instruction directly from the generalissimo, and that it was reaffirmed by his son, General Chiang Ching-kuo, when he became overseer of Taiwan's intelligence services and eventually president of Taiwan. The Chiangs' high-level involvement in the drug trade was no great surprise, because the generalissimo had kept his government afloat in Nanking during the 1930s by sharing Green Gang earnings from drug trafficking, while serving personally as chief of China's opium suppression campaign. This meant he suppressed everyone else's drug profits. True, after decades of effort, the KMT had little believability, but it was the world's richest political party, and is to this day. It had a substantial economic presence in Bangkok in the form of wealthy individuals, powerful community associations, industrial groups, and the underworld syndicates of each dialect group, which shared Taiwan's anti-communist mindset and were encouraged to move drugs through Taiwan. Thus they had parallel financial interest. Although Hong Kong was unmatched as an offshore conduit for heroin, Taiwan provided sanctuary for drug-runners and corrupt Hong Kong police officers on the run, and offered money-laundering facilities that were incomparable because they were impenetrable.

When opium-growing in Mainland China was ended by the communists, the Shan States became the leading Asian drug source. The CIA was backing General Li Mi's KMT remnants in military operations to harass the communists along China's back border. Material provided by a CIA subsidiary called Sea Supply was airlifted to General Li Mi's troops by Air America and other CIA-contract airlines.

Because he portrayed himself as a great enemy of communism, Police General Phao was fully backed and supplied by the CIA. This gave him an additional way to exert pressure on the Overseas Chinese community, by threatening to denounce as a communist sympathizer any businessman who refused to meet his extortionate demands. (It is now generally accepted that no serious communist threat to Thailand ever existed, but was exaggerated to justify the agendas of Phao and the CIA.)

CIA support gave Phao the upper hand over his rival Sarit. Between 1950 and 1953, Sea Supply gave Phao thirty-five million dollars' worth of weapons, communications and transport. The Agency helped Phao create his own armoured division, air force, pocket navy and border police, whose reciprocal responsibilities were to see that Sea Supply shipments reached the KMT opium armies, while nobody interfered with the drug trade. By 1954, Bangkok had become the main source of hard drugs in the Far East, and most of the flow came via General Phao.

Drug profits increased so fast that General Sarit's 'clean' group could not resist scooping up some, which nearly led to civil war. Near Lampang in 1950, a drug shipment travelling south by army convoy ran into a roadblock set up by the police. When the army threatened to shoot, the police pointed out their own heavy machine-guns. The stand-off lasted two days, until Sarit and Phao arrived to escort the drugs personally to Bangkok, where they split the proceeds.

Phao's greed was growing out of control. He bullied wealthy Chinese businessmen into appointing him or one of his associates to the boards of more than twenty corporations. He helped himself to their treasuries and moved huge sums of gold through Overseas Chinese channels to offshore accounts, including major gold bullion deposits in Swiss banks. To terrorize his enemies, he arrested scores of student leaders and dissident intellectuals, many of whom never reappeared and were rumoured to have been cremated alive. At long last, in a comedy of errors, Phao was finally brought down by Sarit, through his own Chinese banker. Everybody has a soft spot.

That rather unusual banker was the Horatio Alger of the Overseas Chinese financial world, a grade school drop-out who became one of the world's richest and most powerful tycoons. While the Thai military dictatorship thought it was taking advantage of his financial wizardry, he was turning his local bank into a world-class multinational, and setting himself and other Chinese like him as free as the birds on Buddha's birthday.

CHAPTER 13

THE GENIUS

HE LIVED IN A BIG MANSION ON WIRELESS ROAD IN BANGKOK, NEXT door to the residence of the American Ambassador, and just across the street from the United States Embassy, which was devilishly awkward. That made it difficult for Washington to come right out and accuse him of being 'the financial kingpin of the heroin trade'.

They had other reasons to be careful of how they handled him. He was among the world's richest Overseas Chinese, one of the top five most powerful leaders of the global Teochiu community. He had built the biggest private bank in South East Asia, one of the most profitable on the planet, and he was the personal banker for everybody who was anybody in the Bangkok military regime. In those days of General Phao, the drug trade was high-level government business, so no Thai banker could avoid all contact or contamination. The people involved were generals and field marshals, after all, not Sicilian thugs in black shirts with mustard-coloured neckties. In Asia, the underworld is just the underwear of the overworld. Why get excited? Anyway, Washington was picking up the tab.

His name was Chin Sophonpanich, the eldest (and only male) of five children born in Bangkok to a Teochiu father and a Thai mother. His official biography dodges around his place of birth, implying that he was born in China. This subterfuge was necessary because Chin's mother was his father's secondary wife, and not pure Teochiu, which might have diluted Chin's ranking in Teochiu circles. More important, as a young man Chin dodged military service by forfeiting Thai citizenship, claiming to have been born in China, in Chao-yang Hsien – one of the seven *hsien* around Swatow. His father, who worked in Bangkok as a clerk, took him to Swatow for several years as a child. Chin claimed he attended primary school there, then dropped out of secondary school due to poverty. When he became rich, Thai citizenship again became desirable, so he went to great expense to acquire it, with the help of powerful friends.

In Bangkok at the age of seventeen, Chin found work as a clerk in a shop. When the business burnt down in 1930, the result of arson, he sailed for China on a Teochiu rice-smuggling junk, and made a number of voyages with smugglers from Swatow to Bangkok. In China, he married Lau Kwei Ying. Each time he returned from a voyage, she became pregnant. Of their four children, only two boys survived, but they were to be his principal heirs. Chin had no stomach for ocean voyages, so when he reached Bangkok in 1936, he gave up the sea and moved in with a friend five years his junior, Udane, the 'adopted son' of General Phin Choonhaven. Chin and Udane had the same ancestral home in China, Chao-yang Hsien, and members of the Chao-yang Hsien Association were the most influential Chinese in Thailand.

Through Udane, Chin found a new Thai wife and work as a clerk-bookkeeper for a building suppliers owned by Udane's uncle. Chin was employed giving quotes, collecting bills and filling orders. Everyone was impressed by his speed and skill with accounts. Despite his very limited education, he was a prodigy with figures and financial concepts. When Udane reported this to his patron, General Phin's ears pricked up and Chin was invited onto the fringes of the powerful circle of colonels and generals of the Rachakrul Ratpack.

During the Second World War, although General Phin and his inner circle of army officers went north to run the occupation of the Shan States, members of Phin's group remained in Bangkok to handle black-market deals with the Japanese military establishment, and to cash in on rice, opium and gold smuggling.

The arrival of the Japanese transformed retail trade in Thailand. Prices shot up. Strategic materials such as rubber, tin and copper wire were in great demand. Traders with access to commodities and construction materials could make a fortune supplying the Japanese. All over South East Asia, the Japanese conquest caused such disruption that warehouses were abandoned or left unguarded, and underworld gangs were quick to loot and stockpile the materials.

Although he had been only a warehouse clerk, Chin was given financial backing to set up half a dozen black-market businesses. He started his own building supply, Asia Company, and made immediate profits, and with them he played the gold market through another company tucked between the jewellery shops in Bangkok's Baan Moh area. Gold prices rose to twenty times pre-war levels. Profiteering on the Chinese-controlled gold market became feverish. Chin was a wizard. He came out of the war a wealthy man, rising from clerk–bookkeeper to financier in only three years (1942–1945). With further backing from General Phin, he set up a number of new companies in trade, construction, insurance, gold and foreign exchange. His connections expanded to include Teochiu rice and gold merchants throughout South East Asia and South China.

Strictly a moneyman, Chin made a point of launching each new venture partnership with others who had practical experience. This allowed him to distance himself and to 'tone down his involvement in certain areas of business,' as one Thai put it. His company for foreign exchange dealings, Asia Trust, was managed for him by a refugee banker from Shanghai.

The wild inflation of the war years increased demand for precious metals. Gold and foreign exchange proved so lucrative that, by 1949, Chin was concentrating exclusively on them. He imported gold from Teochiu sources in Hong Kong and other Asian capitals, and sold it to Chinese. Every Wednesday, he or one of his clerks went to the airport to pick up the latest shipment, rolled it over in the brisk Bangkok gold market, and split the profits. Ultimately, Chin was not working just for himself, or for General Phin, but for the shadowy overlords of the entire Teochiu dialect group headquartered in Swatow and Kowloon.

To stay ahead of rivals, he kept abreast of the Asian gold market by radio. A central bank official said, 'Even government departments were less sophisticated.' Except for the BBC, there was at the time no regular financial reporting service on any wavelength. Chin used a Teochiu shortwave link from Hong Kong, which tied ocean smuggling fleets to shore-based smuggling centres, and kept Teochiu gold traders like Chin fed with commodity prices and fluctuating exchange rates.

To back up shortwave transmissions, subject to the weather, Chin had his own system for cables. Urgent information arrived by cable and wireless at the General Post and Telegraph Office on New Road by the river, in those days an operation worthy of sub-Saharan outposts of the Foreign Legion. Incoming telegrams were typed hunt-and-peck on ancient machines, and these bulletins were delivered hours later by postmen on ruptured bicycles.

Chin's solution was to keep a full-time employee at the post office, who collected cables the moment they arrived and telephoned the information to his boss, giving Chin detailed market intelligence hours ahead of rivals.

After the 1947 army *coup*, General Phin saw to it that Chin got the government monopoly on all gold trading, the monopoly on all foreign exchange transactions, and the monopoly on all Chinese remittances to the Mainland. How could he lose? It was a milk cow with three giant udders. 'First thing every morning, all the bankers and businessmen would come to our office and check the exchange rate quotations,' Chin boasted. 'We became sort of the authority.'

Many Chinese remitted most of their income to their families on the Mainland. Traditionally, if a Teochiu truck driver bought a bit of gold in Bangkok and wanted it moved to his family in Hong Kong or Swatow, it was credited privately through the old boy network without passing through any form of currency control. This was an effortless process, in which a Teochiu financial agent in Bangkok notified his counterpart in Swatow and the value of the gold was credited automatically, minus commissions at both ends. The purpose of the new remittance monopoly in Bangkok was to bypass the old boy network and to funnel all China-bound funds through establishments operated by Chin or other members of Phin's clique. In Chin's hands, the ancient transaction was dressed up with the look of modern banking. Remittances went as bank transfers from Bangkok to Hong

Kong to Swatow. By complicating matters this way, it was possible to charge commissions at each stage, and lots more money was made on the three-stage foreign exchange conversions from one currency to another. What made it especially profitable was that a time-lag was built into the transactions, so that all remittances could be held back to play the gold market in Bangkok, then the gold market in Hong Kong, and finally the gold market in Swatow, rolling over other people's money several times. Because Chin's patrons controlled the Teochiu Association, the Remittance Association, the Ministry of Finance, the police and the whole Thai government, who was to argue?

To handle the Hong Kong transfer and the Swatow end, Chin bought a controlling interest in the Hong Kong and Swatow Bank, located in Kowloon, and imported its manager – Chang Keng Hui – to run the whole operation from Bangkok. When the communists took over the Mainland, including Swatow, Chin changed the name of his Hong Kong operation to the Commercial Bank of Hong Kong, which sounded less parochial. It is now one of Hong Kong's biggest and richest banks.

In 1952, Chin broadened his Western-style banking operations by launching Thai Financial Syndicate (TFS), registered for lending, discounting bills, foreign exchange transactions, dealing in stocks, bonds and precious metals, and importing gold. Who should be its board chairman but Police General Phao, coincidentally deputy minister of finance, who saw to it that TFS was the only legal channel for gold imports to Thailand. TFS and Asia Trust were also the only non-banking financial organizations licensed to deal in foreign exchange.

Because Asia Trust was not a bank, it avoided fiscal regulation. Critics were told it did not qualify as a bank because it did not accept deposits.

Most Asians knew little about Western banking methods before the Second World War, because they had been excluded from using them. Their secrets were carefully guarded. During the war, the seizure of Allied banks in Thailand, and the imprisonment of their Western officers and managers, paid extraordinary dividends. A team from the Ministry of Finance spent the entire war studying the confidential records of Chartered Bank and the Hongkong and Shanghai Bank, learning all they could about Western banking techniques. They were aided by Chinese and Thai former employees of the banks, and were able to interrogate imprisoned British managers. This put the two banks at a disadvantage after the war, while giving Phin's clique exceptional inside knowledge.

Thanks to this knowledge, seven new commercial banks were started in Thailand after the war, among them Bangkok Bank, with offices in a rented two-storey building in Chinatown, downstairs from two other Chin companies. Chin was the bank's director.

Bangkok Bank started as a collaboration between the Phin clique and several other groups who needed an umbrella for their financial dealings. After only a month, Chin had to resign as director, because for him to be the owner of free-wheeling Asia Trust upstairs and director of Bangkok Bank downstairs endangered Asia Trust's freedom from banking supervision. After the 1947 *coup* when General Phao became deputy finance minister, no such pretence was necessary, and Chin resumed his public association with the bank.

Serious problems developed in 1951, because Bangkok Bank suffered a chronic lack of liquidity from being bled by its original owners. Chin was given full control to clean up its act. He brought in professional accountants and money experts from Asia Trust upstairs. The old management was sacked, and Field Marshal Phin boosted capitalization 500 per cent, gaining complete control of the bank.

Chin had been studying Western banking assiduously. He had learned that Western banks accumulated large assets and profits by attracting the small savings accounts of shopkeepers and farmers, paying low interest on these savings, then lending the money out at high rates. Chin went after small Chinese depositors aggressively by offering 3 per cent interest per month calculated daily, which was well above the norm in Thailand.

After making a tour of European banks, he then transformed Bangkok Bank's entire personality by introducing personalized accounts for bigger customers. This made such an impression on Thai and Chinese clients that many moved over from Bank of America and the Hongkong and Shanghai Bank. Overseas Chinese corporations were persuaded to move their business to Bangkok Bank, and its capitalization came to a rolling boil. When Chin could not convince them to move, General Phao found ways to be more persuasive.

To be sure, Chin was not the only Overseas Chinese businessman making use of high-level connections. No matter where they find themselves, Overseas Chinese have always found it essential to buy protection and patronage from ruling élites and senior military officers, who were willing to sit on their boards or share in their profits. Chin took pains to make it seem that he was only cultivating connections like everyone else, but he was widely regarded at the time as General Phao's main business agent and his chief spokesman in Chinese circles. While Police General Phao was a director of Asia Trust, and chairman of Thai Financial Syndicate, another son-in-law of Field Marshal Phin and an aide of General Phao served as their proxies on the board of Bangkok Bank. Chin had become Phao's chief business agent and banker.

With the police general and the field marshal as major shareholders, and the Commerce Ministry providing large deposits, Bangkok Bank was positioned to open its first overseas branches in Hong Kong in 1954 and Tokyo in 1955. Branches in Singapore and London followed in 1957.

Eyeing all this jealously was the rival faction of General Sarit. Although General Phao and General Sarit were both members of the junta, the army general despised the police general. As a prudent banker, Chin was careful not to exclude General Sarit's faction totally. Another director of Bangkok Bank was one of Sarit's closest aides.

Each faction owned newspapers, so Chin's ties to Phao began to draw veiled criticism. A Member of Parliament charged that an opium deal was financed by an 'influential person' using gold bars from Bangkok Bank. It was alleged that 200 kilos of opium had been obtained by General Phao under the pretence of seizure, and the 'reward' to those who told him where to find it was said to have been paid into offshore accounts in gold by Chin Sophonpanich. Sarit's newspaper said: 'A major banking merchant, who was one of the players, departed overseas with money to deposit in foreign banks. Others involved in the incident include influential people in uniform.'

Another scandal broke when General Phao proposed bypassing major currency printer Thomas de la Rue in Britain, and printing Thailand's banknotes locally, which would allow him to manufacture all the money he wished. Chin Sophonpanich was alleged to be Phao's collaborator in the scheme. Sarit's newspaper sneered: 'At the forefront of this activity is a businessman who was of Chinese nationality but later became Thai. He has connections with a bank and the opium trade.'

It was in this way that Sarit used Chin to embarrass and weaken Phao. Chin's defenders insisted that he would never have anything to do with irregular banknotes. They raised no such defence about his alleged involvement in the drug trade. In those days, so many influential people in Thailand were involved with opium traffic that it would have seemed gauche to raise eyebrows. Counterfeiting was another matter entirely. Money was serious.

As we've seen, Phao's police were Thailand's biggest domestic drug traffickers, moving major shipments of opium and heroin in collaboration with the Teochiu syndicates. The border police escorted KMT opium caravans from Burma to police warehouses in Chiengmai, then by train or police aircraft to Bangkok. There it was loaded onto cargo vessels and escorted offshore by the marine police to freighters headed for Taiwan or Hong Kong.

If the opium was for domestic consumption, the border police 'ambushed' the smugglers at the border, and took the load to Bangkok, where they collected a government reward of one-eighth of the retail value. The opium then vanished. Phao personally led some of these staged gunbattles. After the 'capture' of 20 tons of opium in July 1955, Phao authorized a reward of $1,200,000 and hurried to the Finance Ministry, where he signed the cheque. Next, he delivered the reward personally to the 'informant' himself. Phao then claimed that most of the 20 tons had been dumped at sea and that what remained would be sold to pharmaceutical companies to recover the reward money.*

---

* Some time later, I was having lunch in Bangkok with Prince Jimmy Yang of Kokang State, which produces the world's finest opium. Kokang was just east of the Shweli Valley where I spent my childhood. During the season, the hills were mauve with opium poppies. Jimmy was an old friend. His family had ruled Kokang for generations. His sister Olive, known far and wide as 'Miss Hairylegs', commanded the Kokang State Army with a magnum revolver strapped to her hip. She was also well known for her love affair with a chubby Burmese actress.

Since 1962, when Burma became a military dictatorship, many ethnic leaders like Prince Jimmy had to go underground or into exile, and supported their rebel forces by collaborating with the KMT opium armies. Once, Jimmy had to flee for his life and ended up flat broke in Paris, living for a year in a tiny *chambre de bonne* in the Chinese quarter, nearly starving. Now he was prosperous again.

I asked Jimmy if any of General Phao's 20 tons had really been dumped in the ocean.

'Oh, yes! Oh, yes!' Jimmy laughed, looking up moonfaced from a bowl of rice noodles and chicken coconut curry. 'All 20 tons was dumped into the ocean – but luckily there was a ship in the way. Not an ounce got wet.'

Phao's greed now had become so public that even his father-in-law, Field Marshal Phin, finally turned on him. Phao was relieved of his post as deputy minister of finance. General Sarit's newspaper led the attack, accusing Phao of being a CIA puppet. Sea Supply Corporation was said to have participated actively in Phao's drug trafficking. Prime Minister Phibun also denounced Phao's close ties to Taiwan: 'The Kuomintang causes too much trouble,' Phibun said. 'They trade in opium and cause Thailand to be blamed in the United Nations.'

Early one morning in September 1957, tanks from Sarit's First Division moved into traditional *coup* positions. Phao was allowed to leave for Switzerland, while Phibun fled to Japan. The operational independence of Phao's national police was ended, and hundreds of American CIA agents were thrown out of Thailand.

Sarit made himself a field marshal, appointed his crony General Thanom as prime minister, and another crony, General Praphat, as minister of the interior.

At Bangkok Bank, Chin worried that Sarit might simply kill him, take over his bank, and loot it. One of Sarit's followers, a member of the board of the bank, told Chin it might be simpler to resign immediately and name him chairman. After giving the matter some thought, Chin outsmarted them all.

He invited the new interior minister, General Praphat, over for a conversation. His selection of Praphat was said to have been influenced by a Chinese fortune-teller who told him 'the chairman of the bank should be a short, fat person.' Because he resembled the cartoon character, the CIA had given Praphat the codename 'Porky'. He was tough and resourceful, with his own large following. Not even Sarit was likely to challenge anything Praphat did.

During their private conversation, the banker and the general reached an accommodation, and the following day it was announced that General Praphat had been named the bank's new chairman. Whatever it cost, Chin had a new protector. But this did not make him bulletproof.

Sarit was furious. When Chin went to Sarit's mansion (without the usual basket of fruit) to explain Praphat's appointment, the field marshal would not receive him. The message was painfully clear. Prudently, Chin caught the next plane for Hong Kong and five years in self-exile.

In Chin's absence, Sarit's government became just as deeply involved in drugs, although they went about it in a different way, letting others move the heroin while the army and police provided a very expensive military escort.

With Chin out of sight, but the interior minister in charge, Bangkok Bank's fortunes continued to improve, with sixteen domestic branches, four overseas, and declared assets of nearly fifty million dollars.

During his five years of exile, Chin was based in Kowloon, running his Commercial Bank of Hong Kong. Since Mao's victory in 1949, the Teochiu leadership had shifted its global headquarters there from Swatow. In Kowloon, Chin groomed Robin Chan, his eldest son by his first marriage, to take over management of Commercial Bank, and his younger son, who used the Thai name Chatri Sophonpanich, to take over Bangkok Bank.

During his years in Hong Kong, Chin strengthened his Teochiu connections at the source, rose high in the ranks of the Teochiu leadership, and learned much about modern banking methods, computers, telecommunications, and offshore finance. After Marshal Sarit died of natural causes in 1963, Chin waited a few weeks for the body to get cold, then returned to Thailand. It was agreed that General Praphat would remain chairman of Bangkok Bank, but Chin would resume his role as chief executive officer. They worked in harness for the next twenty years as powerbroker and moneyman.

To enhance the international leverage of Bangkok Bank and his Commercial Bank of Hong Kong, Chin arranged to link them to all Teochiu banking nodes in Asia and the West, starting with Singapore and Taiwan. As one of the new leaders of an increasingly high-tech global Teochiu community, he became a financial ambassador, travelling to the Philippines, Malaysia, Singapore and Indonesia, cultivating rich Overseas Chinese who were not Teochiu, such as Indonesian magnate Liem Sioe Liong, a Hokchia. To pursue his own commercial goals, Liem had long collaborated with Teochiu maritime traders throughout the archipelago. He and Chin had much in common. They were both bankers and dollar billionaires. With such vast sums of money, both had a need to keep their personal assets salted offshore. Chin was one of the first to bridge the ancient gap of enmity between dialect groups when he and Liem became friends and lent each other millions of dollars, to cover occasional lapses in liquidity. The cross- tribal collaboration had major significance for world banking by bringing about offshore financial linkages between big Overseas Chinese institutions such as Chin's Bangkok Bank and Liem's First-Pacific.

The strategy of the Teochiu leadership was to create their own multinational banking network around the world, with their own satellite communications. The financial conglomerate built around Bangkok Bank, Commercial Bank of Hong Kong, and other sub-sidiaries and components of the Sophonpanich clan became a giant Teochiu *kongsi*, tied together by interlocking directorships. Its patriarch was the chubby kid with the grade school education who turned out to be a financial genius. Now that he was a banking mogul, honours poured in. In Thailand, Chin became chairman of the Chao-yang Hsien Association, the richest *hsien* association of the richest Overseas Chinese tribe. He also became president of the umbrella organization, the Teochiu Association of Thailand. In Kowloon, he was named permanent chairman of Hong Kong's separate Teochiu Chamber of Commerce. All of this plainly identified him as one of the five most powerful Teochiu in the world, if not number one.

After Chin's death in 1988, following a long illness, management of the bank was inherited by his son, Chatri. Despite ups and downs, in 1993 Bangkok Bank was named one of the world's five most profitable banks by a British credit-rating agency. By 1995, with grandson Chartsiri at the helm, Bangkok Bank had completely outgrown its origins and had matured into a world-class institution. As one of Thailand's two biggest corporations, top ranked for financial soundness, it had assets amounting to one quarter of Thailand's GDP, four hundred domestic branches and more than twenty offices overseas. Its first branch in China was opened in Chin's hometown, as part of the billion-dollar development of Shantou, the Mainland's Special Economic Zone at Swatow. This was a fitting monument to an extraordinary rags-to-riches career. Perhaps an even greater monument was the fact that during Chin's lifetime, Washington, for all its backstage grumbling, never got up the courage to publicly accuse him of anything. Drug Enforcement Agency staff working in the embassy across the street from Chin's mansion complained bitterly, but were kept busy chasing small fry. How could anyone point fingers when General Phao himself had been America's great ally?

Meanwhile, in Indonesia, Chin's banking friend, Liem Sioe Liong, was doing very nicely for himself as well . . .

CHAPTER 14

WHERE THE WHALES PLAY

INDONESIANS ARE LIKE TINY PLANKTON IN A WARM SEA WHERE the great whales bathe. They find it reassuring that the biggest whales – President Suharto's family and friends – swallow nearly everything, after running it through their krill strainers. To them, that means everything is not swallowed by the Overseas Chinese. The role of the Chinese in the islands is exactly opposite to that in Thailand, but the result is the same. Instead of the Chinese controlling the economy and the army providing protection in return for kickbacks, as they do in Thailand, in Indonesia the army controls all commerce, while the Chinese run it for them in return for kickbacks. Here Chinese are not the army's unwilling victims but its eager bedmates; there is no argument over who gets to be on top, which is important for the army's prestige.

Without the Chinese, their management savvy, and their international connections, the Indonesian army would quickly have gone bankrupt, and they know it. Commercial competence is not in their arsenal. Together, the army and the Chinese have become fabulously rich.

In Jakarta they have a word for the intensely clever Chinese who enrich army officers in return for commercial favours: *cukong*. President

Suharto's dear friend, the Chinese banker Liem Sioe Liong, is the *cukong* of *cukongs*. Indonesia's modern history would be totally different without Liem. In the 1940s, when Suharto was a rebel officer fighting the Dutch, Liem and other Chinese businessmen helped smuggle arms, medicines and supplies to the rebel forces, and as the rebel army took over Dutch businesses they taught Suharto and his fellow officers to appreciate the traditional Chinese commercial practices of innovative financing and creative accounting, the value of personal offshore reserves and the importance of losing – or seeming to lose – great sums of money. Since then, Indonesian generals have developed a worldwide reputation for catastrophic financial losses, while rarely being scolded. Astronomers might cite this as evidence of the existence of a Black Hole.

Delegations now arrive from military regimes in other countries such as Burma, hoping to learn how the Indonesian army makes the Chinese equation work so miraculously. They would be better off asking the Chinese, for only the chauffeur knows how to drive. Many Asian countries are frightened of China's future ambitions, and are nervous about the growing economic power of the Overseas Chinese, yet nothing seems to reduce their dependence upon the Chinese. Just the reverse. Already, the big Overseas Chinese financiers are essentially nationless. National governments around the Pacific Rim must cater to them, not the other way around. Suharto's Indonesia is a classic case.

Most Chinese who came to Java before the nineteenth century were Hokkien traders from Amoy, the network once led by Coxinga. Teochiu and Hakka dialect migrants clustered on the bigger islands of Sumatra and Borneo – mostly Hakka in Borneo, mostly Teochiu in Sumatra – smuggling, running gold-mining *kongsi*, working as coolies on estates, or becoming small merchants. Indonesia is a smuggler's paradise. It is the biggest country in South East Asia, with 13,667 islands sprawling over 780,000 square miles, across one-eighth of the earth's circumference. Some twelve thousand of these islands are uninhabited and unpatrolled. Historically, the islands have been important way-stations for Teochiu rice and opium-smuggling junks bound from Siam to Sumatra and onward to Swatow.

In the past, rival sultans ruled different islands, with Arab, Indian and Chinese commercial support. By the time the Dutch arrived and began knitting the islands together into a single colony, the Chinese were in complete control of commerce. Although the Dutch forced the Chinese out of some fields, like a squeezed balloon the Chinese expanded into others. They didn't mind who held the cow as long as they milked it. Chinese served the Dutch as *compradors*, leased the rights to collect tolls and customs duty, took over retail trade and distribution, ran pawnshops, gambling clubs and opium dens. They lent money at high rates to native (*pribumi*) farmers and batik makers, and when the *pribumi* defaulted, gained control of farm production and cottage industries. In defence, the batik traders formed a militant protection society, the Islamic Trading Union, which burned down Chinese shops. The society was banned by the Dutch, but reappeared as the Islamic Union, with two and a half million followers. Its political wing was the Indonesia Nationalist Party (PNI) led by charismatic Bung Sukarno, who became Indonesia's first president.

Because the Chinese were despised and resented, they organized their own *kongsi* with private armies of ten thousand or more in the gold- and diamond-mines of Borneo, and on plantations throughout the islands. The Dutch tried to destroy the *kongsi*, but only forced their private armies underground – their natural habitat. Many Chinese were heavily involved in inter-island trade, which the Dutch naturally regarded as smuggling. But in the fight for independence from colonial rule, smuggling and blockade-running were noble pursuits that became part of heroic legends. Such was the case with Suharto and Liem, and many others.

The first of the big nineteenth-century Chinese trading empires in Indonesia was Kian Gwan (Source of Prosperity), founded in 1863 by Oei Tiong Ham, a Hokchiu immigrant at Semarang in Central Java. He controlled the world sugar market through branches on five continents, then diversified into rubber, shipping and finance, and his success drew Chinese to Semarang like fruit bats to a mango tree.

Semarang was founded in the early 1400s by one of Admiral Cheng Ho's navigators, who had been put ashore because he was ill. Thousands of Chinese migrants followed, mostly Hokchiu from Foochow.

The next Chinese fortunes there grew out of clove-flavoured cigarettes called *kretek*. This was only a cottage industry until the 1920s, when a *pribumi* started a *kretek* factory employing ten thousand people at Kudus, near Semarang. Chinese quickly moved into the *kretek* business and put it on an industrial scale.

Soon afterward, there arrived a twenty-year-old migrant named Liem Sioe Liong, from the port of Fooching. People there speak Hokchia, a subgroup of the Hokchiu. When Hokchia speakers go overseas, they tend to cluster. Today, thanks in large part to Liem, the Hokchia are one of the wealthiest groups of Chinese in the world. Many are in textiles, where they have their own *kongsi*, the Yu Yong, with its own secret army.

Although it is always said that Liem arrived a penniless illiterate, in fact his clan was already among the richest in Semarang, where one out of every eight Chinese was a Liem. They all got together regularly to arrange business deals at their big Liem ancestral temple, built in 1881. Young Liem might have been personally poor at first, but the Liem clan was insurance against starvation for anyone with the superglue trust of *shinyung*.

Liem joined his elder brother, who had a small peanut oil business, and began diversifying. Soon they began supplying cloves to *kretek* factories. Their trade secret was to import cheaper cloves from the great starfish-shaped island of Celebes, where Dutch clove growers were folding up and their plantations were coming under Chinese control. Lower costs were guaranteed by Chinese inter-island trading networks whose fleets of cargo junks were able to pass through colonial Dutch tariff barriers as if they were invisible. It was Liem's shrewd business sense, his thorough knowledge of these traditional maritime channels, and his exceptional Chinese connections throughout East and South East Asia that led to his historic partnership with Suharto.

Suharto was born in 1921, five years after Liem, in a village of bamboo houses near Jogjakarta in Central Java, a hundred miles south of Semarang. Javanese like to think he was really fathered by a sultan of Jogjakarta. Whatever the case, the next sultan (Hamengkubuwono IX) was like a brother to Suharto and later served as one of his vice presidents.

Suharto had a conservative Islamic education, and was so reserved as a boy that he showed no emotion. This served him well.

When Hitler overran the Netherlands in 1940, the Dutch government in the Indies opened the colonial army roster to Javanese. Suharto enlisted, but three months after Pearl Harbor, the Dutch surrendered. Suharto and thousands of others were transferred to the Japanese-sponsored Volunteer Army, PETA. From there, he was sent to military school, graduating just as the Japanese occupation collapsed.

In 1945, before the Dutch could return, the independence leader Bung Sukarno declared Indonesia independent. Hurrying home, Suharto found Jogjakarta in rebellion. The young ninth sultan – his friend if not brother – declared his territory part of the free Republic of Indonesia. When Allied troops arrived to keep order until the Dutch returned, fighting broke out, and Suharto took part, gaining a reputation for cool-headed leadership. But he was less interested in politics than he was in putting his military forces on a firm financial footing with the help of sympathetic Chinese entrepreneurs and their offshore trading networks.

Many ordinary Chinese had suffered terribly in Java during the war. Those who thrived were the foxes who smuggled rice, drugs and strategic commodities, which they sold to the Japanese at a fat profit. There was no interruption in coastal junk traffic on the South China Sea, the Bay of Bengal or the Java Sea. Tens of thousands of tons of black-market rice from Thailand and Vietnam were smuggled to Indonesia by the Teochiu with Japanese collusion. In Asia, the difference between underground and underworld became permanently blurred. Among the leading Chinese merchants in Java at war's end was clove king Liem Sioe Liong, who was secretly helping the independence movement.

When the Allies withdrew in 1946, the Dutch were only back in control of major coastal cities and towns in Java, Sumatra and the Outer Islands, leaving the interior to the rebels, who quickly seized abandoned Dutch plantations and rural enterprises. Rebel officers also found themselves in possession of great warehouses crammed with commodities abandoned earlier by the Japanese. The rebels were unable to administer or to market such a super-abundance. They lacked the experience and networks for international distribution. Suharto travelled to Semarang to make a deal with Liem. He proposed that the Chinese take over responsibility for the management, exporting and marketing of these commodities, while the army retained ownership and provided licences, permits and protection. When the Dutch could be driven out of the remaining cities, the Indonesian army would seize the rest of their factories, companies and other assets, and the arrangement with the Chinese would be extended on a case-by-case basis. Essentially, they were offering to lease the Indonesian economy to the Chinese.

Liem realized that these army officers would be running Indonesia in the future, and his survival and prosperity could depend on their good will. Their prosperity, on the other hand, could be guaranteed by his intervention. He agreed to the arrangement and – as a grand gesture – offered personally to supply Suharto's forces with food, clothing, medicine and arms. The guns could be obtained through Chinese channels from warehouses in Singapore. While the Dutch might regard it as arms smuggling, the independence struggle was making the new Indonesian army a law unto itself.

When independence came in 1949, Suharto was given command of the Diponegoro Division, and controlled all Central Java with the help of his chief commercial officer, Major Humardani. For them, the future was very bright, but not for all their countrymen.

Historically Javanese society was divided between Muslim *santri* landowners, and landless *abangan*, who were only nominally Muslim. The wealthy *santri* identified with the army, while the poor *abangan* identified with the Indonesian Communist Party (PKI). In the Solo River plain in East Java, at the time of independence, clashes occurred between landowners and land-hungry peasants, resulting in the formation of a breakaway PKI government based in Madiun. Although some twenty-five thousand Indonesian soldiers sided with the PKI locally, they were completely flattened by the well-armed Siliwangi Division rushed in from West Java. Many thousands were slaughtered and thirty-five thousand imprisoned in brutal concentration camps. Madiun was the first merciless act of repression that established the Indonesian army's signature. The Indonesian army may be incompetent commercially, but it is not incompetent militarily. Everybody, without exception, is afraid of it. This repression at Madiun created a blood lust between right and left, rich and poor, that has remained in the Javanese personality ever since. In Indonesia, poverty means you are subnormal and subversive.

During the first years of independence, there was a boom for Indonesian exports because of the Korean War. Its end brought an economic slump. When the honeymoon was over, the Western concept of multi-party adversarial democracy proved unworkable in Indonesia, as it did elsewhere in Asia. The chaotic election of 1955 resulted in the collapse of parliamentary democracy and the start of 'Guided Democracy' in which the president, Bung Sukarno, did the guiding and the only thing democratic was hunger. Two years later, he declared martial law.

Looking for ways to paper over its failed promises, Bung Sukarno's government made the leap into deficit financing and distracted its critics with anti-Western rhetoric. The Indonesia army was not happy about Sukarno's growing romance with the left. When the United Nations rebuffed Indonesia's claims to Dutch West Irian in 1957, Sukarno encouraged leftist trade unions to take over all Dutch companies in Indonesia, thus getting the jump on the army. The army, which had exceptional powers under martial law (and did not like leftist anything), took the Dutch firms away from the unions and kept them for itself. This fulfilled the army's long-term economic-seizure strategy and gave it a huge independent source of income and patronage. Executive positions in corporations became available for officers. These officers could keep their posts in executive suites only if the army stayed on top. So the army – already protector of Islam and guardian of the *status quo* – became intensely politicized, and developed its own political and economic agenda in direct opposition to the leftist backers of Bung Sukarno.

Each army division had its own financial office fully occupied in setting up businesses. Lucrative relationships developed between senior officers and Chinese *cukong*, who ran these companies for the army. Officers contributed political connections, approvals, licences and franchises. The Chinese provided money, management skills and import-export connections with Hokchiu, Hakka, Hokkien or Teochiu syndicates, plus discreet offshore-banking facilities. The Chinese were indispensable. Nothing could function without them, especially the new army-owned enterprises. Anybody could concoct a new business, but only the Chinese could make it work.

In the mid-1950s, many centrifugal forces were threatening to break up Indonesia. Sukarno faced resistance from former Dutch colonial army units left behind in strategic areas, and native guerrilla forces in the Outer Islands. Rebellions began that were secretly backed by President Eisenhower in an effort to swat down the leftist gadfly Sukarno.

Sukarno and his supporters were driven deeper into the leftist camp by Washington's hostility, but the Indonesian army remained locked in its lucrative embrace with extremely conservative Chinese whose emotional ties and financial linkages were to Singapore, Hong Kong, Bangkok, Taipei and Tokyo, not to Beijing. Many of the Chinese in Taiwan also were Hokchiu originally from Foochow, so they had strong family and dialect bonds with the big and prosperous Hokchiu community in Java led by Liem. Taiwan recognized this opportunity and scurried to woo the Indonesian army, just as Sukarno stepped up his romance with Beijing. Tokyo, with so much oil at stake, was more subtle.

As a kingpin of the army-*cukong* accord, Liem Sioe Liong was now riding high. Diversifying out of Central Java, he founded Bank Windu Kencana, bought Bank Central Asia, and established his corporate offices in Jakarta's Chinatown. When the Indonesian clove industry came to a standstill because of the US-backed rebellion in the Celebes, Liem switched to importing African cloves from Zanzibar and Madagascar.

Officers of Suharto's Diponegoro Division were now running factories, trading companies and plantations, and they directed the earnings back to their own commands, bypassing the leftist government in Jakarta. Major Humardani, head of the division's financial section, set up a general trading venture and a shipping company as a smuggling cover.

In 1959, Colonel Suharto was denounced for smuggling and relieved of command, but instead of dismissal he was sent to staff college in Bandung. A few months later, promoted to brigadier-general, he became first deputy to the army chief-of-staff, in charge of military intelligence, and was given command of a new rapid-deployment force, KOSTRAD, that had its own black-operations section which dealt in political manipulation. If there is a moral to be found in Suharto's military career up to this point, it is that financial skills were crucial for survival and advancement in the officer corps.

By the 1960s, President Sukarno's health was beginning to fade, along with his legendary virility. Doctors have said the president's kidney trouble was aggravated by his obsession with very young girls. Biologists at the research centre in the vast botanical gardens behind Bogor Palace confided that the president was constantly ordering them to search the archipelago for new kinds of aphrodisiacs. They said the real reason he was unable to achieve a normal erection was because the army had him by the balls.

Under Guided Democracy, power had three legs: the army, Bung Sukarno and the PKI. During the many years since the slaughter at Madiun, misery among Indonesian farmers and workers had regenerated the PKI, now the largest Marxist party outside the Communist Bloc. In return for the mass adulation the party was able to create in the streets, Bung Sukarno gave in more and more to radical PKI initiatives. His dependence on the PKI was encouraged by Foreign Minister Subandrio, an opportunist of the witch doctor variety with a relentlessly ambitious wife, who played the PKI against the army.

Nobody knew how much longer the Bung would last. The army and the PKI developed contingency plans to neutralize each other the moment Sukarno was gone.

The army's universal commercial activities kept soldiers happy, but did little to improve conditions for civilians. Indonesia was a rich country impoverished by mismanagement. Success was measured in kickbacks. Staple foods were in short supply. Inflation was Argentine. To distract the population, President Sukarno contrived a new confrontation, this time with the Federation of Malaysia, composed of the former British territories of Malaya, Singapore and North Borneo. He denounced the Federation as an 'imperialist plot', and mobs stormed the British embassy. In protest at Malaysia's seating on the Security Council, Indonesia withdrew from the United Nations. American and British companies in Indonesia were taken over. Beijing noisily supported Jakarta. The idea of an alliance between Red China and leftist Indonesia caused a lot of adrenaline to flow in Washington and London.

The army did not pursue the Malaysian confrontation vigorously, however, for the simple reason that it was bad for business. General Suharto's black operations chief, Ali Murtopo, secretly contacted Malaysian and British officials and went to Bangkok to negotiate with them, as well as holding secret talks with Taipei and Tokyo.

By 1965, the PKI and the army were circling each other warily like judo novices, each convinced that the other was plotting its downfall. Rumours of foreign conspiracy were fuelled when Foreign Minister Subandrio revealed a draft diplomatic cable allegedly written by

British Ambassador Sir Andrew Gilchrist to the Foreign Office, which implied that some sort of 'operation' was being planned by the British and US embassies, and 'our local army friends' were involved.

Army chief General Yani denied rumours of a so-called Council of Generals involved in such a plot – within the army, Yani's circle was regarded as particularly corrupt and self-indulgent – but many people were persuaded by the conspiracy rumours, including a member of the presidential bodyguard, Lieutenant Colonel Untung. On more than one occasion during the eight months between March and October 1965, Untung overheard the president exclaim bitterly about an army plot, and wish aloud that somebody would rid him of Yani and his clique once and for all. At one point, the president even asked Lieutenant Colonel Untung if he was 'prepared, if ordered, to take action against the generals.' Untung said he was. Something had to be done urgently, but exactly what and when was left pregnantly vague.

Compared to Sukarno, who was a house-of-mirrors, Untung was a straight-up fellow. Untung consulted only members of his own army cabal, most of them in Central Java. No action was taken until the last day of September 1965, when Untung and his friends set out to kidnap and, if necessary, kill the seven generals, to block the conspiracy. He took it for granted that the president would endorse his actions once they had been carried out successfully.

However, evasion was such a fundamental part of Sukarno's nature that, after tossing all these balls up in the air, he let them come down on their own. He liked to nudge destiny, not pre-empt it. Part showman, part shaman, even the generals were spooky of him.

Several days before, a fortune-teller had warned General Suharto that it would be wise to spend Thursday, 30 September 1965, in a place where two waters joined. Suharto knew a perfect spot, not far from Jakarta, where a small river emptied into the South China Sea. His family could enjoy the beach while he taught his son how to fish from the riverbank. Suharto spent Thursday morning inspecting troops brought to Jakarta for the big parade to be held on Armed Forces Day, 5 October. At his modern house in the plush suburb of Menteng, his wife, Tien, gathered their children, while servants put a hot picnic in a multi-level aluminium tiffin-carrier. On their way to the beach, somebody knocked over the tiffin-carrier, and the scalding sauces splashed over his son's bare legs. The boy howled all the way to the army hospital. The general followed his trolley, then stayed by his bed. In the corridor, he encountered Colonel Latief, one of the men preparing to purge the general staff that night. Suharto was not on their list.

The decision to proceed with the kidnappings was only made late in the afternoon of 30 September. The plan was for Colonel Untung to contact the president and tell him that the kidnappings would take place before dawn, so he should withdraw to Halim Air Base outside Jakarta, where he could be flown to safety if necessary. Battalions 454 and 530 from Central Java would seize downtown installations, including the radio station. The palace would be secured by Brigadier General Supardojo, who had flown down secretly from Borneo to take part. When all seven generals had been dealt with, Sukarno would be asked to go on the radio and assure Indonesians that it had been necessary.

Colonel Untung could not find the president. Bung Sukarno had decided, on the spur of the moment, that he urgently needed the ministrations of his Japanese wife, and wandered off without telling the palace guard where he would be.

The plotters assembled their strike force at Crocodile Hole on the edge of Halim Air Base, seven miles south of Jakarta. Most were from the presidential bodyguard. Despite the planned show of force in the city centre, the conspirators were so undermanned that the actual kidnapping of the generals was left to Untung's subordinate, First Lieutenant Arief. He divided the strike force into seven squads, then also stayed behind while his subordinate Second Lieutenant Mukidjan, took charge. It was not an auspicious beginning.

The squad assigned to General Yani reached his house at 4 a.m., and took up positions while Lieutenant Mukidjan and a sergeant told the guards they had an urgent message for the general from the president. The guards were overpowered. Inside, they found Yani's seven-year-old son, Eddy, up early, and sent him to awaken his father. As Yani emerged from his glass-doored bedroom, they told him he was needed at the palace. When they would not let him change his pyjamas, Yani knocked the lieutenant down and slammed the glass door shut behind him. A burst of Sten fire through the glass killed Yani instantly. His body was dragged out and thrown in a truck.

The second was easier. General Soeprapto answered the door himself, and was dragged away in his sarong.

General Parman, chief of intelligence, was accustomed to the president summoning him at odd hours. He changed clothes, but before he left, he whispered to his wife to get in touch immediately with Yani. Yani was already dead.

General Soetojo was tricked into opening his bedroom door, tied up and thrown into a truck.

General Pandjaitan tried to fight them off, but his Sten gun jammed, and he was shot dead.

General Harjono also was shot.

The one remaining general was Defence Minister Nasution. Not one of Yani's circle, Nasution was a hero of the independence struggle, and he lived in a house surrounded by the villas of diplomats. His guards were deceived and overwhelmed, and hearing noises, Mrs Nasution opened her bedroom door and was startled to find an armed man facing her. She slammed the door. There was a burst of Sten fire through it. From another bedroom, Nasution's sister appeared in panic, holding the general's youngest child, Ade Irma. When she tried to cross to Nasution's bedroom the marauders opened fire, hitting the little girl and wounding her aunt.

Mrs Nasution led the general out back to a wall, where he clambered over and fell into the garden of the Iraqi ambassador, breaking his ankle. He dragged himself into the bushes and lay hidden.

In a pavilion at the far end, the general's elder daughter sought refuge with Nasution's adjutant, Lieutenant Pierre Tendean. She hid under his bed while he grabbed his rifle and ran out. In the dark, he was mistaken for Nasution, wounded, and hauled off.

Three generals dead, three captured, one escaped, an adjutant kidnapped by mistake, and a child dying.

The raiders drove back to Crocodile Hole, where they were awaited by their commanders and a throng of young peasant men, women and girls brought in from the countryside months earlier by the PKI for para-military training at the air base. Street rabble and village girls, they did not know who the prisoners were. They were told they were traitors.

The three corpses were dumped down a well. The three generals who were still alive were kicked and beaten, then shot and thrown down the well. Nasution's aide, Lieutenant Tendean, was given special treatment. One overzealous PKI cadre produced several straight razors and ordered girls to take turns slashing Tendean. Later reports of atrocities, eyes being gouged out and sexual organs sliced off, had to do with the young lieutenant. Tendean's remains were then thrown down the well and the hole filled with trash and dirt. It was dawn.

At 5.30 a.m. General Suharto was awakened by worried neighbours who had heard shooting, then one of his staff drove up with news of the kidnappings. With Yani dead and others missing, Suharto assumed command. He drove himself to KOSTRAD headquarters opposite the presidential palace, overlooking the central square filled with heavily armed Battalions 454 and 530. In his office, he began making phone calls.

It was only at 6 a.m. on 1 October that President Sukarno finally was tracked to his Japanese wife's bedroom. When Colonel Untung told him about the killings, Sukarno balked at giving him the ringing endorsement he desperately needed.

To avoid attention, the president was driven to Halim Air Base in a Volkswagen Beetle. At a house on the base, President Sukarno, his friend Air Vice Marshal Dhani, and PKI chief D. N. Aidit were passive bystanders. They had all been asleep in unlocked houses, like the generals. Aidit ordered his party to remain calm.

Downtown, General Suharto was piecing events together. Several of his phone calls went to Liem Sioe Liong, seeking advice. KOSTRAD officers were arriving for normal duty. At 8.00 a.m., Suharto learned that Defence Minister Nasution was in hiding at a safe house where his broken ankle had been set in a cast. Nasution was brought to KOSTRAD, where he and Suharto lived around the clock for the next three months.

It took a while for Suharto to realize that he was now the most powerful senior general in Indonesia, aside from the defence minister, and that little stood in the way of his taking over the government himself, if he proceeded with his characteristic prudence.

Emissaries from the president reached KOSTRAD and told Suharto that the president wanted someone else to assume command of the armed forces. Suharto sent back the message, 'No!' The navy and police were now with him.

Suharto sent those that had worked before with Batallions 454 and 530 into the square to talk the troops into standing down and having breakfast. The sun was hot, but it took all day. By 6.00 p.m., the troops in the square were wolfing down food. The centre of Jakarta was cleared without bloodshed.

Suharto passed word to President Sukarno that he should leave Halim Air Base for some neutral place, such as his palace at Bogor. He complied. When the president's plane was gone, General Suharto's forces attacked the air base, which quickly capitulated.

The bodies of the missing generals and Nasution's aide were discovered two days later. Scuba divers brought the remains up from the well a piece at a time, while television crews conveyed it all live. Suharto's propaganda staff went to great lengths to let Indonesians know that this was the grisly work of the PKI, which they said had been trying to seize power. The official line was that all the victims had been brutally tortured and mutilated by some two thousand communist cadres, including crazed members of the PKI's women's auxiliary. These women and girls, the army said, had carried out demonic rituals, including gouging out the generals' eyes and slicing off their genitals with straight razors.

Army newspapers carried details as part of a witchhunt to destroy the Communist Party once and for all. Foreign journalists got all the help they wanted. The Armed Forces Day celebrations on 5 October became a heroes' funeral. General Nasution, whose little girl was near death, gave a bitter oration. The country was in shock, and the shock was manipulated calmly from KOSTRAD headquarters. Bung Sukarno did not attend the funeral, a public-relations gaffe that permanently damaged his mystique.

This chance was not to be wasted. The army rounded up thousands of communists and suspected leftists. Ordinary people were encouraged to arrest and kill anyone they thought might be sympathetic to the PKI, unleashing communal violence across the archipelago. Much of the carnage was provoked by General Nasution, enraged by the death of his little girl, Ade Irma: 'There must be no more hesitation . . . this communist group has committed murder, torture, terror and treason against our state and government.' Later, his rage cooled, but the murders went on and on, including many little girls like Ade Irma. It was many months before all the killings ended.

In the Solo River plain, a PKI stronghold since the Madiun affair

years earlier, soldiers armed *santri* Muslims and sent them out to kill
communists, most of them dirt-poor *abangan*. But it was not
exclusively a Muslim vendetta. Roman Catholic students left their
dormitories at night to join in the execution of truckloads of
'communists' rounded up earlier in the day. Many whose names were
on PKI rolls had no idea what communism was. They only knew it as
an organization of poor people. Its membership included many
teachers, and when the bloodbath ended, forty thousand teachers had
been killed or imprisoned. Whole villages thought to be communist
were given mass executions, men and women were made to kneel by
pits, thumbs wired behind their backs, then beheaded. Rivers were so
full of corpses and parts of corpses that people stopped eating
freshwater fish for fear of swallowing human carrion. On Bali,
islanders went on a rampage, provoked by Hindu priests calling for
human sacrifices. The army only intervened early in 1966. By then the
death toll had reached half a million.

In Singapore, it was easy to get the impression from the international
press that Chinese in Indonesia were the main target, and that
hundreds of thousands of Chinese were being butchered. This was part
of the army's effort to establish that the PKI, leftist Chinese, and Beijing
itself, were behind the Untung business. Many newspaper editorials
said this was the kind of punishment the Chinese fifth column and the
communists richly deserved.

In fact, relatively few Chinese were butchered, and some of that
bloodshed was provoked by KMT agitators sent from Taiwan, who
deliberately inflamed Indonesians against pro-Beijing communities in
Medan and Makassar, by shouting Maoist slogans while denouncing
Muslims in the same breath – something no Overseas Chinese survival
expert would ever do. In the Medan riots, two hundred Chinese died.

The KMT had been unusually active in Indonesia because of Bung
Sukarno's rapid drift toward Beijing, and was a discreet supporter of
General Suharto through his right-wing Chinese allies, including Liem.

Elsewhere, the Chinese were mainly targets of looting and extortion,
not homicide. It was in Bali that they suffered most from communal
violence. In Aceh and in Borneo, tens of thousands of Chinese were driven
from their homes because of tribal rivalries – not politics. A lot of Chinese
were attacked by Indonesians at the urging of rival *kongsi* and rival

dialect groups. If General Suharto was seizing this opportunity to purge Indonesia of its entire left wing, his conservative Chinese supporters were not going to miss the chance to purge their own rivals, political and otherwise. Rich Chinese left quickly for Singapore or Hong Kong, to come back when it was over. Thousands of poor Chinese fled to the Mainland aboard refugee ships sent by the PRC. By making it seem primarily an anti-Chinese bloodbath, the army used racism and anti-communism to disguise what was essentially a great wave of repression, intended to silence permanently all opposition to army rule in the islands, regardless of ethnic group.

In March 1966 – six months after Untung's fiasco – Bung Sukarno was holding a meeting of his advisers at Merdeka Palace when an aide told him that unidentified troops were surrounding the palace. Sukarno panicked and fled to Bogor, followed by Foreign Minister Subandrio and others. The troops were those of General Suharto, who had removed their patches to disguise their identity. While the smell of fear was still in the president's nose, three tough generals followed him to Bogor to spell things out. They told the president that unless he co-operated immediately, the army would remove him by force the following day. There was a lot of shouting, but they were finally able to get him to understand that in a few hours he would be killed. Then they stood over him while he signed a document transferring all presidential authority to General Suharto, although it was another twelve months before General Suharto officially became acting president of Indonesia.

After all the blood and cruelty, Indonesia's fundamental problems remained unchanged by this *coup*. While Bung Sukarno had given perks and import licences worth millions of dollars to his girlfriends and cronies, at the grassroots the problems were rice and fuel. During 1965, prices went up more than 500 per cent. Foreign trade came to a halt. Hard currency reserves evaporated. Payments on foreign debts totalled five hundred and thirty million dollars. Revenues from oil and rubber were barely four hundred million dollars. The undeniable truth was that the army had long been running the rice trade and the fuel trade, and was more on the take than Bung Sukarno. During nearly a decade in control of most commerce, the army had blamed its failures on Sukarno and the PKI. But these scapegoats were no longer available.

The army was chiefly to blame for the shortage of hard currency, because it controlled revenues from a large part of the economy, and had withheld them from the central government during its long contest with Bung Sukarno. The army had crippled the commodity market by playing games with rice and sugar; games in which the Chinese syndicates had gladly participated. The army was also mismanaging Indonesia's oil industry so that it was mysteriously misplacing billions of dollars.

Once General Suharto assumed the presidency, the army's monopoly of the Indonesian economy became unabashed, with blatant takeovers of businesses from the cronies of Bung Sukarno. In effect, the army seized all the assets of the domestic opposition, redistributed the franchises among its officers, and let them arrange their own *cukong* management. Through corporate shells and joint ventures, and huge new 'post-*coup*' infusions of Japanese, Overseas Chinese and Western capital, military officers converted licences, contracts, export credits and franchises into lush income.

The National Logistics Board (BULOG) was given monopoly control of all rice, sugar, wheat and flour, including purchasing, importing, marketing and pricing – all financed by the Bank of Indonesia. Thanks to BULOG, Indonesian rice farmers became debt-slaves like the rice farmers of Thailand. Chinese control of rice production in both countries allowed them to limit Indonesian production, pushing up prices, while scalping rice that was smuggled to Indonesia from Thailand. Indonesia got ripped both for legal and black-market supplies. Such mismanagement nearly destroyed domestic rice producers. But it enabled BULOG officials and their Chinese agents to make wild profits.

President Suharto was not entirely in the dark about BULOG's failings. One of the richest Chinese in Indonesia, Go Swie Kie, an intimate of Suharto and Liem, was BULOG's exclusive agent for the import of rice and sugar. BULOG even granted massive credits to an army-owned corporation to manufacture 'artificial' rice. Apparently, this was to be done entirely with smoke and mirrors. Although huge sums changed hands, no factory ever went into production.

Participants in even the biggest scandals were rarely scolded, much less jailed or shot. President Suharto was an exceptionally calm, self-disciplined leader, and as he matured over the decades into one of

Asia's elder statesmen, he continued to demonstrate a paternalistic affection for his military children.

Nobody could top Suharto's old army comrade General Ibnu Sutowo, who could make millions vanish in front of your eyes, then reappear in somebody else's pocket. He made ten billion dollars vanish while he was head of the state-owned Pertamina oil company in the 1970s, after which he became a consultant, advising others on his methods. Whatever became of the money nobody got mad at Ibnu.

Following the death of Ibnu's personal assistant, Haji Thahir, his widow laid claim to eighty million dollars that Haji had in his personal bank accounts at Chase Manhattan and the Hongkong and Shanghai Bank. Haji's widow said her husband had done everything with Ibnu's full knowledge, as part of the routine financial arrangements of President and Mrs Suharto and their Chinese financial adviser, Liem Sioe Liong. Multiple books had always been a part of Chinese accounting.

Suharto rarely revealed his role in any of these business deals, but he was sometimes embarrassed by the antics of his inner circle, his family or his Chinese partners. Humardani, one of the 'financial generals' who had risen through the ranks with Suharto, formed a partnership with two *cukongs* – Bob Hasan and Sukatia – to launch a shipping line in association with Japanese investors. Part of the profits from such deals were turned over to a charity run by Mrs Tien Suharto. This, in turn, led to Mrs Suharto being criticized by the Sydney *Morning Herald*, in an article on Indonesian patronage that provoked a diplomatic furore between Jakarta and Canberra.

Liem Sioe Liong, the wizard behind it all, became so fantastically rich he was outgrowing the islands. When General Suharto toppled Bung Sukarno in 1965–66, Liem was already a multimillionaire with diversified holdings. Two years later, he tightened his grip on the global clove trade by locking up 90 per cent of the output of Zanzibar and Madagascar, and then acquiring Indonesia's clove-import monopoly for companies run by himself and Suharto's half-brother. As part of the deal, Liem was guaranteed a selling price double whatever he paid in Zanzibar or Madagascar.

Liem was also given the flour and cement monopolies for Indonesia, and was granted huge government credits and export licences that enabled him to move into rubber and coffee without risking a rupiah of his own. From there he branched into textiles, car assembly, insurance, property development, timber, rubber, mining, retailing and finance, and his Bank Central Asia became one of Indonesia's largest private banks.

Unlike some *cukong* who succeeded largely because of their army connections, Liem's participation in a venture became a guarantee of solid management talent, financial soundness, and long-term strategic thinking. His durable association with President Suharto helped move Indonesia out of the postwar tourist genre of shadow puppets and onto the world stage as an increasingly major player in the future of the Pacific Rim. Coming up in Liem's footsteps were scores of other world-class conglomerates, like the Lippo Group, which are helping to drive the Asian boom. Liem is no longer merely the *cukong* of *cukongs*. He has become one of the world's wealthiest Overseas Chinese. In the 1980s, as he expanded overseas, his conglomerate ranked as a major international financial industrial group. He was listed as one of the twelve richest bankers in the world, with known assets in excess of one billion dollars. His Salim Group is by far the biggest private player in the Indonesian economy, its 1993 sales totalling at least nine billion dollars.

In a manner suitable for one of the world's wealthiest supra-nationals, Liem subcontracted most of his domestic industries, while he personally concentrated on borderless high finance. Liem's offshore corporate structure has been built around the holding company, First Pacific. Through it, he acquired California's Hibernia Bank, which took over the financing of Liem's American and European trade, and handles the three hundred and thirty million dollars per year wheat exports to Indonesia destined for Liem's Bogasari mills, which produce most of the noodles consumed in the islands.

Liem is naturally concerned about the political risks of keeping all his holdings in Indonesia when the matter of succession after Suharto is so uncertain. First Pacific gives Liem a vehicle to operate in finance and banking throughout the Pacific Rim at a time of explosive growth and the rapid emergence of the new borderless capitalist class that is largely Overseas Chinese. In addition to big capital inflows from Japan, Europe and North America, First Pacific Finance has taken substantial offshore deposits from Indonesia, the Philippines and South Korea. Some of this capital movement is linked to the succession issue.

Nobody has forgotten the fate of Bung Sukarno's cronies.

As Liem's business empire becomes fully supranational, he is less vulnerable. So far, he has avoided the requirements of the 1974 regulations requiring 30 per cent public ownership of his domestic companies. But a future government may crack down. Accordingly, First Pacific and the Salim Group are extremely secretive. Liem is sensitive about his company's big investments in Mainland China, where he has spent a hundred million dollars transforming his ancestral hometown. South East Asian politicians complain that investment is slowing down in their countries while it is rushing to China. For Overseas Chinese, this trend could become dangerous.

Nobody in Jakarta admits openly to being fearful of a drastic change after President Suharto's departure – the army will decide who rules next – but nobody is taking chances. Millionaire generals and government officials in Jakarta are seeking havens offshore. A lot of it is going into First Pacific's coffers. The Overseas Chinese are not particularly worried. They have already bought off every army faction and possible successor, and they are sitting on top of the flight capital.

It is the extreme disparity between *cukong* like Liem and the great majority of impoverished Indonesians that makes them seem like whales and plankton. There is now a McDonald's in Jakarta, but very few Indonesians earn enough each day to buy a Big Mac. Yet it is argued that without such gifted men as the *cukong*, nothing whatever would work in the islands, and the future would sit rusting in the rainforests.

CHAPTER 15

A PLACE IN THE SUN

THINGS ARE A LITTLE DIFFERENT FOR THE OVERSEAS CHINESE IN Malaysia. They're rich, but it's a nervous rich. Getting beheaded can do that to you.

In Malaysia, anti-Chinese sentiment is closer to the surface than elsewhere in South East Asia. At independence from Britain in 1957, Malays found themselves a minority in their own homeland, where Chinese made up 37 per cent of the population, Indians 11 per cent, and the last 3 per cent were a mixed bag, so together they outnumbered Malays. Ethnic paranoia has a thin skin, allergic to Chinese domination of the economy, and easily irritated by firebrands. Malays feared a complete Chinese takeover. As a scholar summed up their insecurity, 'There is no earthly reason why we should simply lie back and let the Chinese have Malaysia. Although many have been here a long time, it isn't their country. It is ours, and has been since the Chinese were living in caves in North China and we were hooting in the trees in our rain forests. They are welcome to do business here if they live elsewhere.'

So one of the richest, friendliest, prettiest countries on the Pacific

Rim, the choice of hundreds of Western companies as their Asian base, suffered a neurosis about Chinese being a fifth column. Despite Malay sensitivity on this issue, few nations in the world enjoy such a strong sense of domestic tranquillity, thanks to the affable, upbeat nature of the population – compared to brooding, excitable Java – and to the fact that Chinese in Malaysia typically mind their own business. Under tight British rule, and during early years of independence, peaceful accommodation made ethnic compromise work well here. But by the late 1960s, a new generation of Malay élite was chafing to seize power from their own old guard and to squeeze the Chinese out. They wanted to take wealth and patronage out of Chinese hands, with no certainty that this would make things work better, and no guarantee that the imagined benefits would ever trickle down to Malays in general. What they wrongly interpreted as a purely anti-Chinese pogrom in Indonesia in 1965–66, gave some aggressive but shortsighted Malay extremists the idea of provoking a similar crisis in their own country. The Chinese did not make matters easier, for traditionally they would rather bribe politicians than kiss them. At a moment of political uncertainty in 1969, a handful of chauvinists provoked an outburst of gruesome rioting by hooligans that left hundreds dead, and for the last quarter century an uneasy tension has remained just below the surface. The Chinese are never entirely certain the nightmare won't recur.

Fortunately, that tension has now begun to subside. After twenty-five years of asserting Malay predominance, political leaders are coming around to a more positive view of the mix that Malaysia needs, to carry its phenomenal economic boom into the new century. The result is that this exceptional country has steered itself clear of the reefs, and found what may be snug harbour. But not without a few harrowing moments along the way.

Malays usually blame the British and the Overseas Chinese for crippling their initiative and enterprise. Of course, the British and Chinese blamed the Malays for tropical lassitude. The colonial food chain set the British on top, the Chinese in the middle, with Malays on the bottom. The British needed the Chinese as middlemen, but they cultivated the Malay élite as a buffer between them and the lower orders. While the Chinese admired and imitated British culture, they displayed indifference, disdain and condescension towards Malays. As a result, both the British and the Chinese gave the Malays an inferiority complex, which caused deep anxieties. Vengefulness did not emerge as a national force until well after the British left, when the Chinese began to get involved in Malay politics. Abruptly, the Malay attitude towards them changed from envy to anger.

For social as well as economic reasons, most Chinese clustered in the thriving commercial centres of Penang and Kuala Lumpur, which meant that they outnumbered the Malays in these two most important locations. Selangor state, the site of the federal capital, Kuala Lumpur, was rich in tin deposits. In the late nineteenth century, Chinese tin miners had arrived and fought a six-year civil war over who could control Selangor's tin deposits. On one side was the Ghee Hin *kongsi*, mostly Hokkien. Fighting them was the Hai San *kongsi*, primarily Hakka. Eventually, the Hokkien group and its Malay allies won. This established Hokkien Chinese firmly on top in the Malay Peninsula and in the capital region. The Hakka did not get their revenge until a century later.

Furtive, sometimes bloody struggles between rival Chinese groups became part of life in Malaysia thereafter. In the richest market, Singapore, Hokkien had to share tax farming with the Teochiu, squeezing out Cantonese and Hakka altogether. In Perak state, in the north, tin mining was ruled jointly by rival Hokkien and Hakka groups. Never were their quarrels over politics, just over money.

Politics only came into it briefly in the 1930s, when KMT agents from Nanking tried to take over Malaya's Chinese guilds and associations. The KMT was so notoriously corrupt that even anti-communist Chinese resisted their embrace. During the Japanese occupation, the Communist Party of Malaya (MPC) was the only established resistance. Many in its ranks were frustrated Hakka, whose ambitions in life had been blocked by Hokkien domination of the economy. British secret agents joined in guerrilla operations with the MPC. The Japanese fought back by cultivating latent anti-Chinese sentiments among rural Malays, which after the war helped to polarize ethnic hatreds. The Malays resented Chinese war profiteering, Chinese guerrilla atrocities, and the ability of wealthy Chinese to buy their way out of Japanese forced labour battalions.

At the war's end, Chinese in the MPC tried to use constitutional means to oppose the restoration of British rule, supported by a coalition of left-wing and liberal groups. So, even before the Cold War began, communism and the Chinese became linked in Malay minds.

The British themselves forfeited every opportunity to encourage Malayan-born Chinese to see themselves as Malays. London was never interested in teaching the Chinese or the Malays to govern themselves, expecting them only to co-operate with their colonial masters. As a consequence, when Britain withdrew after the war, neither the Chinese nor the Malays were adequately prepared to govern themselves, or to work together.

At first, the British planned to create a union. The sultans would cede their jurisdiction while conferring citizenship upon all people born in Malaya or resident there for ten years, meaning Chinese and Indians would be nearly half the voting population. This distressed the Malays, who were fearful that the better-organized and economically dominant Chinese would take over the government. These fears were inaccurate. The Overseas Chinese are not even interested in Chinese politics, except as it impacts on profits. Unaccustomed to being involved in political decisions of any kind, the Chinese in Malaya foolishly did not get behind the Union plan. While the Chinese were dithering, influential Malays forced the British to agree to an alternate plan for a Federation. Under Federation, the sovereignty of the sultans would continue, and under the new constitution Malays would be given preferential treatment in all things. Citizenship would be strictly limited, and the non-elective legislative council would be dominated by Malay officials and Malay aristocrats. London acted hastily to appease them, leaving the Chinese to suffer the consequences.

The MPC tried to capitalize on Chinese feelings of alienation by stepping up its organization among the work force. When European planters resisted, the MPC used terror tactics learned from British agents during the occupation. British and Gurkha troops struck back, beginning a long guerrilla war. Malays saw The Emergency not in communist terms, but as a Chinese attempt to seize power.

Leading the insurgents was Chin Peng, a brilliant young Hakka. Son of a bicycle-shop owner in Perak state, he joined the MPC as a teenager, and quickly rose to a senior post. When the Japanese arrived,

Chin Peng organized an underground, working with Britain's Force 136. By the end of the war, he was a national hero, decorated by Lord Mountbatten. No fanatic, he was a gentle, patient man, who spoke English, Malay and four Chinese dialects.

When London agreed to drop the Union plan and adopt the Federation, Chin Peng felt that his high-level British friends had betrayed him. He then discovered that long before the war, the British Secret Service had planted a mole in the MPC. This double-agent, Lai Tek (also known as 'Mr Wright'), repeatedly betrayed party members to the Japanese during the war in exchange for his own liberty. Before he could be brought before a postwar party tribunal to answer the charges, Lai Tek vanished, with all the party funds. His escape appeared to have been arranged with help from British Intelligence.

In a transparent attempt to buy him off, Britain chose this moment to award Chin Peng the Order of the British Empire. He rejected the OBE and went back to the jungle with four thousand of his guerrillas. A reward of eighty thousand dollars was offered for him, dead or alive, but he was never caught. The Emergency lasted twelve years and cost millions of pounds. The majority of victims were Chinese who did not co-operate with one side or the other. Between 1950 and 1952, more than half a million Chinese regarded as potential subversives were forcibly resettled in controlled areas and some ten thousand were deported to Mainland China. When everyone wearied of the issues involved, Chin Peng and five hundred of his men withdrew to southern Thailand. They continued to fight sporadically until 1960.

While there were subtler issues involved, Chin Peng's insurrection was portrayed by London as a crude Marxist terror. As a result, anti-communism with anti-Chinese undertones remains strong in Malay party politics today. Since its formation, the United Malays National Organization (UMNO) has warned all Malays to halt 'the devastating ignominy of race extinction'. Only Malays are allowed to join the party.

Just as UMNO was an exclusive club for Malay leaders, the 'rival' Malayan Chinese Association was a club for wealthy Hokkien community leaders, including Western-educated Chinese who spoke English and whose Anglophile views made them 'safe'. Other Chinese were simply subordinated by the Hokkien élite.

Because these political parties and the similar Malayan Indian Congress (MIC) were essentially racial clubs, some channel of political collaboration between the ethnic groups was needed. As an experiment, in 1954 the three big parties – UMNO, MCA and MIC – set up an Alliance Party, which turned out to have broad appeal to voters.

Its leader was the president of UMNO, Tunku Abdul Rahman, a popular British-trained lawyer and public prosecutor. The Alliance won an overwhelming majority in the election of 1955, and two years later when Malaya became independent, Rahman was its first prime minister and foreign minister.

Chinese businessmen gave major contributions to the Alliance, allowing the Malays who dominated the Alliance to make liberal use of Chinese money. In return, the Malayan Chinese Association gained strong influence in government, with control of the strategic ministries of Finance, and of Commerce and Industry. There was a direct correlation of money and influence. After the 1969 riots, when the Chinese became less enthusiastic donors, the Malay leadership began to squeeze the MCA out of high government posts. By 1974, they had lost the ministerial portfolios and did not regain them. All a question of cash flow.

After being subordinate so long to colonial governments, Malays had exaggerated expectations that independence would make them masters of their economic destiny and their homeland. It did not turn out that way, although Malaya enjoyed more than a decade of peace and prosperity before there was serious trouble.

In 1959, Singapore, too, became a self-governing state, under Prime Minister Lee Kuan Yew, a Hakka. Communist influence on the island was strong and growing, and Lee pushed for a merger with the Malayan Federation to block the communist rise. A Singapore referendum on union with Malaya resulted in a clear victory for Lee.

However, when the expanded Federation of Malaysia came into existence in September 1963, including Singapore, the marriage was not a success. Instead of solving problems, the participation of Singapore with its predominately Chinese population, again provoked Malay fears of a Chinese takeover, and disputes immediately broke out between the federal authorities in Kuala Lumpur and Lee's state government in Singapore. Kuala Lumpur asked Singapore to leave the

Federation. Singapore had no choice but to secede. Unlike Malaysia and Indonesia, Singapore then became a paragon of interracial harmony and economic success.

While Singapore prospered, Malays remained obsessed with the Chinese issues. Politicians demanded that the Malay language (not English or Chinese) be used exclusively in government and in schools, even those with only Chinese pupils. Abdul Rahman was unwilling. He felt that Malays (particularly the wealthy, educated élite in the UMNO) were spoiled by the easy abundance of their lives in a rich, well-watered land. He had less confidence in their commercial abilities than in their tantrums.

But Abdul Rahman represented the past. A new generation was coming into the upper ranks of political power, not reluctant to use chauvinism as a political weapon. While the old generation worked out deals, alliances and compromises in smoke-filled rooms, the younger party members preferred direct agitation. Muslim revivalism also played a part. The radical Pan-Malaysian Islamic Party gained ground by stirring ethnic hatreds among its members, who were typically poor and uneducated.

Efforts to preserve communal harmony were not succeeding. The Chinese continued to strengthen their economic position, while that of the Malays deteriorated. Rural Malays did not benefit from any of the government's loudly touted achievements. The growth of tele-communications during those years made many more Malays aware of the disparity. Chinese businesses in Malaysia were always politically vulnerable because few had Malay partners and few hired Malays. Larger firms could afford Malay sleeping partners in order to exercise political leverage, but most Chinese enterprises were organized around a single family, and were disinclined to bring in outsiders. In any case, Chinese thought Malays made poor employees, because they were too fun-loving. This provoked resentment among Malays, who felt that their advancement was being blocked for ethnic reasons.

In the 1969 elections, the Alliance lost the two-thirds majority needed to push through constitutional amendments without a referendum, and lost control of a number of constituencies, including Selangor and Kuala Lumpur. Its inability to form a Malay-dominated state government in Selangor created the impression that the Chinese majority there might gain political control of the federal capital. This had just enough truth in it to make a dangerous weapon.

On 9 May 1969, a boisterous mob, including Chinese students, marched on the home of Selangor Chief Minister Harun Idris, a humourless Malay chauvinist, to remind him that he was now out of a job. Racial insults were yelled at Malay bystanders, and Chinese kids in the group shouted, 'Kuala Lumpur is Chinese now,' while young Indians shouted, 'Malays are powerless.'

Idris responded angrily, calling Malays to a mass rally on 13 May. Five thousand came from all parts of Selangor state, many of them hooligans armed with freshly sharpened parangs and other lethal weapons. Idris and other Malay politicians inflamed the mob by repeating the earlier insults and by suggesting that pork-eating Chinese communist infidels were trying to 'seize power'. The Chinese, Idris raged, needed to be taught a lesson. Two Chinese observing the rally from a van parked near by were hacked to death and their van burned. The mob raced to a public market, where more than two hundred unsuspecting Chinese men and women were butchered, many of them beheaded and dismembered. Chinese girls were gang-raped and slashed. Motorists were pulled from their cars and beheaded. Chinese triad gangs and street-toughs struck back, invading a movie theatre and stabbing to death Malays in the audience.

The army was called in, but only Malay units, which treated the Chinese as the only 'troublemakers'. Chinese houses were torched during curfew hours, and those who fled the flames were shot by the soldiers for 'violating curfew'. Only later were ethnically mixed forces brought in to quiet international criticism. Four days of communal rioting in and around Kuala Lumpur left between fifteen hundred and two thousand dead, mostly Chinese. Malay soldiers took more than a hundred Chinese corpses to a leprosarium, where they were buried in a mass grave (the government grudgingly confirmed this). The sons of two senior Malay army officers confided later that 'hundreds' of other bodies were trucked into the rainforest, doused with gasoline, and burned. Officially, only 196 bodies were recovered.

Prime Minister Rahman was forced by Harun Idris and other hardliners to proclaim martial law, declaring the Chinese communists were making an armed bid to overthrow the government.

Malay political leaders were unanimous in blaming the Chinese. A Chinese political leader, Dr Tan Chee Khoon, countered that the *coup* actually had been staged by Malay extremists inside the government, not by Chinese – it was a palace *coup*, not a revolution – but that fell on deaf ears.

In fact, there had been an abrupt change in government, as Malay hardliners took over from moderates, in the atmosphere of wild alarm triggered by the violence. Abdul Rahman remained for the moment as figurehead prime minister, but his executive powers were taken over by a junta headed by the tough deputy prime minister, Tun Abdul Razak. It was Razak who had called out the Malay army units that added to the violence. The palace *coup* by Razak and his group ended efforts at ethnic compromise and began a long period of Malay aggrandisement. Rahman was attacked for being pro-Chinese, and for giving the Chinese too much face. Humiliated and neutered like an old dray horse, he retired in September 1970. The constitution was amended to make it a seditious act to question the special position of the Malay people, even in Parliament. In rich, peaceful, laid-back Malaysia, as in so much of the rest of Asia, multiparty, multi-ethnic democracy was shelved. For the time-being, Razak was the strongman, but his days also were numbered.

Ironically, not even Razak was completely untainted by Chinese connections. He was a son-in-law of Senate Speaker Mohamad Noah, who had been involved in many business dealings with Chinese tycoons, among them Lim Goh Tong, one of the world's richest Chinese and the developer of the Genting Highlands Resort – a pleasure palace for those very same pork-eating infidels.

Perched on the summit of the jungle-covered Ulu Kali mountain, overlooking Kuala Lumpur, is the site of the Genting Highlands Casino-Hotel. It takes half a day to drive up there, through rainforests noisy with hooting gibbons. The last few miles to the hotel-casino cuts through eerie cloudforest, where moss-covered trees and giant ferns are perpetually wet and chilly. At the summit the hotel-casino is a four-hundred-bedroom mass, squatting like a frog on a broad concrete lily pad, the whole affair crowned by the sort of huge neon sign that Chinese billionaires seem partial to. Near by is a small lake and a helicopter pad. Helicopters made the trip from Kuala Lumpur to

Genting in minutes. It was the only casino in Malaysia.

Although the country's official religion is Islam, which forbids gambling, Malaysia prudently legalized gambling in order to regulate and tax the industry. Laws passed in 1982 prohibit Muslims from entering any gambling establishment, so the casino at Genting primarily benefits Chinese residents, and non-Muslim Asians and Westerners living around the Pacific Rim who feel burdened by their disposable income. Still, Muslims flock to Genting in ever increasing numbers to enjoy the rest of the resort's facilities, which include hotels, golf course, monorail, and theme parks. By 1995, Genting had grown into Malaysia's leading company, capitalized at over $6 billion, with more than 80 per cent of its revenues coming from gambling. It was one of Malaysia's top five taxpayers, bringing in a deluge of foreign exchange. Genting was widely regarded as one of the best run companies in South East Asia, and indeed had to be well managed for its gambling licence came up for renewal every three months.

The man who created Genting out of virgin rain forest, Lim Goh Tong, was cut from the same homespun as his old friends and fellow billionaires, Chin Sophonpanich and Liem Sioe Liong. A Hokkien born in 1918, he came to Kuala Lumpur on the eve of the Second World War to work for an uncle who was a government contractor. During the war, Lim made a lot of money selling food, machinery, and scrap iron on the black market and to the Japanese. The money he made enabled him to go into construction in a big way during the postwar boom, specializing in giant government infrastructure projects. These came his way because he was generous with his political donations. Lim is famous for his knack of making people feel good. He was soon the head of the Chinese Chamber of Commerce in Selangor state, leader of the Hokkien community in Kuala Lumpur, and one of the most influential Chinese in Asia. He cultivated friendships across the spectrum, including Malay sultans, and the Speaker of Parliament, Mohamed Noah, who also happened to be chairman of UMNO and father-in-law of two future prime ministers, Abdul Razak and Hussein Onn. Such friendships were helpful when Lim needed government permission to build his resort at Genting. Twelve thousand acres were acquired on the top of Ula Kali mountain. Lim shared ownership with Mohamed Noah, and with the sultans of

Pahang and Kedah. In time, Genting Highlands became a public company, but Lim retained controlling interest.

Lim's partnership with Mohamed Noah was no accident. As an upcoming young civil servant in Johore after the war, Noah was cultivated by many Chinese businessmen and bankers. With their generous financial support, he became a prominent national politician and chairman of UMNO, and by 1970 was wealthy enough to retire from politics and go into business, leaving government to his two sons-in-law. Chinese, Japanese and Western investors all competed to have Noah as their Malay partner. From the examples of Lim and Noah, it is possible to see why a lot of younger Malay politicians felt left out. They arrived at the banquet too late.

Strongman Razak, a British-educated member of the Malay aristocracy, devoted his attention to national development, with development aid from the Islamic world. Malaysia recognized Beijing, and said it considered Taiwan part of the People's Republic. This was a slap in the face for Taipei, which had a long history of covert meddling in Malaysian affairs. Taiwan was the chief offshore base of the Hokkien networks that were the dominant Chinese group in Malaysia. Thus a rebuff of Taipei was a warning to all Hokkien.

In 1971, the Trade and Industry portfolios were taken out of Chinese control and given to UMNO members. Three years later, Razak also took over the Finance portfolio, which had been Chinese for nearly twenty years. In this way, official Chinese participation in national economic management came to an end.

Razak's strategy for economic development was based on the grand idea that Malay poverty could be ended by moving Malaysia into the industrial age. This was used to justify a curious set of New Economic Policies (NEP) designed to give Malays a bigger share of the nation's wealth with more jobs and executive positions. Simply put, the government intended to take wealth out of Chinese hands and put it under the control of the Malay élite, increasing the patronage they could bestow on their constituents. The Malay élite were no longer content just being sleeping partners.

Direct expropriation of Chinese wealth and companies would have stampeded the Chinese. So a graduated approach was taken by the New Economic Policies, initially affecting only foreign investors.

Progressively, more and more domestic companies would find themselves in a half-nelson. Eventually the Malay élite would be able to gain control over old Chinese firms, and would have unprecedented access to capital, much of it Chinese in origin.

Malaysia was beginning to boom, with petroleum leading the way, but without an industrial base the boom could not be sustained. A national oil company, Petronas, enabled the government to bring under its supervision all joint ventures with multinational oil companies. But the government's management was erratic and shortsighted, like a child learning to ride a bike. When oil income was high, Malaysia cut back incentives to foreign investors. When oil prices fell, the government anxiously boosted the incentives.

Until 1975, the only requirement for manufacturing was that new companies wanting government incentives must get approval, and reserve at least 30 per cent of equity for Malays. This left most older Chinese firms beyond government supervision, because they were already in business and did not want the incentives. However, then the rules were changed to include many long-established Chinese companies as well.

Most were old family businesses, and did not exist just to maximize profits. Instead they were elaborate social security systems linking generations together. After the rules were changed in 1975, Malays could choose any profitable Chinese company and demand 30 per cent ownership, virtually at gunpoint. The government also insisted upon the right to choose the Chinese company's Malay partners, to appoint it distributors, and to set the share price of the firm. After many years of risk-taking, hard work, and the forsaking of luxuries for the long-term benefit of the family, there was bitter resentment among older Chinese at what was being done to them. They simply could not relinquish 30 per cent of the family firm to outsiders. The Malay politicians who drafted the new law knew this, but the most efficient, most profitable companies in Malaya were precisely these old Chinese family firms.

Prime Minister Razak died of leukaemia in 1976, just as the new rules went into effect. Expecting the worst, many wealthy Hokkien immediately left Malaysia, taking the portable assets with them to less vulnerable places around the Rim, planting one foot in Hong Kong,

Taiwan or Singapore, the other in Los Angeles, San Francisco or Vancouver.

Razak's brother-in-law, Hussein Onn, briefly became the new prime minister, then retired to make way for Dr Mahathir bin Muhammed. Over the next twenty years, Mahathir came to embody Malay aspirations as no leader before him. He put it in gospel: 'We are the Negroes in this country . . . Here, the Blacks are in charge . . . No other country has tried this kind of experiment. We are doing it very nicely, very slowly. I am not anti-Chinese in any way, but I feel Malays must have a place in the sun, otherwise there is going to be bitterness.'

A complex, intense man, Mahathir's style was abrasive at times, but refreshingly forthright. When Vietnamese boat people stormed ashore in Malaysia in 1978 – most of them Chinese – and other countries were slow to keep promises to resettle the refugees, Mahathir simply announced that any refugee found on Malaysian beaches would be shot. There was immediate action by the international community. He got results. Critics labelled him a demagogue and called him 'tyrannical, power-mad, and ruthless'. They joked that Mahathir's parents forced him to study medicine, when what he really wanted was to be a housepainter in Vienna. But when the jokes grew stale, they conceded that he was a new kind of politician for Malaysia, personally upright and incorruptible at a time when the country was awash with money and possibilities for personal gain. As he matured in office, Mahathir earned much of the credit for the boom that moved Malaysia out of the Third World and into the forefront on the Pacific Rim. He was remarkably successful in attracting foreign investment to supplant Chinese domination of the economy. Malaysia became the top choice of many Western companies seeking a congenial and peaceful Asian base. When Mahathir sought new ways to generate income, radical ideas were tried. Some succeeded, others failed.

Secretly, Mahathir set out to corner the world tin market. The plan was for Malaysia to make large, secret purchases of tin on the London Metal Exchange, to provoke a worldwide price increase. They could do it cheap by buying on margin. Traders in tin futures either would default on forward contracts or would be obliged to meet the contracts by buying tin from Malaysia at much higher prices. As such schemes depend on circumstances remaining fixed, the plan can fail.

Mahathir and his finance minister secretly began buying tin futures on margin. Indeed, prices started to rise. Malaysia held 50,000 tons of tin off the market to keep prices up – but before they could reap profits, other tin producers, including the United States, started selling off their strategic stockpiles. The tin market crashed, and Malaysia lost some two hundred and fifty million dollars (similar schemes to support rubber prices also failed).

Fortunately, Malaysia was so rich in resources that mistakes like these could be made without lasting damage. It is the main preoccupation of all governments to make themselves look good, while trying to keep mistakes to a minimum.

The craving of Malays to be on equal economic footing with the Chinese entrepreneurs (but without getting up early in the morning) required a lot of pump priming. To that end the government of Abdul Rahman had allocated 124 million dollars to set up Bank Bumiputra (the bank for native sons) to provide start-up loans for Malay businesses. Thanks to oil profits, Bank Bumi grew into the nation's biggest. A Malay was named the bank's president, but the general manager was Chinese, and so was one of its principal financial backers. Great expectations were created that Bank Bumi would help tip the economic scales in favour of the Malays. Instead, it became a source of easy money for the risky pet projects of the Malay élite.

Bank Bumi was at the top of a house of cards. Few of its Malay officials had any previous experience in money management. They were given responsibility for vast sums from public revenues, including the life savings of countless poor *bumiputra* families, and were told to maximize profits. With minimal supervision, the bank's officials took bizarre risks. They loaned money to individuals and corporations without collateral and with little regard for default. Bank Bumi was, above all, a funnel for patronage.

An irresistible temptation came in the late 1970s, when Hong Kong's property market boomed. A Bank Bumi subsidiary, Bumiputra Malaysia Finance (BMF), began investing heavily in the Hong Kong property market through various channels, including the Carrian Group of George Tan. It was George Tan who pulled the rug out.

George Tan Soon-Gin was the smooth-talking son of a Mainland Chinese taxi-driver, and never made a move without first checking his *feng shui* and numerology. Early on, Tan drifted to Singapore, applied for citizenship, and got a job as a construction company bookkeeping clerk. For kicks and contacts, he joined several dialect associations and secret societies that provided him with introductions to wealthy, lonely Overseas Chinese. George cultivated anyone with money, especially older Chinese who felt let down by their own children. At the end of 1971, with mysterious financial backing, he moved to Hong Kong, where he took a job at another construction company while he boned up on the real estate market. Then he went into property development in a big way. He called his company the Carrian Group.

Although he had little money of his own, George had access to a lot of Chinese flight capital looking for a discreet way out of Malaysia. For a while he could do nothing wrong. He went to the track with the chairman of Hongkong Bank, bought chunks of Kowloon's Golden Mile, bought a kinky piece of Nikatsu, a Japanese company that specialized in pornographic movies. Tan's Carrian Group became the hottest thing in Hong Kong – and Hong Kong loves a new rage. He also cultivated the head of Bank Bumi's Hong Kong subsidiary, Bumiputra Malaysia Finance – calling him 'uncle' – and persuaded him to lend Carrian more than one billion Hong Kong dollars. With this money, George bought a three-hundred-and-fifty-million-dollar property in California, a huge real estate parcel in Florida, a majority share of Hong Kong's fourth largest shipping fleet, half of China Underwriters Life, 27 per cent of Union Bank, and other properties. As more money poured in, he also bought Gammon House, a thirty-nine-storey tower in Central Hong Kong, paying nearly one billion Hong Kong dollars. A few months later, he resold the property for what he claimed was a fat profit. This secured his reputation as a wheeler-dealer.

Nobody knew where George was getting the money. It was whispered that he was sitting on more than one billion dollars in dirty loot. Some thought it was Teochiu heroin profits from the Golden Triangle, or black money being laundered through the real estate shell game, but when Britain began negotiations with China in 1982 for the reversion of Hong Kong, the stock market plunged, real estate prices collapsed, and the Hong Kong dollar fell. George's bubble burst. His Carrian Group went bankrupt.

George had borrowed huge sums from BMF without collateral. There were tangled transactions between BMF and The Carrian Group involving consultant fees, concealed payments to shadow companies, and diversion of money. In Kuala Lumpur, Bank Bumi's head office became worried. A senior officer sent to investigate BMF's Hong Kong operations was found dead in a banana grove, strangled with a bathrobe belt from a nearby hotel. Merchant bankers who had been putting together a rescue package to save Carrian vanished. The murder spoiled any idea of corporate rescue. Police opened BMF's filing cabinets and found that its lending to Carrian had been much bigger than anyone had ever imagined. There was a whole separate set of books for loans to Carrian. The Carrian Group was liquidated, with outstanding debts of 1.3 billion dollars.

Malaysian officials denied culpability. Prime Minister Mahathir rushed through a new Official Secrets Act. Board members of Bank Bumi said they were completely unaware. Challenged in Parliament, Mahathir accepted that crimes had been committed, but 'legally it was within the law, [so] we cannot take them to court.' Despite these disclaimers, the former chairman of Bank Bumi insisted that 'no important decisions are taken without the agreement or knowledge of the government or of the central bank.'

To save Bank Bumi, Mahathir forced Malaysia's national oil corporation to purchase 90 per cent of the share capital and to buy BMF's problem loans. A BMF official who went to jail for four years in Hong Kong insisted that he acted only on direct orders from Mahathir and that a number of senior Malay government officials close to Mahathir had received kickbacks from George Tan.

The political opposition in Malaysia alleged that UMNO ran Bank Bumi as a huge slush fund to dispense patronage, kickbacks, credit lines, and favours. According to this view, the Malay élite were simply emulating traditional Chinese business practices. In other words, there was nothing unusual about the Bank Bumi affair except for George Tan's sudden bad luck. After proclaiming special rights and privileges to protect and enrich the Malay people as a whole, only a few were being protected and enriched. Under one-party rule, these few were able to avoid any public peer review. The most embarrassing aspect of the Bank Bumi scandal, some said, was that the Malays needed Chinese help to be wicked.

Enormous power had become concentrated in the hands of UMNO leaders and heads of key government agencies. Many members of the Malay élite were enriched in the process, but the average wage for ordinary Malays remained only one notch better than Indonesia. A Western economist observed wryly that making millionaires by patronage was neither fair nor prudent.

Mahathir's determination to industrialize Malaysia did pay off in many important ways. Foreign companies operating in Malaysia were given lavish concessions, and were rarely bothered by the continual infighting between UMNO factions, or the skirmishes between UMNO and the Chinese establishment. Foreign investors could repatriate capital, profits, dividends, royalties, fees and commissions in any currency. For five years their profits were exempted from tax up to 100 per cent of capital expenditure. And, after all, Malaysia was beautiful, clean, friendly and a superb place to live and raise children.

To generate employment among Malays, the government encouraged American and Japanese multinationals to help develop labour-intensive, export-oriented industries with Malay partners and shareholders. Free Trade Zones were established. Textiles and electronics were favoured. Along the way, Malaysia began to boom, overtaking Hong Kong, Singapore and Taiwan as the largest producer of semi-conductors in the world. Whatever Mahathir's people were doing wrong, they were doing a few things right.

None of the mistakes has been fatal, and the jungle has quickly grown over those scars. The national flower of Malaysia is money, and it is blooming everywhere. With oil, tin and rubber revenues, plus massive investments from Japan and the United States, Malaysia has enjoyed amazing economic progress in the last two decades, with an annual growth rate now running at nearly 10 per cent. Along the way the UMNO leadership has had to cope with unexpected challenges – not from the Chinese, but from Malays themselves, including ethnocentrists, Islamic fundamentalists, and religious cults, whose fanaticism threatened to derail the new prosperity. This has been a sobering discovery, an epiphany which has taught that Malaysia's greatest strength comes from its diversity. The old Alliance Party idea has been revived by UMNO in the form of a new National Front coalition, with the Malaysian Chinese Association as its ethnic Chinese component.

Similarly, thanks to an explosion of common sense among students, new generations of non-Malays (both Chinese and Indians) are making the effort to be fluent in the national language, Bahasa Malaysia, eliminating one of the most emotional issues. For its part, the government, after downgrading the use of English in order to favour the Malay mother tongue, has seen the need to strike a better balance to assure full employment in high-tech industry. Meanwhile, a strong Malay middle class has emerged, more confident of its influence, less insecure about ethnic issues, and with a more cosmopolitan world-view. Tactfully, both Mahathir and Deputy Prime Minister Anwar Ibrahim have begun to encourage Malays to learn from other cultures, to see Islamic values as universal values, and to appreciate that Malaysia's unique character can only be damaged by catering to narrow ethnic or religious interests.

The UMNO government may be militant, but it is not military. Occasional policy failures or economic miscalculations can cause it embarrassment, to which Asian military regimes remain insensitive. One benefit is that the social atmosphere of Malaysia is more relaxed and wholesome, and its residents – regardless of ethnic ties – can drive down the street, pursue their livelihoods, and go to bed at night without dread. Mahathir's period in power has established Malay prestige without the stengun or the jackboot, in an atmosphere of civility that is remarkable for Asia and rare anywhere in the world.

As a refuge for Chinese flight capital after Hong Kong's reversion in 1997, Malaysia is not at the top of anyone's list. To set out a welcome mat, yet keep things under control, a Special Economic Zone has been set aside on the big island of Labuan off Borneo, which is being developed with Chinese money as a sort of New Singapore. The example of Genting Highlands proves that such a collaboration can work well. If it does, Malaysia could just succeed in having it both ways.

CHAPTER 16

THE SHARP END OF THE DRAGON

STROLLING THROUGH A HONG KONG GARDEN, YOU MIGHT COME unexpectedly upon a stone zigzag footbridge, crossing a pond full of flashing gold carp to an island robed in the long green gown of a willow. Bad spirits travel in straight lines, so when you cross a zigzag bridge, all the evil influences are blocked. You arrive at the other end cleansed. If they ever build a proper bridge linking Hong Kong to the Mainland, it should be this kind. The harbour tunnel was built without a zigzag, which may account for the presence of mean spirits in Government House. Many rich refugees in the great exodus from China in 1949 came out with only the bad spirits clinging to their backs. They brought no baggage, because their great fortunes had already been transferred to offshore bank accounts. They prepared the way carefully: first rescue the money, then the women and children.

The Shanghai millionaires who fled to Hong Kong in 1949 were China's financial brains and managerial élite, bankers and industrialists with generations of family and clan experience in economics. They came from the Yangtze delta, the sharp end of the dragon. They fled offshore to escape Chiang Kai-shek as much as Mao Tse-tung, so instead of heading for Taiwan they ran to Hong Kong, which was still a sleepy colonial outpost with more rickshaws than telephones. Once out from under the heavy KMT thumb, and safe from communist cadres, they turned the crown colony into an unparalleled base of international finance.

They were the first Chinese to master modern Western banking and commercial practices, so they could play the global financial game by Western rules. They were on top of new waves of technology in the Sixties, Seventies and Eighties that ushered in historic changes in the forces that drive the world economy. Barriers between national financial markets dissolved, and a truly global capital market emerged. New electronic banking and information technology made it possible to link together Overseas Chinese banks and financial institutions in Tokyo, Hong Kong, Taipei, Bangkok, Singapore, Manila, Kuala Lumpur and Jakarta, creating the high-speed links of a new Offshore China, one without borders.

These boys from Shanghai were the vanguard of the great Asian boom. They did not create the boom, or develop the technology, they just happened to be present when the Great Depression and two world wars shattered the Western colonial order, littering the landscape with unclaimed treasure. Throughout Asia, ownership was turned upside down. Whole colonial economies had their pockets emptied. The Dutch-built economy in Indonesia, after being abandoned by the Japanese, was simply seized by the Indonesian army, who leased it to the Chinese. Elsewhere the transfer was less formal. White and black money gushed or crept out of hiding-places, seeking new ones. Opportunities were everywhere, and there were no rules and few witnesses. The Overseas Chinese were the only ants at the picnic. They found themselves with so much capital they did not know how to handle it. Pawnbrokers and moneylenders do not moult into stockbrokers overnight. It was the boys from Shanghai who showed them the way. No study of the Overseas Chinese would be complete without understanding the crucial financial role of the Shanghai boys. They were and are the financial pointmen of the new age of borderless global capitalism; they taught Chin Sophonpanich how to do it, and Liem Sioe Liong as well; they figured out how to liberate the Chinese-owned domestic banks of South East Asia from the military regimes of each country; and they are behind the new global economics of speculation, where industry takes a back seat to fast profits from stocks, bonds, currency manipulation and real estate.

More than one Chinese billionaire now has his own communications satellite up or on the way. But behind the glossy exterior of their banks on both sides of the Rim, they still make use of arcane Chinese connections, tribal loyalties, business webs, secret syndicates, numerology, geomancy and shamanism, which Westerners only dimly comprehend. They grafted the best the West had to offer onto their own very ancient root stock. Today *guanxi* and *feng shui* move around digitally through silicon chips and fibre optics. This gives Overseas Chinese a powerful advantage as the Asian boom makes the Pacific Rim the biggest growth area for the new century.

They all started as pawnbrokers, doing business only within their own tribe. Pawnshops selling gold and making small loans were the traditional way for a wealthy family to roll over surplus profits. By Southern Sung, there were pawnshops and money-changers all over China, financing the needs of peasant farmers, petty traders and artisans. As trade expanded, they issued paper drafts that could be redeemed for copper or silver in other towns. Yet paper money was trusted only if you knew the clan that issued the banknote. You automatically distrusted the pawnshops of other dialect groups. The most successful moneylenders were chains run by well-known clans, operating on 'unlimited liability', meaning that any banker who accepted deposits and then made a bad loan was personally responsible.

Same-native-place ties played a crucial role. A Hokkien firm in one city did not export goods to a Teochiu firm in another. As merchants travelled in search of goods and markets, members of the same clan or guild could draw upon a line of credit wherever they went. To default on such a loan was rare, for that would jeopardize the *shinyung*, or personal trust, that provides the only social security in Chinese life.

One of the richest networks in imperial China was the Shansi remittance bank chain run by the Kung family, which was vital to government fiscal operations throughout the empire. The Kungs dealt only with other Shansi banks, which had branches all over China.

The great rivals of the Kungs of Shansi were the banking clans of Ningpo, the major smuggling centre near Shanghai. Ningpo was dominated by powerful families. Thwarted scholars from these clans went into commerce. Their families set up the young men in business, investing capital in new enterprises. Way back during Southern Sung, Ningpo had served as China's main trading port with the outside world, in competition with Amoy, Chuanchow and Canton. In the eighteenth century, when Canton had the imperial monopoly on foreign trade, Western ship captains scouted up the coast for a harbour where they could smuggle goods into China without paying off the taipans. Ningpo was their choice. Not only was it safe in all weather, but its merchants had easy access to the superb silks and teas of Hangchow and Suchow.

Centuries of smuggling and pay-offs made the bankers of Ningpo more resourceful than their rivals. Their best-known moneylending syndicates were the Fang, Hsu, Shih, Yeh and Yen clans, which had branches in cities and towns across the Yangtze delta. In order to head off runs on one bank that could bankrupt the whole group, they set up guilds to secretly cover bad debts.

In the second half of the nineteenth century, when Shanghai began to grow into China's most important centre of foreign trade, Ningpo bankers were the first to start branch offices there, getting the jump on their rivals from Suchow. In Shanghai they came into contact with the colonial branches of Western banks. The Ningpo bankers were intensely curious. But the Westerners and Chinese kept a hostile distance, for fiscal as well as racial reasons. The gulf between them was not bridged for another century. This was their first experience with the English branch-banking system, which depended on speedy remittances over vast distances. Western banks had limited-liability and banking disclosure laws, which reduced the risk to individual owners. Thus, British banks were able to attract deposits from all directions, while the Chinese continued to depend on narrow ties of family, clan and *kongsi*. These foreign banks enlisted influential Chinese as agents and *compradors*. As the *compradors* learned Western banking, they began to influence conventional Chinese ways of doing business.

By the beginning of the twentieth century, Shanghai was a major international city. Through its harbour passed a huge volume of foreign, regional and coastal trade. There were telegraph connections to all the world's financial centres. All manner of silver coins became the medium of exchange for silk, tea, cotton, opium and flesh. Ningpo banking clans now had branch networks in Shanghai and in all of China's commercial cities. In each city, they issued their own Ningpo credit notes, in whatever currency was favoured locally. Overseas, they had branches in Japan, the Philippines, Indochina, Singapore, Sumatra and Ceylon. Everywhere, they were noted for their secretiveness and fierce regional loyalty. A Ningpo man – *comprador*, bank manager, shipper or shopkeeper –always employed only fellow Ningpo natives.

They were only kept out of international banking by lack of information and experience in the inner workings of Western private and clearing banks. These were closely guarded commercial secrets. But gradually Chinese accountants employed by Britain's Chartered Bank, and the Hongkong & Shanghai Banking Corporation, were hired away to manage Ningpo-owned banks, taking secrets with them. Sometimes the rich *compradors* of these same Western banks retired to start their own native banks, which they made into replicas. Millions of dollars also came from wealthy Overseas Chinese who wished to keep their money on deposit in their ancestral homes. These funds were invested in Shanghai industry, producing a prewar generation of Chinese capitalists like the Soongs, whose wealth and assets began to rival the biggest Western financial houses. By the 1940s, Shanghai had four Chinese central banks, fourteen foreign banks, and 388 Chinese-owned banks.

On the death of Dr Sun Yat-sen in 1925, when Generalissimo Chiang gained control of the KMT, the Ningpo bankers made him an irresistible offer: they would help to underwrite his northern campaign to bring all of China under his control, if he would make Shanghai his first stop and purge the city of communists and labour unions. Chiang, who qualified as a native of the Ningpo region, marched his armies into Shanghai, where he set himself up in league with the banks and the underworld – which was every bit as right wing as the bankers. He became known as 'the Ningpo Napoleon'. Under his Nationalist regime, the Ningpo clans gained the edge in China in the 1930s.

Then the generalissimo began to cannibalize his backers. He drew fifty of Shanghai's richest merchant groups into a federation. Included were the Silk Merchants' Guild, the Flour Merchants' Guild, the Tea Merchants' Guild, the Bankers' Association, and the Native Banks' Guild. These groups were China's richest men, and held most of its commercial capital and property. A delegation from the federation offered to 'lend' Chiang three million Chinese dollars, in return for continuing to 'protect' them from the communists. A few days later, another loan of seven million was made, then another of fifteen and another of thirty, to install Chiang's Nationalist government upriver in Nanking.

If these financiers originally expected the generalissimo to be their saviour, they now learned that he was to be their tormentor. From the late 1920s until his death in the 1970s, Chiang's fee to protect everyone from the communists and then the Japanese came to hundreds of billions of dollars, and the 'protection' was completely illusory.

Take the case of Fu Tseng-yao, head of the Shanghai Chamber of Commerce, general manager of the Commercial Bank of China, and managing director of the China Merchants' Steam Navigation Company. Chiang asked Fu for a loan. When he refused, Chiang ordered Fu's arrest and the seizure of all the banker's property. Fu fled into the International Settlement, and for safekeeping made over all his holdings to foreigners. Eventually, he realized there was no escape, and made a huge personal donation to Chiang's coffers. Chiang then added a little touch of his own, putting the Chamber of Commerce under the direct supervision of his friends from the Green Gang.

When next he found himself short of cash, Chiang issued short-term government bonds, using soldiers and gangsters to force everyone from small shopkeepers to bank presidents to buy them. When one millionaire refused, his son was kidnapped. Another merchant's son was arrested as a counter-revolutionary, but released when his father made a big donation to Chiang. A cotton-mill owner paid nearly a million dollars to free his imprisoned son. Another paid half a million for his missing three year old. Extortion-by-kidnap became a hallmark of the KMT. To outwit the regime, Shanghai bankers stepped up efforts to learn all they could about Western banking methods in an effort to shield their assets by getting them offshore. It was terror from Chiang Kai-shek, not Mao Tse-tung, that gave the bankers of Shanghai a thirty-year jump on Chinese bankers everywhere else.

In its heyday in the 1930s, Shanghai was the preferred residence of expatriates in Asia. Along the Whangpoo River, the Bund looked like the shelf where Queen Victoria kept her hatbox collection. Squat stone buildings housed banks from New York, London and Paris. Chinese-owned department stores were jammed with dry goods and foreign luxuries. At night, Nanking Road was smeared with neon like cheap lipstick, and handmade motor cars nudged their way through ragged crowds, while their occupants stared straight ahead. Great fortunes were being made in rubber, coal, iron, soybean, flour, noodles, silk, cigarettes and opium. Her sycamore-lined boulevards, brothels and nightclubs were sprinkled with a world-weary milieu of Old China Hands, White Russians, French, British, Americans, Persian Jews – dealmakers and fugitives from all over the world.

Much was lost or destroyed when the Pacific War began, yet when it ended, Shanghai was still fabulously rich. In the postwar years she was still the industrial giant of China, with half of China's foreign trade. Surprisingly, much of this wealth came not from silk but from cotton, which had been cultivated and woven in China since the Han Dynasty. Ming emperors wore cotton underwear, not silk. As mechanized mills were introduced in Shanghai, China's textile industry spawned financial empires, some of which still are among the biggest in the world today. Instead of trusting their wealth to Western banks or to the Chinese bank of a rival clan, the cotton clans started their own.

Bankers had not been the only victims of KMT extortion. The textile tycoons also were kept in a hammerlock. After the war, Finance Minister T. V. Soong created a state enterprise called China Textile Industries, nationalizing all former Japanese-owned mills, nearly half of China's spinning capacity. Supplies of raw cotton to everyone else were tightly rationed; pricing and distribution were dictated by the government; private holdings of foreign exchange were prohibited. In self-defence, the textile barons kept large secret reserves salted outside China, but these could not be tapped without risking revealing their existence to Soong, who would immediately seize their assets. Several industrialists were prosecuted for attempting to get around Soong's regulations. Like the Shanghai bankers, the textile tycoons frantically sought a safe haven. One of those persecuted was Jong Hong-yuan, whose family ran one of China's biggest textile conglomerates. He was arrested in Shanghai for the unauthorized purchase of Hong Kong dollars to pay for a supply of imported cotton. After payment of a half-million US-dollar 'fine', Jong was given a 'suspended sentence'.

The moment he was free, he fled to Hong Kong, where he set up the Da Yuan Cotton Mill and started over. The smart textile money followed him. The decision had been made. They would all get out. Most would go to Hong Kong. They were not fleeing the communists, they were fleeing the Nationalist KMT.

A few tried to relocate elsewhere in South East Asia, only to regret it. A younger son of one of Shanghai's richest cotton tycoons set up a factory in Bangkok in partnership with a member of the Thai royal family. After 'meeting various government restrictions', the company was permitted to start business. Soon the royal partner ran up such huge debts on equity that the company went bankrupt. The Chinese partner was left with the bill, and could not leave Thailand until his family paid everyone off. He had been royally plundered.

Those who remained in Shanghai gossiped about the heavily armed KMT troops emptying gold from the vaults of Shanghai's four central banks, loading the ingots and bars in stout canvas bags onto KMT ships for the escape to Taiwan, just before the Red Army rolled into town.

The Soongs got out early. Eldest sister Ai-ling Soong was the real business brain of the family, using government and underworld connections to create an immense fortune. Her husband H. H. Kung, scion of the great Kung banking clan of Shansi, was already one of the richest men in China. While he was finance minister of the Chiang regime, Kung sat on China's hard currency and gold reserves, while printing worthless paper money for everyone else. The Soong and Kung portfolios were discreetly converted to investments in North and South America, including industries, railways and airlines in Guatemala, Colombia, Brazil and Argentina. The rest was tucked away in Canada and the United States.

As the communists approached and the Nationalists looted, the time came for Shanghai's bankers and industrialists to make a decision. Should they emulate the cotton tycoons and flee to Hong Kong? Capitalists faced an uncertain future on the Mainland. Those who fled to Taiwan would become slaves of the KMT.

This was not a question of politics. What difference was there between being stripped by communists or Nationalists? Everyone talked about China as a nation, without meaning a word of it. The only nationality was the tribe. The only passport was money.

The sensible choice was Hong Kong. The British colonial govern-ment would leave you alone, and taxes were low and easy to avoid. Between 1945 and 1951, nearly one and a half million Chinese refugees flooded into the colony. Most came in the last months of 1948 and the first months of 1949. The notion that everyone fleeing the Nazis or the Reds was poor and helpless is sentimental nonsense.

How much flight capital arrived in Hong Kong in the 1949 stampede is impossible to measure, because banking statistics were not published there before 1964. The KMT claimed that it was sixty billion Hong Kong dollars in the form of cash, gold, commodities and shares. By some estimates, flight capital forms nearly half of Hong Kong's annual national income.

With the closure of the Mainland, the entire Overseas Chinese remittance system came into jeopardy. Beijing tried to direct the flow through communist financial channels. Taiwan redirected all it could to tame banks in Taipei. Hokkien and Teochiu banks elsewhere funnelled their remittances into Hong Kong where the money piled up and was kited and rolled over hundreds of times before trickling into family coffers. The build-up of flight capital in Hong Kong became so great that it spilled over into London, Zurich, Liechtenstein, Luxemburg, the Channel Islands and Bermuda.

The first wave to arrive in Hong Kong was the élite that had planned long in advance; the second wave was the élite that had hesitated, then fled in haste. The middle class was swept along in a third wave. The poor came in late, if they came at all.

Refugee businessmen arrived by plane, looking like conventioneers, not coming to get rich but to stay rich. Eight planeloads from Shanghai arrived each day. Among them were thousands of well-educated professionals and managers. At the top of the heap were the bankers. They brought Shanghai's financial brains in their carry-on luggage, and changed Hong Kong for ever. They knew all about money, how to get it, how to move it, how to hide it, how to make it do gymnastics. When they got out of bed in the mornings, they hit the floor running. Green tea does that to you. Their intense drive to resecure their endangered fortunes moved Hong Kong overnight from the age of the pith helmet to the age of satellite communications, or so it now seems in retrospect. Time is measured differently in Hong Kong.

Aside from local Cantonese, Hong Kong already had a large Teochiu population, and sizeable communities of Hokkien, Hokchiu, and other Fukienese, many of them earlier refugees from the Chiang regime. But until 1949 there was no equivalent group from Shanghai. Only a few of the new arrivals from Shanghai already had Hong Kong connections.

You could tell at a glance that the Shanghai Boys were not from Hong Kong. They looked like Boston bankers starting over in Atlanta. Like Mormons, they were easily identified on the Star Ferry by their well-tailored clothes, trim haircuts – and, of course, their sibilant Wu dialect. They were more cultivated, more efficient, more elegant than the 'uncouth, lazy and mean-spirited' Cantonese who, in those days, filled the ghettoes of Kowloon and the noisy streets of Victoria. These Cantonese rivals also wore Western clothes, but something about the fit never seemed right. While many Shanghai tycoons spoke English like Oxford dons, the Cantonese, however rich, spoke it like waiters, each sentence slapped down like a menu with an explosive 'WAH!' Eventually, the sober professionalism of the Shanghai Boys caught on and became the new image of Hong Kong in the 1980s and 1990s.

When the Korean War started, the United Nations imposed a trade embargo on the People's Republic, so Hong Kong's role quickly changed from that of an offshore entrepôt to manufacturing and financial centre. Expatriate Shanghai textile families led the manufacturing boom, while expatriate Shanghai bankers took the lead in finance. They started new businesses on credit, using somebody else's money. They had a bolder attitude toward finance than Westerners, and were only conservative about their personal assets. The assets of others could be used with wild abandon. They could do ten million dollars' worth of business with one million capital. When they went bankrupt, it wasn't their money anyway. Their personal fortunes remained safe.

They were so far ahead of the rest of Asia in their experience with Western banking, that they had no anxieties about dealing with Westerners. They did not hesitate to approach Hong Kong's staid British banks. The British bankers were impressed, and lent them the money they needed to restart their industries, but soon were horrified by their abnormally high rate of borrowing. The Shanghai Boys merely moved to the Bank of China and to the Commercial Bank of Chin

Sophonpanich. Because of this hesitation, Western banks suffered, while Chinese banks became giants with branches throughout Asia.

Forget the sweaty noodle-shop image. The economic impact of the Shanghai Boys gave Hong Kong a significant lead over the rest of Asia. By 1962, more than half its exports were textiles. Even with quotas, England and America were the biggest customers. Among the Shanghai refugees were the Fang brothers, S.C. and S.H., members of one of the most important families in Asia's textile industry, which is the most important in the world. Before the Second World War, they were cotton traders 30 miles outside Shanghai, with credit lines to the Ningpo banking family of the same name. After fleeing to Hong Kong, the Fangs built a global textile business with four hundred and fifty million dollars in annual sales. Their products were not soup-stained silks. Normally, they supplied fashion leaders like Calvin Klein. In North America, they started a line of their own retail shops called Episode, that filled the gap between designer originals and upmarket chains such as Limited. They were far-sighted. Before they fled to Hong Kong in 1949, the Fang brothers ordered hundreds of cotton spindles and had them shipped to Hong Kong for 'storage'. In the mid-1960s, as the spinning industry was reaching saturation in Hong Kong, the Fangs moved into clothing manufacture. When labour costs began rising, and Washington imposed restrictions on textiles from Hong Kong, S.C. and S.H. moved operations to Thailand, Malaysia, the Philippines, Panama – nine countries in all. Looking for a still-cheaper place, they discovered South Carolina, one of America's low-wage areas. There they were not troubled by US protectionism.

Anxious not to be caught by another shift in the political winds, other Shanghai Boys also set up subsidiaries elsewhere – Singapore, Taiwan, Thailand, Malaysia, Indonesia, the Philippines, Canada, the United States and Europe. They watched Japanese buy properties around Diamond Head and Waikiki, and flew off themselves to buy properties around Puget Sound. Vancouver became Hongcouver, the Asian bolt-hole. Old Shanghai banking families with corporate offices in Hong Kong and subsidiaries in Malaysia bought banks in Beverly Hills, shopping centres in Fort Worth, and acreage in Florida. In England, they bought townhouses in London's West End, country cottages in the Lake District. Their girls were at Stanford, Chicago,

Columbia, Oxford, the Sorbonne. Their sons were at Cambridge, Caltech, MIT and Harvard Business School. Contingency planning.

Kipling once asked of Hong Kong, 'How is it that everybody here smells of money?' A century later, economist Milton Friedman had the answer. Hong Kong, he said, was 'a one-legged man, winning a two-legged race.' The smell of money was his sweat.

Overwhelmed by the one-legged man, many of Hong Kong's old Noble Houses lost their nerve. In self-defence, the British focused their energies on a small group, which left the field wide open to the Shanghai Boys. Overseas Chinese money flowed in from all around the Pacific Rim. Black money was everywhere, flowing through arteries offshore, looking for a bigger return, a place to hide, or a laundry. Regional networks took care of moving it around. Deals that began in Sumatra could move in hours through Singapore to Hong Kong, London and New York, and never leave Chinese hands. Some governments set up their own national banks, like Malaysia's Bank Bumiputra, to break the Chinese grip, but a one-legged man is harder to trip.

The mass movement of huge sums offshore only became a world-wide phenomenon in the late 1960s, when multinational corporations began using Hong Kong, Liberia, Panama and Bermuda to hide profits and to conduct transfer-pricing schemes. The Chinese were twenty years ahead.

The idea of offshore investing is to make as much money as possible while paying as little tax as possible – remaining invisible so nobody knows you did it. Overseas Chinese investors turned this into fine art. With one hand, they controlled the fastest-growing economies in the world. With the other, they moved their personal assets offshore through private Chinese bankers and fund managers. Their capital moved effortlessly across political boundaries creating a borderless economy, long before the concept became fashionable in the West. By the 1990s, there were thirty-three offshore tax havens, such as the Cayman Islands, crowded with bank branches. The banks were followed by fund managers, and the offshore fund business became one of the world's great growth industries. Again the Overseas Chinese were decades ahead.

Rapid developments in information technology during the same period made it easier for individuals and small companies to avoid taxes and regulations by turning the paper-chase into a computer game. Information, capital, gold and foreign exchange flowed freely. It was simple to hide ownership of private companies. Hong Kong became a world financial centre partly because its telecommunications networks were superior to those of the international financial centre in London. The colony's system of taxes ignored interest and earnings, as well as profits derived from overseas operations, and limited the government's share of profits to 16.5 per cent.

A large part of the Hong Kong business community was totally occupied making money for invisible customers without attracting the taxman in any jurisdiction. This is one of the roles of the precious metals trade, as embodied in Hong Kong's Gold and Silver Exchange. The exchange maintains an elaborate system of self-regulation to assure that its members meet their commitments, much like the guilds of Ningpo oversaw the workings of their native banks. But beyond that the exchange reveals no interest in where business really originates, and it keeps no records of transactions. In this way it assures that gold will continue to be an ideal way to hide wealth.

As a meeting point for East and West, Hong Kong remains unrivalled. Even members of the families of the ruling Politburo in Beijing make use of Hong Kong invisibility to hide their investments, privately engineered arms deals, or dabbling in the heroin trade. Like the Shanghai élite before them, the communist élite are patiently laying the groundwork to secure their personal wealth offshore – not in Hong Kong but through Hong Kong – before Beijing takes formal control and the opportunity is lost.

As the 1997 handover approaches, some of what the Shanghai Boys fled – malignant bureaucratic supervision and intervention – began to catch up. Because of these apprehensions, Hong Kong holding companies and trusts began shifting to the British Virgin Islands or to the Cayman Islands. For the time being, their administration and management remained in Hong Kong. Why was the Caribbean going Chinese? Thailand, Indonesia and Malaysia were uncertain havens. Singapore had the most to offer, but demanded a lot in return. Smart survivors never put all their children in one lifeboat – and, whatever happens in Hong Kong after the handover, of one thing you may be sure: the Shanghai Boys *will* survive, and prosper.

CHAPTER 17

THE FALL OF THE HOUSE OF CHIANG

THE SAME CANNOT BE SAID FOR THE TWO GREAT FAMILIES OF Taiwan, however: the Soongs and the Chiangs. And things started so well for them.

When young Charlie Soong arrived on the east coast of the United States in 1878, most Americans had never seen a Chinese, but they were ready to fall in love with China. As it turned out, Charlie and his children, through their partnerships with American presidents, generals and journalists, would become the most powerful Chinese in the world for the better part of the twentieth century. Americans were swept up in a consuming passion to evangelize the world, to convert all Asians and Africans into Christians, and to change their governments into democracies. The Methodist Church was actively involved in this movement, and they saw Charlie as a piece of clay they could mould into their ideal of what all Chinese would become.

Charlie did not join the Methodists for religious reasons. For him, it was like joining a triad. If he had gone to San Francisco or Vancouver, he would have found triads and benevolent societies well established. But there were none in the American south. Like a triad, the Methodist

Church offered friendship, support and protection. The church gave him valuable connections, help with his career, and financial aid from rich men such as Durham industrialist, Julian Carr. It was Carr who later set Charlie up as a Bible publisher in Shanghai and got him started in the noodle and the cigarette businesses. The Methodists sent Charlie back to China as a native missionary. They never questioned whether he was sincere or opportunistic. They did not see him as a Rice Christian. There was a bit of opportunism on both sides. In terms of money and political power, the experiment was a great success. In terms of saving China, it was a disaster.

The American love affair with China, like any love affair, involved a lot of fantasy and wishful thinking. Hucksters on both sides of the Pacific found it easy to take advantage. Charlie Soong and his children gave Methodists (and Americans in general) a feeling that they had special connections in China. In a way they did, because Charlie was secretly active in the patriotic Hung League and the Teochiu syndicates through his friendship with Dr Sun Yat-sen, who married Charlie's daughter, Ching-ling. Eldest daughter Ai-ling was married to one of China's richest bankers, H. H. Kung. When another daughter, May-ling, married Generalissimo Chiang Kai-shek, the family circle expanded to include the Shanghai Green Gang, a criminal organization heavily involved in racketeering and drug trafficking. As a young man, Chiang Kai-shek had been a Green Gang gunman involved in armed robberies and shootings, and he remained subordinate to Green Gang boss Tu Yueh-sheng till the Second World War. Thus, when Chiang Kai-shek took over the Kuomintang Party from Dr Sun, following his death in 1925, the KMT became criminalized.

After that, the close connection between the KMT and America through Madame Chiang and the Soong family was given two faces. On the surface, it looked like a good, clean, wholesome Christian connection between powerful Methodists in China and powerful Methodists in America. But beneath the surface were a lot of shady political and financial deals that made the Soongs very rich, and kept Chiant Kai-shek in power for an unnaturally long time. Many Americans in China before and during the Second World War knew that the KMT was corrupt and criminal, but these people did not have influence in Washington or New York. The British in particular despised the generalissimo, but in those days, Soong influence in America was so great that nobody dared to criticize them in public. There were careers to be made in politics, business and journalism by pushing a 'Christian partnership' between Washington and the Kuomintang. Nobody spoke about gangsters.

Those who did speak out, such as General Stilwell and diplomat John Service, had their careers and reputations destroyed. President Truman formed a sour opinion of the Soongs and called Chiang 'Generalissimo Cash-My-Check'. Americans in Chungking nicknamed him 'Chancre Jack' after his previous wife, Jenny Chen, let it be known that the generalissimo had given her gonorrhoea. In short, the Soongs and Chiangs had a lot of skeletons in the closet. But anyone who mentioned them could be certain of violent reprisals. This would turn out to include murder, by a Chinese hit team, in an American suburb.

As a publisher of influential magazines, Henry Luce became a leader of the China Lobby. The son of Methodist missionaries in China, he believed that he had inside knowledge of the Orient, while the Soong family played him like a harmonica. He was dazzled by Madame Chiang and thought her brother T. V. Soong was a financial wizard. Luce was a strong-willed, stubborn and single-minded man who became convinced that together he and the Soongs would rescue China from godless communism. His magazines – *Time*, *Life* and *Fortune* – published many articles glamorizing the Soongs and Chiangs, and did much to convince Americans to support the KMT. President Roosevelt also thought he understood China, because his family had made its fortune in the opium trade with Shanghai. The Soongs and the China Lobby convinced Roosevelt to back the KMT against the Japanese. Once Americans became involved with Generalissimo Chiang, they could not shake him off. By the time FDR realized that Chiang was still a gangster, it was too late (Roosevelt briefly considered having the generalissimo assassinated).

The Christian image of the Chiangs and Soongs was so deeply planted in American minds that it is still around today. If even half of what they said had been true, faith in them would surely have been justified.

Charlie's daughter May-ling was the Soong who exercised the most influence on American attitudes toward China. As a child she attended school in Georgia, where she developed a charming but manipulative personality much like Scarlett O'Hara's. Going on to Radcliffe, she matured into a very attractive, exceptionally intelligent and politically astute young women. She had an uncanny ability to beguile men and women. Thousands of American men seriously thought she was a Christian goddess defending China from the devil. Cynical men of long experience, such as General Claire Chennault of the Flying Tigers, confessed that they were secretly in love with Madame Chiang. One pilot related that when she commended him for a daring mission, she gave him such a look that his knees went rubbery. For thirty years running, millions of Americans voted her the woman they most admired on earth. They agreed that Washington should give hundreds of millions of dollars to the Soongs and Chiangs to save China. They did not realize that Madame Chiang had nothing to do with the real China. She was strictly ornamental.

May-ling's brother, T.V., also was skilled at manipulating Americans – particularly businessmen and politicians. T.V. was personally afraid of Generalissimo Chiang and his gangster associates, so he spent a lot of time in Washington as China's foreign minister and prime minister. He played poker with US government officials, including Cabinet members, and cultivated powerful journalists such as Stewart and Joseph Alsop. He gave many of them gifts that were calculated to impress without provoking unbearably guilty consciences. In return, he obtained military and financial support for Chiang's KMT and deals for the Soong family. Once, he got millions of dollars to buy American tanks for the Chinese army, but then said the ship was lost at sea. As it turned out, the tanks were phantoms, the ship never existed, and T.V. had pocketed the money.

During the 1940s, T. V. Soong was described as the richest man in the world. Sister May-ling also invested millions of dollars in American property. Eldest sister Ai-ling was in charge of the family finances, while two other brothers – T. A. Soong and T. L. Soong – started banks in New York and San Francisco to cloak Soong holdings in America. The only Soong who was not involved was sister Ching-ling, widow of Dr Sun Yat-sen. She had broken with her family when Generalissimo Chiang criminalized the KMT in 1926. For decades, she remained

relatively poor, sometimes with little to eat, although she was
honoured as Sun's widow and eventually became a figurehead in the
People's Republic. As the only sincere one in her generation, she was
despised by her brothers and sisters.

A lot about the Soongs, Kungs and Chiangs was hidden from the
American public; not the least of it was the fact that Western-style
democracy had no place in their plans for China. They saw themselves
as China's newest imperial dynasty, not as temporary power-holders
to be voted out of office. But as always happens in a dynasty, there was
the ticklish question of who would ultimately become the generalissimo's successor. The family power struggle became a hard-fought
contest between the generalissimo's wife and his son by a previous
wife.

Chiang Ching-kuo (known to everyone as 'CCK') was the
generalissimo's only son and heir, though there was also an adopted
son, Chiang Wei-kuo, the illegitimate child of Chiang's best friend.
CCK was the child of Chiang's first (and only legitimate) wife, the
result of an arranged marriage in his ancestral village; long after that he
took up with a woman named Jenny Chen, then dumped her for a
bigamous political marriage to May-ling Soong.

As an heir apparent, CCK was never promising. At age sixteen, after
getting in trouble for running with hooligans, he was packed off to
Russia to study at Sun Yat-sen University, which welcomed Chinese
revolutionary cadres. Graduating in 1927, he asked his father for
permission to come home to China, but was refused. The generalissimo
was busy exterminating the communist faction of the KMT in
Shanghai with the help of the Green Gang. In Moscow, CCK was
infuriated by news of his father's anti-communism and publicly
denounced him. Still in the Soviet Union eight years later, CCK married
an orphaned Russian girl. In 1937, he was finally allowed to return to
China at the age of twenty-eight, accompanied by his wife and two
infant children. Greeting them at the airport, the generalissimo
gestured toward May-ling Soong and said, 'Now come meet your new
mother.' CCK snapped, 'That's not my mother,' and stalked away. It
was the beginning of a power struggle that would provoke moments of
high drama, and last until the Three Generation Curse finished them all
off.

CCK had an uphill struggle to prove himself, after his brush with communist heresy. He joined the KMT, and his father used him as a bludgeon, sending him here and there as his personal enforcer, to block the activities of rivals. Whenever politicians or underworld figures in different Chinese cities did not keep up their kickbacks to the regime, CCK was sent in with a team of security thugs to crack down.

CCK's adopted brother enjoyed a more genial relationship with Madame Chiang and the generalissimo. While CCK was short, chubby and uncertain, Wei-kuo was a handsome bon vivant, bright and humorous. During the years CCK was in Russia, Wei-kuo stayed at the generalissimo's side, until arrangements were made for him to undergo training with the 98th Regiment of Hitler's *Wehrmacht*, with whom he took part in the invasion of Austria in 1938. In 1940, he returned to China and was stationed at Chiang's wartime capital in Chungking, while CCK trudged the provinces. Because Wei-kuo spoke English, May-ling arranged for him to escort Wendell Willkie on his tour of China. Entertaining Willkie lavishly in Chungking, May-ling confessed to the former US presidential candidate in her silkiest Georgia drawl that he was a very 'disturbing influence'.

In the summer of 1943, all members of the family who were not already licensed Christians joined the Methodist Church on the generalissimo's orders, in a baptism ceremony at Chungking. CCK's Russian wife, known in China as Fang-liang, and his adopted brother Chiang Wei-kuo, were reluctantly baptized at the same time. The baptisms were a publicity stunt arranged to coincide with the start of May-ling's triumphal 1943 tour of America which climaxed in her stay in the Roosevelt White House and her appearance before a joint session of Congress. CCK was bitter about being forced to go through the baptism charade, but May-ling's tour paid off with a fresh deluge of American aid, and a grudging invitation for the generalissimo to attend the Cairo Talks, which made him seem to be on confidential terms with the Big Three – Roosevelt, Churchill and Stalin.

Despite the financial success of her 1943 American tour, the Chiangs' presence at the Cairo Talks was a fiasco. Thereafter, the generalissimo seemed disenchanted about May-ling's fabled ability to wind Americans around her finger. He began to regard the Soong clan as a dangerous nuisance. When Chiang's secret police chief, Tai-li, learned that Roosevelt had secretly ordered Chiang's assassination, and suspected the Soongs of involvement, May-ling's leverage with the generalissimo diminished sharply. Chiang took up again with Jenny Chen. Jenny, a reed-thin, pretty girl who was taken out of a Shanghai brothel to be the generalissimo's mistress or common-law wife during the 1920s, was believed to have borne him a daughter during the Second World War, when she was briefly reinstalled in Chungking, but the fate of the child is unknown.

Chiang began to lash out at the rest of May-ling's vicious clan. This squabbling grew out of the fact that the Soongs had long been channelling American aid funds into their private bank accounts, rather than turning the money over to Chiang. As premier and foreign minister, T. V. Soong was able to withhold a larger share than other members of the family thought equitable. The generalissimo wanted to pry the foreign-aid portfolio out of T.V.'s hands, but was afraid of completely losing Washington's financial and military support. As a safeguard, T.V. hastily moved his base of operations to America, where he was out of reach of Chiang and his secret police. The moment the war ended, however, the generalissimo struck back, charging T.V., his sister Ai-ling, and her husband, H. H. Kung, with corruption, and expelling them all from China. Before they fled, the Kungs arranged for their son David to become general manager of the family's Shanghai holding company, Yangtze Development Corporation, which had an enormously lucrative monopoly on importation of American humanitarian aid supplies.

Shanghai was a Soong stronghold, and one of their loyalists became the postwar mayor, K. C. Wu, a cultivated, urbane man popular with Western diplomats and businessmen. Wu had extremely good American connections and ivy-league credentials from Princeton. After she married the generalissimo in 1927, May-ling had insisted on Wu becoming Chiang's English-language secretary, which allowed her to put words in his mouth (Chiang spoke no English). During the war, Wu became mayor of Chungking. At the Cairo Talks he was Chiang's official translator, working closely with May-ling.

It has always been implicit that there was a special relationship between May-ling and K. C. Wu. This was a consistent undercurrent during the decades of her loveless political marriage to the generalissimo which many assume was never consummated. That would hardly be surprising, if any credence were given to what Jenny Chen said about the generalissimo giving her gonorrhoea the year before. Certainly K. C. Wu was in continual liaison with Madame Chiang from 1927 to the early 1950s, and was one of her closest advisers and intimates, if nothing more.

In the late 1940s, the generalissimo tried to regain control of Shanghai from the Soong clan by appointing his son – now General Chiang Ching-kuo – as the new anti-corruption tsar. CCK was ordered to erase all vestiges of the Kungs in particular, crack down on the black market, jail all unscrupulous speculators, and assist in the economic 'reformation' of Shanghai's underworld – which meant bringing all rival forces into line with the KMT. Using secret police as shock troops, CCK made this a personal vendetta against the entire Soong clan and its supporters. Anyone suspected of having dealings in the black market, or in currency speculation, was given a choice of co-operation or death. His men held street-corner tribunals and sidewalk executions. When his agents followed a tip and discovered a huge cache of bootleg American and European humanitarian aid goods on the premises of Yangtze Development, CCK gleefully arrested general manager David Kung, Madame Chiang Kai-shek's favourite nephew.

May-ling was in Nanking, hosting a diplomatic supper, when she received a phone call from Mayor K. C. Wu advising her of David's arrest. She flew into a rage and confronted the generalissimo, punctuating her shrieks with a few high-speed cosmetic bottles. Chiang wiped his hands of the whole business. Flying down to Shanghai, May-ling confronted CCK personally and demanded David's release into her custody. Checking with his father, CCK received chilly instructions to back off. For CCK, this was a serious loss of face, one he chalked up to his father's insufferable concubine and her backstairs collaborator, K. C. Wu. May-ling hurried David Kung onto a plane for Hong Kong, with connections to Florida.

By then, China's long civil war was drawing to a close, but the generalissimo had chosen a new stronghold to which he could withdraw. After the Japanese surrender in 1945, KMT forces had rushed to Taiwan to reclaim the island for China. Chiang's crony, General Chen Yi, was appointed governor, and immediately began looting. The island was rich by comparison with the Mainland. Fifty years of Japanese rule had left the Taiwanese more prosperous, modern and educated than their Mainland cousins. The Taiwanese were mostly coastal Chinese from across the strait in Fukien province who had been settling the big island since Coxinga's days. In the mountains lived a few aboriginals like the Ainu of Japan, remnants of an ancient Pacific culture. The KMT considered the majority Fukienese population of Taiwan to be irrelevant, and insisted that 'native Taiwanese' were only 'sub-human bush-people'.

General Chen Yi's henchmen, including Mainland gangsters, engaged in wholesale extortion, kidnapping, embezzlement and black marketeering. Any Taiwanese who dared to complain was branded a communist and a traitor, had his property expropriated, and was clapped in jail. In a few months, Taiwan was ruined. Food ran out, cholera and bubonic plague struck. Despite their fear, people began to protest. On 28 February 1947, KMT soldiers beat a street vendor. When an angry crowd gathered, the soldiers shot them down, touching off riots that escalated into island-wide rebellion and demands of self-rule. Buying time, General Chen Yi began negotiations, while KMT reinforcements poured over from the Mainland. Fifty thousand troops were unleashed against the civilian population. All doctors, lawyers, journalists, teachers and students were rounded up and shot, wiping out a generation of leaders. Mass executions took place everywhere. An assistant US navy attaché saw civilians 'bayoneted . . . without provocation . . . students tied together, being driven to the execution grounds . . . One foreigner counted more than thirty young bodies – in student uniforms – lying along the roadside east of Taipei; they had had their noses and ears slit or hacked off, and many had been castrated. Two students were beheaded near my front gate.' More than fifty thousand civilians were slain, none of them 'aboriginals'.

Compared to the 1989 crackdown at Tienanmen, this was a major bloodbath. Yet there was no great international outcry against the KMT. The Mainland was in chaos, and the Chiang regime was in full retreat. What happened on Taiwan seemed secondary. The fate of Nationalist China also seemed increasingly irrelevant. When Chiang fled to Taiwan in 1949, few thought his regime would survive on the island more than a year. Britain recognized the new communist government of Mao Tse-tung. It seemed only a matter of time before the United States would follow suit. The Truman State Department notified its diplomatic posts to expect the fall of Taiwan to the communists and said America would not provide Chiang with military aid or advice.

This posed an immense public relations problem. As in the past, Chiang relied on May-ling and her American admirers to rally Washington politicians and the press behind the 'Christian Hope of China'. May-ling had flown to America in late 1948 to seek support. American conservatives, aroused by her exhortations, Henry Luce's magazines, and an all-out campaign by the China lobby, counter-attacked, provoking fears of a worldwide communist takeover. Millions of dollars were spent by the Soongs and their allies on a nationwide media blitz. Much of this, as Truman grumbled, was funded by stolen US foreign aid money, redirected at Americans.

In an effort to dress up the KMT's image in American eyes, in December 1949, May-ling badgered the generalissimo into appointing former Shanghai mayor K. C. Wu as the new governor of Taiwan, minister without portfolio, and member of the standing committee of the KMT Central Executive. She made it sound as if Wu, the Princetonian, would be running Nationalist China from then on. Wu hastily introduced reforms. But the Chiang regime was saved instead by the outbreak of the Korean War in June 1950. Thereafter, American policy was reversed and Washington committed itself to defending the Nationalist regime. Taiwan was to become America's 'unsinkable aircraft carrier'. The Seventh Fleet moved into the Taiwan Strait, and a new programme of large-scale US military and economic assistance pumped whole blood into the KMT's well-perforated veins. The CIA made Taiwan its primary operational base in Asia for the next forty years, and the KMT was given precious time to secure its grip.

When May-ling rejoined the generalissimo on Taiwan in 1950, it was only to reclaim her part of the throne and to resume the struggle for her political survival, again under attack by her stepson. Had she remained abroad any longer, her political influence in Taiwan would have withered, as her supporters in the so-called Palace Clique were squeezed out of their posts one by one. If she did not have adequate leverage when the generalissimo died, CCK would be victorious in the succession struggle, and May-ling's power base could not survive his vengeance. Each time she turned her back to visit the United States, CCK moved up another rung and busied himself weeding out vestiges of Soong influence.

In May-ling's absence during all of 1949, CCK had become the generalissimo's personal assistant. He had also been made chief of security overseeing the Political Department of Taiwan's Defence Ministry; the secret police apparatus on the island, it was modelled on Moscow's NKVD. Secret police terror was crucial to the maintenance of KMT control on Taiwan. The island remained under martial law, with sandbagged machine-gun emplacements at strategic points in and around the city of Taipei, and checkpoints on every road. Coincident-ally, this job also put CCK in direct charge of the KMT opium armies in the Golden Triangle.

On a personal level, CCK was able to use his new job to get revenge on Governor K. C. Wu, for his humiliation in Shanghai.

The enlightened Wu was attempting to create a new Nationalist China, under a more liberal regime. He had been allowed to proceed with these reforms only while the generalissimo was desperate to regain American military and financial aid. The moment this aid was resumed, the need for liberal window-dressing ceased, and Wu became expendable. But there was more to it. Whatever K. C. Wu's private relationship with Madame Chiang, it was widely assumed that on the death of the ageing generalissimo, May-ling hoped to hold onto power herself, and would appoint Wu as her prime minister. CCK's dread of this prospect suggests that it was taken very seriously. Soon after he became chief of security, CCK arrested one of Wu's oldest friends on trumped-up charges of communist collaboration. The man was sentenced to death. Governor Wu angrily confronted CCK, then went to see the generalissimo. The death sentence was commuted. Once again, CCK felt humiliated.

During his conversation with the generalissimo, Wu said, 'If you really love CCK, you should not put him in charge of the secret service.' In his high-pitched voice, Chiang screamed at Wu to shut up. When he learned that Wu had tried to unhorse him, CCK was so enraged that he had agents rig the steering of the governor's car, nearly killing Wu and his wife. The accident badly frightened the couple. In a letter of resignation, Wu told the generalissimo, 'You loved your son more than the people, and the party more than the nation.' In public, Wu said he was resigning because of asthma, and applied for a passport to go to the United States for a cure. CCK blocked his departure for months, while secret policemen dogged his steps. Only after May-ling intervened personally were Wu and his wife permitted to leave. But Wu's son was kept hostage to guarantee his father's silence. After they left, Wu's name was blackened in the Taiwan press. Evidence was cooked that Wu had embezzled government funds.

When the end of the Korean War in 1953 reduced American anxieties about the Far East, and made the KMT vulnerable to criticism once again, Wu counter-attacked. With surprising candour, he told the American press that Taiwan was a Soviet-style dictatorship, corruption was rife at the top, and everyone on the island lived in terror of the secret police. Privately, he told political and business leaders about CCK's drunken binges, which he said had begun with stupefying bouts of vodka in Moscow in the late 1920s, and talked about CCK's use of secret police terror to carry out furtive love affairs in Taipei. In one liaison with an opera singer, he claimed, CCK had got rid of the singer's previous lover by jailing him as a communist. In the course of these affairs, it developed that CCK had fathered two illegitimate children – hardly the sort of man that puritan Yale whiffenpoofs like Henry Luce should want running China, Wu said.

The candour was wasted. By this point, a CIA agent in Taipei named Ray Cline had established a close personal bond with CCK, so for some hardline strategists in Washington, it made more sense to have CCK win the power struggle, and to keep Taiwan under the thumb of 'dedicated anti-communists.' Indeed, when May-ling flew off to America for a long visit, Washington pressed for CCK to be named deputy head of the National Defence Council, with control of all KMT political, military and security operations, which gave Ray Cline indirect influence over the entire establishment. When the two countries signed a mutual defence treaty in Washington, CCK was the one courted, not May-ling. Outwardly, she remained the world's most famous and influential Overseas Chinese, but behind the scenes she was losing her grip.

May-ling had to find a new champion to replace K. C. Wu. The generalissimo was becoming senile, so he was no longer vulnerable to her Olympian rages, but he was still able to make trouble. When she returned to Taiwan late in 1954 to help celebrate Chiang Kai-shek's sixty-seventh birthday, the doddering generalissimo stayed foxily out of sight in the terminal while CCK and his son, Chiang Hsiao-wu (called Alex), walked out to the plane to greet May-ling. While the cameras whirred, she had no choice but to go tight-lipped through the arrival ceremony, but as a put-down it was staggering. She fought back by starting to work on the generalissimo's adopted son, General Chiang Wei-kuo, in an attempt to make him her new cat's paw.

Wei-kuo's first wife had died, reportedly from drugs taken to induce labour so their child would be born on the generalissimo's birthday. May-ling persuaded Wei-kuo to marry one of her closest friends, in what was seen as a blatant power play. But the marriage definitely was not a love-match, and the couple soon separated.

As May-ling and the generalissimo never had any children, and Wei-kuo had none that survived, the only heirs in the third generation were the children of CCK and his Russian wife, three boys and a girl. The generalissimo picked their names, each containing the character 'Hsiao', meaning 'filial piety'. He wanted them never to forget which ancestor to worship. Half Russian, half Chinese, they had a difficult time fitting into a singularly xenophobic society. Instead of iron discipline, CCK's children were indulged by everyone, including 'Grandmother' May-ling. The elder boys earned reputations as dangerous troublemakers, consorting with gangsters and prostitutes (as grandfather had in Shanghai half a century earlier), while emulating their father's drinking bouts.

The eldest, Hsiao-wen, was expelled from the Army Academy after repeatedly going AWOL on drunken sprees in triad brothels. CCK sent him to America, where he was booted out of Georgetown University and the University of California. His father then set him up as the office manager of Taiwan Power Company, a government enterprise, but by 1970 booze, syphilis, and diabetes had turned him into a vegetable. As Chinese sources put it, 'not simply a case of debauchery.'

CCK's second child, and only daughter, studied in California and married the son of Defence Minister Yu Ta-wei. Yu faded from prominence in 1964 when CCK swallowed his job.

The third child, Hsiao-wu or Alex, was born in 1945. Unlike his older siblings, Alex and his little brother, Hsiao-yung, were educated entirely in Taipei. Surrounded by people anxious to profit by ties to the Chiangs, the boys were pandered to by the worst elements. Alex developed into a chain-smoking alcoholic with a nervous twitch. He hung out with professional killers on the nightclub circuit, and surrounded himself with aspiring actresses, singers and teenage junkies. He loved guns and reputedly had a taste for sadism. No-one dared to contradict him.

His little brother, Hsiao-yung, was by most accounts completely different: intelligent, quick-witted, well groomed and polite.

May-ling doted on the two younger boys, but as they grew up, she fixed on Alex as the most likely to succeed to the throne. If she was going to lose the struggle to CCK, it would not be for long. She knew that CCK was a severe diabetic, a condition aggravated by his heavy drinking and obesity, and he would not be on the throne long before his poor health intervened, and Alex would take over.

When the generalissimo died in April 1975, at the age of eighty-seven, CCK became president of Nationalist China. May-ling attempted to have herself appointed the new chairman of the KMT Party, but was outmanoeuvred by CCK and his supporters. Three weeks later, CCK became KMT chairman. After a bitter quarrel, he demanded that she go into exile. At seventy-eight, May-ling was frail and ill. She flew to New York and became a recluse at David Kung's sprawling estate in Lattingtown, Long Island. Wei-kuo's estranged second wife came to stay with her there. Only bodyguards and doctors were allowed inside its perimeter. The only influence she had left in Taiwan was through her so-called 'Palace Clique of Eunuchs', led by Chin Hsiao-yi.

Chin was a cold-blooded political lizard of the variety commonly found clinging to the lacquered rafters of the Forbidden City in the days of imperial China. He had been Chiang Kai-shek's Chinese-language secretary in the 1950s, and was one of the High Mandarins allowed to be present at the deathbed of the generalissimo. As recorder of the great leader's will, he could claim a position as guru and oracle, passing on to ordinary mortals what was really meant by the mumblings of an old man who had become increasingly incoherent after the Korean War. In those days, May-ling was able to manipulate policy by choosing who should be the generalissimo's English-language and Chinese-language secretaries. In this manner, she could put the generalissimo's 'decisions' in her own words, and shade meanings to suit her interests.

Enemies called Chin Hsiao-yi 'the last eunuch of the Chiang Dynasty'. In his years of service, he became very rich, and he tried to please Madame Chiang in every possible way. All her publications and public statements were carefully groomed by him, and during her absences he was her spokesman in Taiwan. As a sinecure, she got him a post as head of the Palace Museum, which contained treasures that had been collected by the Manchu Emperor Chien Lung, and had originally been the nucleus of the National Museum of Peking. As the Japanese had advanced into North China in the 1930s, Chiang Kai-shek had had the treasures moved to Nanking. His agents had then hauled the crated art works to Szechuan Province for the duration of the war. Many masterpieces had disappeared in the process, sold to wealthy con-noisseurs overseas. Nearly a quarter of a million paintings, porcelains, jades and bronzes had finally been spirited away to Taipei in 1949, where Chin became the sole individual controlling their fate. His position as head of the Palace Museum gave him enormous prestige, while keeping him out of the direct line of fire. Given the respect that Chinese accord to art and culture, the arrangement was ingenious for May-ling.

Four years after the death of Chiang Kai-shek, Taiwan exploded. The political opposition, mostly Taiwanese-born Fukienese – survivors of the 1947 bloodbath – had gradually gained a voice as the 'Tangwai' or 'outside party'. They were allowed to exist as evidence of democracy, but were kept entirely powerless. KMT stalwarts grew alarmed when the Tangwai began holding rallies around the island. One such rally was planned for December 1979 in Kaohsiung, Taiwan's second largest city, to mark the anniversary of the UN Universal Declaration on Human Rights. The rally was outlawed, but ten thousand protesters gathered anyway. Provoked by KMT thugs, rioting began, and scores were injured. Police jailed most Tangwai leaders. The Chiang family felt threatened more by Taiwanese than by communists.

One Tangwai leader, Lin Yi-shiung, was nearly beaten to death by government agents. His mother tried to notify Amnesty International. The following day, Lin's seven-year-old twin daughters, and his sixty-year-old mother, were stabbed to death in their home. A third child almost died. According to the US embassy, the killers were members of the Iron Blood Patriots Society, and had been ordered by one of their senior members – Alex Chiang – to 'teach Lin a lesson'.

As heir apparent, Alex was rising fast. The year of the Lin murders, he was assigned by President Chiang to oversee the weekly meetings of the National Security Council, and report back to his father. Alex personally sanctioned the Bamboo Gang and the Iron Blood Patriots as paramilitary branches of the secret police, to carry out missions overseas that might embarrass the regime if its own agents were caught. In return, they were promised a share of KMT heroin smuggling to America. Previously, the Bamboo Gang's thousand members had only been engaged in gambling, prostitution, extortion and murder. When Alex let them in on the KMT heroin trade, membership jumped to forty thousand.

Gang boss Chen Chi-li could not swim, so he was called 'Dry Duck'. Alex was regularly inebriated at Dry Duck's nightclubs and brothels. He never paid for drinks or women. On these nightclub prowls, he was often accompanied by his uncle, General Chiang Wei-kuo, who shared his taste for movie starlets. They became blood brothers of Dry Duck. Thanks to President Chiang's family, the Bamboo Gang soon had gunmen and heroin brokers based in the United States, and wherever else adequate cover was provided by a community of Overseas Chinese.

Because they were a supposed ally in the battle against communism, the KMT discovered that it could carry on illegal activities – military espionage, heroin smuggling, kidnapping and murder – inside the United States with no serious consequences. They did so for forty years.

In 1975, a military attaché at Taiwan's embassy in Washington offered three million dollars to an FBI informant to buy the latest wire-guided torpedoes. The attaché also proposed buying atomic weapons and guided missiles. President Ford blocked prosecution because Washington did not want bad publicity about an 'ally'. Because he could no longer be covert, the admiral was recalled to Taiwan.

One of CCK's first responsibilities after becoming chief of security in the early 1950s had been the supervision of the KMT opium armies in the Golden Triangle. Since then, the Taiwan government had become a major heroin marketer all over the world. General Tuan collected the opium tar each season and brought it by pack train to the Thai border for processing into morphine base and various grades of heroin. In Chiengmai, General Lee acted as chief broker. Both Generals Lee and Tuan have said they reported directly to CCK, which meant that a second generation of the Chiang family was now personally involved in heroin trafficking. While Thailand and Hong Kong were the main Teochiu trans-shipment points, Taiwan was the main Hokkien drug base. Previously, this was regarded as private enterprise by syndicates. But in the fall of 1977, American agents discovered that Taiwan was using diplomatic pouches to smuggle heroin to the US. KMT government officials and diplomats were handling the drugs personally. Again, Washington covered up the scandal. In American and Canadian cities, the heroin was sold by Chinese street gangs, including the Bamboo Gang. Even today, more than 80 per cent of the 2,000 tons of heroin coming out of the Golden Triangle each year is shipped to America by Teochiu syndicates through Hong Kong, or by Hokkien syndicates through Taiwan. Taiwan's share of the two-hundred-and-fifty-billion-dollar-a-year trade poured black money into the coffers of the Chiang regime. These drug profits are part of Taiwan's huge hard currency reserves. Taiwan's known reserves are not as big as those of Japan, but Taiwan has a smaller population, so its reserves are larger per capita. Its unacknowledged reserves in black money derived from drugs, product counterfeiting, and underworld activities, including money-laundering, are perhaps equal to Japan's. 'Taiwan's economic miracle is built on illegal businesses,' admitted a Taiwanese banker. The 'parallel' economy may make up 40 per cent of the whole. This includes an underground futures market, an off-exchange stock market, black-market foreign exchange networks, and an underground banking system. The old gag is that Taiwan is the world's largest Chinese laundry.

Another aspect of the KMT dominance: since 1929, the KMT has insisted that all Overseas Chinese are citizens of China under the legal protection of the KMT. As the Overseas Chinese population in the

United States passed the eight-hundred-thousand mark and became more wealthy, they were also more influential. By Taiwan's logic, the KMT had the right to exercise political thought-control over all Overseas Chinese. Anti-KMT activity of any kind was seditious.

Every KMT intelligence organization had secret agents and informers in America to keep an eye on the Chinese communities. They posed as businessmen or students. Most were trained by the Garrison Command under General Wang Ching-hsu ('Big Wang'). Six other bureaux sent agents to America to monitor anti-KMT dissident groups.

In one case, Chen Wen-chen, a Taiwanese citizen, was a professor at Carnegie-Mellon University in Pittsburgh. On a visit to his family in Taiwan in the summer of 1981, he was picked up by agents of Big Wang. Informants had heard the professor criticize the KMT for violation of human rights following the Kaohsiung Riots. The next day, Chen was found battered to death on the campus of National Taiwan University, his back broken. The KMT said he had committed suicide by throwing himself off a roof. General Big Wang said Chen was 'full of remorse' for aiding the opposition. American investigators discovered that the Iron Blood Patriots, who had murdered the Lin family under orders from Alex Chiang, had beaten Professor Chen and thrown him off a building – also on orders from Alex Chiang. Despite US Congressional hearings, no action was taken by Washington.

Alex was untouchable. Among other things, he had himself named director of the Broadcasting Corporation of China, the KMT radio service, which gave him droit de seigneur on all aspiring pop singers on the island. Then word got around that Alex had May-ling's political blessing. At the urging of his formidable step-grandmother, he became politically ambitious, and involved himself in KMT party politics, using his own patronage to build a power base of military, security, political and business leaders. Alex's father, the president, was in deteriorating health due to complications from diabetes and alcoholism. Although May-ling was in her eighties and had undergone two mastectomies and other surgery, she pulled strings from her reclusive exile in Long Island. The old campaigner was determined to outlive her hated rival, and to see her grandson on the throne. Then she could make a triumphal return.

Early in the 1980s, the family was angered by the publication of a slim Chinese-language biography of CCK that discussed his sex life and his illegitimate children, and a magazine article describing CCK's attempts to murder K. C. Wu. Both the book and article were written by Henry Liu, a former KMT propagandist who had been a paid informant in America both for Taipei and for Beijing's spy services, sometimes simultaneously. After becoming American citizens, Liu and his wife were now running a small shop on San Francisco's Fisherman's Wharf. At heart, Liu was a journalist, however, so he continued to write about President Chiang's private life. He accepted bribes to tone down his treatment, but this produced mixed results. Now that he was an American citizen, Liu thought nothing bad could happen to him.

In July 1984, members of the Chiang family talked to heads of Taiwan's secret agencies about how to silence the writer. Some Asian news reports said Madame Chiang was angered by a rash of bad publicity about the Soong family and discussed this by telephone with Alex Chiang. Henry Liu was known to be preparing a biography of K. C. Wu that might raise eyebrows about Wu's relationship with May-ling. CCK and Wei-kuo were also said to be enraged by the prospect of more muckraking. Whoever inspired him, in the end it was established that Alex Chiang personally ordered the killing of Henry Liu.

The murder was coordinated by Admiral Wang Hsi-ling ('Little Wang'), the director of the intelligence bureau of the Ministry of National Defence, which had earlier been scolded by the American government for heroin smuggling. Admiral Little Wang's superior was General Big Wang, who had arranged the torture of Professor Chen before his murder.

As Little Wang put it: 'There is a traitor in the United States. Despite [our] support . . . he has thrown in his lot with the communists. He has . . . recently written a book entitled *The Biography of Chiang Ching-kuo* in which he maliciously slanders our national leader. This . . . has triggered [others] to publish stories that denigrate this government and smear the image of the nation . . . [Now] this traitor is preparing to write . . . *The Biography of K. C. Wu*, which will further denigrate our leader . . . Liu must be killed. If he survives, matters will get out of hand.'

Then Little Wang added nostalgically, 'A guy like Henry would have

been killed long ago if a Chief of Police like Tai Li were [still] alive.'
Those were the good old days.

Bamboo Gang boss Dry Duck was told to arrange the killing. As a
longtime intimate of Alex and his uncle Wei-kuo, there was no
question of Dry Duck's loyalty. In return, his gang would be allowed to
take over all KMT heroin deliveries to America. So pleased was Dry
Duck that he personally financed the San Francisco murder, refusing
reimbursement or per diem.

Henry Liu was murdered in his garage on 15 October 1984. Dry
Duck's boys arrived on bicycles, shot him once in the head, and twice in
the stomach.

The clumsiness of the killers led to their immediate exposure and the
identification of high-level participants, including Admiral Little
Wang, General Hu Yi-men, deputy director of intelligence at the
Defence Ministry, and Colonel Chen Hu-men, a deputy chief of the
defence intelligence bureau. Among other acts of folly, the killers
placed a trans-Pacific phone call to the offices of Taiwan's defence
intelligence bureau, to boast that the murder had been carried out
successfully. This call was routinely monitored by spy satellites of
America's National Security Agency. Only hours after the murder,
Washington knew all about it, and about who was involved, on both
sides of the Pacific. Although the Taiwan government tried to make it
seem that only three officials were culpable, in fact its entire national
security organization had been fully informed throughout. A few
months later, General Big Wang, head of the combined national
security and intelligence operations, bragged at a liquid lunch with US
officials that he, too, had known about the murder in advance.

American demands for punishment led to the trial and imprisonment in Taiwan of Admiral Little Wang, General Hu Yi-men and
Colonel Chen Hu-men, as fall guys for the rest. Word spread all over
Taiwan, then all over Asia, that they had received their orders from
Madame Chiang's playboy grandson. Alex Chiang's wings melted and
he fell suddenly from grace. His identification with the murder caused
such intense embarrassment to both Chiang and Soong families (and
their constituencies) that Alex was hustled off to Singapore as a trade
representative, to get him out of sight. His status evaporated overnight.

After the Liu murder, President Chiang spent the remaining four years of his life in a vigorous effort to rehabilitate his public image and that of the KMT. At the end of 1985, he formally announced there would be no family succession. In July 1987, he ended martial law for the first time since 1945. However, the same year, his adopted brother General Chiang Wei-kuo, blood brother of the imprisoned Bamboo Gang leader, was appointed by CCK as secretary-general of the National Security Council – not a move to inspire confidence.

There was a frantic eye-gouging scramble for power in Taiwan after CCK's death in January 1988. May-ling, now in her nineties, sought to sabotage the nomination of the chosen successor, President Lee Tung-hui, as acting chairman of the ruling KMT. She wanted to be named honorary chairman herself and to have control vested in members of her Palace Clique. But she was outmanoeuvred once again.

At her insistence, Alex Chiang was allowed back from Singapore in June 1988, to run for a seat on the KMT Central Committee (along with his kid brother, Hsiao-yung, and two of CCK's illegitimate sons). Uncle Wei-kuo ran for election to the KMT Standing Committee. The Chiangs were attempting a comeback. But even the corrupt KMT had had enough. Alex was forced to back out. Wei-kuo was shunted off to the Central Advisory Committee, a KMT retirement home. President Lee cut a deal with May-ling. In exchange for her endorsement of him as Party Chairman, she could retain her honorary position as the Advisory Committee's chairman. If she refused, she would lose even that withered appendix of prestige.

A pariah in Taiwan, Alex Chiang again went into exile, this time to Japan, where he drowned his sorrows for the last time in 1991. His death marked the fall of the House of Chiang. All that remained of the KMT was a police state, and even that was a spent cartridge. It was only a matter of time before the people of Taiwan would eject it, and start life over.

CHAPTER 18

RESHAPING AMERICA

MANY THOUGHTFUL CHINESE ARE SERIOUSLY WORRIED ABOUT what will happen in the next few years. Those on the Mainland fear that the lid will blow off its pressure-cooker economy, and that the resulting chaos may bring civil war, which could involve other countries in a regional conflagration. Those on Taiwan fear what will happen to them if Mainland chaos and military actions result in an attempt to seize their island. In Hong Kong, the immediate fear is of what will happen when the crown colony reverts to Beijing's control in 1997, followed two years later by Macao. Tienanmen Square is still fresh in everyone's mind. Similarly, the Chinese in Indonesia fear what could follow President Suharto's departure, while those in Malaysia worry about the escalating chauvinism of the Malay élite.

The sum of all these fears is that many Chinese want out now. Those people are doing everything possible to migrate to Canada, Australia, the United States, New Zealand, Britain, or to continental Europe (in that order) – as far from China as they can get. If they cannot leave, or don't want to leave until the last moment, they are taking precautions, such as moving their money to Zurich, the Caymans or New York. At the same time, paradoxically, Western businessmen are equally frantic to get into China. All *they* stand to lose is their shirts.

Such worries have provoked a major surge in Chinese emigration during the 1980s and 1990s, with tens of thousands leaving Asia each year, both legally and illegally. It is only a preview of the flood that will come if their fears prove true – and for the destination countries, the results will be both good and bad.

On the positive side, most of the legal immigrants in the new wave are of a completely different type from those who left Asia during exoduses of the past. The new arrivals are predominantly middle-class professionals, business managers, engineers, doctors, nurses, computer wizards, and other well-educated, talented individuals accompanied by their families – the kind of people any country is lucky to get. Most are affluent. Many are rich. A few are super-rich. In a phrase, the Overseas Chinese are currently the world's richest and most desirable immigrants. At a time of prolonged recession and disenchantment in the West, they have much to contribute, including their entrepreneurial energies. They have invested billions of dollars in their new homelands, and are changing the skylines, politics and cultures of their three favourite destinations: Los Angeles, San Francisco and Vancouver. Although most people are not yet fully aware of it, because the impact is still in its early stages, the United States and Canada are literally being reshaped and recharged by Asian wealth and vitality, and what is being called the 'brain gain'.

On the downside, some of the tycoons and their lieutenants are men with ties to the syndicates and triads that make up the Asian underworld – as we've seen, it's sometimes as hard to separate the noble from the ignoble in Asia as it is to separate scrambled eggs. There were already many triads, tongs and syndicates in the US and Canada, not only of the traditional variety, but newer groups such as Taiwan's Bamboo Gang, which carried out the murder of journalist Henry Liu in San Francisco. However, a major geologic shift is now taking place, as well. The most established Asian syndicates have been transferring part of their treasury to safety in North America and Australia, to create a secure strategic base for the twenty-first century, much as they once kept a secure base in the Goto Islands off Japan. In the long term, this could mean subtle but profound changes for Canada and the US.

In times past, the Chinese were welcomed in the West only as labourers, never as neighbours. The reception was particularly hostile in England. The first to appear, in the eighteenth century, were Chinese sailors on East Indiamen, and they did not stay long. There was a grand total of seventy-eight Chinese in England in 1851, and by 1931 the tally had risen only to about two thousand, who mostly operated restaurants, groceries and hand laundries. While huge numbers of coolies were shipped all over the world to work in plantations and mines, none was brought to England. Over the years, to be sure, a few wealthy Chinese students came to Oxford or Cambridge for their higher education, but most hurried home the moment they had their degrees or had passed the bar. During the First World War, one hundred thousand Chinese were shipped to Europe in labour battalions, but the survivors were all sent back. In the Second World War, twenty thousand Chinese seamen (mostly from Shanghai) were based in Liverpool, but only a handful stayed. By 1950, there were few Chinese left anywhere in the United Kingdom. In the years since, a modest flow of Chinese has arrived in a second wave scattered from London to Glasgow, most of them rice farmers from Hong Kong's New Territories, who had been put out of work by the rise of the Teochiu rice cartel in Thailand. The Chinese are now the third largest ethnic minority in England, after West Indians and East Indians, but in actual numbers they total only about one hundred thousand, mostly in London. England has fretted a good deal, however, over the prospect of a great third wave of Hong Kong refugees in 1997. To slow the rush, London offered to grant British citizenship to fifty thousand people in Hong Kong and their dependents, but this opportunity was so greatly oversubscribed that a quarter of a million immigrants may be at the gates in 1997. How many will choose to remain is another question, for they can use their British papers to establish residence elsewhere in the European Community, where the weather, and the welcome, may be more benign.

In some ways, first-wave Chinese who emigrated to Canada, the US and Australia during the nineteenth and early twentieth centuries were better off. There was more room in the wilderness, so they could make money for a few years before whites became envious and rose up against them. They came for the gold rushes of the 1860s, and stayed to build the transcontinental railways, roads and telegraph lines. San Francisco was seen as the Golden Mountain of Chinese mythology. Most of these men spoke the Taishan variety of Cantonese, because they came from counties south-west of Canton, where they were rounded up by recruiters from Hong Kong and crossed the Pacific on British or American steamers. Poorly prepared for frontier life, they spoke no English, but they worked hard for little money and made few complaints. Some gold-rush towns had large Chinese populations. Sooner or later, however, their gold and silver claims were jumped by white gangs. Others started commercial fishing ventures, to supply Chinese merchants in San Francisco, Seattle or Victoria, until the whites burned their boats.

When a recession swept the west coast in the 1880s, jobs became hard to find. In San Francisco and Seattle, when white businessmen hired Chinese workers because they were cheap, demagogues whipped up mobs of unemployed whites in a Yellow Peril frenzy. Chinatowns were put to the torch, and vigilantes staged 'pigtail-cutting parties' that did not stop with the pigtails. In Montana and Wyoming, Chinese were beheaded, castrated or burned alive on bonfires. Others were humiliated by mobs. Anti-Chinese rioting around Seattle aroused so much horror that President Cleveland was obliged to take action. Thousands of Chinese fled back to Asia. From a high of 107,488 in 1890, the number of Chinese in the US dropped by almost half in 1920, to only 61,639. New arrivals were blocked by the Chinese Exclusion Law passed by Congress in 1882, which barred entry to all but teachers, students, merchants and tourists. During 1891, there were forty thousand Chinese arrivals; six years later, there were only ten.

Canada was never as hostile, and Chinese merchants and republican fund raisers such as Dr Sun Yat-sen were still allowed entry to Victoria and Vancouver, until 1923, when Ottawa passed its own Exclusion Act, which barred Jews, East Indians, West Indians and Chinese. In Australia, the pattern was similar. In the nineteenth century, most Chinese Down Under worked in the goldfields of Victoria or New South Wales. Many returned to China, or moved to mines in New Guinea. 'White Australia' became the national policy. Few Chinese ever got as far as New Zealand, except by accident. Even in Hawaii, where Cantonese and Hakka farmers had been among the first outsiders to settle, white planters raised impenetrable social barriers against them, until the new US exclusion laws blocked further entry.

Most Chinese never intended to stay in North America in the first place, whether they were welcome or not. They saw themselves as temporary sojourners who would one day return to their ancestral homes. Those who did remain started self-protection societies, tongs, triads and masonic orders, and secluded themselves in urban ghettoes, where they lived a life apart. They were blocked from many occupations, and could not enrol their children in white schools, or buy property outside Chinatown. Only Chinese who served in the US army in the Second World War were allowed to bring their wives to America.

The Canadians were the first to rethink these racist immigration policies, and in 1947 Ottawa repealed its Chinese Exclusion Act. As word got out, small numbers of Chinese immigrants and sojourners began to arrive. The policy was modified again in the 1960s. Instead of quotas based on race, immigrants were selected on humanitarian grounds, or for the economic contributions they could make, or to allow relatives to join family members already in Canada.

Soon afterward, in 1965, as one of the Johnson-era initiatives to end racial discrimination, the US Congress passed a similar new immigration act that abolished national quotas and gave preference to scientists, technicians, professionals and skilled or unskilled workers. Canberra followed suit in 1973 by dropping its White Australia policy.

This second wave of Asian migrants included many refugees fleeing the Indochina War. Hanoi followed its victory in the south by expelling or persecuting ethnic Chinese, who long had had a tight grip on commerce there. As Saigon fell, one group of twenty Chinese businessmen offered to pay an American charter airline pilot one million dollars each in cash if he would fly them to Costa Rica immediately. (Because he already had other heavy commitments, he refused.) Other second-wave migrants came from Taiwan, Hong Kong, and a few from the Mainland. They had little education, but since they spoke mostly Cantonese dialect, they fitted into existing Chinatowns.

In the early 1980s, after Britain agreed to relinquish Hong Kong to Beijing's control in 1997, the third wave began, and it was very different. Any optimism felt by residents of the Crown Colony about their future was shattered by the Tienanmen Square crackdown in 1989. Many remembered what had happened in Shanghai after the communist victory in 1949, when Mao's promise that it would remain a free city lasted only three months. From then on, anyone with money was victimized. Businessmen and professionals have been the most anxious, because they have the most to lose. At the very least, they want to get their families to safety in English-speaking countries that offer political stability, economic opportunity, and a good educational system. Even pro-Beijing politicians in Hong Kong are worried about the future, and are scrambling to get themselves set up in British Columbia; for instance, a leader of one of Hong Kong's biggest pro-Bejing political parties quietly applied for Canadian citizenship. When word got out, he withdrew his application, but his wife and son went ahead with the move, which gave him an escape hatch if he needed it.

The anxiety that hit Hong Kong has now washed over Taiwan and the Mainland, as well as Indonesia and Malaysia, although for a different reason there. The end result is that throughout much of East and South East Asia, everyone is jittery, precautions are paramount, and flight has become fashionable.

Canada is their first choice, Australia second, the US third. The appeal of Australia is partly in its proximity; professionals in Hong Kong or Taiwan who are able to get their families or children settled in new homes and schools in Sydney or Brisbane can fly back and forth to visit without crossing so many time zones. If chaos comes, the parents can join their children with a new life already in place.

Unlike the illiterate coolies of gold-rush days, a lot of the new migrants are ready to invest large sums of money to guarantee a warm welcome in their new country. Some purchase big houses and flashy cars, but most of them are earnest middle-class families that have worked hard and saved all they could, only to face the prospect of losing everything after 1997. After selling Asian houses and apartments, many have two hundred and fifty thousand dollars or more in liquid assets with which to start again.

They leave Asia with great expectations, and when they arrive, the experience can be deflating. As credit ghosts, and conspicuously Asian, they have trouble getting mortgages, or even decent rental housing.

Finding a job is tougher than expected, thanks to the long recession. In booming Asia, many people have not even been touched by the recession, so when it comes, reality hits hard. They are discouraged by the dramatic fall in income and status. When they do find a job, it may be menial compared to their earlier career. High-powered factory managers sometimes end up chopping vegetables, parking cars or pumping gas. Chinese who start businesses as part of a deal for their immigrant visa, run into strong labour unions, high wages, costly welfare packages, environmental controls and byzantine government regulations – things that did not interfere in Asia.

Many do it for their children. Chinese think in terms of generations, and like to prepare the future of their children and grandchildren. They do not realize how much the US and Canada have changed since Eisenhower and Mackenzie King. For a traditional Confucian family, the trauma of adjusting to decadent Western attitudes toward sex, alcohol, drugs and life in general, can be disastrous. Chinese boys and girls quickly adopt Western mannerisms and cease showing respect toward their elders. They become deaf to parental reasoning, and ignore traditional moral sanctions. Parents who threaten to punish their children discover that in America today, nobody can raise a hand to a child. When that point is reached, sometimes in less than a year or two, traditional Chinese family life collapses, and the primary motive for emigrating to the West becomes meaningless. Instead of the children becoming more secure, they become estranged. Many migrants regret the move, and think they would have been better off moving to Singapore, where Confucian family values apply, and Western youth-culture has had little impact.

Professional women who had servants in Asia to look after homes and children, end up toiling in Sacramento or Toronto, trying to make ends meet while their children treat them with contempt.

In frustration, while wives and children remain in North America, husbands often go back to Taipei or Hong Kong or Bangkok to resume the high-paid managerial jobs or professional careers they had left behind. To maintain contact with their families, and to avoid forfeiting their immigrant status, the husbands have to return to Canada or the US every several months. If a husband cannot avoid forfeiting his immigrant status, his family remains in place, so the escape route exists. Thousands of middle-class Chinese immigrants have returned to work in Asia this way, earning them the sobriquet 'astronaut', because they spend so much time in orbit. They have become Overseas Chinese in reverse – living overseas and sojourning in Greater China.

When the children are old enough to be left on their own, more and more Chinese professional women now do the same: leave the kids in Toronto, Sydney or Los Angeles, and return to Asia. Both parents become astronauts. This reveals one of the hidden attractions of Canada and Australia over the United States. The US is the only country in the world that obliges all its citizens to pay income taxes no matter where they live. Citizens of Canada and Australia do not have to pay income taxes if they live somewhere else. For astronauts with high-paid executive jobs in Asia, this is a godsend.

Parents with the foresight to recognize the downside of emigration to the West, set things up that way deliberately. They do not emigrate themselves, but place their children in colleges or private secondary schools in Australia, New Zealand, Canada, the US or Europe, often buying a house near by to serve as a home away from home, and remain at work in Asia. Instead of the parents flying back and forth, the children do, becoming 'parachute kids' – each school break, they drop in as if by parachute. Skylanes over the Pacific are full of jumbo jets carrying astronaut parents one way, parachute children the other. It is estimated that there are forty thousand parachute kids in the US from Taiwan alone.

Some 'astronauts' spend so much time in the air that they no longer see much point in having a particular passport. They have joined the ranks of the 'permanent tourists', or 'PT' who never stay long enough in any country to require special visas, or to become liable for taxes as residents. In the decades ahead, this custom could become so widespread that it will transform attitudes about national identity. Thanks to high-speed communications, faxes, modems, electronic mail and easy air travel, families can be scattered without feeling so out of touch. (As a precaution, some Chinese discreetly acquire second passports from countries such as Paraguay or Belize, which sell citizenship and driver's licences to whoever has the money – although such documents immediately identify the bearer as suspect.)

The third-wave immigrants are well-educated people who have

made a success of their lives in Asia, where they have contributed to the booms in several countries, and they have scrimped and invested to build significant personal resources. They have begun to breathe new life into Canada and the US buying homes in all neighbourhoods (not just in Chinatowns), pouring money into local economies, and bringing Asian banks, insurance companies, computer manufacturers and other firms along in their wake.

Vancouver is the most striking example. Its proximity to Asia, plus its mild climate and beautiful setting, make it favoured by Chinese over all other destinations. In 1991 alone, the total net worth of entre-preneurial immigrants to British Columbia was 1.4 billion Canadian dollars. More than 75 per cent of Vancouver's immigrants have been Asian. Once, although it was already an international trade centre of sorts, Vancouver seemed parochial and outside the mainstream, unable to shed its image as a north woods town dependent on minerals, forestry and fisheries. That has now changed.

Chinese see Vancouver not only as a place of refuge, but as part of their overall future strategy. Many of the new immigrants have ties to family-held corporations all over East and South East Asia. Others are advance agents for Asian conglomerates, whose motive is to establish a secure Canadian presence, and to make Vancouver their stronghold. Where Western corporations once shifted labour-intensive sub-sidiaries to poor Asian countries, businesses in those countries are now setting up Western subsidiaries. All manner of Asian companies are hoping to build global empires, as Japan slows down its own push. Europe and North America are the main targets. What started with textiles, toys and electronics, now includes Asian banks, insurance companies, law firms, appliance makers, food producers, transporta-tion, aircraft manufacturers and professional services. The Chinese running most of these companies are tough, shrewd executives with long experience, backed by very canny, very big, Chinese money. For them Vancouver is an important part of a new Pacific Rim strategy, one of the legs of a financial tripod with its other feet in China and South East Asia. What the Overseas Chinese have done to turn Hong Kong and Singapore into leading world financial centres, they intend to do for Vancouver.

The fact that several of the richest and most powerful of the

Overseas Chinese have decided to seek Canadian citizenship supports the conclusion that British Columbia (BC) has been chosen as their strategic base in North America for the twenty-first century.

Vancouver is uniquely placed, and BC wide open, underdeveloped, and oddly vulnerable to economic and political takeover. Compared to one of America's states, a Canadian province has great independence from the central government in Ottawa, and BC has only a very thin layer of Anglo political control. The province has long been run by socialist or liberal-populist governments, which enlarged their constituency by pushing through social welfare programmes that catered to blue-collar labour, paid for by mortgaging the province's abundant natural resources, largely to Japan. Unions are very strong in BC, to the point that they have frightened away high-tech industry that has settled instead in neighbouring Washington State.

The Overseas Chinese, with their own agenda and their own traditional structures, generally do not make use of public welfare programmes, and are therefore immune to BC's wasting disease. While Anglo vitality remains dormant, the Chinese develop and operate a parallel economy, gradually gaining economic leverage and the political swat that comes with it – as they have done so thoroughly in Thailand, for example. Big money is hard to resist, and the Chinese are pouring money into BC, with benefits already apparent to all. Once addicted, nobody will want to turn off the dollar flow.

Changes are clearly visible in the streets of the city. Vancouver's Chinatown on Pender Street had been in decline for decades, and efforts to turn it into an ethnic tourist attraction in the 1980s failed. The new immigrants ignored the old ghetto and instead set about remodelling Vancouver as a whole. Wealthier Chinese bought big homes all over the city, but most headed for the inner suburb of Richmond, which was then completely transformed. Richmond is now one-third Chinese and is on a roll. Shopping districts have bloomed with high-quality Asian boutiques, restaurants, opera and movie theatres. The old KMT-dominated Chinese Benevolent Association has been displaced by a new Chinese Cultural Centre that offers language classes and stages Chinese opera, Dragon Boat festivals and Chinese New Year parades. Two radio stations and a TV channel carry Chinese programming. Once-drowsy Vancouver stays wide awake into the night.

Among the world's richest Chinese who have picked Canada as their new strategic base are Li Ka-shing, Stanley Ho, James Ting and Michael Huang.

Hong Kong property baron Li Ka-shing bought the sprawling site of Vancouver's 1986 Expo (previously the railway yards) and is re-shaping the entire south side of the city with towering high-rises and a spectacular waterfront of parks and marinas. Reputedly the world's richest Chinese, with a fortune valued at eight billion dollars, Li Ka-shing is currently the top tycoon of the global Teochiu network, and one of its senior patriarchs. His saga is yet another of a man fleeing China to make his fortune offshore. Li came to Hong Kong in 1939 as Japanese forces spread down the coast and Swatow was singled out for a pounding. Although the Li family arrived as refugees, the Teochiu were the second biggest dialect group in Hong Kong, in effect the second biggest labour union, so the Li clan were not without friends, or *guanxi*. In the 1950s, with a little seed money borrowed from the enormous Teochiu purse, Li Ka-shing started a factory to make cheap plastic flowers, toys, buckets, and other household items.

'Plastic flowers are better,' he said, 'because you can wash them and they last for ever.' All over the world, shoppers thought he had a point, so by 1958 he was a plastic-flower millionaire. These proceeds he invested in Hong Kong real estate, at a time when Chinese were just discovering that property could be bought and sold like plastic flowers. In those days, the venerable Hongkong & Shanghai Bank, which had once snubbed Chinese customers, was facing a pinch. They went after Li's business, and helped him acquire 22 per cent of Hutchinson Whampoa, one of Hong Kong's oldest British trading houses, on easy terms.

Li's oldest son now lives in Vancouver, holds Canadian citizenship, and is overseeing the North American end of the family enterprises. In the past, Vancouver was predominantly Cantonese. But Li Ka-shing's choice of Vancouver has now made it the North American stronghold of the Teochiu dialect group.

Macao gambling tsar Stanley Ho, whose hotels, jetfoils and casinos earn the Portuguese enclave most of its annual revenues, has long held dual British and Portuguese citizenship, and owns lucrative casinos in Lisbon and major properties in China and Australia. It runs in the family. Ho's father was chief *comprador* for the Sassoons, Iraqi Jews who made a great fortune as traders in Shanghai and Hong Kong. His grand-uncle, Sir Robert Hotung, knighted by King George V, was the wealthiest property owner in Hong Kong earlier this century, and chief *comprador* of Jardines-Mathieson. In his own right, Stanley Ho made a fortune trading with the Japanese in Macao during the Second World War, and soon became one of Asia's high rollers. As a corporate wheeler-dealer, in the 1990s he has been involved in complex multinational deals that came under scrutiny by regulatory agencies because of allegations of gross market manipulation, which Ho consistently denied. If things go sour in Hong Kong and Macao, Ho could easily move his headquarters to Lisbon or to London – or, for that matter, to any other country in the European Community. But Ho prefers to regard the entire Pacific Rim as his own green baize gaming table, and has now opted for Canadian citizenship.

Clearly, Vancouver – once the Edwardian wallflower of the Pacific North-west – now has her dance card full and is in for a breathless waltz into the new century.

Similar changes are happening in Seattle, San Francisco and Los Angeles, where Asian flight capital, and affluent new-wave immigrants with big Chinese money, are transforming downtown business districts and many suburbs. The old Los Angeles Chinatown has been superceded by suburban Monterey Park, east of LA in the San Gabriel Valley, where well-heeled Asian professionals live while working for defence contractors and the aerospace industry. More than twenty Asian banks have opened in the Los Angeles area, with ten more in San Francisco, for a total of thirty in California, and an estimated twenty-seven billion dollars has been pumped in by Asian investors. Monterey Park is the first city in the continental US to have an Asian majority – but it will not be the last. Other nearby towns such as Alhambra are now one-third Chinese, and an increasing number of Southern California housing developers are having their architects work with Chinese geomancers in the placing of doors and windows, so they can boast that their houses have been designed with *feng shui* in mind.

Nobody is quite sure how California's Chinese are spending their millions. The wealthy Hokkien immigrants from Taiwan are fiscal conservatives, less ostentatious than their Hong Kong counterparts, and go about their investments and business strategies discreetly. Some are buying warehouses, filling them with Asian textiles, toys, electronics and heavy machinery, then marketing the goods around the US.

A lot of Chinese prefer the ambiance of San Francisco, where they have bought homes with views in Sunset, San Bruno or Burlingame, more agreeable environs than the crowded storefronts of the original Grant Street Chinatown. Whites who worried in the past about immigrants lowering standards in their neighbourhoods are now alarmed because incoming Chinese are raising the standards, causing property values to soar. The newcomers are better dressed than the locals, serious professionals with a keen business sense and a shrewd knowledge of how capitalism really works. This arouses more than a little envy.

One-quarter of San Francisco's residents are now Chinese (78,000 households, by latest count). They own more than one-tenth of downtown San Francisco. Li Ka-shing has a great deal of property in the Bay Area. Near by in Silicon Valley, firms founded by Chinese such as Wang, Everex and Tseng Laboratories have played major roles in the growth of the computer industry. Chinese are also buying up real estate in other major cities, including Seattle, Portland, Houston, Austin, New Orleans and Boston, but politically and culturally their greatest impact is in California, where the effect is like a brain transplant. Although Asians are still only about 10 per cent of the state's population, in 1993 they provided 36 per cent of all new students at all nine campuses of the University of California. Among all college graduates over age twenty-five in California, 34 per cent were Asians (whites were only 25 per cent). More than half the Asians in California high schools were taking college preparatory courses, while only 34 per cent of whites were. Not all these bright Asian children are from wealthy families – many live in poverty but have their sights set very high. No matter how poor they are, Asians are determined to make their own lives much better.

Regrettably, the positive impact of Asians on the West Coast is not the case in New York. There, after early signs of promise, the Chinese backed away from plans to upgrade Chinatown in Lower Manhattan. This is inevitable, because New York in the 1990s is no longer receptive to small business; manufacturing is discouraged and support goes to high-tech industries and the service sector. Decaying public transportation, collapsing social services, dilapidated housing, and official indifference, discourage all but the big players. Serious Chinese investors are putting their money elsewhere. Ignoring Chinatown completely, Hong Kong billionaire Y. T. Cheng, who owns the Renaissance and Stouffer hotel chains, has taken control of Donald Trump's troubled Riverside South project, which plans a two-and-a-half-billion-dollar apartment complex along the Hudson River.

Those Chinese who remain active in Chinatown are often either slum landlords and sweatshop owners, or fast-buck real estate speculators taking advantage of the proximity of Chinatown to the high-rent district of Wall Street. Chinatown used to be only six crumbling blocks of slums filled with ageing bachelors. When US immigration laws changed in 1965, the number of garment factories there jumped from eight to five hundred, which employed twenty thousand Chinese women, all newcomers. Hundreds of Chinese food shops opened to feed them. By 1980, Chinatown had a hundred and fifty thousand residents and was encroaching on Little Italy. For a while, there seemed a chance that the ghetto could become an ethnic showplace, but like a defective braid of firecrackers on Chinese New Year, those hopes fizzled out.

Chinatown remained a dump. Branches of Asian triads involved in drugs, prostitution, gambling, money-laundering, car theft and illegal immigration, made Lower Manhattan their base on the East Coast (and Monterey Park on the West Coast). In between, they bought motels, restaurants, brothels, gambling joints and nightclubs, strung like costume jewellery along major highways from coast to coast and north to south. In rural areas of California and Florida, New Jersey and Illinois, huge Chinese-owned farms supply fresh produce for Chinese restaurants –and sometimes provide safe havens for triad pushers and hitmen.

The traditional tongs in America, such as the Hong Leong Tong, are branches of worldwide clan organizations that have existed for many generations; the Hong Leong extended family includes many millionaires and more than a few billionaires, including some of the greatest family fortunes in Asia. The extent to which huge global tongs become involved, even parenthetically, in rackets depends on their internal policing, and on whether a bad seed temporarily gains control of one branch of a tong. In the 1980s and 1990s, the rise of big money in Hong Kong, Taipei, Bangkok and Singapore has brought some of America's tongs under the influence of drug-rich Asian racketeers. Tongs (and the less-visible triads) typically occupy a role as community service organizations, and protectors of Chinatown business interests, but this sometimes simply provides cover for protection rackets. US narcotics investigators identified the Luen Kung Lok Triad, for instance, as a major supplier of heroin to New York in the 1980s, the drugs distributed from an eleven-storey building on Mott Street in Chinatown. Chinese gangs have largely displaced the Cosa Nostra in the US heroin trade. In the 1990s, more than 70 per cent of the heroin reaching the East Coast is China White from the Golden Triangle.

New York is awash with Chinese illegals, brought in by plane, truck and ship, people who have paid from fifteen to thirty-five thousand dollars per person to triads and syndicates that operate a worldwide traffic in humans, stolen cars and drugs. In 1992, more than a hundred thousand Chinese were smuggled into the US, most of them ending up in New York City, where they provide labour for sweatshops, slumlords and gang bosses. The major syndicates have tramp steamers plying the Pacific, Atlantic and Indian oceans on perpetual smuggling operations. They carry heroin to Antwerp and live bodies to Long Island, and then go back to Asia loaded with stolen BMWs, Mercedes, Cadillacs and Porsches, which are smuggled into South China and sold to the nouveaux riches. The bosses of these smuggling networks are wealthy Overseas Chinese businessmen based in regional drug centres like Mae Sai, in Thailand. On the surface, they may be involved in hotels, banks, tourism and manufacturing, but they put their disposable income into trawlers and tramp steamers, which are operated for them by street-tough lieutenants called snakeheads.

Young men in Mainland China's Fukien and Kwangtung provinces scrounge together enough money from relatives and friends to make a downpayment of five to six thousand dollars. Like coolies a century ago, they guarantee to pay the rest of their 'credit ticket' out of their wages once they reach America, a payback that can take five years or more. In effect they become bond slaves, who know they will be murdered if they don't pay off. Any trouble and the snakeheads will throw you overboard, fracture your spine, or sever your tendons, so you never work again. Packed like anchovies into the holds of ships, they are taken around the world, surviving on meagre rations of water, noodles and rice, until they disembark one night off Mexico, Canada or the US. Few speak English. Lucky ones end up toiling long hours in Chinatown restaurants, bakeries or sweatshops, sleeping in three-tier bunks in ghetto flophouses. If they don't get sick working fourteen hours a day seven days a week, they eventually pay off their passage and get on with their own lives. This means sending money home to reimburse family and friends, and serving as an anchor to windward in North America for other relatives who may follow in their footsteps. If they get caught, no problem – the US government does not have enough space to lock them up, so when their trial date comes up, they just don't show. Few are ever sent back.

In terms of the coming Pacific century, New York is not an example of the future but of the past. The future lies on the West Coast, where Chinese money and talent are beginning to have an impact on political life. In 1987, Vancouver businessman and philanthropist David Lam See-chai was named Lieutenant-Governor of British Columbia, the first Chinese appointed to such a high office. In the October 1993 Canadian national elections, seven Hong Kong-born candidates contested seats, and Raymond Chan of Richmond, the Vancouver Chinese suburb, was successful. In a recent race for mayor of Los Angeles, Michael Woo, who is of Cantonese origin, made a strong showing.

This is just the beginning. With their easy access to major financial resources, Asian-Americans will play a bigger role in local, regional and national politics. There are those who boast that before the middle of the twenty-first century, the US could have its first Asian-American president. Maybe not, but whoever is in the White House will have a lot of powerful Chinese constituents.

CHAPTER 19

MONEY HIDES A THOUSAND FLAWS

_____

BY THE 1990S, MAINLAND CHINA WAS EXPERIENCING THE BIGGEST consumer boom in world history. It was already the third largest economy in the world, after the United States and Japan, and by 2010 could be number one. This turnaround from poverty happened in less than fifteen years. In 1978, when the change began, China's economy as a whole started to grow at nearly 9 per cent a year, a rate that doubles the economy every eight years. Its empty shops became crowded with consumer goods and eager customers. Streets once packed with Red Guards were jammed with more and more foreign cars pushing through the bicycles and buses. Billboards everywhere touted products that a few years earlier only the Communist Party élite could afford. By 1993, China's growth increased to 13 per cent, and by 1994 to 19 per cent, making it the world's fastest growing economy three years in a row. The South China coastal provinces of Kwangtung and Fukien grew even faster, at over 30 per cent. Interior provinces like Szechuan were also experiencing astonishing growth. Dramatic changes all over the country unleashed social and political forces that seemed to career out of control. Reports of violence and warlordism leaked out of certain areas. A Party document warned that Beijing was losing its grip, and that China might blow apart, breaking into new groupings.

In China, it is customary to expect earthquakes when farmyard animals begin to exhibit strange conduct for no apparent reason, and roaches head for the hills. Such signs were everywhere. Chinese yuppies were washing their hair in Proctor & Gamble shampoo, starting their day with Nescafé instant coffee, driving to work in new Toyotas with electronic pagers clipped to their shirt pockets, then heading for karaoke bars where they mixed Hennessey brandy in Coca-Cola. They bought new jeans and pullovers by mail from Lands' End catalogues, and ordered tanga panties from Victoria's Secret. Exuberance and confidence were in the air that could not be matched in Detroit or Philadelphia. On a more profound level, life expectancy, which was thirty-five years when Mao took over in 1949, had risen to seventy by 1991. As average earnings passed the $1,400-a-year mark, the majority of people in China for the first time were able to buy such basic consumer items as refrigerators. Given a population of over 1.2 billion, this meant that more human beings were escaping from poverty in one brief period than at any previous time in history. On a graph, it would look like a giant pig passing through an anaconda. Explosive hiccups could be expected, but China's long-term economic prospects were nothing short of fantastic. Economic news of this magnitude helped to jolt the West out of its traumatic depression. The enormous vitality of Greater China and Asia as a whole could stimulate worldwide prosperity for many decades ahead.

A Klondike gold rush got underway, as Western companies competed for a foothold on the Mainland – China already was the biggest market for American aircraft, power-generating plants and telecommunications – but everywhere Western companies looked, the Overseas Chinese were there first. During the 1980s and 1990s, it was the Overseas Chinese who fuelled and managed the Mainland China boom. However, they were also the first to be alarmed (and excited) by the disintegration of central government control in Beijing. As other foreign investors continued full speed ahead, some leading Overseas Chinese tycoons pulled back, and shifted assets elsewhere in expectation of violent upheaval following the death of Deng, possibly including the fragmentation of the Mainland. Visionaries foresaw a realignment of China's national boundaries, with South China again becoming a separate nation, or several separate nations. A policy paper in Taiwan predicted a future union between the island nation and Fukien province across the strait. Unlike the break-up of the Soviet Union, which left most of its fragments impoverished, many of the new Chinese states could be rich and powerful in their own right. Given their historic fear and loathing for the central government, the great syndicates of Fukien and Kwangtung could well be looking forward to secession. Some analysts thought the People's Liberation Army held the key, but the PLA is known to have its own regional power clusters, and its own centrifugal forces.

It bears repeating that Overseas Chinese money is smart money. If you tracked their investment as a single block of economic activity, the way it is possible to track US or Japanese financial activity, it would emerge that their business ventures around the Pacific Rim, and, increasingly, worldwide, have usually been one jump ahead. Overseas Chinese money moves quickly and is extremely sensitive to changes in political climate. They have excellent channels of intelligence on the Mainland through their clan and dialect networks, and they know that strategy is only half the job. The other half is rapid reaction. Even the Japanese cannot match them for quick response.

Since 1949, China had achieved equality, but without freedom or prosperity. The Party was discredited by the Great Leap and the Red Guard movement. Communist doctrine was in shreds, and ideology and terror were no longer adequate glue. The centrally controlled economy was foundering. Facing collapse on Soviet lines, in 1979, Deng and the Party leadership decided to save themselves and to preserve their control, by sacrificing communism. They rallied support by providing unprecedented material benefits, and setting loose free enterprise. Like emergency-room doctors trying to revive a patient, they clapped electrodes to the body and gave it a magnum jolt of greed. In Beijing, dictatorship of the right easily replaced dictatorship of the left, proving that their chief concern was not ideology but control. Economic liberalization caused so much excitement that nobody noticed Mao rolling over in his sarcophagus. It also masked the personal financial cravings of the Party leadership. Greed was always the monster in the Confucian closet.

Deng and his associates had been dazzled by the extraordinary economic performance of Hong Kong, Singapore and Taiwan. They were particularly inspired by Singapore's authoritarian Chinese government, which combined rapid economic growth with strict political and social control. Singapore invoked Confucian values as a means of maintaining social order through a strict hierarchical system. In recent decades, Lee Kuan Yew's shrewd and eloquent political philosophy had a growing impact on Beijing and on other Asian governments, including ever-recalcitrant Hanoi and Rangoon. The most influential thinker of the new Asian Renaissance, Lee became the unseen hand behind the Mainland boom and the emergence of a Greater China.

In conscious emulation of Singapore, Deng reshaped the Mainland into a new kind of Confucian dictatorship, an enlightened totalitarian state devoted to profit. Chinese communism is no longer equality without freedom or prosperity, but prosperity without equality or freedom. Those with enough money do not crave equality, and can buy all the freedom they need.

For the first time since the fourteenth century, China's central government actively encouraged citizens to engage in private trade and commerce in pursuit of profit. The moongate was cracked open slightly to foreign firms. This experiment began in the most fertile of places: Kwangtung and Fukien provinces, where the enterprising capitalist spirit of Yueh and of Southern Sung persists to this day. Fourteen cities along the coast were made 'open cities' and given special trade status and tax breaks to encourage foreign investment. Nine of these are in the southern provinces and include Ningpo, Shanghai, Wenzhou (Wenchow), Fuzhou, Guangzhou (Canton), Zhanjiang (Chan-chiang), Beihai (Pei-hai) and Hainan. All of them are ancestral homes of the Overseas Chinese. Deng also gave generous economic privileges to Szechuan, his home province in China's south-west, traditionally one of the richest regions in the interior.

Four Special Economic Zones (SEZ) were created with even greater economic privileges. Three of the four SEZ were located in Kwangtung province: Shenzhen borders on Hong Kong's New Territories; Zhuhai is at the mouth of the Pearl River across from Macao; and Shantou (Swatow) is the Teochiu homeland. The Party was blunt about its choice of Shantou: 'Being the native place of many Overseas Chinese, it can make use of funds of Overseas Chinese and foreign nationals.' Fukien has a single SEZ at Xiamen (Amoy).

The creation of Special Economic Zones appealed directly to the tribal loyalties of Hakka, Hokkien, Hokchiu, Henghua, Teochiu, Cantonese and Hainanese. Who could resist a blunt plea to pour money into the ancestral home? It worked wonders.

While hundreds of millions of Chinese are still desperately poor, this rapid change has created in them the hope that with hard work and with luck they now have a chance, where before there was none. The universal message is that anyone can prosper, even get rich, although some will get richer faster. The illusion of equality has been replaced by the illusion of equal opportunity. That those who are clever, ruthless or criminal get rich faster, acknowledges a fact of life that the Chinese have always known and which no government has been able to alter. Whether cadres or mandarins, some are always more equal than others. As the Chinese say, 'Money hides a thousand flaws.'

One immediate result of these changes was a surge in criminal activity. Big morphine-base and heroin shipments began to move directly overland to Hong Kong from the Burmese and Lao sections of the Golden Triangle. This direct route through south-western China bypassed Thailand, and thus avoided the traditional pay-offs to Thai military and police commanders.

After 1949, Kwangtung and Fukien provinces had been starved by Beijing to punish the coastal Chinese for their chronic disloyalty to the centre, and to favour provinces in the interior whose loyalty and patriotism were less in doubt. Both coastal provinces had their factories and infrastructure moved inland, on the pretext of the danger of an invasion from Taiwan. Nobody had forgotten how the Manchu regime had ordered everyone to move inland to starve Coxinga of support, this causing terrible suffering and dislocation. The chief assets of Fukien and Kwangtung had always been their overseas networks. From 1949 to 1979, these networks were regarded as inherently subversive, because their loyalties were tribal and could not be shifted to the Party centre.

In 1979, Deng's decentralization of control over China's economy reversed the bloodflow. Provinces that had been ruthlessly cut back like sycamore trees were allowed to regenerate their commercial limbs, and encouraged to reactivate their ties to overseas networks. Beijing simultaneously went out of its way to mellow relations with neighbouring countries, to encourage commerce by disarming regional critics. All the Overseas Chinese syndicates had maintained active underground ties to their ancestral homelands through Hong Kong. As China opened up, the big harbours of Fukien discreetly renewed direct syndicate connections with Taiwan, Japan and South East Asia. Cantonese and Teochiu syndicates stepped up smuggling operations into Kwangtung from Hong Kong.

When Deng's economic liberalization was paralleled by the fall of the House of Chiang on Taiwan in 1984, it became politically correct for Overseas Chinese to openly and aggressively re-establish ties with the Mainland.

Since 1979, China has received nearly sixty billion dollars in foreign business contracts and nearly the same amount in loans from foreign bankers, commercial lenders and international financial institutions. More than 80 per cent of this capital came from or through Overseas Chinese sources. Of Mainland enterprises with significant foreign equity, 75 per cent are financed by Overseas Chinese. Two-thirds of this money comes from Overseas Chinese in Hong Kong and Taiwan alone. Investment in China from Hong Kong and Taiwan is ten times that of investment from Japan.

Unlike big American firms that rushed to Beijing in the 1980s to make deals that often turned sour, the Overseas Chinese went back to their ancestral villages to make deals with their tribes. Bitter experience had taught them to 'stay small and far from the centre'. Many Overseas Chinese were motivated by sentiment, but they were also driven by tribal self-interest, which perpetually seeks to renew and enlarge tribal leverage in the ancestral heartland. Up to a point, they saw and continue to see the Mainland as a gold-rush opportunity. That 'point' will be reached when political turmoil on the Mainland cancels out the financial advantages. Their heavy investments in China must be seen as a gamble that might pay off in the liberation of their ancestral province, as a major player in a future China, or as an independent state. In China what has happened before can always be encouraged to happen again. Chinese have learned to take the long view.

While they contributed money to the republican movement and to the defence against Japan, they have no history of seeking Mainland business opportunities outside their native counties. High-flyers among them are drawn by the highest rate of return. But they all know that if Beijing comes unglued, their investments will be in jeopardy. It should come as no surprise, then, that they are not investing their own money in the Mainland; wherever possible, they are acting as *compradors* in deals involving other people's money, and making a healthy profit. Their own money remains safely offshore.

For what little comfort it gives Indonesian or Malaysian chauvinists, the Overseas Chinese tycoons claim to be raising most of their investment funds for China offshore, and not withdrawing them from their adopted countries. Nobody will ever know with any certainty whether this is true, given the notorious obscurity of Chinese bookkeeping methods. While they have deep attachments to their ancestral villages, most expatriate Chinese do not feel strongly about China as a nation. Some 90 per cent are now citizens in their host countries. Thus it cannot be said that sentiment toward their native place represents disloyalty toward their adopted home. Many Chinese in Malaysia, for instance, feel a deep obligation to their ancestral roots, but consider Malaysia – not China – to be their real home.

The resources at their command are enormous. The GNP of the fifty-five million Overseas Chinese (Taiwan and Hong Kong included) is in the neighbourhood of four hundred and fifty billion dollars, one-quarter larger than Mainland China's GNP. They have one of the world's deepest pools of liquid capital. Bank deposits in Taiwan alone exceed three hundred billion dollars; add gold bullion hoards and black-money holdings, and the figure for ready capital is at least twice that. Worldwide, the Overseas Chinese probably hold liquid assets (not including securities) worth two trillion dollars. Japan, with nearly twice as many people had only one-third more assets (three trillion dollars in 1990). The existence of this invisible offshore empire with dynamic underground linkages and vast financial reserves, may explain why the earth wobbles on its axis.

This capital flows through the unique social system of *guanxi*, connections. Anything can be financed by *guanxi*. Hundreds of books have been written about it in Chinese, but it still takes a lifetime to master the intricacies. *Guanxi* grew out of an agricultural society in which people swapped favours with neighbours, relatives and friends of friends. Like fishermen, Chinese make nets of *guanxi* in which knots are tied with marriage, school, clubs, secret societies, both forward and backward in time. You can collect *guanxi* built up by your mother or grandfather. It can be inherited or conveyed. Under communism, business was not arranged for profit but for *guanxi*, a different kind of collateral that bypasses official channels. *Guanxi* eases pain. It stops bullets. Feuds are ended by calling in someone obliged by *guanxi* to both parties, who negotiates a settlement. Some Chinese keep records of *guanxi* in ledgers. A Singapore programmer has developed software to keep track of *guanxi*. It is a different form of computer networking.

For Chinese, said Lee Kuan Yew, 'networking is the natural thing to do.' He urged Overseas Chinese to take advantage of *guanxi* to create a solid commercial relationship with Mainland China. These great root systems running deep into the Mainland, he said, were still very strong.

'This *guanxi* capability will be of value for the next twenty years at least,' Lee said, so every opportunity should be seized. 'The Anglo-Saxons do it, the Jews do it, so do the Hindus and the Muslims.' Rich means never having to apologize.

Guanxi is the only way business can be conducted inside China. It gives you the best ventures, the best choices, the best prices. *Guanxi* is vital in places where there have been few, if any, legal controls. In such a place, you are completely adrift without *guanxi*.

Western firms feel uneasy operating in China's weak legal system. They claim that Overseas Chinese have an unfair commercial advantage because *guanxi* protects them, like wearing a garlic necklace in Transylvania. But there is nothing arcane about *guanxi*; today's wealthy Overseas Chinese weave the same webs at Cambridge, Harvard or Wharton. It works like a drift net throughout the Pacific.

Fully 30 per cent of Hong Kong's currency circulates on the Mainland through *guanxi* channels. Taiwan entrepreneurs, mostly Fukienese, have invested over four billion dollars on the Mainland, mostly in their ancestral districts. Bangkok Bank opened a branch in Shantou SEZ at Swatow, close by the ancestral home of Chin Sophonpanich. From Malaysia, lottery-wizard Vincent Tan won rights to manage a government lottery in Guangzhou (Canton), certain to pay off handsomely. Indonesia's Liem Sioe Liong became a major developer in Fukien. His efforts are centred on Fuching, his home town just south of Foochow. Even before Indonesia and China normalized relations in 1990, Liem was pouring money into Fuching, earmarking eighty-nine million dollars to build a 10-mile highway, dozens of sprawling apartment blocks, office buildings and factories, and a marble-lobbied three-star hotel. Another high-roller is billionaire Stanley Ho, the Macao casino boss who is involved in hydrofoil rapid transit schemes all over the Pearl River delta, and who is spending vast sums improving Macao's infrastructure in advance of its takeover by Beijing. When everyone banquets on Beijing duck, these men expect to be sitting above the salt.

Top members of the Communist Party leadership have been involved in backstage business deals with Overseas Chinese that seem inappropriate for veterans of the Long March. Tracking these discreet deals is sometimes tricky or roundabout. For example, Hong Kong Overseas Chinese billionaire Robert Kuok holds 13 per cent of Citic Pacific, an investment company in Hong Kong with strong links to China's ruling State Council. Citic is essentially a vehicle to enable top Beijing cadres to make huge offshore investments for their own profit, and is overseen by China's Vice President Rong Yiren, a close crony of Deng. The Rong family (also called Jong, Yung, or Wong) ran one of China's biggest textile conglomerates in Shanghai before the Second World War. When the communists took over, most of its sons fled – the eldest to Brazil, another to the US, a third to Australia. The youngest was one of the Shanghai Boys who started over in Hong Kong. But another son stayed behind in Shanghai, and eventually became vice-minister of Textile Industries. He vanished in the Cultural Revolution, but was restored to grace by Deng, which created a deep *guanxi* bond. Vice President Rong's Shanghai financial and industrial know how, the strategic worldwide placement of his family and his *guanxi* with Deng, made him the perfect man to direct the ruling élite's international financial activities under Citic cover. Citic was managed by Larry Yung, the Vice President's son. In 1994, Citic paid four hundred and thirty million dollars for half of Discovery Bay, a large luxury residential development on Hong Kong's Lantau Island. If nothing else, it could be a pleasant retirement home for any of Deng's family who survive his passing, and who do not sprint for Switzerland. By 1995, it was estimated that the Deng family's interests in fourteen publicly listed Hong Kong companies were worth more than two billion dollars.

One of the best connected Overseas Chinese players is Hong Kong property baron Li Ka-shing, who has signed deals to build a port in Shanghai, shopping centres in Beijing and a highway to Swatow in Teochiu country. As one of the richest Teochiu in the world, Li Ka-shing commands enormous *guanxi*. His connections in the PRC are of particular interest. In Beijing, he teamed up with Deng Zhifang, son of China's maximum leader, to make joint acquisitions of Tung Wing Steel Holdings, and Kader Holdings. When Deng's daughter, Deng Lin, discovered that she was an artist, Li cut the ribbon at her exposition in Hong Kong, while David Tang, proprietor of the élite China Club, picked up the dinner-party tab. Nobody could do enough. As an emblem of her transition from cadre to *arriviste*, she wore a gold Rolex. She could afford more than one, because she sold her large *oeuvres* for over forty-five thousand dollars a pop. The tapestries she designed, said one art critic, looked 'like they came off a totem pole somewhere in North America.' Unlike Deng's daughter, Li Ka-shing just wore a cheap wristwatch, and his taste in fine art and plastic flowers were considered to be on the same aesthetic plane. But a wise cook first feeds the emperor's children.

Whenever Li Ka-shing needed anything, he simply phoned Beijing to talk to Deng Senior. He was one of forty-four Hong Kong Chinese anointed as 'advisers' to Beijing in ceremonies at the Great Hall of the People. All were self-made tycoons wary of democratic reforms. Most Overseas Chinese are of two minds about democracy and reforms, because they see the two as very different. Many leading 'pro-democracy' groups are passionate about reforms, but they are not similarly passionate about Western-style democracy. In public, they speak of 'democracy' rather than 'reform' because it gives them cachet with America. In private, it is reform they want. Few Asians who have given the matter any serious thought have any real enthusiasm for Western-style democracy, especially the American variety, which they regard as deeply flawed and overrated.

Beijing welcomes Overseas Chinese entrepreneurs like Li Ka-shing,

Robert Kuok and Liem Sioe Liong precisely because they are not Chinese citizens, merely distant relatives. Deng was never a permissive man. Journalist Jacques Marcuse, long based in Beijing, knew Deng for years, and described him as 'ruthless and fanatical'. Deng's position on discipline was somewhere to the right of the Duke of Chou, and his attitude toward private business was as hostile as that of the First Emperor (except when it came to his own private business). China's inefficient state enterprises are protected against competition so that they will yield huge profits and tax revenues to the regime, while providing crucial political patronage in the form of jobs. As Professor Jenner argues persuasively, the Beijing regime has 'as strong an interest as any of its predecessors in preventing the development of large and well-capitalized private businesses.' The First Emperor, Jenner said, would have been fascinated by the new technology now flooding China, but he would have been shocked that it was not being used to give the regime even greater control of the people. It is, though, indirectly: the money earned by the new technology has given the failing regime a new lease on the Mandate of Heaven.

The Chinese Communist Party was always deeply hostile to homegrown private enterprise. Despite appearances to the contrary, Beijing is even more hostile today, as it is increasingly threatened by centrifugal forces. Deng's idea was to turn lead into gold with the help of foreign-based tycoons. The last thing he wanted was a strong domestic bourgeoisie – witness the continued harassment of middle-class intellectuals and students.

As distant relatives, the Overseas Chinese were the perfect touch. By pushing the right buttons and setting up each SEZ in a calculated location, they could be induced to invest billions in improving China's rickety infrastructure, thus creating millions of jobs and flooding the Mainland with residual benefits – while acting as *compradors* to attract huge joint ventures with Western and Japanese investors. All in a satisfyingly Chinese manner. If there was a change in the political weather, they could be expelled, and their new Mainland assets nationalized. It has happened in the past to generations of Chinese entrepreneurs, so there is no reason to believe that the ancient cycle will magically stop now. Because they are uniquely aware of the hazards, the leading tycoons are extremely wary: they concentrate their attention on infrastructure improvements in their native places, but elsewhere stick to joint ventures with non-Chinese investors, so their personal capital is not in jeopardy.

Nobody is fooled by Beijing's friendliness. Since 1949, the Party has deliberately sought to attract Overseas Chinese remittances and investment. It has catered to relatives on the Mainland, treating them as a privileged class. They had their own stores, for luxuries not available to the masses; construction materials were made available so they could build fine houses with money sent from abroad. They were encouraged to lavish foreign remittances on consumer goods, bringing the regime much needed revenue. To create the right impression on families overseas, they were permitted to maintain ancestral tombs, ancestor worship and geomancy. Government-sponsored investment companies were set up in Fukien and Kwangtung to encourage Overseas Chinese to put significant sums into the Mainland. In the difficult years of the 1950s and 1960s, remittances and injections of capital from expatriates were the main revenue of the two provinces.

'Overseas Chinese families', explained a *People's Daily* editorial in 1956, 'are divided into two parts: the main labour force, which is overseas, and the dependents, who are in China . . . Mishandling of the problems of [relatives] in China has an immediate effect on the attitudes toward China of the Overseas Chinese.' This, it said, was why Beijing 'veered from left to right, and alternated between severity and leniency.' By playing them like trout in a mountain stream, the Overseas Chinese could be induced to jump directly into the wok – to participate in 'socialist construction'.

All that is new in the 1990s is the more aggressive welcome. No longer were the Overseas Chinese just 'the main labour force, which is overseas.' They had quietly become one of the world's wealthiest clubs. In Hong Kong, in the spring of 1993, Deng inaugurated an exclusive key club, pairing Asia's biggest tycoons with firms owned by the Chinese government. Called the New China Hong Kong Group, it was the first officially sanctioned club for Overseas Chinese investors committed to spend billions on the Mainland. Among them were rich men from Singapore, Taiwan, Indonesia, Thailand and Hong Kong. A few tycoons had cold feet and stayed away.

Deng's campaign of economic liberalism has spawned a new

generation of Mainland millionaires who see the Overseas Chinese as their role models. Some are low-brow hustlers and foxes, while others are simply 'talented people' (*neng ren*). Perhaps the richest private businessman to emerge in the first wave was Zhang Guoxi, with more than fifty million dollars in assets. Zhang's Guoxi Group exported expensive Buddhist shrines and intricate wood carvings, but he then expanded into real estate and trade. An adept politician, he kept officials happy with the traditional tools of philanthropy, flattery, banquets and subterfuge. These new millionaires do not express gratitude toward Beijing except when they are hosting obligatory banquets. The long history of official treachery is too well known. Zhang takes a lot of precautions: 'For the past nineteen years, I have worked with my head under my arm.' He had bodyguards, and slept with a rifle and a double-barrels shotgun beside his bed. His wife and children established a home overseas. He was ready to bolt offshore himself if there was a crackdown. Like so many, he tucked vast sums overseas to set up his own tontine. He was confident of his family's future, in or out of China: 'My wealth will provide for my offspring for at least ten generations.'

The biggest Mainland operators were corrupt government officials and children of Politburo members like Deng. When he said 'to get rich is glorious', Deng added that not everyone could get rich at the same speed. People generously assumed he meant that some people were more aggressive or unscrupulous. But favouritism also plays a role. As part of the move to a free-market economy, in 1985 Beijing created a dual price system. Influential people could buy commodities from the state cheap and sell them dear on the free market. Deng and Premier Li Peng's sons were both involved. They got so rich that they were able to buy their way into any deal they wanted. All this was reminiscent of years of KMT rule, when similar corruption was institutionalized, the juiciest morsels going to Generalissimo Chiang, T. V. Soong, H. H. Kung, and their children. At the top in Beijing, as in Tokyo and elsewhere, the exposure of corruption is a toothpick, not a bludgeon. Purification is for religion, not for government. Children of the Politburo may feel safe because they have millions offshore, but a sudden political reversal could take them by surprise, as Deng himself was caught off guard twice in the Cultural Revolution.

Half of all Mainland business deals involve blatant corruption. Foreign investors find they pay more in bribes than on labour, land and materials. In the import–export trade, side deals are so banal that tens of billions of dollars in black money have ended up parked in offshore accounts. The method is called 'mis-invoicing', in which exports are understated and imports overstated. Contracts are 'stir-fried' – that is, written for 10 per cent above the negotiated price, with the difference to be salted offshore. The Cantonese adage applies: 'Hot wok, cold oil, food no stick.'

Mimicking the Overseas Chinese, the new Mainland élite hides its money offshore, causing one of the greatest financial riptides in history. Millions pour in the top, while billions pour out the bottom. In the undertow, some nine billion dollars in China's projected foreign exchange earnings in 1990 ended up in third-country bank accounts. By 1992, the total had risen to over twenty-eight billion dollars. At that rate, it may soon hit forty billion dollars a year.

Like Overseas tycoons, Mainland nouveaux buy steel mills in America, paper mills in Canada, and hotels wherever they find them. Although the Japanese got stung buying Rockefeller Center and bushels of American hotels in the 1980s, the Chinese are picking up the same properties for white-elephant prices. As one boasted, they don't buy American hotels from the Japanese, they steal them.

Not to be left behind in the quick march, the People's Liberation Army has invested tens of millions of dollars in Hong Kong properties, some of it proceeds from foreign arms deals for drugs. When Burma's impoverished military regime recently used Golden Triangle heroin profits to buy one billion dollars in Chinese arms, the money went to the PLA and its Party *compradors* through the banking channels of BCCI, the Bank for Credit and Commerce International. Much of it washed right out again to private offshore accounts. The Bank of China, Beijing's main international bank, found it necessary to open a branch in the Cayman Islands tax haven in 1992.

For the time being, Hong Kong is the main window to the offshore world. Mainlanders are quickly enlarging their stake there. At the end of 1993, there were more than fifteen thousand Mainland Chinese-owned companies in Hong Kong, energetically penetrating all sectors of the economy and employing some 4 per cent of the work force. More than four billion dollars' worth of Hong Kong properties were owned by Mainlanders. State-backed Mainland investors set up shell companies there to make secret investments. Bank of China had become the number-two bank in Hong Kong. Once into the offshore *guanxi* network, Mainlanders, like their Overseas role models, have no difficulty crossing national borders or getting around national laws. Frontiers and national laws do not exist for offshore operators. Back when Taiwan had strict monetary controls, a briefcase full of dollars deposited with gold merchants in Taipei could be retrieved the next day in Hong Kong. Money moved from Singapore to Zurich by way of Hong Kong with a single phone call, bypassing strict currency controls. The system works the same for Chinese in Bangkok, Paris, Pasadena or Vancouver.

China's government bankers joined in the feeding frenzy. To avoid central government control, they told Beijing they were lending to each other, when in fact they were lending to friends and clans, financing real-estate ventures and foreign currency speculation. The money supply tightened and Beijing had to print more money. The money supply then rose by half in 1992, with inflation over 20 per cent. In 1993, inflation hit 30 per cent. Since government loans are controlled at 10 per cent, this protected money-losing enterprises. To get government loans, private companies were registered under the names of state enterprises, with kickbacks going to the *compradors*.

In their eagerness to be part of the free market, one local government bank issued ten billion dollars in letters of credit, with nothing to back them up. Another one hundred and seventy-four million dollars in public funds was lost when a private businessman, Shen Taifu, issued unregulated bonds to investors and squandered the proceeds.

As the profit motive careened out of control, Beijing intervened. Assigned to clean house was Vice Premier Zhu Rongji, a shrewd, tough, former mayor of Shanghai, and possible successor to Deng as maximum leader. In July 1993, he was named Governor of the Central Bank. In the summary style of the Duke of Chou, he sent out teams to investigate financial corruption, threatening that anyone defying central authority 'will have his head chopped off'. Prudently, he did not at first mention the families of the Politburo.

Two months later, in September 1993, eight accountants and

bankers found guilty of embezzlement and fraud were executed with a bullet in the back of the neck, which is more cost-effective than beheading. Times have changed. China's executioners once had the right to sell the victim's blood for medicinal purposes. Now fresh kidneys and other human organs are sold on the international organ market. In the early spring of 1994, Shen Taifu, who had sold so many unregulated bonds, was given the death sentence. The speed and severity of these punishments was unavoidable, because Zhu's authority depended on Deng's backing and might not survive Deng's passing.

Vice Premier Zhu was also given the dangerous job of remodelling China's tax system, the most unpopular of all his economic reforms. 'Three Japanese governments have fallen because of attempts to reform the taxation system,' Zhu cracked. 'I, myself, have already started preparing for my own demise.'

Corruption was rampant. As China's Special Economic Zones boomed wildly, many of Hong Kong's shadier businesses moved to Shenzhen, which became an exotic offshore-banking market, a market for stolen cars, and a new base of Teochiu heroin operations. The Pearl River gushed black money. Shenzhen's banking sector laundered the money through the Hong Kong dollar-lending business. Joint ventures financed by banks in Shenzhen took on a comic opera quality, with a strangely costumed cast – off-the-shelf companies registered in Jersey, Guernsey, Monaco, Panama, Luxemburg, Liberia and the Caymans – all with a distinctly Asian look.

Shenzhen bankers had themselves driven to work in near-mint condition Jaguars and 'previously owned' Mercedes-Benz sedans provided by Overseas Chinese stolen-car syndicates. Fishing-boats towed some of these hot cars ashore in giant balloons, floating just below the muddy surface. The wife of a Shenzhen bank manager did her shopping in a late-model BMW with a sticker that said 'New York Athletic Club'.

Rural areas took the bit in their teeth and launched their own enterprises, which challenged the central government's turgid monopolies. Wisely, Deng had abandoned the agricultural commune and restored the family as the main unit of production. Most farm commodities price controls were dropped. Rural incomes then rose

sharply in many areas. Ambitious peasants became overnight entrepreneurs, setting up small rural industries, bribing officials to divert
price-controlled raw materials from state factories. These rural
enterprises now account for over 30 per cent of the Mainland's
industrial output, and fund local schools, welfare, health and transportation programmes through the tontine system: If the enterprise does
well, all live well; if it does poorly, all live poorly. This encourages a
renewed family-oriented spirit, and managers of successful rural
enterprises are both heroes and champions, for 'when the belly is fat,
the emperor is far away.'

As certain provinces and urban areas prospered faster than others
(notably those with strong Overseas Chinese connections), poorer
regions felt left out and farmers rioted in protest. Privatizing the
communes brought out rural triads who had the secret resources to
grab the best assets. People with influence and *guanxi* – Party cadres,
relatives, cronies – bought tractors, trucks, wells, pumps and processing equipment at two-thirds off. Some financed the deals with easy
credit from state banks, then defaulted on the loans. Peasants, anxious
to make a killing before the government changed its mind, chopped
down or slaughtered anything that could be marketed. More aggressive rural entrepreneurs bullied and exploited those who hesitated.
Gangs secured agricultural monopolies of melons or mangoes. Ancient
loyalty bonds reappeared, further weakening Party control. Local
leadership was needed, because nobody knew what to expect if what
everyone most feared (and wanted) happened, and the collapse of
Beijing rule was followed by chaos and violence. After the collapse of
the Han and Sung dynasties, strong local leaders saved many
communities from disaster.

To ordinary Chinese, however, chaos is always just around the
corner. Historically, the centre either remained in absolute control or
everything fell apart. Deng's liberalization policies decentralized
control, loosening the regime's grip. This resulted in some provinces
becoming independent kingdoms, commercially. For example, on
Hainan Island, one of the fourteen free trade zones set up in 1984, local
officials imported thousands of tax-free mini-vans, then sold them to
the rest of China at hugely inflated prices.

When taxation and other economic powers were decentralized,

Beijing had to bargain with each province each year for central government revenues. Accordingly, remittances to Beijing dropped by half. Provincial officials rolled these revenues over, causing fiscal overheating. The central government tried to recapture direct control of local taxation and the distribution of public funds, arguing that this was necessary to spread prosperity more evenly, by reappointing sums from richer to poorer areas. Whether the poorer areas would ever actually see the revenue was uncertain.

The rise of local autonomy poses grave danger to Beijing because of the violent centrifugal forces at work. The Party can issue orders, but if they are not obeyed and implemented by the provinces, or by the military, the result may be a slide beyond fiscal chaos and political anarchy to national disintegration. At a time when Deng's death was imminent and Beijing's authority over the southern provinces was in ever-growing doubt, China was in danger of splitting into pieces. A September 1993 report published by China's Academy of Social Sciences sounded the alarm. 'Until now, policy makers did not realize the danger of the central government's rapid decline of power, or they did, but have not come up with an effective way to halt the trend.' The report raised the spectre of warlordism, and predicted that on Deng's death China might 'move from economic collapse to political break-up, ending with disintegration.'

The Party naturally tries to link its fate to that of the nation and the economy, predicting disaster should its rule collapse. Yet the downfall of the ruling Party does not necessarily mean economic disaster. Just the reverse has been the case so far. Although the Party clings to the Forbidden City, it is terminally ill. In China today, success is all that matters. Many people might prefer the current chaos to continue. Instability means opportunity. Some observers also predict that the intense competition among provinces will prevent any one province from gaining pre-eminence.

The worst-case scenario is a reassertion of 'stupefying tyranny' by Beijing. It may be hard to believe China's rulers would crack down on the south, and throw out the boom-baby with the bath-water. But in fear of itself, China has often cut off its own genitals. The determination of the central regime to regain control must never be underestimated. Beijing is not kinder, nor gentler. Thousands of executions take place across China each year.

Like the Duke of Chou, when the Party offers the public a choice of tyranny or chaos, no real choice is intended. China has the world's longest continuous tradition of tyranny, which mesmerizes the entire society. In 1990, a secret internal report warned that the official debunking of Mao Tse-tung was a technique easily turned against the current leadership. The last thing Deng wanted was to be vilified after his death. Quickly, Mao was rehabilitated as an icon of national unity. From now on, Great Helmsmen and Paramount Leaders will go into a Pantheon instead of the trash bin. Confucius has also been recruited as a top cadre, and emperors resurrected as tourist attractions to glamorize the role of absolutism. Autarchy has always been used to bind the nation together. No longer is anything said about 'running dogs of the capitalist warmongers, fascist bandits and insects,' or about heroic peasant rebellions. The last thing Beijing needs now is a peasant uprising. Some signs indicate that one may already have started.

Despite Overseas Chinese efforts to portray themselves as modern and liberal (in the sense of urbane), no Overseas Chinese billionaire became rich by being democratic or expansive. Confucianism itself is a celebration of inequality. Few educated Chinese reformers would voluntarily extend voting rights to 'muddy legs', the uneducated peasants who are China's great majority. The Chinese élite's idea of democracy is more like that of Thomas Jefferson than of Andrew Jackson. Wise and virtuous leaders, selected by their peers, should decide the course of action for the good of all and the good of the nation. In that sense, Singapore's Lee Kuan Yew is the Jefferson of the Pacific Rim. Ultimately, though, China is most at home with tyranny. The use of force to repress opposition or dissent never worries the centre. In China's experience, leadership gains nothing by showing weakness, hesitation or compassion.

Deng's passing may have no immediate visible effect. Since 1949, it has taken the outside world many months to discover crucial leadership changes in Beijing, such as Mao's physical collapse at the end of 1965. 'Nothing at all will happen,' said one Chinese observer, speaking of Deng's death. 'Everything is in place ... Our country resembles a freight train tearing along at 200 kilometres an hour. There isn't the time to worry who is the driver, and he really doesn't matter anyway, as long as the train stays on the rails.'

Lee Kuan Yew predicted that 'a triumvirate of sixty year olds' would emerge as the new leadership, backed by the PLA. A few months later, one of the three would become supreme. There would be no change in economic policies, he said, but a 'tightening of social discipline and party control'. Whip-cracking. China would remain a hierarchical society, with one-party rule, but a few minor parties would be 'in control' of major urban areas. These would include Dalian and Tientsin in the north, Shanghai in the centre, and Hong Kong in the south. This was as close as Lee would come to conceding the likelihood of fragmentation, or the emergence of regional power centres. To regain public confidence, he said, the new leadership would launch a great campaign, introducing a judiciary and a constitution, with 'a semblance of participatory government'. Something, in other words, along the lines of his own Singapore.

Interestingly, Singapore has allied itself with North China in the matter of commercial ethics. South China's business environment, by contrast, is fast and loose. Deals are made in a fluid, open-ended way, often involving bribes, kickbacks, and under-the-counter manipulation. Unlike South China, Singapore's successful effort to attract multinationals and to build large state-controlled companies, required strictly honest and efficient conduct, so the Singapore-style manager is not at ease with the ethics of a place like Shenzhen.

There is no doubt how Deng would like China to evolve, because the role model is so obvious. He once mourned, 'If I had only Singapore to worry about.'

As role models go, Singapore is one of the best. Its economic strength grew from a robust mixture of multinational corporations and government-linked companies. Its 'free-market' capitalism is actually carefully controlled and directed by the government. To attract the multinationals, Singapore offered tax breaks and created a superb infrastructure, with world-class education, hospitals, roads, utilities, transport, telecom, port, airport – and a surprisingly efficient civil service. Nobody stands in line long in Singapore.

No other government in the tropics functions so briskly or openly. In Singapore you can win bids for government contracts even when your competitor is a company owned by the government. Bribery of government officials simply does not happen. In a country so proud of its living conditions that it is illegal to chew gum, it has been a long time since anyone proffered a bribe. Technology has been given preference, producing one of the best educated work forces in the world. No militant labour unions, strikes, rabble-rousing opposition parties – nothing is permitted to endanger Singapore's stability and financial success. Singaporeans are not only citizens of the same country, they are all owner–members of the same *kongsi*; they all work for the same paternal corporation, the Singapore tontine. The ruling People's Action Party is its custodian. Most Singapore-based Overseas Chinese strongly support the government's authoritarian approach, based on Confucian ideas of rule by a benign hierarchy. Its success is obvious. The opposite extreme is available in Shenzhen for anyone who wants it. After sampling life in other Asian capitals, a large number of Old Asia Hands have gravitated to Singapore. They find that life on the island is sweet, streets are clean, flowers bloom everywhere, there is no litter or crime, and the mingling of races works better than elsewhere on the Rim.

The Singapore government made itself an energetic partner in expediting new enterprises. It constructed factories so that new companies did not have to waste time putting up a building from scratch. Its Economic Development Board took care of arranging tax concessions and agency approvals. Texas Instruments and Hewlett-Packard were just two of dozens of high-tech firms that chose Singapore for their Asian plants. Three thousand other foreign companies have set up operations there, eight hundred of them from America. More than 80 per cent of the capital in Singapore's industrial base has come from foreigners. Multinationals are not known for their loyalty. If they stay in Singapore, it is not an accident.

In place of socialism or communism, paternalistic Singapore bullied its own population into shaping up and looking after itself. Citizens were unable to dodge contributing part of their earnings to a retirement fund for their own benefit. In 1992, this took 34 per cent of a worker's salary. Like a Confucian elder brother, the government alters the amount depending upon whether the island's economy is thriving or faltering. When there is a recession, less is taken, so that people have more to spend, and the economy is stimulated. It works, which is the ultimate test.

Singapore is widely regarded as the most successful economy in the world. Purists argue that it is not a free market success story because so much of it has been guided. On the other hand, South Korea grew under a succession of military regimes. Taiwan succeeded despite the incompetence of the KMT, while Hong Kong's free-for-all has had a human cost that is absent from Singapore.

However, to declare Singapore as a role model for the future of Mainland China stretches believability. Chinese enjoy fantasy as much as anyone, but they prefer to do their dreaming in bank vaults. The massacre at Tienanmen led most Chinese to the conclusion that twentieth-century politics had become meaningless in any case, and should be left to the old fanatics in Beijing. Everybody else should simply get on with making money. If China was reborn in Singapore's model, fine. If not, Shenzhen's model would do just fine.

Economic collapse would come only if foreign capital stopped pouring in. Since most foreign capital came through Overseas Chinese hands, Beijing was not likely to interfere much in what happened along the South Coast.

In the words of Deng's daughter, Deng Lin, the artist, Tienanmen Square and the Cultural Revolution were 'accidents of little importance' that were 'just plain bad luck'. China needed time, she said, to acquire absolute stability. Doubtless she was paraphrasing the Duke of Chou, three thousand years ago. But then she went on. 'It's a good thing for the Chinese to get rich,' she explained. 'Money is the best antidote to anti-establishment activities.'

Perhaps. But in February 1995, as Deng lay in his death bed, his successors began the long-expected purge of his family's business associates. Denouncing 'commercial corruption', Beijing arrested Zhou Beifang, a partner of Deng's son, Deng Zhifang. This was followed by the abrupt retirement of his father, Zhou Guanwu, an old comrade-in-arms of Deng Senior. The Zhou family had long enjoyed a free hand in running Shougang, one of China's biggest steel industries. Another Shougang investor was Li Ka-shing, whose Orient Plaza project on prime real estate in downtown Beijing suddenly was halted following charges of bribery and the arrest of city officials. Stock prices fell sharply in Hong Kong, in fear of possible further casualties at Citic and other major players. And where it will stop, nobody knows.

EPILOGUE

SUNRISE ON THE RIM

THE BOOM ON THE MAINLAND IS EXHILARATING TO OVERSEAS Chinese everywhere. They are proud that after centuries of humiliation China is regaining greatness at breathtaking speed – economic greatness, first, but with political leverage as a consequence. The older generation of expatriates, who have felt discriminated against in Western and Asian societies, hope a strong China will change all that. Others fear that it will.

Asians are particularly nervous about China's military potential. Since 1990, her defence spending has doubled on tanks, ships and aircraft. Her military strategists talk of the need to secure the Strait of Malacca. The Strait of Malacca? It has been six centuries since China last took a military interest in the Strait, under Cheng Ho. Now a Chinese radar base and listening post has been built on Burma's Cocos Island in the Bay of Bengal, to monitor international shipping in the Strait. Since several South East Asian nations have been buying military hardware and enlarging their navies and air forces in expectation of some future confrontation over oil rights around the Paracels in the South China Sea, this end-run by China may be intended to serve notice that ASEAN (Association of South East Asian Nations) will also have to watch its back.

Much depends on how Tokyo works out its future relationship with Beijing. What Japan does to remain number one or number two could be the key to war or peace in the Pacific century. After coasting for decades with one of the world's lowest defence budgets, Japan grew to become the third largest military spender after America and the USSR. Then, with the Soviet collapse, it became the second largest. Fear and aggression sleep in the same bed. Tokyo fears Chinese competition more than it does American sanctions. It also fears Beijing's military ambitions. On the flip side of the coin, other nations worry that a Japan provoked by China will reawaken Japanese militarism. The fear of China going rogue is balanced by the fear of Japan going rogue again. Hard times in Japan, political scandals, short-sighted American demands, and artificial pressure on the yen, serve as reminders of diplomatic and intelligence blunders by Washington in the 1930s and 1940s. Japan's militarists have not vanished for ever; some members of the Diet still insist that the Rape of Nanking never happened. Others argue that Japan was not defeated, but made a strategic surrender to conserve its remaining assets and thus recover much faster, to triumph another day. Indeed, fifty years after the war it 'lost', Tokyo is in its strongest position ever.

It is the possibility of a secret pact between Beijing and Tokyo that most worries Washington intelligence analysts. Such a possibility will depend on who emerges victorious in Beijing from the musical chairs following Deng's departure.

China's neighbours watch closely the growing evidence that the Mainland could fragment into several nations. The possibility of civil strife is serious; after briefly putting on the brakes in 1994, as inflation caused the economy to overheat, Beijing decided that further restraint might provoke open revolt, and allowed the gold rush to resume. To hide its chagrin, the regime claimed that prices had increased at a slower rate in the second quarter than in the first, although the consumer price index was 22 per cent higher than at the same time the previous year. If Beijing had to resort to such subterfuge to hide the failure of its efforts, then it might still be devoured by the tiger it is riding.

Some nations, including Japan, might be discreetly encouraging the centrifugal forces, as part of a longer-term strategy to break up the new economic giant. A separate South China could subdivide into three or more smaller states based on Kwangtung, Fukien, and the Shanghai provinces of Chekiang and Kiangsu. Hong Kong is already destined to merge with Kwangtung in 1997. Shanghai will continue to be Hong Kong's main economic rival below the Yangtze. Meanwhile, Taiwan strategists speak of a union with Fukien province. Since Beijing has made clear that it will not tolerate Taiwan declaring itself a sovereign nation, the Fukienese majority on the island may be content to seek union with Fukien, in return for being acknowledged as a semi-autonomous region of Greater China. Such grand dreams in the former Soviet Union have turned sour because of poverty. Prosperity could make the difference in China.

Whether we see an independent South China, or three independent countries based on Hong Kong, Shanghai and Taipei, the result would be a victory for the Overseas Chinese. It would also reduce the challenge to Japan by diffusing China's power among several capitals.

Whatever happens in terms of military balance, Overseas Chinese are excited about China triumphing over Japan economically. Western and Japanese firms watch jealously as the Overseas Chinese exploit their *guanxi* connections to snap up the best deals on the Mainland. Tokyo is responding to the challenge by making a new push in South East Asia, but ironically, wherever they go, the Overseas Chinese control the ground floor. In Thailand, for instance, they are the shoehorns for Japanese firms waiting to enter the Thai market, and are content to serve as frontmen there for Japanese corporations. The phenomenal growth of the Thai economy, and of an educated urban middle class, has been led by approximately thirty huge con-glomerates, of which all but two are owned by Thai-Chinese. The founding families, mostly Teochiu, have brought in executives from international business schools, but retain core control. As we have seen, the Chinese in Thailand traditionally made deals with a handful of top political and military leaders, but the recent growth of multi-party politics in Bangkok has obliged them to underwrite an ever greater number of generals and politicians. A dramatic increase in heroin traffic from the Golden Triangle has generated fabulous wealth for the top four or five Teochiu syndicates and their Thai military and police protectors, but growth and prosperity in legitimate business has now become so great that the Teochiu are letting the drug trade shift into the hands of syndicates on the Mainland – and of the Burma army, which is using drug profits to remodel Burma's tourist image.

As part of its drug-money-for-weapons deal with the Chinese military, the Burma army regime has opened its border to Chinese traders and entrepreneurs. The army's objective is to copy the Suharto regime in Indonesia by leasing Burma's economy to the Chinese, while raking off the lion's share of profits for the officer corps, and while retaining for themselves the primary power of any government, which is the exclusive right to inflict pain and punishment. In response, Chinese from Yunnan are buying up the best property in Mandalay and other cities and towns, elbowing Burmese shopkeepers aside. In Rangoon, dilapidated British colonial buildings are being bulldozed to make way for hundreds of new hotels financed by Overseas Chinese investors from Singapore, Malaysia and Thailand. In one of the world's poorest and most desperate countries, such a radical change is startling, but to Burmese, at least, the message is frighteningly clear: when Chinese money moves in, the effect is like a plague of locusts.

'Before we can do anything to stop them,' a Burmese intellectual complained, 'all our teak forests will be gone, and the Golden Triangle will be turned into a golf course. That's one way of ending the drug trade, but I'm not sure it's the best way.'

Indeed, there are already 'Golden Triangle' resort hotels in North Thailand, and 'Golden Triangle' tour boats on the Mekong that invite you to go swimming on the same sandbars where the druglord Khun Sa fought machine-gun battles over mule trains loaded with opium tar, morphine base, and Double-UO Brand China White.

In Indonesia, prosperity has gradually reduced the dependence of the government on the Chinese *cukong*. It has also freed the *cukong* to go offshore, and turn their wealth and privileged connections to their personal profit. Nevertheless, the top twenty conglomerates still have tight connections to the Suharto family, personally or through interlocking directorates. Despite public posturing, there has been little serious industrial development. Much Indonesian wealth is quietly slipping out of the country. Not everyone is happy with this situation.

Recent outbursts of Muslim labour unrest in Sumatra fixed their attention on Chinese shops and businesses. Nothing can be done about the army's corruption, so mobs take revenge on the Chinese. Whether or not Suharto serves out his current term, which ends in 1998, there may be catastrophic reprisals against members of his family, against *cukong* such as his personal favourite Liem Sioe Liong, and against Chinese in Indonesia in general. The word is out that Suharto's choice of successor will depend primarily on which military man can best guarantee the safety of Suharto's family and friends.

Whatever vendettas occur in Indonesia may be dwarfed by vendettas in China, where the safety of Deng's family and other members of the Politburo is not at all certain. Years of tyranny, whether in China, Indonesia, Thailand or Burma, invite grisly reprisals. Like Suharto, Deng is counting on the army to keep order.

Nobody trusts Beijing, least of all the Overseas Chinese. If the Mainland becomes too rich and powerful, it may cause trouble for Overseas Chinese in their adopted countries. Member countries of ASEAN compete with Beijing for international development funds. Angry voices claim that the huge sums the Overseas Chinese pump into the Mainland come at the expense of other Pacific Rim countries. The Overseas Chinese reply that they are raising the money offshore, not looting it from their adopted homelands. They also insist that their investments are for commercial reasons, not out of allegiance to ancestral loyalties, although most of what they invest goes into their ancestral districts, where sweetheart deals are to be made. They point out that over 90 per cent of all Overseas Chinese have become citizens of their host countries.

'This danger shouldn't be underrated,' warned Singapore's Lee Kuan Yew. 'If relations turn sour between any ASEAN country and China, those ethnic Chinese who have invested in China will be criticized for disloyalty.'

So far, only a dozen or so Overseas Chinese tycoons routinely operate on a global scale, although many more have moved a large part of their personal wealth out of domestic holdings and into international channels, from Canada to the Netherlands. Many use Hong Kong as a source of easy finance, as an offshore nest, or as a discreet conduit for investments in the China market. The Overseas Chinese role model is an urbane global financier with a townhouse in London, penthouses in Singapore and Hong Kong, a beach house in Hawaii, at least one high-rise property in Vancouver, a horse ranch in Australia, a cattle ranch in Florida, banks in California, Luxemburg and the Caymans, a yacht on the West Indies, and a conglomerate stuffed with off-the-shelf companies registered in Panama, Liberia and Andorra.

Until they know the outcome of the succession in China and in Indonesia, Overseas Chinese want to remain highly mobile intermediaries, whose personal wealth stays safely salted away, earning high interest. They have done their damage control in advance, and hope to be watching events from those self-same high rises in Vancouver. They shed no tears for nationalism. Mobility is everything. The amount of Chinese capital moving around the Pacific Rim has reached astonishing proportions. Shrewder investors are placing chips on both sides of the Pacific. The objective remains to generate as much personal wealth as possible, preferably offshore, preferably black.

'When you reach this stage,' one said, 'craving US citizenship becomes pointless. I spend so little time in any one place that citizenship no longer matters.'

To them nationalism is a vanity and a prejudice, like racism, which they cannot afford. They are a moral community whose members feel bound to each other and, more so than most ethnic groups, responsible for each other's survival, at least within each dialect group. The conflict between them and China's central government is unlikely to heal. Even if they end up with complete control of China's coastal provinces, ingrained fear will keep them on guard. It would be prudent and practical for the West to recognize these ancient undercurrents, and to adjust strategies accordingly. But Western attention is focused elsewhere.

America insists that China install a democratic system modelled on Western concepts of universal justice and morality. Asians respond that trust and justice are not abstractions, and only tyranny and corruption are absolute. Taiwan shows how a government shielded and enriched by America did nothing to advance democracy, until that protection was removed; now the KMT buys time from the firing squad by showering its citizens with liberties.

Authoritarian leaders such as Lee Kuan Yew and Dr Mahathir

Muhammed put reform and prosperity ahead of political liber-
tarianism. The last thing any Asian country needs at this point in time,
they argue, is the sort of loud, adversarial media politics that stalls
forward progress in Washington, London, Paris and Rome.

Most Asians are extremely poor and terrified of violence. Desperate
people will back anyone who claims to have a solution. Asian regimes
use the craving for prosperity to build a consensus for authoritarian
rule. The success of Singapore demonstrates that getting there quickly
and surely requires a firm hand. This had also been the lesson of South
Korea, which achieved major improvements in the quality of life at the
cost of personal liberties. Prosperity eventually brings latitude, latitude
allows more freedom, and freedom necessarily precedes democracy.
Yet both Singapore and South Korea are denounced in the West for not
following democratic models – models that have repeatedly failed
elsewhere. The frenzy in America over the caning episode in Singapore
in 1994 shows how the fantasy of the free spirit is related to the fantasy
of the free lunch.

With their tradition of evangelism, and the conviction that they have
the mandate of heaven, Americans are in the habit of forcing their
vanities down the gullets of other people. Much of Lee Kuan Yew's
advice to the West about China has to do with letting the Mainland
have its own particular nationalism, and with ceasing to press China to
behave according to what the West sees as 'universal' moral principles.

Like it or not, Asian tradition puts the rights of the group ahead of
those of any individual. This is crucial in China, a nation always on the
verge of famine, always tending to fragment. If individuals do not meet
their obligations to the group – in agriculture, in flood control, and so
on – chaos follows. There is an obligation to contribute, not a right to
defy. Confucianism is an attempt to rationalize Chinese society, a
nearly impossible task given its disparities. The idea of a single
monolithic China is the propaganda of a ruling élite, to foster the ideal
of uniformity.

Lee Kuan Yew urged the United States to befriend China, rather than
trip it up with threats of trade war. Would the West really prefer it if
Beijing lost control, China disintegrated, and the chaos of the warlord
years resumed? The Japanese learned that there are many Chinas, not
just one. Aside from its tragic impact on the Chinese people, whose life

has recently taken such a promising turn, chaos there would cause severe headaches for China's neighbours. A Beijing preoccupied with prosperity is much less likely to make trouble. The West's best interest therefore lies in encouraging China's prosperity.

And prosperity there will be, whether the West encourages it or not, co-operates with it or not, plans for it or not. The age of Sun Tzu has returned. It is sunrise on the Rim. The year 2000 is the Chinese Year of the Dragon – an auspicious beginning for what may also be the Century of the Dragon.

NOTES

CHAPTER 1

Professor Creel's books about ancient China remain the best general introduction.

p. 9: For the full T'sao T'sao anecdote, see *Romance of the Three Kingdoms*, translated by C. H. Brewitt-Taylor, or the fine new translation by Moss Roberts.

p. 10: Yu the Great's dates are traditionally given as 2205–1766 BC. Recent discoveries show that the annals are surprisingly accurate.

p. 11: The Shang kings had a good reputation until the eleventh century BC. Then, the *Documents* and the *Odes* assert that they fell into bad habits because of alcohol.

p. 12: Feeding people has been one of China's greatest problems, so theft, corruption, or mismanagement quickly cause disaster. Only severe discipline could prevent this. As Creel sums it up in *Origins*, King Wen of Chou established a regime of 'exceptionally harsh discipline.'

p. 12: 'If it is reported . . .'; 'Small faults . . .'; 'A woman with a long tongue.'; '. . . tranquil and orderly.' All from Creel in *Origins*.

p. 13: The quick death sentence by Confucius is mentioned in Ssu-ma Chien. I relied primarily on translations by Watson, and Yang and Yang.

p. 14: In China there is a saying, 'If he is not our kin, he is sure to be of different mind.' Everyone with the same surname is a potential ally. Those who are not kin, or born in the same village, are potential enemies. See Hsu for more.

p. 14: When a usurper named Ch'en seized power in the state of Ch'i, he adoped the name T'ien (Heavenly), which sounds the same but is written differently, and traced his ancestry back to god himself, in the form of the millet god Ti. Thus the house of T'ien was made to seem a heavenly family, more divine than the house it had overthrown. (A Tang historian said Sun Tzu was related to this T'ien clan.) See Hsu for more.

p. 15: Many centuries later, discussing guerrilla warfare strategy with Red Army commanders, Mao Tse-tung reminded them, 'We are not the Duke of Chou.' He meant the duke who hesitated to attack, not the earlier one who obliterated fifty rebel states.
p. 15: Lucien Pye affirms that corruption, bribery and conspiracy were the order of the day.
p. 15: Hsu mentions that a duke of Ch'i won a struggle for the throne only after exhausting all his wealth feeding the poor, and during a famine the rich Han clan fed the entire state of Cheng by distributing rice to each family. This won them such acclaim that they were able to make the chancellorship their hereditary office.
p. 16: Losing always has been especially tough in China. In Spring and Autumn, fallen aristocrats were paraded through villages in dunce hats, as in the Red Guard movement 2,500 years later. The defeated Duke of Yu and his chief minister were presented to a rival as slaves. Toppled rulers were ritually murdered. Some had their livers eaten. Ordinary citizens of vanquished states became convicts. See Hsu for more.
p. 16: Griffith describes the 'corrosive influence' of this new class of wandering scholars upon feudal ideas and institutions. As greedy and cynical opportunists, they 'carried out schemes of the blackest treachery.' States devoured each other 'as silkworks eat mulberry leaves.'
p. 18: Some readers may find it difficult to believe that corruption in China can be so profoundly and completely institutionalized. However, approaching the question from a completely different point of view, the normally circumspect *Economist* was moved to remark, on 29 January 1994: 'Corruption is more than a poison afflicting Chinese business life. It is Chinese business life.'

CHAPTER 2

Until recently, scholars were not certain whether Sun Tzu was an actual historical figure or simply legendary. Therefore little credence was given to any of the random clues about his life scattered through Chinese literature. Some thought that he and Sun Pin were the same man, and offered possible explanations for this. All books discussing Sun Tzu and published before 1993 reflect this uncertainty. But the discovery of the trove of manuscripts in a tomb at Lin-i in Shantung in 1972, established that Sun Tzu was real, and that Sun Pin was a separate person whose own long-lost treatise of the same name, *The Art of War* was recovered from the same tomb. With this evidence it is possible to give greater credence to the literary clues we have about Sun Tzu, his origins, and his dates, fitting the clues into the broad framework of Ssu-ma Chien's chronicle of that period. For a discussion of the Lin-i documents, see Loewe, and Ames, also Yates.
p. 19: My account of Wu Tsu-hsu is drawn from Ssu-ma Chien.
p. 20: According to Ssu-ma Chien, a psychopath named Chuan Chu was hired to serve as a waiter, take the knife from the fish, and stab the king.
p. 21: According to a Tang history, Sun Tzu was born in Tung-An, the modern city of Hui-min in Shantung, where his father became military governor early in the reign of Duke Ching (547–489 BC). We know that he was a contemporary of Prime Minister Wu Tsu-hsu, who died in 485 BC. Sun Tzu must have been born no later than 535 BC or he would have been less than twenty-three years old when he appeared before King Ho-lu in 512. It seems likely that when his family fled to Wu, they lived on a farm three or four miles west of the capital, because a source cited by Griffith claims that Sun Tzu's tomb or burial mound was situated there, and the tomb would have been placed at or near his family home. Once *The Art of War* became famous, its author was known only as Master Sun (Sun Tzu) and his personal or 'style' name, Ch'ang-ch'ing, was used only

by intimate friends. Because he was the strategist of Wu state, some sources refer to him as Sun Wu, further complicating matters. See Balmforth.

p. 21: Two years after becoming prime minister, in 512 BC according to Ssu-ma Chien, Wu persuaded the king to read Sun Tzu's treatise, and this resulted in an invitation to court, where the famous scene with the concubines is said to have unfolded. After being hired as strategist, Sun Tzu led his first military campaigns in 512 or 511 BC.

p. 23: My account of dialogues between Sun Tzu and King Ho-lu comes from Ssu-ma Chien.

p. 23: Of the missing manuscripts of Sun Tzu and Sun Pin found in Shantung in 1972, Yates says, 'These texts are genuine and therefore may be relied upon for important information concerning the Warring States period ... the most spectacular are the versions of the *Sun Tzu* and the long-lost *Sun Pin Ping Fa*.'

p. 26: My account of Fan Li also comes from Ssu-ma Chien. Fan Li and Wu Tzu-hsu each also wrote an *Art of War*. See Yates.

p. 27: A variation on this famous medical analogy was repeated in the 1940s by Generalissimo Chiang Kai-shek, who said, 'The Japanese are only a disease of the skin, while the communists are a disease of the heart.'

p. 27: Professor Kierman describes the famous suicide of Wu Tzu-hsu in 485 BC in *Four Warring States Biographies*. See also Ssu-ma Chien.

p. 28: This colourful advice from Fan Li was in a letter he wrote to one of Sun Tzu's colleagues, Wen Chung, chancellor of Wu state.

p. 28: Details of Fan Li's escape are from Ssu-ma Chien; added touches from Swann.

p. 28: Yates says that among the artefacts found at Lin-i were more than two hundred bamboo strips on which are written some 2,300 characters – about one third of Sun Tzu's *Art of War* as we know it – including fragments of the familiar thirteen chapters plus five chapters never seen before, a biographical passage, and references to other chapters not yet found. This suggests that the original treatise was eighty-two chapters in all. The work we know is a shortened version, perhaps chosen by a later admirer. From various clues it seems portions were composed before 500 BC, while others were written half a century later, after 453. Assuming that he was at least in his twenties in 512 BC, Sun Tzu must have lived into his eighties to complete the final parts of his treatise after 453.

p. 30: J. J. L. Amiot's translation is in *Memoires Concernant l'Histoire, les Sciences, les Arts, les Moeurs, les Usages, etc. des Chinois*. Paris, 1782.

p. 30: This extract from the Lin-i artefacts is from Balmforth.

p. 31: For a discussion of strategy as seen by Clausewitz and Moltke, see Aron, Asprey, Cowley, Earle, Hackett, Kennedy, Paret, Presseisen, and Rapoport.

p. 31: My selections from Sun Tzu were rephrased to eliminate military terms. The most commonly available translations are by Griffith and Wing. A different approach was used by Thomas Cleary in the Shambhala edition. Yet another interpretation of Sun Tzu can be found in Wee, Lee and Bambang. Ames includes the new material from Shantung.

CHAPTER 3

Very little has been written in the West about Sun Pin. The outstanding exception was Edmund Elliott Balmforth, a China scholar and linguist who spent his career as an intelligence officer for the US army in Asia and at Fort Holabird, then returned to Rutgers to teach military history and prepare a doctoral dissertation on Sun Pin. Balmforth's work (available from University Microfilms) is a rough text, with some contradictions, but Balmforth was aware of the Lin-i discoveries and painstakingly compiled fascinating material.

p. 33: The opening image is from the Tang poet Li Po. Sun Pin's story comes from Ssu-ma Chien, with embellishments from Balmforth.

p. 33: Sun Pin, who was born approximately 135 years after the presumed date of Sun Tzu's birth, would have been a fourth- or fifth-generation descendant, perhaps a great-great-grandson or grandnephew.

p. 33: Griffith says Sun Pin was born between the towns of O and Chuan, near P'o Hsien in modern Shantung. But Balmforth says he was born between Tung-a and Yang-ku, 40 miles south-west of modern Tsinan in Shantung. Balmforth probably has it right.

p. 33: 'When they shake the sweat off . . .' Creel, *Origins*.

p. 33: According to Ssu-ma Chien, his uncle was named Sun Ch'iao. Balmforth says the uncle was a bureaucrat in the Ch'i state government.

p. 34: Chinese sources have many more details of Sun Pin's life than about his illustrious ancestor. See, for example, Su Haichen's *Wiles of War*, which recounts the rivalry between Sun Pin and Pang Chuan. Ghost Valley and the Master of Ghost Valley (Kuei-ku-tzu) are famous in Chinese military history. Another celebrated pupil, Chang I, later organized the Ch'in state military alliance that vanquished all rivals to set up the first Chinese empire.

p. 34: A disciple of Confucius conned five states into an ingenious game of military dominoes to save the state of Lu from defeat. See Balmforth.

p. 34: Wu Ch'i has been called 'second only to Sun Tzu' for the popularity of his own treatise on warfare. His story is well told by Sadler. Unlike Sun Tzu, the treatise attributed to Wu Ch'i is thought to have been compiled after his death by pupils of his academy. Notes on strategy were expressed in aphorisms to make them easier to memorize.

p. 34: Ta Liang was near K'aifeng, in modern Honan province.

p. 35: Hulsewe's study shows that usually only one foot was cut off, to hobble convicts but still permit forced labour. Mildest of the Five Punishments was branding the face with the name of the crime; after that cutting off the nose; then removing one foot, or both feet; next the genitals – castration, emasculation, or both. Kneecapping by slicing a tendon was reserved for cases where revenge was more important than utility. Some scholars thought Sun Pin's legs were amputated, but as Balmforth explains, the word *pin* meant crippling by kneecapping. The word can be written in two forms, with the *ku* (bone) radical, or the *jou* (meat) radical, both meaning kneecap. One implies removal of the bone, the other the slicing of the tendon. Regarding Sun Pin, Ssu-ma Chien uses the term *pin-chiao*, explicitly meaning the kneecap was removed. But this probably was an error, given Sun Pin's high level of activity thereafter. Ssu-ma Chien may have drawn the wrong conclusion because of his own mutilation; the historian was castrated for speaking too boldly in defence of a general being criticized at court.

p. 36: The prince was said to be related to Sun Pin. They were descended from the ducal Ch'en clan that once ruled the state of Ch'en, but fled to Ch'i to escape punishment after a family quarrel, and changed their name to T'ien. (See my notes for chapters 1 and 2.) One branch became generals and eventually produced Sun Tzu and Sun Pin. The other branch were bankers and property owners who became enormously popular with the ordinary citizens of Ch'i because they made loans that could be paid back at substantial discounts and sponsored merchants who sold goods at fair prices. Twice when the growing wealth and power of the T'ien clan was threatened by the private armies of rich rivals, commoners took their side. Eventually, the T'ien clan overcame all competition and gained control of Ch'i, one of the richest states in China. So the prince's patronage of Sun Pin was all in the family.

p. 37: '. . . marked for life . . .' is from Ssu-ma Chien.

p. 38: 'To unravel tangled yarn . . .' is from *Wiles of War*. Ssu-ma Chien actually says, 'You do not ward off an invasion by seizing your enemy's halberds.'

p. 38: For Mao's account, see his *Problems of Strategy in Guerrilla War Against Japan*.

p. 39: This exchange with the king is retold in *Wiles of War*.

p. 40: There are various accounts of the famous Battle of Maling, all compiled long afterward. They differ mostly in their descriptions of the terrain chosen for the ambush, which the compilers had not visited. Balmforth gives a comparison. While Sun Pin is not mentioned in these accounts by name, references to T'ien-ch'en Ssu in *Stratagems of the Warring States* probably refer to Prince T'ien Ch'i, and therefore can be taken to mean the prince and his personal adviser.

CHAPTER 4

As professor Hsu expressed it, selling a king can be infinitely more profitable than selling pearls and jade.

p. 42: In the 1930s, after his sister May-ling married Generalissimo Chiang, banker T. V. Soong became prime minister of the Nationalist regime at Nanking.

p. 43: The bargain was struck with Lady Huang, childless wife of Prince An-kuo.

p. 44: Some scholars wonder if this pregnancy story was invented later by the First Emperor's critics as a way of casting doubt on his legitimacy. What better insult than to suggest that he was the bastard son of a detested merchant?

p. 44: According to mythology, the house of Chin began when the granddaughter of a legendary ruler swallowed a bird's egg and became pregnant. Actually, it began when a petty horse-trader was given an estate to raise horses for the Chou royal house. This fief, called Chin, grew by 677 BC into a feisty frontier state battling the Jung nomads, and was regarded as a place full of ruffians. Human sacrifice continued there longer than in other states, and even as late as 210 BC, when the First Emperor died, many of his concubines and tomb builders were buried with him. But Chin was by no means backward in laws or culture. See Hulsewe.

p. 45: Bodde notes that Confucius was referring to businessmen like Lu when he condemned 'men of false virtue.' Such a man, said Confucius. 'assumes an appearance of virtue which his actions belie, and his self-assurance knows never a misgiving. Thus he ensures his reputation and that of his clan.'

p. 45: The First Emperor reigned supreme until his death eleven years later at age forty-nine. The birth of his empire makes 221 BC the most important date in Chinese history before the great upheavals of the twentieth century. From Chin the name China first appeared in Greek and Roman texts, although the Chinese themselves always called it *Chung-kuo*, the Central Country or Middle Kingdom. The death toll in 130 years of military campaigns leading to Chin's final victory was around 1.5 million.

p. 45: Lu was removed from office and sent to his home state, Honan, where he was given a huge estate with income from a hundred thousand households. But after a year, the First Emperor feared that Lu might inspire a rebellion, so he exiled him to Szechuan, and along the way Lu drank poison. See Crump.

p. 46: See Hulsewe for a fascinating account of the system of laws and punishments.

p. 46: Li Ssu added immeasurably to China's unity by standardizing the written script, which (with a few modifications during the Han dynasty) remained in use to the twentieth century.

p. 47: More books were destroyed by imperial order during the Han dynasty, and as recently as Manchu emperor Chienlung. But this incident made Chin, and the First Emperor, targets of scorn by Confucians ever after.

p. 47: Chin's north-south freeway had a centre lane for royal vehicles, outside lanes for ordinary people. The wheelbase of chariots and wagons later was standardized by Han at 4.92 feet, to fit the same ruts everywhere.

p. 48: Dun Li gives a refreshing portrait of the growth of trade and commerce, and the power of wealthy merchants. His picture is quite different from the traditional idea of the 'four classes' in China.

p. 49: For the First Emperor's fruitless search for the elixir, and his fascination with the seacoast, see Twitchett and Loewe, volume I. Ssu-ma Chien implies that the wizard Hsu Fu had made a detailed study over many years and knew exactly where he was going and what he would find when he got there. Professor Needham, volume 4, conjectures that such early voyages might have reached North America, beginning as far back as 1000 BC. Needham is not speaking of a large-scale migration, but the arrival from time to time of small groups of Chinese with high culture, making the crossing on Yangtze sailing rafts, helped along by the Kuroshio and North Pacific currents. They would have been unable to return to China directly because contrary winds and ocean currents would force them south.

p. 50: The detail about the rotten fish is from Jenner.

p. 50: For the comic opera downfall of Chin, see Twitchett and Loewe, volume I.

CHAPTER 5

Bentley's engaging book gives a vivid account of cultural and trading contracts across Central Asia over the centuries.

p. 53: For an account of the military feats of Wen-ti and Wu-ti, see Lœwe in Kierman and Fairbank, *Chinese Ways in Warfare*.

p. 53: 'When Han arose . . .' is from Swann.

p. 53: China's relations with neighbouring peoples changed greatly. Soldiers, officials, diplomats and colonists travelled far greater distances at the initiative of the Han government.

p. 55: 'Over that corridor [the steppes] mounted warriors could move faster than anywhere else in the world and from it they could strike north or south into either hemisphere.' (Chambers).

p. 55: 'North we can flee . . .' and 'Just because . . .' are from Bentley.

p. 56: 'Do you suppose . . .' is from Ssu-ma Chien.

p. 56: Deodotus, satrap of Bactria, and others ruled a Greco-Bactrian kingdom till 151 BC when they were overrun by Scythians. The Yueh-chih nomads then drifted in and took over. Eventually the Yueh-chih moved on to Afghanistan, where they established the Kushan dynasty.

p. 56: Chang Chien's tales and rewards are recounted by Ssu-ma Chien.

p. 59: For an account of the Chinese military expedition to Ferghana, see Loewe in Kierman and Fairbank, *Chinese Ways in Warfare*.

CHAPTER 6

Professor Wang Gungwu's studies of Chinese merchant society form the backbone of modern scholarship on the Overseas Chinese. See also Swann for a feast of anecdotal material on money and food in ancient China.

p. 61: 'Small, crowded . . .' 'Indolent and easygoing . . .' and 'Worth a thousand catties . . .' are from Ssu-ma Chien.

pp. 61–2: For an account of Yueh's feats, see Dun Li, and Needham, volume 3. Pelliot also concluded that Chinese merchant seafarers were voyaging across the Indian Ocean to Arabia and Africa early in Han.

p. 62: Needham quotes an eighth-century source as saying that Yueh warships had three decks, bulwarks, and catapults for cannon.

p. 62: '. . . the wanderers of Yueh . . .' is from Needham, volume 3.

p. 63: Not all immigrants to Yueh were exiled merchants. Swann says that during a three-year famine caused by flooding of the Yellow River, which reduced the population of North China to cannibalism, the government authorized resettlement in the south, in the Huai and Yangtze valleys.

p. 63: Wang Gungwu describes how scholars and bureaucrats secretly invested their money with merchants.

p. 64: So complete was the Mongol genocide that 'few houses were left standing and not a dog barked.' (Dun Li)

p. 65: 'They never look down . . .' Ssu-ma Chien.

p. 65: The need to keep money out of rash hands was reemphasized recently by Singapore's Lee Kuan Yew, in defence of the one-party system on the island. Lee warned that reckless introduction of a multiparty system would risk an uncontrolled spending spree that would dissipate Singapore's massive foreign exchange holdings, worth $75 billion and reduce the island to the status of a common debtor nation. Confucianism does not apply to making money but to protecting assets.

p. 66: In the seventeenth century, Italian banker Lorenzo Tonti developed a financial arrangement whereby participants shared certain benefits until one of them died or defaulted, whereupon his advantages were redistributed among the remaining members; the last survivor getting all. Hence, a *tontine*. In a rolling Chinese tontine, benefits pass from generation to generation, administered by succeeding patriarchs. Singapore is a Chinese tontine.

p. 66: See Wang Gungwu for a close study of Chinese guilds and other mutual-aid societies.

p. 67: Purcell says kongsi armies of 10,000 or more were typical in Borneo.

p. 67: This period of prosperity was during the southern 'empires' of Liu Sung (420–479), Liang (502–557), and Ch'en (557–589).

p. 68: In AD 760, thousands of Arab and Persian traders were killed in a riot in a Yangtze River seaport. When the rebel Huang Chao, a former salt merchant, sacked Canton in 878, he executed 120,000 foreigners because they were 'too wealthy'. Magistrates and interpreters were specially assigned to cope with foreign traders, and often had to settle disputes according to Islamic law. In 847 a Muslim passed the Chinese civil service exams with the highest honours.

p. 68: There was also heavy trade with Korea and Japan, which adopted the Chinese script, Buddhism, and the trappings of Tang court life. One of the leading Korean merchants was shipowner Chang Pogo, who operated out of Wando island off the south-western tip of the peninsula. See Needham.

p. 69: 'Our enemies become richer . . .' is from Dun Li.

p. 69: Sung's credo was that pleaure and long life were more important than anything else. Dun Li calls it 'disarmament beside the wine cups.' 'To get rich is glorious' is merely Deng's paraphrase of the Sung credo.

p. 70: Ibn Batuta told how 'The sailors also have their children in such cabins; and in some parts of the ship they sow garden herbs, vegetables, and ginger in wooden tubs.' See *Junks and Sampans of the Yangtze*, by G. C. E. Worcester, for a description of life aboard a floating colony of large and small junks.

p. 70: 'The ships which sail the southern sea . . .' is from Needham, volume 4.

p. 71: 'Profits from maritime commerce . . .' is from Wang Gungwu.

p. 72: In Chinese he was call P'u Shou-keng. P'u is thought to be the Chinese transliteration of Abu.

p. 72: 'Lived a life of luxury . . .' is from Dun Li.

CHAPTER 7

Professor Needham's volume 4, has the most complete survey of Chinese seafaring and shipbuilding, including many details on Cheng Ho.

p. 74: Wang Gungwu tells of the merchant Wan-san, a native of Wu-hsiang, who offered to feed the army of the founder of the dynasty; later, using his own money, he helped to build one third of the wall around the capital. But the wealth and influence of Wan-san made the emperor suspicious. Only the intercession of the empress saved his life. He was sent into exile to Yunnan where he died.

p. 76: Lucien Pye emphasizes that despotism in China has its roots in this fear of imminent chaos. The two feed upon each other.

p. 77: 'Powerful as the emperors are . . .' is from Dun Li.

p. 79: Ma Ho was the second son. He had four sisters. There is an entry on Cheng Ho in the *Dictionary of Ming Biography*. My information comes from the Cheng Ho Memorial at Kunyang on the south bank of Lake Tien Chih.

p. 79: His family records say, 'When he became an adult, he grew to be 7 feet tall and had a waist about 5 feet in circumference. His cheeks and forehead were high but his nose was small.' Historian Huang Sheng-tseng insisted that Cheng Ho was in fact closer to 9 feet tall and had a girth of 90 inches.

p. 80: That first Ming emperor abolished the post of prime minister in order to rule directly. This created a problem for subsequent Ming emperors, who were overwhelmed by their responsibilities. They became increasingly dependent on personal favourites, including eunuchs, who gained a sinister influence behind the scenes.

p. 80: Yung Lo's navy at maximum strength included 400 warships of the Nanking fleet, 2,700 warships on the coasts, 400 armed transports for grain shipments, and the pride of the navy – 250 treasure ships, each manned by a crew of 500. See Needham.

p. 80: In 1957 a wooden rudder 11 metres long was found near Dragon Bay shipyard, clearly intended for a ship around 150 metres long. Typically, these great junks had flat bottoms planked with pine. Their great strength derived from fourteen bulkheads, like the partitions between sections of bamboo. These bulkheads made watertight compartments possible, so a damaged ship could stay afloat.

p. 81: Cheng Ho's ships carried drinking water in big white gourds, which doubled as life preservers. To this day, Chinese residents in Thailand still bring well mud from China.

p. 81: Kuo Chung-li was attached to three expeditions; he and Ma Huan recorded observations of foreign countries. Kung Chen and Fei Hsin both wrote their own books. Kung Chen became private secretary to Cheng Ho.

p. 82: Wang Taiyuan's book is discussed in Wang Gungwu.

p. 82: Because of the missing archives, there has always been some confusion about the real purpose of Cheng Ho's voyages, beyond mere flag waving. But an understanding of the economics of patronage and foreign trade monopoly in the Ming court makes it apparent that this inspired the missions. Merchants, mandarins and eunuchs represented three power centres in continual rivalry. The mandarins and eunuchs took advantage of commercial enmities to turn leading merchants against each other.

p. 86: Emperor Yung Lo's policy of keeping the Shan-Tai-Lao princes divided led to his support of a pretender in Malacca to block the ambitions of Siam at the lower end of the Malay peninsula.

p. 88: It was probably the appearance of Cheng Ho's fleets that made Portugal's Prince Henry and others aware that very large ships with multiple masts could be built and sailed into the wind. Till then Europeans had built single-masted ships that could only sail downwind. Thus it was an indirect result of Cheng Ho that Vasco da Gama and the Cabots were able to make their great voyages. Prince Henry, who inspired these changes, was an avid reader of the chronicles of travellers to Asia, among them the narrative of Nicolo di Conti, who visited South China in 1438.

p. 88: One squadron may have stayed behind to explore further. Needham mentions that a Portuguese sailing with Vasco da Gama down the west coast of Africa, in 1420, reported sighting a junk flying through a squall off the Cape.

p. 88: Where Cheng Ho did not go personally, he sent small squadrons. Needham says one may have reached Australia.

p. 89: In the PRC since 1949, Cheng Ho has regularly appeared on stage in the play *Cheng Ho Sails to the Western Ocean.*

CHAPTER 8

Keene, and Crozier, provide dramatic accounts of Coxinga and his rebellion. My brief summary of General Hu's adventures is drawn from the wonderful narrative of Hucker in Kierman and Fairbank. I merged the two stories because both concern the same maritime trade network under different dynasties, and reveal how deceit and treachery were not the characteristics of a single regime.

p. 90: 'As soon as the fog lifted . . .' is from Keene.

p. 91: Only the emperor's sudden death ended Eunuch Wei's career, when his enemies forced him to commit suicide.

p. 92: The Siamese king did well enough out of the deal to continue providing false documents of tribute through the nineteenth century. See Suehiro.

p. 92: 'More like merchants . . .' is from Spencer and Wills.

p. 93: Chinese syndicates formed alliances with Japanese, Muslim and European traders. They found it difficult to compete with the Europeans, who were sponsored and armed by their government. Chinese in Macao, Manila and Malacca did not have official Chinese backing, so they acted humble and kept their operations secret.

p. 94: Chinese, mostly Hokkien from Amoy, lived for centuries in the Goto Islands off Kyushu under the protection of the Japanese, who found them useful collaborators in trading with China. Hsu Tung and Wang Chih both used the Goto Islands as a base. In his turn, Li Tan exchanged presents, social visits, and banquets with Lord Matsuura, daimyo of Hirado, and his samurai. Other Hokkien communities grew around the fishing village of Nagasaki, which developed into a major entrepot only after Portuguese traders and missionaries settled there in the 1570s. One of Li Tan's brothers was godfather of the Chinese community at Nagasaki. Another brother in Fukien took care of business at their home base of Amoy.

p. 94: Hucker, in Kierman and Fairbank, calls General Hu's performance 'a masterpiece of dirty work, far beyond the unsophisticated capacity of a mere military man.'

p. 96: The emperor died the following year, and without his protection Grand Secretary Yen Sung was purged.

p. 98: Cheng's ambition was not to save the bungling Ming dynasty, but to outmanoeuvre his business rivals and take over the entire maritime trade. Some of Li Tan's lieutenants were still in control of parts of the network in Amoy.

p. 101: Crozier, Keene, Spencer and Wills, all give various accounts of the mother's dramatic death.

p. 101: The Ming pretenders were no saints. At different times each of them had betrayed their dynasty, helping to bring about its downfall.

p. 101: Coxinga's severity turned a number of offices against him, men who could not accept discipline, but who were valuable and talented. He had a cousin and an uncle executed for treachery and another uncle disgraced. See Crozier.

p. 102: Coxinga gave the Manchu a serious fright, and could easily have won the day if he had pressed his advantage from the start, taking Nanking before the Mongol-Manchu cavalry arrived. He was a better admiral than a general.

p. 102: 'When the city . . .' is from the Dominican, François de Rougemont.

p. 102: My summary of the Mongol tactics and Coxinga's defeat is from the Ming loyalist Huang Tsung-shi, in his work on Coxinga.

p. 103: Coxinga's message to the Spaniards, carried by Vittorio Ricci, said in part: 'I have hundreds of thousands of good soldiers, and a large number of war and merchant ships at this island. The distance which separates us from our kingdom is not great; indeed, if we set sail in the morning, we could arrive there by evening.'

p. 103: Medical evidence from the signs and symptoms points to a type of malaria known as malignant tertian, caused by the parasite *Plasmodium falciparum*, which begins with mild fevers but changes suddenly into terminal illness, with the failure of liver, kidneys, and respiration, inflammation of the brain, violent seizures, coma and death.

p. 103: For the Japanese, Coxinga was a dashing hero doing noble deeds in an exotic foreign setting. This fame came through Japan's greatest playwright, Chikamatus Monzaemon. His *Battles of Coxinga*, first produced in 1715, had a lasting impact in Japan.

p. 104: In 1700 the desecrated graves of Coxinga and his son near Amoy were officially restored by the Manchu. By 1787 he had become one of the Manchu's 'loyal and pure' historical figures. On Taiwan they built a temple to him. The Japanese resurrected him as a hero during their occupation of Taiwan after 1895. The KMT and the communists both invoke him. But it is to the Overseas Chinese that he truly belongs.

CHAPTER 9

For general background on Chinese migration to South-east Asia, main sources are Purcell, Skinner, Wang Gungwu and Wu and Wu.

p. 109: The dialects of South China are actually distinct languages. Nothing like them exists in North China, where there are fewer differences from district to district.

p. 112: The Hung League or so-called Red Gang should not be confused with the Green Gang, which was a modern criminal organization in Shanghai, although there was an overlap in membership. Pockmarked Huang, one of the founders of the Green Gang with Tu Yueh-sheng ('Big Ears') was also a major figure in the Hung League in Shanghai, as well as chief of detectives for the French Concession.

p. 113: Dr Sun Yat-sen and Charlie Soong were Hakka who belonged to the Three Harmonies triad.

pp. 114–15: Wu and Wu give examples of the violent clashes between syndicates and dialect groups. Also Purcell.

p. 116: Junks rarely travelled in convoy because most harbours had only enough cargo for one ship at a time.

p. 117: 'I know not whether . . .' is from Song.

p. 118: Ni Hoe-kong, Captain China of Batavia and head of the Hokkien community in the islands, tried to escape disguised as a woman, but was caught by the Dutch, tortured and banished to Amboina. Somewhat late in the day the Dutch governor began to worry about the effect this pogrom would have on trade, and what the Emperor of China might do. An obsequious letter was sent to Peking, but the emperor was unconcerned about citizens who left China.

p. 120: See Wang Gungwu, *China . . .* , for an account of how the Chinese looked upon Western colonial capitalism.

p. 120: The abolition of slavery in the West Indies (1840s), Peru (1855), then the rest of the Americas, and the end of convict labour in Australia (1840s), brought an acute demand for cheap labour. In 1900 Nord-Deutsche Lloyd offered to carry coolies free, to drive competitors out of business.

p. 120: Until 1870 it was illegal for Chinese to leave China; during earlier periods of migration, the men usually went by themselves.

p. 121: According to the Institute of Southeast Asian Studies, Singapore, while the Chinese were 39 per cent of the population of Malaya in 1932, they were less than 3 per cent in the Dutch East Indies; 12.2 per cent in Siam; 1.6 per cent in French Indochina and 1.6 per cent in Burma. This may seem small, but it added up to 4.5 million Chinese.

p. 121: One Chinese tycoon kept an orangutan addicted to brandy.

p. 121: When Sun Yat-sen set up a Singapore branch of his revolutionary organization in 1907, Tan and other wealthy Overseas Chinese joined, cutting off their Manchu queues and contributing money. The birth of the Republic of China caused great optimism, however shortlived.

p. 121: For a well-rounded biography of Tan, see Yong.

p. 121: Amoy University opened in 1921 with Tan's crony, Singapore publisher and author Lim Boon Keng (pen name Wen Ching), as president. As a powerful Hokkien patriarch, Tan Kah-kee was able to persuade the Nationalist regime in Nanking to take over support of Amoy University, freeing him to devote the rest of his life to philanthropy.

p. 123: Economist Sakaiya Taichi observed, 'If material acquisition is the instrument of human happiness, one must beautify the actions that go along with the creation of wealth.'

CHAPTER 10

p. 125: After the First World War the West obliged Japan to relinquish these German leaseholds in Shantung, but Chinese frontmen enabled Japan to hold on to them indirectly. See Beasley.

p. 126: With Tokyo's encouragement, Mitsui made secret loans to Sun Yat-sen and other Chinese conspirators. Japan always preferred a weak and divided China, and doubtless still does.

p. 126: Manchuria was to be the exclusive domain of the Japanese army. Manchurian opium and heroin were the chief source of revenue to pay for the army's campaign to seize power from the civilian government in Tokyo. But the army lacked management savvy. Tokyo bureaucrat Kishi Nobusuke (later a postwar prime minister) advised the Kwantung Army to have Nissan administer Manchuria's development. He chose Nissan because his uncle headed the conglomerate. See Beasley, Montgomery, Duus and Herries.

p. 127: Paret discusses the racial background. Kennedy, in *Rise and Fall*, explains why the West was too preoccupied to notice.

p. 127: Even during the Great Depression, when there were food shortages in Japan, Japanese colonists in Manchuria earned high salaries and had abundant food, including all the butter, flour, sugar, bamboo shoots, tofu and mushrooms they wanted. See Cook.

p. 128: A member of Black Dragon, Kita Ikki, spelled out future strategy when he argued that the Meiji Constitution should be set aside in favour of a military regime that would nationalize property, limit wealth, end peerage and parliamentary systems, and expel the West from Asia. He recruited young officers to carry out terrorist acts to cause such panic that military dictatorship would become necessary. Sakaiya points out that the fat salaries of generals went unremarked.

p. 128: After receiving threats from the army, the Tanaka Cabinet blamed the warlord's murder on Manchurians. When the next government tried to crack down on the militarists, Prime Minister Hamaguchi was mortally wounded by an assassin.

p. 128: Ishihara was a close friend of Tsuji. For insights into the psychology of purification, see Saburo and Gluck.

p. 129: Gangster Ku Chu-chuan was the Shanghai harbour boss; his brother Ku Chu-t'ung was the KMT general. See my *Soong Dynasty* for a full account of the gangster role of the KMT. See Herries' *Soldiers of the Sun*, for the Japanese army's role in drugs. The Japanese army estimated that it earned $300 million a year from narcotics in China; see also Kaplan and Dubro.

p. 130: 'Almost all other countries . . .' is from Saburo.

p. 130: Among the zaibatsu that became involved in South-east Asia early in the century were Mitsui and Mitsubishi. Mitsui had offices in Manila, Cebu, Iloilo, Davao, Bangkok, Jakarta, Medan, Surabaya, Palembang, Semarang; Mitsubishi in Manila, Singapore, Jakarta, Surabaya and Bangkok. Mitsui Bank, Yokohama Specie Bank (now Bank of Tokyo) and Bank of Taiwan, financed Japanese ventures in South China and South-east Asia. See Duus and Yoshihara. Total Japanese investment in South-east Asia by the late 1930s was only a third of US investment, a fifth of British. Bartu notes the subversive use of Spanish fly, while Robertson describes the strategic positions of the Overseas Chinese on the eve of the war.

p. 133: 'It was not inevitable . . .' is from Cook.

p. 134: See Paret for a discussion of US and Japanese delusions about China.

p. 134: See Akira in Goodman, on barbarity.

p. 135: After attacking Pearl Harbor, Japan posed as the injured party. Psychiatrist Okonogi Keigo explains, 'Japanese psychology is so structured that people can only admit their own aggression by placing those who attack (or thwart) them in the position of powerful and unfair assailants and by casting themselves as weak victims whether or not it is actually the case . . . A classic example is in the imperial proclamation of the opening of hostilities in the Pacific War and the attack on Pearl Harbor, made to settle old scores with fiendish America and Britain.'

pp. 135–6: See Herries, McCoy, Robertson, Alletzhauser, Hall, Kaplan and Dubro, for accounts of Japanese intelligence operations and subversion at the start of the war.

p. 136: 'They wanted opium . . .' Kempeitei agent Uno Shintaro, in Cook.

pp. 136–7: Tsuji wrote proudly of his role in *Singapore: The Japanese Version*. These extracts are from Tsuji's pamphlet, titled *Read This Alone – and the War Can Be Won*. The morbid poetry is from eighth-century poet Yakamochi Otomo; the lines were set to music in 1937 and after 1943 preceded Japanese radio reports of battles. For background, see Turnbull.

p. 137: Statesman Ito Hirobumi once explained to journalist George Morrison how Japanese regard Chinese as hopelessly corrupt: 'An imperial ordinance that the officials shall be virtuous, upright, and incorruptible cannot transform men who are hopelessly corrupt with the corruption carried to them by hereditary transmission through hundreds of generations.' See *Dragon Lady*.

pp. 137–8: See Cook for poignant and chilling insights into Japanese experiences during the war.

p. 138: See McCoy, *Southeast Asia Under Japanese Occupation*, for Chinese experiences during the conquest.

p. 139: 'Who are the Chinese . . .' is from Tsuji, in *Singapore*.

pp. 139–40: See McCoy, and Goodman, for details of the terror.

pp. 140–41: Japanese army officers were ordered to pay their own way in the field, so they had to extort money. Not unlike the Nazi Holocaust, for which there was no budget, Sook Ching had to be paid for from confiscated property.

p. 141: See Cook for the horror stories. Projects included excavating ten kilometres of tunnels and chambers for the Matshushiro Underground Imperial Headquarters in Japan. Korean labourers digging a bunker there for Emperor Hirohito were all murdered on 15 August 1945, to keep them from revealing that the emperor had planned to flee.

p. 142: 'There were always pariahs . . .' Uno Shintaro, former Kempeitei agent, quoted in Cook.

p. 142: See McCoy for a description of Chinese-Japanese rice smuggling. Mitsui ran the wartime rice monopoly in Indochina. Many Japanese army and Mitsui officials exploited price differences in the black market to enrich themselves, in collaboration with corrupt Chinese.

p. 143: After foolishly abandoning Sun Tzu in favour of Clausewitz and Moltke, the Japanese High Command then forgot Clausewitz: 'The first, the supreme, the most far-reaching act of judgement . . . is to establish . . . the kind of war on which they are embarking; neither mistaking it for, nor trying to turn it into, something that is alien to its nature.' Uncertain whether to take seriously General MacArthur's posturing for the American public, Tokyo allowed itself to become spellbound by his island-hopping, and failed to react in time to the much greater danger posed by Admiral Nimitz. See Paret.

CHAPTER 11

Skinner, Wu and Wu, Purcell and others provide the broad background of Chinese migration to Thailand.

p. 147: If Thailand seems docile, it's an illusion. Sukkothai was founded around 1220, after the Khmers were neutralized; Chiengmai was founded in 1296, after the Mon were defeated. Many Tai principalities became involved in the wars and political intrigues of the Mongol khans, and later the Ming emperors. Siam controlled Laos, Cambodia, eastern Burma, and much of Malaya till Westerners took most of it away in the nineteenth century.

p. 147: The Chinese adviser to the Siamese king was called the *uparat*, an Indian term roughly equivalent to 'godfather' – only one step removed from regent.

p. 147: According to Purcell, King Narai was the leading merchant in the kingdom. Skinner said King Narai's junk fleet was operated for him by Chinese. Every rich Chinese was ennobled to obligate him to safeguard the interests of the country. As one Westerner remarked, 'From the moment Chinese are presented with a noble title, they become slaves of the King; the more so if they are made his officers.' See Skinner, *Leadership and Power*.

p. 148: It is said that the ruling Chakri family has Chinese blood; Chinese women were in its harems. Chao Phya Chakri, who founded the dynasty, was the son-in-law of a Teochiu, and had a Chinese name as well as a Siamese name. See Purcell.

p. 150: For the names of some of the Chinese families that adopted Thai identities, see Fallows.

p. 150: For the rags-to-riches story of Khaw Soo Cheang, see Cushman. Chinese daughters made desirable wives because of their pale skin and their innate business acumen, highly prized in a country where wives run the family economy. Chinese sons are prized as husbands because of their many financial connections.

p. 151: Imports came under British control, and European trading houses took over rice exports, teakwood and tin mining. Chinese were left only with the rackets, but these provided between 40 and 50 per cent of total state revenues. See Skinner, Suehiro, and McVey, *Southeast Asian Capitalists*.

p. 151: One reason Chinese governments suddenly became so concerned about their nationals living overseas was that their remittances became a major source of official revenue and graft.

p. 152: 'Jews of the East' is quoted in Alexander.

p. 152: See Cushman for the plot against Rama VI (King Vijiravudh).

p. 152: In 1917 King Vijiravudh took Siam into the First World War on the side of the Allies. The war produced the first low-visibility Chinese multinationals linking several Asian countries, dealing in rice, shipping, insurance and banking, conglomerates outside the traditional channels tied to Siam's royal household. These included groups tied together by Teochiu, Hakka and Cantonese syndicates, and headed by prominent families with branches in Bangkok, Singapore, Hong Kong, and Shanghai. See Yoshihara, and also McVey.

p. 153: Pridi was the son of a rice trader from a small village north of Bangkok. He probably had Chinese blood, but that's commonplace. After the First World War he attended Chulalongkorn Law School, a seedbed of liberalism, and the École de Science Politique in Paris, where he became very close to the father of the future King Ananda. When Pridi returned to Thailand he worked at the Ministry of Justice, lectured at his old law school, and became the leader of a band of liberal and humanistic reformers. He also became the chief target of intense right-wing conspiracy. See Kruger.

p. 153: In retrospect it is astonishing how completely foreign governments were deceived into thinking for two decades that Marshal Phibun was the actual military dictator of Thailand; this is a testament to the cleverness of the men who operated behind the scenes, pulling his strings.

p. 155: For the cannibalism episode, see Swinson.

p. 156: Tsuji and Tai Li would have made an interesting postwar team, but before they could get up to much Tai Li was killed in the explosion of a plane booby-trapped by Mao's spy chief, Kang Sheng.

CHAPTER 12

Skinner (*Leadership*) and McCoy (*Politics of Heroin*) are essential reading for any understanding of how things work in Thailand. For more recent developments in the Golden Triangle, see Lintner. In this chapter I have drawn on material about General Phin and his clique that appeared in the *Bangkok Post* on 9 April 1988, in its lengthy obituary of banker Chin Sophanpanich, a valuable historical document. By fitting these different pieces together, we see the interplay between military strongmen and the Chinese business community. McVey concludes that the Phin clique 'lost power' while Sarit and his followers were in the driver's seat; in fact, only Phao's group dropped out, while Phin's and Sarit's cliques remained fastened together in a cat's-cradle of backroom financial dealings.

p. 159: General Phao's career gets close attention from McCoy.

p. 160: 'I discovered . . .' is from the *Bangkok Post*. 'Otherwise they would be killed . . .' is from McCoy.

p. 160: The actual circumstances of the king's death have never been revealed to the public because of political and family considerations, but are widely known. There was never any evidence linking Pridi to the king's death; that was a red herring to damage Pridi and neutralize his anti-Chinese reform movement. See Grey for some interesting details.

pp. 161–2: See chapter 11 for the wartime growth of the Teochiu rice monopoly.

p. 162: See Skinner for some discussion of how Phin and Phao gained control of Chinese enterprises.

pp. 163–4: In Skinner, Udane is referred to as 'Leader Wang'. This is obvious when you compare the biography in Skinner with the Udane biography in Yoshihara. The tight relationship between Udane and Field Marshal Phin is attested to by the *Bangkok Post*. Udane became so wealthy and powerful that he was decorated by King Bhumiphol with the Order of the White Elephant.

pp. 165–6: During conversations I had with General Tuan and General Lee in the 1960s, in Chiengmai and in North Burma, both were surprisingly forthcoming abut the chain of command in Taiwan and about their working relationship to the CIA.

p. 166: See McCoy for an account of the feud between Phao and Sarit over drugs.

CHAPTER 13

Biographical information in this chapter, and many financial and political details, were drawn from the elaborate obituary of Chin published as a special supplement by the *Bangkok Post* on 9 April 1988. Chinese eulogies often contain surprising information not found elsewhere.

p. 167: His Chinese name was Chin Tan Piak.

p. 168: Skinner says he was born in Bangkok of a Thai mother.

p. 168: Chin claimed to have been educated at Chak Ching Primary School in Chua Awa village near Swatow, and went on to attend Lak Sow Secondary School in the same area for a few years before poverty forced him to seek work. But that was all the formal education he had. He later donated money to these schools. After the Second World War he built a small school there. *Bangkok Post*. See also Skinner.

p. 168: His Chinese wife died in Hong Kong in 1979.

p. 168: The most important persons in Chin's early career in Thailand, according to the *Bangkok Post* obituary, were Udane and Udane's uncle, a Teochiu merchant who owned an insurance company and a builders' supply warehouse. Both were under the protection of Sahas Mahakun, the richest and most powerful Teochiu in Thailand at that time. Chin was given a job handling accounts at the warehouse.

p. 169: 'Tone down his involvement . . .' *Bangkok Post*.

p. 169: In 1943 the Ministry of Finance issued war bonds at 3 per cent annual interest over an eight-year maturity, with the attractive option of redemption in gold. When the bonds matured in 1951, the value of gold was more than six times higher than that stipulated. Speculation was wild. Among Chin's new companies were Mahakij Construction, Thai Dawee Poi (rice) Trading, Krungthep Suwan Panich in the gold trade, Asia Trading for general commerce, and Asia Trust for foreign exchange.

p. 171: Chin's acquisition of the bank was helped by Panthip Boriphat, a member of the Thai Royal Family. Panthip later became chairman of the board of the bank. See Phipatseritham and Yoshihara, *Business Groups*.

p. 171: In the mid-1960s, Asia Trust successfully applied for a commericial banking licence. By then, Chin and his circle had sold most of their shares. One of Chin's managers at Asia Trust was Wallop Tarnvanichkul, a refugee from Shanghai. Wallop acquired Asia Trust from Chin and obtained a banking licence with the help of Police General Prasert, a member of the Sarit faction, turning it into Asia Trust Bank.

p. 172: Part of the ideal to reduce Bangkok Bank was partnership with the Ministry of Commerce, which involved putting on the board of directors some of General Phin's men (including Major General Siri Siriyothin, Colonel Pramarn Adireksarn, and General Phao's man, Police Major Pansak Visedphakdi – all members of the Rachakrul Group). Like General Phao, Colonel Pramarn was married to one of General Phin's daughters. The partnership with the Ministry of Commerce was possible because in the military regime General Siri was deputy commerce minister. It was General Siri who suggested to the Japanese government that they allow Bangkok Bank to open a branch in Tokyo.

p. 173: Rivalry between the two groups came to a climax in 1955 and 1956 when an aggressive campaign of innuendo was waged by Sarit in his newspaper, *Sam Seri*. Phao used his own newspaper, *Pao Thai*, to fight back.

p. 173: 'A major banking merchant . . .' *Sam Seri*, 17 September 1955.

p. 173: 'At the forefront . . .' *Sam Seri*, 26 October 1955.

p. 175: When Sarit became the new strongman, his director general of police explained that five or six syndicates controlled smuggling in the north, operating 'with police influence behind their backs', and that his wave of arrests were part of a larger campaign to fire or transfer all those police involved. Police Brigadier General Thom Chitvimol was indicted for his involvement in a six-ton opium shipment. See McCoy, *Politics of Heroin*.

p. 175: Blocked from access to Bangkok Bank's large accumulated reserves, Sarit had no choice but to generate his own income. A number of army officers were sent to Hong Kong, Taipei and Singapore to take orders, while others flew to Chiengmai to set up buys with KMT generals Lee and Tuan, with representatives of Shan rebel armies, and with the Haw Chinese (Yunnanese) brokers who travel through the Golden Triangle each season buying small quantities of opium tar from rural shopkeepers. In Chiengmai, where I had dinner with General Lee one night in a walled compound with heavily armed guards standing on the roofs, the general brushed the new government off as a 'change of faces'. McCoy says Marshal Sarit and General Praphat – new chairman of Bangkok Bank – were for continuing the lucrative arrangement with the Teochiu syndicates, but Prime Minister Thanom was worried about the new government getting a bad name. A compromise was agreed by which the Thai army and police would no longer engage directly in drug transactions, but would provide protection.

'They guarantee not to kill us,' Prince Jimmy Yang told me. 'They provide the hazard, then they protect us from the hazard. We all take out policies. The premiums are very, very dear.'

Prime Minister Thanon's son Narong married Police General Praphat's daughter. A senior Thai narcotics official (Police Colonel Pramual Vangibandhu), who was arrested for drug dealing, charged in the Thai press that 'Narong has a nationwide network of trafficking. Most of the drug shipments by boat to Hong Kong and South Vietnam belong to him.' See McCoy. Thai police and military officials repeatedly stated that bank chairman General Praphat received a share of profits from the narcotics trade, as he did from most other businesses in the kingdom.

p. 176: Chin boasted in an *Insight* magazine interview of lending millions of dollars to Liem, and vice versa.

p. 177: US government leaks to the press over many years referred to a 'powerful financial kingpin in the drug trade' who lived next door to the American ambassador, but never mentioned a name. When I asked a Drug Enforcement Agency source in Bangkok to identify the alleged kingpin, the source said it was Chin Sophonpanich.

CHAPTER 14

Crouch, Purcell, Robison and Suryadinata (*The Chinese Minority*), provide the broad background of the Chinese in Indonesia.

p. 181: See Willmott's *The Chinese of Semarang* for more details, and McVey's *Southeast Asian Capitalists* for the success of the Hokchiu.

p. 182: MacDonald recounts Suharto's early life. Robison and Yoshihara remark on the Sultan of Jogjakarta's Japanese connections.

p. 183: It must be emphasized that smuggling is commonplace in Indonesia and is not regarded as particularly criminal; in a huge archipelago, interisland trade is by ship, and much of that is surreptitiously to avoid paying kickbacks. While government was controlled by the Dutch, and the islands were in rebellion, Javanese and Sumatrans saw smuggling as patriotic. Indonesia is on several main Chinese smuggling routes from Amoy and Swatow to Singapore and Malacca. So smuggling is simply 'the import sector'.

pp. 183–4: See Robison for Liem's help to Suharto. Purcell says most Indonesian Chinese stayed neutral during the revolution. Indonesians wanted them to boycott the Dutch. But the Chinese wondered if they were not better off under Dutch rule. Either way they did not feel brave. If they defied authority, they were subversive. If they supported authority, they were opportunistic. If they stayed aloof, they were interested only in profit. So they were abused by all sides. It was impossible in Dutch territory to boycott the Dutch, or in republican territory to avoid collaborating with the rebels. See Coppel for this dilemma.

p. 185: When Dutch enterprises were taken over by local trade unions, General Nasution ordered these properties placed under military supervision. See Coppel, Sundhaussen and Robison.

p. 186: Under martial law business and government became one. For any business to prosper, you needed connections. The bigger the business, the higher the connections, the bigger the bribes. In the old days, Malay sultans gave concessions to court favourites, who sold them to the Chinese. President Sukarno's plan was to take the import sector out of Chinese hands and put it into Indonesian hands. It failed because once the new import licences became available they were obtained by well-connected Indonesian fixers who sold them to the highest bidder, inevitably Chinese. See MacDonald.

p. 186: In 1958 a scandal broke over the smuggling of army operations chief Ibnu Sutowo, who handled the Sumatra end of Suharto's smuggling network. To shield the military from criticism, Ibnu was suspended from the army but he was allowed to continue running Indonesia's army-controlled oil companies (the former Royal Dutch Shell fields), which were the single most valuable resource the nation had. One year later, the smuggling scandal spilled over onto Suharto, and he was removed from command, but he, too, sidestepped serious trouble. The army was able to protect its own. See MacDonald.

p. 187: When the military showdown with the Dutch over West Irian began in 1962, General Suharto was given command of the entire campaign. Under American pressure Holland finally capitulated to an Indonesian takeover. As the Dutch withdrew, an enterprising young Chinese businessman named Robin Loh made a fortune selling abandoned Dutch heavy equipment to Suharto's army. Just how the equipment came into his possession to sell has never been explained, but Robin Loh was a friend of Liem, who was in partnership with General Suharto. Afterward, Loh moved to Singapore and went heavily into shipping, becoming a main link between Liem Sioe Liong of Bank Central Asia and Chin Sophonpanich of Bangkok Bank.

p. 187: See Coppel for Murtopo's secret talks. See Hughes and Sundahaussen for different versions of the Gilchrist episode. The letter was on British embassy stationery, dated 24 March 1965, but stationery could have been stolen in 1963 when mobs looted the embassy.

p. 188: Sir Andrew denied having written such a message.

p. 189: See Crouch for a discussion of why Suharto's name was not on the list to kill. Anderson and McVey's study of crucial events is still fascinating.

p. 191: Sukarno's Japanese wife, Dewi (Nemoto Naoko), was partying at the Hotel Indonesia. Sukarno was driven there and waited at the hotel until midnight for Dewi to conclude her party. Then the two went to her house to party some more. Thirty years later she is still a celebrated courtesan; in 1994 a book of recent nude photographs of her was published in Japan.

p. 192: Any PKI mobilization plans would have been known in advance because army informers had burrowed deep into the party apparatus over the years. Had there been any such alert, General Yani and his intelligence chief would not have been caught sleeping.

p. 194: It was not until May 1967 that Sukarno was stripped of all his titles; he remained under house arrest until his death in June 1970. See Crouch.

p. 195: One import the Chinese completely dominated was rice, brought from Siam and Indochina, where the Teochiu had a monopoly both on wholesale and intermediate trade. In 1973 BULOG's price-gouging caused bloody riots. Mobs went on a rampage, burning and looting Chinese shops. The Suharto government cracked down on the Javanese farmers, rather than on BULOG and its price-gouging Chinese brokers. See Crouch. Liem Sioe Liong also became involved. When BULOG decided to establish flour milling in Indonesia, the licence was given to a Singapore company, Prima. Liem saw no reason why Prima should get the contract, so he set up Bogasari flour mills, in partnership with President Suharto's half-brother, 26 per cent of profits going to Mrs Tien Suharto's charities. Bogosari immediately got a huge government credit, and BULOG's licence to do all flour milling for heavily populated western Indonesia. Prima found its hands tied in many ways, gave up and sold out. See Robison and Crouch.

p. 196: Ibnu had a gift for wheeling and dealing. He married into a politically powerful South Sumatran family. Given the task of converting Shell's oil fields into Pertamina, he turned to the Japanese, who were eager to help. Sasakawa Ryiochi, former Sugamo

Prison cellmate of Prime Minister Kishi, triumphed over all rivals by introducing President Sukarno to the beautiful eighteen-year-old Nemoto Naoko. President Sukarno made the girl his third wife – renaming her Dewi – and as a reward gave Sasakawa the exclusive agency for Indonesian oil exports to Japan. Sasakawa set up a meeting between Ibnu and Nishijima Shigetada, a Japanese secret agent during the Pacific War with excellent connections in Jakarta and Tokyo. Nishijima brought in financier Kobayashi Ataru, one of the Four Heavenly Kings who underwrote the political careers of LDP leaders. They offered a Japanese credit of $53 million to be repaid by fixed percentages of Indonesian crude. Pertamina became a honeypot, providing two thirds of Indonesia's export earnings. Ibnu ran Pertamina like a men's club, with pretty girls and free junkets to Bali. Oil companies dealing with him got a much higher percentage per barrel than in the Middle East. Ibnu took short-, medium- and long-term loans, kept hidden in six separate sets of books. When the oil crisis of 1973 hit, he was unable to raise more loans to pay off the ones he already had. Pertamina fell behind in payments of $40 million to Republic National Bank of Dallas and Toronto Dominion Bank. The Texas bank threatened to take Ibnu to court. Through cross-default clauses, if a borrower defaults on one loan, all his other loans can be called in. To everyone's astonishment, Pertamina was found to be $10.5 billion overdrawn. The Indonesian Central Bank had to rescue the honeypot. But Ibnu went unscolded, and became a leading consultant on how to do business in Indonesia. See Robison, and Yoshihara, for more details.

p. 197: One of Liem's closest associates was banker Mochtar Riady (Lee Mo Sing). A Henghua from Fukien province, Riady built his own Lippo Group into one of Southeast Asia's biggest conglomerates, rivalling his patron's Salim Group. Riady eventually became so wealthy in his own right that he ranked as one of the world's richest Overseas Chinese. The Henghua are the second-most powerful Chinese group in Indonesia. See McVey (*Southeast Asian Capitalists*), Willmott (*Chinese of Semarang*), MacDonald, Robison, and Yoshihara.

pp. 197–8: Although the bulk of Liem's capital came from monopolies secured through political connections, the Liem group and the Lippo group eventually became so big they were no longer dependent on favours from Indonesian generals. However, the close relationships continued, with one of President Suharto's sons, a daughter, and his half-brother still among Liem's business partners. See Robison, and Yoshihara.

CHAPTER 15

Jesudason and Means provide the best background on the Chinese predicament in Malaysia.

p. 201: See Mak for the early Chinese infighting.

p. 203: Chin Peng's story is told by Williams.

p. 206: See Means, and Shaplen, for varying accounts of the bloodshed and beheadings. The Malay élite was frightened by the gruesome outcome of the riots, and tried hard to downplay their own role in inciting mob violence. Nevertheless, the riots provided an excuse for the Razak palace *coup*.

pp. 208–209: The stories of Noah and Lim were drawn from McVey, Yoshihara, Jesudason, Means and Clad.

p. 211 'We are the negroes . . .' is from Jesudason.

p. 211: The tin scheme is recounted by Jesudason, and by Schlossstein.

pp. 212–14: Jesudason gives the best reprise of the Bank Bumi scandal.

p. 215: Clad says rival UMNO factions quarrelled over the bank, bargaining for credit lines for their respective protégés. Many big banks had their fingers burned by the Carrian affair, including Barclays, Peking's Bank of Communications, West Deutsche Landesbank, Bankers Trust, France's Paribas, and the Hongkong & Shanghai Bank. Some sixty banks had lent money to Carrian. Ten years later, in April 1994, the *Asian Wall Street Journal* reported that Daim Zainuddin was helping Hasan Abu Samsudin acquire 100 per cent of Bank Bumi, privatizing the bank by making it part of Landmark BHD, a company started by a Hakka. See Clad, and Rafferty.

CHAPTER 16

The story of Hong Kong's growth from colonial backwater to global financial centre is best told by Welsh in *A Borrowed Place*. See Rafferty for a lucid account of the growth of Western banks in Hong Kong and Shanghai, out of facilities provided by big hongs like Jardine's, Dent's, and Russell's. With support of the colonial government, in 1864 Dent and others formed the Hongkong and Shanghai Banking Corporation. By Chinese it was called Wayfoong, meaning Abundance of Remittances. No other local bank was able to develop more than limited business with the Chinese. Today, there are Chinese on the board, but all are non-executives. Michael Sandberg, chairman from 1977 to 1986, arranged the appointment first of Y. K. Pao as non-executive deputy chairman, followed by Li Ka-shing.

p. 219: For how banking worked in imperial China, see Willmott, *Economic Organization*.

p. 220: Wong Siu-lun shows how Ningpo banking clans gained control of nineteenth-century Shanghai and turned it into China's financial centre.

pp. 221–2: For the bizarre financial politics of nineteenth-century Ningpo and Shanghai, and the emergence of the gangster-backed Chiang Kai-shek dictatorship, see my *Dragon Lady* and *The Soong Dynasty*.

pp. 223–4: The importance of cotton to Shanghai's wealth is studied by Dietrich in Willmott, op. cit.

p. 225: Between 1945 and 1951, Hong Kong's population jumped from 600,000 to over 2 million. The figures on flight capital are from Wong, op. cit.

p. 227: The expansion of the Fang textile family into North America is described in *Forbes*, 20 January 1992, and in *Fortune*, 31 October 1994.

p. 228: 'One legged man . . .' is from Sampson, *Money Lenders*.

pp. 228–9: See Yoshihara for insights into how Chinese money moves around the Rim. Other details on the movement of Chinese offshore capital are drawn from the *Asian Wall Street Journal*, 18 October 1994, and the *Far Eastern Economic Review*, 5 March 1992.

CHAPTER 17

Until the 1990s, news reports on political developments in Taiwan (including dissident journals) were completed in Hong Kong by Father Edward Kelly, and were circulated to subscribers under the name *Yuan*. This provided a valuable resource for outside observers. Much of the information in this chapter came from *Yuan*.

p. 231: Although Charlie Soong and Dr Sun were Hakka, they had strong ties with the Teochiu syndicates thanks to their anti-Manchu activities and their connections in the foreign settlements of Shanghai, where the Teochiu were active as compradors for branches of Western companies headquartered in Hong Kong.

p. 232: Jenny Chen (Ch'en Chieh-ju) was sent to America after the war to get her out of the way, and attended Columbia University where she wrote a book about her marriage to the generalissimo. The book was suppressed with the payment to Jenny of a large sum, and she resettled in California. Nevertheless, a few copies survived.

p. 232: In his unpublished memoirs, General Frank Dorn, who served on Stilwell's staff in China during the Second World War states that FDR secretly instructed Stilwell to look into various possibilities of killing Chiang, and several American officers were considered for the job of heading the team to carry out the assassination. One possibility was to arrange for Chiang's plane to crash while flying over the Hump to India. FDR later rescinded the order.

p. 234: See Boorman for a sanitized biography of Chiang Ching-kuo. Henry Liu's biography in Chinese provides the seamier side.

p. 236: The 'special relationship' between K. C. Wu and Mme Chiang was to be one of the subjects of Henry Liu's biography of Wu, on which Liu was working at the time of his murder.

pp. 237–8: Several years later, General Chen Yi was himself arrested and executed by the KMT as a communist traitor.

p. 238: 'Bayoneted, without provocation . . .' is from Kaplan.

pp. 240–41: K. C. Wu gave Henry Liu lengthy tape-recorded interviews and access to his personal archives. For Wu's repeated skirmishes and CCK see *Mother Jones*, May 1985, and *San Jose Mercury*, 9 March 1988.

p. 241: Wu wrote an article for *Look* in 1954 titled 'Your Money Has Built a Police State in Formosa.'

p. 242: My profile of CCK's sons is drawn from unpublished fragments of Henry Liu's work, from Kaplan, and from *Yuan*, volumes 4–9. The eldest, Hsiao-wen, died in 1989. 'Not simply a case of debauchery . . .' is from *Yuan*. Hsiao-wu died in 1991. According to *Yuan*, the youngst son, Hsiao-yung, left Taiwan after the Henry Liu scandal and settled in Canada.

p. 243: My accounts of the power struggle between CCK and Mme Chiang after the generalissimo's death is drawn from Henry Liu's works and from *Yuan*. The Profile of Chin Hsiao-yi is developed from newspaper articles about him collected and republished in *Yuan*.

p. 245: 'Teach Lin a lesson . . .' is from Kaplan.

p. 245: The Bamboo Gang's role in the heroin trade is from *San Jose Mercury*, 9 March 1988. Kaplan provides a fine indictment of KMT subversive activities in the United States. See also the San Francisco *Focus*, April 1985.

p. 246: The rule of thumb is that declared assets are less than half of the whole. As London's *Financial Times* put it, 65 per cent of the world's money is thought to be in hiding. See also the *Economist*, 6 November 1993.

p. 248: See *Yuan* for newspaper stories from Taiwan and Hong Kong alleging a possible role for Mme Chiang and Chin Hsiao-yi in arousing family anger against Henry Liu. As Kaplan rightly says, in the end it was Alex Chiang who set the murder plot in motion, and Admiral Wang who actually got the family's sanction and commissioned the killers. Admiral Wang, a former naval aide to the Generalissimo and Mme Chiang who worked for five years out of the Chiang family residence, was put in charge of all Taiwan's covert activities in America. See also the hearings into the Liu murder of the US House of Representatives and the Taiwan indictment of the Bamboo Gang leader. Also indicted were Admiral Wang; General Hu Yi-men, deputy director under Wang; and Colonel Chen Hu-men, who gave the killers a colour photo of Henry Liu.

p. 248: 'A guy like Henry . . .' is from San Francisco *Focus*, April 1985.

p. 250: Aside from using terror to maintain its grip, the reason behind the strange staying power of the KMT is the fact that drug profits and other black money from product counterfeiting and money laundering have made it the world's wealthiest political party, outdoing even Japan's well-funded LDP.

CHAPTER 18

Much of the information in this chapter is drawn from a landmark study of the exodus of Chinese from Hong Kong, undertaken by the University of Hong Kong. The study, *Reluctant Exiles? Migration from Hong Kong and the New Overseas Chinese*, includes contributions from scholars all over the world, edited by Ronald Skeldon. This is a major work, highly recommended to readers seeking a better understanding of one of the more important developments of our time.

p. 256: Tsang Yok-sing's red face was reported in the *Far Eastern Economic Review*.

p. 261: Li Ka-shing details are from Rafferty and Morris.

p. 261: Stanley Ho details are from Lomax, and the *South China Morning Post*.

pp. 263–4: For a curbside look at life in New York's Chinatown, see *The New Yorker*, 10 June 1991, and 17 June 1991.

CHAPTER 19

pp. 267–8: My figures were drawn from a number of sources, including the International Monetary Fund, the *Economist* and the *Asian Wall Street Journal*.

p. 271: For recent changes in the heroin trade see Bertil Lintner's reportage in the *Far Eastern Economic Review*.

p. 274: The computer *guanxi* database is being developed under the auspices of the Singapore Chinese Chamber of Commerce.

p. 276: 'Like a totem pole . . .' is from the *Asian Wall Street Journal*.

p. 277: Dr Jenner's book, *The Tyranny of History*, shows him to be less optimistic about the future than most observers. Nobody ever erred by being pessimistic about Beijing.

p. 278: 'Divided in two parts . . .' is from Fitzgerald, who reminds us (as does Jenner) that there is nothing really new in Beijing's attitude.

p. 279: 'For the past 19 years . . .' is from the *Chinese Science Monitor*, 3 February 1993.

p. 279: See Hinton for early examples of misbehaviour by the princelings.

p. 280: My figures on the financial riptide are from the *Asian wall Street Journal*, 4 October 1993.

p. 282: Hinton describes the effects of the boom in China's rural areas.

p. 285: 'Nothing at all will happen . . .' is from the *Nouvelle Observateur*, 13 April 1994.

p. 286: Lee Kuan Yew's predictions were published in the *Economist*, 11 September 1993.

p. 286: Unlike European social programmes, Singapore's are not subsidized by taxes, and usually break even or turn a profit.

p. 288: 'Just plain bad luck . . .' is from the *Nouvelle Observateur*.

BIBLIOGRAPHY

Adams, James Ring, and Douglas Frantz. *A Full Service Bank: How BCCI Stole Billions Around the World.* New York: Simon & Schuster, 1992.

Alexander, Garth. *The Invisible China: The Overseas Chinese and the Politics of Southeast Asia.* New York: The Macmillan Company, 1973.

Alletzhauser, Albert J. *The House of Nomura.* New York: Little, Brown and Company, 1990.

Ames, Roger T. *Sun Tzu: The Art of War.* New York: Ballantine Books, 1993.

Anderson, Benedict R., and Ruth T. McVey. *A Preliminary Analysis of the October 1, 1965, Coup in Indonesia.* Ithaca: Cornell University Press, 1971.

Aron, R. *Clausewitz Philosopher on War.* New York: Simon & Schuster, 1983.

Asprey, Robert B. *The German High Command at War: Hindenburg and Ludendorff Conduct World War I.* New York: William Morrow and Company, 1991.

Axelbank, Albert. *Black Star Over Japan.* London: George Allen & Unwin, 1972.

Azia, M. A. *Japan's Colonialism and Indonesia.* The Hague: Martinus Nijhoff, 1955.

Balmforth, Edmund E. 'A Chinese Military Strategist of the Warring States: Sun Pin.' New Brunswick, N.J.: doctoral dissertation, Rutgers University, 1979.

Banks, David J., ed. *Changing Identities in Modern Southeast Asia.* The Hague: Mouton Publishers, 1976.

Bartu, Freedman, *The Ugly Japanese: Nippon's Economic Empire in Asia.* Tokyo: Yenbooks, 1993.

Baruma, Ian. *A Japanese Mirror: Heroes and Villains of Japanese Culture.* London: Cape, 1984.

Beasley, W. G. *Japanese Imperialism, 1894–1945.* Oxford: Clarendon Press, 1987.

Benedict, Ruth. *The Chrysanthemum and the Sword.* New York: Houghton Mifflin, 1946.

Bentley, Jerry. *Old World Encounters.* San Diego: University of California Press, 1993.

Blaker, James R. *The Chinese in the Philippines.* Columbus: Ohio State University, 1970.

Blusse, Leonard. 'Batavia, 1619–1740: The Rise and Fall of a Chinese Colonial Town.' *Journal of Southeast Asian Studies*, vol. 12, no. 1, March 1981.

Bodde, Derk. *Statesman, Patriot and General in Ancient China.* New Haven: American Oriental Society, 1940.

Bonavia, David. *The Chinese.* New York: Lippincott and Crowell, 1980.

Boorman, Howard L., ed. *Biographical Dictionary of Republican China.* 5 vols. New York: Columbia University Press, 1979.

Bozan, Jian, Shao Xunzheng, and Hu Hua. *A Concise History of China.* Beijing: Foreign Languages Press, 1981.

Brewitt-Taylor, C. H. *Romance of the Three Kingdoms.* Shanghai: Kelly & Walsh, 1925.

Brown, I. *The Elite and the Economy in Siam, 1890–1920.* Singapore: Oxford University Press, 1988.

Buchan, Alastair. *War in Modern Society.* New York: Harper & Row, 1966.

Bunbongkarn, S. *The Military in Thai Politics 1981–1986.* Singapore: Institute for Southeast Asian Studies, 1987.

Burnell, Elaine H. *Asian Dilemma: United States, Japan and China.* Santa Barbara: The Center for the Study of Democratic Institutions, 1969.

Burstein, Daniel. *Turning the Tables: A Machiavellian Strategy for Dealing with Japan.* New York: Simon & Schuster, 1993.

Byron, John, and Robert Pack. *The Claws of the Dragon: Kang Sheng.* New York: Simon & Schuster, 1992.

Chan, Albert. *The Glory and Fall of the Ming Dynasty.* Norman: University of Oklahoma Press, 1976.

Chang, Pao-min. *Beijing, Hanoi, and the Overseas Chinese.* Berkeley: Center for Chinese Studies, 1992.

Chesneaux, Jean. *Popular Movements and Secret Societies in China, 1840–1950.* Stanford: Stanford University Press, 1976.

Chesneaux, Jean. *Secret Societies in China.* London: Heinemann Educational Books, 1971.

Chie Nakane. *Japanese Society.* London: Penguin Books, 1973.

Chin Ko-lin. 'Chinese Triad Societies, Tongs, Organized Crime, and Street Gangs in Asia and the United States', doctoral dissertation, University of Pennsylvania, 1986.

Chitoshi Yanaga. *Big Business in Japanese Politics.* New Haven: Yale University Press, 1968.

Choate, Pat. *Agents of Influence.* New York: Simon & Schuster, 1990.

Clad, James, *Behind the Myth.* London: Grafton Books, 1991.

Clapham, Ronald. *Small and Medium Entrepreneurs in Southeast Asia.* Singapore: Institute of Southeast Asian Studies, 1985.

Cleary, Thomas. *The Japanese Art of War.* Boston: Shambhala, 1991.

Cleary, Thomas. *Mastering the Art of War. Zhuge Liang's and Liu Jian's Commentaries on the Classic by Sun Tzu.* Boston: Shambhala, 1989.

Cleary, Thomas. *Sun Tzu and the Art of War.* Boston: Shambhala, 1988.

Cleary, Thomas. *The Tao of Politics.* Boston: Shambhala, 1990.

Clutterbuck, Richard. *Conflict and Violence in Singapore and Malaysia, 1945–1983.* Singapore: Graham Brashe, 1984.

Cohen, Eliot A., and John Gooch. *Military Misfortunes: The Anatomy of Failure in War.* New York: Vintage Books, 1991.

Cook, Haruko Taya, and Theodore F. Cook. *Japan at War: An Oral History.* New York: The New Press, 1992.

Coppel, Charles A. *Indonesian Chinese in Crisis.* Kuala Lumpur: Oxford University Press, 1983.

Cowley, Robert, ed. *Experience of War.* New York: W. W. Norton & Company, 1992.

Creel, H. G. *The Birth of China.* New York: Frederick Unger, 1954.

Creel, H. G. *Origins of Statecraft in China.* Volume 1: *The Western Chou Dynasty.* Chicago: University of Chicago Press, 1970.

Crouch, Harold. *The Army and Politics in Indonesia.* Ithaca: Cornell University Press, 1978.

Crozier, Ralph C. *Koxinga and Chinese Nationalism.* Cambridge: Harvard University Press, 1977.

Crump, J. I. *Chan-kuo Ts'e.* Oxford: Clarendon Press, 1970.

Cushman, Jennifer. *Family and State: The Formation of a Sino-Thai Tin-Mining Dynasty, 1797–1932.* Singapore: Oxford University Press, 1991.

Darling, Frank C. *Thailand and the United States.* Washington, D.C.: Public Affairs Press, 1965.

Deane, Hugh. *Good Deeds and Gunboats: Two Centuries of American-Chinese Encounters.* San Francisco: China Books & Periodicals, 1990.

Dixon, N. *Military Incompetence.* Aylesbury: Future Pubs, 1979.

Dudden, Arthur P. *The American Pacific.* Oxford: Oxford University Press, 1992.

Duus, Peter, Ramon H. Myers, and Mark R. Peattie, eds. *The Japanese Informal Empire in China, 1895–1937.* Princeton: Princeton University Press, 1989.

Earle, E. M. *Makers of Modern Strategy: Military Thought from Machiavalli to Hitler.* Princeton: Princeton University Press, 1944.

Elliott-Bateman, M. *Defeat in the East: The Mark of Mao Tse-tung On War.* London: Oxford University Press, 1967.

Faligot, Peter, and Remi Kauffer. *The Chinese Secret Service.* New York: William Morrow and Company, 1987.

Fallows, James. *Looking at the Sun.* New York: Pantheon Books, 1994.

Fitzgerald, Stephen. *China and the Overseas Chinese: A Study of Peking's Changing Policy.* Cambridge: Cambridge University Press, 1972.

Friedman, George, and Meredith Lebard. *The Coming War with Japan.* New York: St Martin's Press, 1991.

Gale, B. *Politics and Public Enterprise in Malaysia.* Singapore: Eastern Universities Press, 1981.

Gibney, Frank. *Japan: The Fragile Super-power.* New York: New American Library, 1979.

Gibney, Frank. *The Pacific Century: America and Asia in a Changing World.* New York: Charles Scribner's Sons, 1992.

Gill, R. *George Tan: The Carrian Saga.* Petaling Jaya, Malaysia: Pelanduk Publications, 1985.

Gill, R. *The Making of Malaysia.* Petaling Jaya, Malaysia: Pelanduk Publications, 1985.

Gluck, Carol. *Japan's Modern Myths.* Princeton: Princeton University Press, 1985.

Goldberg, Michael A. *The Chinese Connection.* Vancouver: University of British Columbia Press, 1985.

Goodman, Grant K., ed. *Imperial Japan and Asia: A Reassessment.* New York: Columbia University Press, 1967.

Goodrich, L. Carrington. *Dictionary of Ming Biography 1368–1644.* New York: Columbia University Press, 1976.

Griffith, Samuel B. *Sun Tzu: The Art of War*. Oxford: Oxford University Press, 1963.

Hackett, R. F. *Yamagata Aritomo in the Rise of Modern Japan*. Cambridge: Harvard University Press, 1971.

Hall, D. G. E. *A History of South-east Asia*. London: Macmillan, 1981 (fourth edition.)

Hall, Kenneth R. *Maritime Trade and State Development in Early Southeast Asia*. Honolulu: University Press of Hawaii, 1985.

Harries, Meirion, and Susie Harries. *Sheathing the Sword*. London: Hamish Hamilton, 1987.

Harries, Meirion, and Susie Harries. *Soldiers of the Sun: The Rise and Fall of the Imperial Japanese Army*. New York: Random House, 1991.

Hasegawa Keitaro. *Japanese-Style Management*. Tokyo: Kodansha International, 1986.

Hearings and Markup before the Committee on Foreign Affairs and Its Subcommittee on Asian and Pacific Affairs, House of Representatives, Ninety-ninth Congress, 1985. 'The Murder of Henry Liu.'

Heinlein, Joseph J. Jr. *Political Warfare: The Chinese Nationalist Model*, doctoral dissertation. Washington, D.C.: The American University, 1974.

Hewison, K. 'The Financial Bourgeoisie in Thailand,' *Journal of Contemporary Asia*. vol. 11, no. 4.

Hidemasa Morikawa. *Zaibatsu: The Rise and Fall of Family Enterprise Groups in Japan*. Tokyo: University of Tokyo Press, 1992.

Higgott, R., and Robinson, R., eds. *Southeast Asia: Essays in the Political Economy of Structural Change*. London: Routledge & Kegan Paul, 1985.

Hill, Hal, ed. *Unity and Diversity: Regional Economic Development in Indonesia Since 1970*. Singapore: Oxford University Press, 1991.

Hinton, William. *The Privatization of China: The Great Reversal*. London: Earthscan Publications, 1991.

Holt, C., ed. *Culture and Politics in Indonesia*. Ithaca: Cornell University Press, 1972.

Hookham, Hilda. *A Short History of China*. New York: New American Library, 1970.

Hoover, Gary, ed. *Hoover's Handbook of World Business, 1992*. Austin: The Reference Press, 1991.

Hsu, Cho-yun. *Ancient China in Transition: An Analysis of Social Mobility 722–222 BC*. Stanford: Stanford University Press, 1965.

Hucker, C. O. *Chinese Government in Ming Times*. New York: Columbia University Press, 1969.

Hucker, C. O. *The Traditional Chinese State in Ming Times*. Tucson: University of Arizona Press, 1961.

Hughes, John. *Indonesian Upheaval*. New York: David McKay Company, 1967.

Hulsewe, A. F. P. *Remnants of Ch'in Law*. Leiden: E. J. Brill, 1985.

Jackson, Tim. *The Next Battleground: Japan, America and the New European Market*. Boston: Houghton Mifflin Company, 1993.

Jayapal, Maya. *Old Singapore*. Singapore: Oxford University Press, 1992.

Jenkins, David. *Suharto and His Generals: Indonesian Military Politics 1975–1983*. Cornell Modern Indonesian Project Monograph No. 64. Ithaca: Cornell University Press, 1987.

Jenner, W. J. F. *The Tyranny of History: The Roots of China's Crisis*. London: The Penguin Press, 1992.

Jensen, Irene. *The Chinese in the Philippines During the American Regime: 1898–1946*. San Francisco: R. and E. Research Associates, 1975.

Jesudason, James V. *Ethnicity and the Economy: The State, Chinese Business and Multinationals in Malaysia*. Singapore: Oxford University Press, 1990.

Johnston, Alastair I. *The Role of Violence in Traditional Chinese Strategic Thought.* Department of Government, Harvard University, July 1993.

Jomini, Baron Antoine Henri de. *The Art of War.* London: Greenhill Books, Lionel Leventhal Limited, 1992.

Kaplan, David E. *Fires of the Dragon.* New York: Atheneum, 1992.

Kaplan, David E., and Alec Dubro. *Yakuza.* Reading: Addison-Wesley Publishing Company, 1986.

Kearns, Robert L. *Zaibatsu America.* New York: Macmillan, 1992.

Keene, Donald. *The Battles of Coxinga.* London: Taylor's Foreign Press, 1951.

Keijzer, Arne J. de. *China: Business Strategies for the '90s.* Berkeley: Pacific View Press, 1992.

Kennedy, Malcolm. *A History of Japan.* London: Weidenfeld and Nicolson, 1963.

Kennedy, Paul. *Grand Strategies in War and Peace.* New Haven: Yale University Press, 1991.

Kennedy, Paul. *The Rise and Fall of the Great Powers.* New York: Random House, 1987.

Kierman, Frank A. Jr. and John K. Fairbank, eds. *Chinese Ways in Warfare.* Cambridge: Harvard University Press, 1974.

Kierman, Frank A., Jr., ed. *Ssu-ma Chien's Historiographical Attitude as Reflected in Four Late Warring States Biographies.* Seattle: University of Washington Press, 1962.

Krirkkiat Phipatseritham and Kunio Yoshihara. *Business Groups in Thailand.* Singapore Institute of Southeast Asian Studies, 1983.

Kruger, Rayne. *The Devil's Discus.* London: Cassell, 1964.

Kunio Yoshihara. *The Rise of Ersatz Capitalism in South-East Asia.* Singapore: Oxford University Press, 1988.

Lau, D. C. 'Some Notes on Sun Tsu.' *Bulletin of the School of Oriental and African Studies.* vol. XXVIII, 1965.

Lethbridge, H. J. *Hard Graft in Hong Kong.* Hong Kong: Oxford University Press, 1985.

Li Chi. *The Beginning of Chinese Civilization.* Seattle: University of Washington Press, 1957.

Li, Dun J. *The Ageless Chinese: A History.* New York: Charles Scribner's Sons, 1965.

Li Shijun, Yang Xianju, and Qin Jiarui. *Sun Wu's Art of War and the Art of Business Management.* Kunming: Feng Publishing Co., 1984.

Lim, T. G., ed. *Reflections on Development in Southeast Asia.* Singapore: Institute of Southeast Asian Studies, 1988.

Lim, L. Y. C., and L. A. P. Gosling, eds. *The Chinese in Southeast Asia.* Singapore: Maruzen Asia, 1988.

Lim, M. H. *Ownership and Control of the One Hundred Largest Corporations in Malaysia.* Kuala Lumpur: Oxford University Press, 1981.

Limlingan, V. *The Overseas Chinese in ASEAN.* Manila, Vita Development Corporation, 1987.

Lintner, Bertil. 'The Politics of the Drug Trade in Burma.' Paper delivered December 1992 at the conference 'The State, Order and Prospects for Change in Burma,' Brisbane, Australia.

Liu Zongren. *Two Years in the Melting Pot.* San Francisco: China Books and Periodicals, 1988.

Liu, C. P. *A Military History of Modern China, 1924–1949.* Princeton: Princeton University Press, 1956.

'The Living Tree: The Changing Meaning of Being Chinese Today.' *Daedalus: Journal of the American Academy of Arts and Sciences*. Spring 1991, vol. 120, no. 1.

Loewe, Michael. *Everyday Life in Early Imperial China During the Han Period* 202 BC–AD 220. New York: Dorset Press, 1968.

Loewe, Michael. 'Manuscripts Found Recently in China.' *T'oung Pao*. vol. LXIII. Leiden: E. J. Brill, 1977.

Lomax, David. *The Money Makers*. London: BBC Publications, 1986.

Lord Russel of Liverpool. *The Knights of Bushido*. London: Corgi Books, 1958.

Ma Hong, ed. *Modern China's Economy and Management*. Beijing: Foreign Languages Press, 1990.

MacKie, J. A. C., ed. *The Chinese in Indonesia*. Honolulu: University Press of Hawaii, 1976.

Mak Lau Fong. *The Sociology of Secret Societies: A Study of Chinese Secret Societies in Singapore and Peninsular Malaysia*. Kuala Lumpur: Oxford University Press, 1981.

Makarim, N. 'Companies and Business in Indonesia,' unpublished doctoral dissertation. Harvard Law School, 1978.

Martin, H. D. *The Rise of Genghis Khan & His Conquests of North China*. Baltimore: Johns Hopkins University Press, 1950.

McBeath, Gerald A. *Political Integration of the Philippine Chinese*. Berkeley: Center for South and Southeast Asia Studies, University of California, 1973.

McCoy, Alfred. *The Politics of Heroin: CIA Complicity in the Global Drug Trade*. New York: Lawrence Hill Books, 1991.

McCoy, Alfred, ed. *Southeast Asia Under Japanese Occupation*. New Haven: Yale University Press, 1980.

McDonald, Hamish. *Suharto's Indonesia*. Victoria: The Dominion Press, 1981.

McVey, Ruth T., ed. *Indonesia*. New Haven: Yale University Press, 1967.

McVey, Ruth T., ed. *Southeast Asian Capitalists*. Ithaca: Cornell University Press, 1992.

Means, Gordon P. *Malaysian Politics: The Second Generation*. Singapore: Oxford University Press, 1991.

Michio Takeyama. *Harp of Burma*. Tokyo: Charles E. Tuttle 1966.

Mills, James. *The Underground Empire*. New York: Doubleday & Company, 1986.

Mills, J. V. G., trans. *Ma Huan's Overall Survey of the Ocean's Shores (Ying-Yai Sheng-Lan)*. Cambridge: Hakluyt Society, 1970.

Montgomery, Michael. *Imperialist Japan*. London: Christopher Helm, 1987.

Morris, Jan. *Hong Kong*. New York: Vintage, 1989.

Mote, F. W. *Intellectual Foundations of China*. New York: McGraw-Hill, 1989.

Naylor, R. T. *Hot Money and the Politics of Debt*. London: Unwin Hyman, 1987.

Needham, J. W. *Science & Civilisation in China*. vol. 4, part 3, 'Civil Engineering and Nautics.' Cambridge: Cambridge University Press, 1971.

Needham, J. W. *Science and Civilisation in China*. vol. 5, 'Chemistry and Chemical Technology.' Cambridge: Cambridge University Press, 1986.

Nitobe Inazo. *Bushido: The Soul of Japan*. Tuttle: 1969 (reprint of 1905 edition).

Okazaki Hisahiko. *A Grand Strategy for Japanese Defense*. Boston: University Press of America, 1986.

Overholt, William. *China: The Next Economic Superpower*. London: Weidenfeld & Nicolson, 1993.

Pan, Lynn. *Sons of the Yellow Emperor*. Tokyo: Kodansha International, 1990.

Paret, Peter, ed. *Makers of Modern Strategy: Machiavelli to the Nuclear Age*. Princeton: Princeton University Press, 1986.

Posner, Gerald L. *Warlords of Crime: Chinese Secret Societies*. New York: Penguin Books, 1988.

Presseisen, Ernst L. *Before Aggression: Europeans Prepare the Japanese Army*. Tucson: University of Arizona Press, 1965.

Purcell, Victor. *The Overseas Chinese in Southeast Asia*. Kuala Lumpur: Oxford University Press. 1980 (reprint.)

Pye, L. W. *Chinese Commercial Negotiating Style*. Cambridge: Oelgeschlager, Gunn & Hann, Publishers, 1982.

Pye, L. W. *Asian Power and Politics: The Cultural Dimensions of Authority*. Cambridge, Mass.: Belknap Press, 1985.

Rafferty, Kevin. *City on the Rocks: Hong Kong's Uncertain Future*. London: Penguin Books, 1991.

Ramsey, S. Robert. *The Languages of China*. Princeton University Press, 1978.

Rapoport, Anatol, ed. *Carl Von Clausewitz on War*. London: Penguin Books, 1988.

Reingold, Edwin M. *Chrysanthemums and Thorns: the Untold Story of Modern Japan*. New York: St Martin's Press, 1992.

Roberts, Moss, trans. *Romance of the Three Kingdoms*. Berkeley: University of California Press, 1993.

Robertson, Eric, *The Japanese File*. Hong Kong: Heinemann Asia, 1979.

Robison, Richard. *Indonesia: The Rise of Capital*. Sydney: Allen & Unwin, 1986.

Saburo Shiroyama. *War Criminal: The Life and Death of Hirota Koki*. Tokyo: Kodansha International: 1977.

Sadler, A. L. *Three Military Classics of China*. Sydney: Australasian Medical Publishing Company, 1944.

Sakaiya Taichi. *What Is Japan?* New York: Kodansha International, 1993.

Salmon, Claudine. 'The Contribution of the Chinese to the Development of Southeast Asia.' *Journal of Southeast Asia Studies*, vol. 12, no. 1, March 1981.

Sampson, Anthony. *The Arms Bazaar*. London: Hodder and Stoughton, 1977.

Sampson, Anthony. *The Money Lenders*. London: Hodder and Stoughton, 1981.

Schell, Orville. *Discos and Democracy*. New York: Doubleday, 1989.

Schell, Orville. *Mandate of Heaven*. New York: Simon and Schuster, 1994.

Schell, Orville. *To Get Rich Is Glorious: China in the 80s*. New York: New American Library, 1986.

Schlossstein, Steven. *Asia's New Little Dragons*. Chicago: Contemporary Books, 1991.

Seagrave, Sterling. *Dragon Lady: The Life and Legend of the Last Empress of China*. New York: Knopf, 1992.

Seagrave, Sterling. *The Marcos Dynasty*. New York: Harper & Row, 1988.

Seagrave, Sterling. *The Soong Dynasty*. New York: Harper & Row, 1985.

Sebeok, Thomas A., ed. *Current Trends in Linguistics*, vol. II, *Linguistics in East Asia and South East Asia*. The Hague: Mouton, 1967.

Shaplen, R. *A Turning Wheel*. London: Andre Deutsch, 1979.

Shi Nai'an and Luo Guanzhong. *Outlaws of the Marsh*. Beijing: Foreign Languages Press, 1988.

Silverstein, Josef, ed. *Southeast Asia in World War II*. New Haven: Yale University Press, 1974.

Simoniya, N. A. *Overseas Chinese in Southeast Asia*. Ithaca: Cornell University Press, 1961.

Skeldon, Ronald, ed. *Reluctant Exiles? Migration from Hong Kong and the New Orleans Chinese*. London: M. E. Sharpe, 1994.

Skinner, G. William, ed. *The City in Late Imperial China*. Stanford: Stanford University Press, 1977.

Skinner, G. William. *Leadership and Power in the Chinese Community of Thailand*. Ithaca: Cornell University Press, 1958.

Skinner, G. William. *A Report on the Chinese in Southeast Asia*. Southeast Asia Program, Department of Far Eastern Studies, Ithaca: Cornell University, 1950.

Song, S. O. *One Hundred Years of History of the Chinese in Singapore*. Singapore: University of Malaya Press, 1967.

Spector, Ronald H. *Eagle Against the Sun*. London: Penguin Books, 1987.

Spence, Jonathan D., and John E. Wills, Jr., eds. *From Ming to Ch'ing*. New Haven: Yale University Press, 1984.

Steinberg, D. J., ed. *In Search of Southeast Asia*. New York: Holt, Rinehart and Winston, 1985 (revised ed.)

Steiner, Stan. *Fusang: The Chinese Who Built America*. New York: Harper & Row, 1979.

Storry, Richard. *Japan and the Decline of the West in Asia*. London: Macmillan, 1979.

Sucheng Chan. *Asian Americans*. Boston: Twayne Publishers, 1991.

Suchit Bunbongkarn. *The Military in Thai Politics, 1981–1986*. Singapore: Institute of Southeast Asian Studies, 1987.

Suehiro Akira. *Capital Accumulation in Thailand: 1955–1985*. Tokyo: The Centre for East Asian Cultural Studies, 1989.

Sun Haichen. *The Wiles of War*, Beijing: Foreign Languages Press, 1991.

Sundhaussen, Ulf. *The Road to Power: Indonesian Military Politics, 1945–1967*. Kuala Lumpur: Oxford University Press, 1982.

Suryadinata, Leo. *China and the ASEAN States: The Ethnic Chinese Dimension*. Singapore: Singapore University Press, 1985.

Suryadinata, Leo. *The Chinese Minority in Indonesia*. Singapore: Chopman Enterprises, 1978.

Swann, Nancy Lee. *Flood and Money in Ancient China: The Earliest Economic History of China to A.D. 25*. Princeton: Princeton University Press, 1950.

Swinson, Arthur. *Four Samurai: A Quartet of Japanese Army Commanders in the Second World War*. London: Hutchinson, 1968.

Tate, D. J. M. *The Making of Modern South-east Asia*. Kuala Lumpur: Oxford University Press, 1979.

Taylor, Robert H. *The State in Burma*. London: C. Hurst & Company, 1987.

Thamsook Numnonda. *Thailand and the Japanese Presence, 1941–1945*. Singapore: Institute of Southeast Asian Studies, nd.

Thurow, Lester. *Head to Head*. New York: William Morrow and Company, 1992.

Tsuji Masanobu. *Singapore: The Japanese Version*. London: Constable and Company, 1962.

Tsuji, Masanobu. *Underground Escape*. Tokyo: Asian Publications, 1952.

Turnbull. C. M. *A History of Singapore, 1819–1975*. Oxford: Oxford University Press, 1959.

Twitchett, Denis, and Michael Loewe. *The Cambridge History of China*, vol. I, *The Ch'in and Han Empires*. Cambridge: Cambridge University Press, 1986.

Twitchett, Denis, and John King Fairbank, eds. *The Cambridge History of China*, vol. II, *Late Ching, 1800–1911*, part 2. Cambridge: Cambridge University Press, 1980.

Van Wolferen, Karel. *The Enigma of Japanese Power*. London: Macmillan, 1989.

Vogel, Ezra F. *The Four Little Dragons*. Cambridge: Harvard University Press, 1991.

Vogel, Ezra F. *Japan as No. 1*. Cambridge: Harvard University Press, 1979.

Wang Gungwu. *China and the Chinese Overseas.* Singapore: Times Academic Press, 1991.

Wang Gungwu. *Community and Nation.* New South Wales: Allen & Unwin, 1992.

Wang Hiujong and Li Boxi. *China Towards the Year 2000.* Beijing: New World Press, 1989.

Watson, B. *Records of the Grand Historian of China.* New York: Columbia University Press, 1961.

Wee Chow Hou, Lee Khai Sheang, and Bambang Walujo Hidajat. *Sun Tzu: War and Management.* Singapore: Addison Wesley Publishers, 1991.

Welsh, Frank. *A Borrowed Place: The History of Hong Kong.* New York: Kodansha America, 1993.

Wesley-Smith, Peter. *Unequal Treaty 1898–1997.* Hong Kong: Oxford University Press, 1980.

White, Gordon. *Riding the Tiger: The Politics of Economic Reform in Post-Mao China.* Stanford: Stanford University Press, 1993.

Wilkinson, Endymion. *Japan Versus Europe.* London: Penguin Books, 1980.

Williams, Lea E. *The Future of the Overseas Chinese in Southeast Asia.* New York: McGraw-Hill, 1966.

Willmott, Donald E. *The Chinese Semarang.* Ithaca: Cornell University Press, 1960.

Willmott, W. E., ed. *Economic Organization in Chinese Society.* Stanford: Stanford University Press, 1972.

Wing, R. L. *The Art of Strategy: A New Translation of Sun Tzu's Classic 'The Art of War.'* New York: Doubleday, 1988.

Wong Siu-lun. *Emigrant Entrepreneurs: Shanghai Industrialists in Hong Kong.* Hong Kong: Oxford University Press, 1988.

Wu Yuan-li and Chun-hsi Wu. *Economic Development in Southeast Asia: The Chinese Dimension.* Stanford: Hoover Institution Press, 1980.

Yamamura, K., and Y. Yasuba, eds. *The Political Economy of Japan.* Stanford: Stanford University Press, 1987.

Yang Hsien-yi and Gladys Yang. *Szuma Chien: Selections from Records of the Historian.* Beijing, Foreign Languages Press, 1979.

Yates, Robin D. S. 'New Light on Ancient Chinese Military Texts.' *T'oung Pao*, vol. LXXIV. Leiden: E. J. Brill, 1988.

Yawnghwe Chao-Tzang. 'Mystification and Rationality: Legitimacy and the State in the Third World.' *Journal of Contemporary Asia*, vol. 22, no. 2, 1992.

Yawnghew Chao-Tzang. 'The Political Economy of the Opium Trade: Implications for Shan State.' *Journal of Contemporary Asia*, vol. 23, no. 3, 1993.

Yeap, J. K. *The Patriarch.* Singapore: Federal Pubications, 1984.

Yong, C. F., and R. B. McKenna. 'The Kuomintang Movement in Malaya and Singapore, 1912–1925.' *Journal of Southeast Asian Studies*, vol. 12, no. 1, March 1981.

Yong, C. F. *Tan Kah-kee: The Making of an Overseas Chinese Legend.* Singapore: Oxford University Press, 1980.

Yoshida Shigeru. *The Yoshida Memoirs.* Boston: Houghton Mifflin, 1962.

INDEX